T0320470

Managing Security Issues and the Hidden Dangers of Wearable Technologies

Andrew Marrington
Zayed University, UAE

Don Kerr
University of the Sunshine Coast, Australia

John Gammack
Zayed University, UAE

A volume in the Advances in
Information Security, Privacy,
and Ethics (AISPE) Book Series

www.igi-global.com

Published in the United States of America by
    IGI Global
    Information Science Reference (an imprint of IGI Global)
    701 E. Chocolate Avenue
    Hershey PA 17033
    Tel: 717-533-8845
    Fax: 717-533-8661
    E-mail: cust@igi-global.com
    Web site: http://www.igi-global.com

Library of Congress Cataloging-in-Publication Data

Names: Marrington, Andrew, 1982- editor. | Kerr, Don, 1952- editor. |
   Gammack, John, 1960- editor.
Title: Managing security issues and the hidden dangers of wearable
   technologies / Andrew Marrington, Don Kerr, and John Gammack, editors.
Description: Hershey, PA : Information Science Reference, [2017] | Includes
   bibliographical references and index.
Identifiers: LCCN 2016033132| ISBN 9781522510161 (hardcover) | ISBN
   9781522510178 (ebook)
Subjects: LCSH: Wearable technology--Security measures. | Wearable
   technology--Social aspects. | Wearable technology--Risk assessment.
Classification: LCC QA76.592 .M36 2017 | DDC 004.167--dc23 LC record available at https://lccn.loc.gov/2016033132

This book is published in the IGI Global book series Advances in Information Security, Privacy, and Ethics (AISPE) (ISSN: 1948-9730; eISSN: 1948-9749)

British Cataloguing in Publication Data
A Cataloguing in Publication record for this book is available from the British Library.

Advances in Information Security, Privacy, and Ethics (AISPE) Book Series

ISSN: 1948-9730
EISSN: 1948-9749

MISSION

As digital technologies become more pervasive in everyday life and the Internet is utilized in ever increasing ways by both private and public entities, concern over digital threats becomes more prevalent.

The **Advances in Information Security, Privacy, & Ethics (AISPE) Book Series** provides cutting-edge research on the protection and misuse of information and technology across various industries and settings. Comprised of scholarly research on topics such as identity management, cryptography, system security, authentication, and data protection, this book series is ideal for reference by IT professionals, academicians, and upper-level students.

COVERAGE

- Tracking Cookies
- Privacy Issues of Social Networking
- Cookies
- Electronic Mail Security
- Technoethics
- Data Storage of Minors
- Device Fingerprinting
- Risk Management
- Access Control
- Security Information Management

IGI Global is currently accepting manuscripts for publication within this series. To submit a proposal for a volume in this series, please contact our Acquisition Editors at Acquisitions@igi-global.com or visit: http://www.igi-global.com/publish/.

Titles in this Series

For a list of additional titles in this series, please visit: www.igi-global.com

Security Management in Mobile Cloud Computing
Kashif Munir (University of Hafr Al-Batin, Saudi Arabia)
Information Science Reference • copyright 2017 • 248pp • H/C (ISBN: 9781522506027)
• US $150.00 (our price)

Cryptographic Solutions for Secure Online Banking and Commerce
Kannan Balasubramanian (Mepco Schlenk Engineering College, India) K. Mala (Mepco Schlenk Engineering College, India) and M. Rajakani (Mepco Schlenk Engineering College, India)
Information Science Reference • copyright 2016 • 375pp • H/C (ISBN: 9781522502739)
• US $200.00 (our price)

Handbook of Research on Modern Cryptographic Solutions for Computer and Cyber Security
Brij Gupta (National Institute of Technology Kurukshetra, India) Dharma P. Agrawal (University of Cincinnati, USA) and Shingo Yamaguchi (Yamaguchi University, Japan)
Information Science Reference • copyright 2016 • 589pp • H/C (ISBN: 9781522501053)
• US $305.00 (our price)

Innovative Solutions for Access Control Management
Ahmad Kamran Malik (COMSATS Institute of Information Technology, Pakistan) Adeel Anjum (COMSATS Institute of Information Technology, Pakistan) and Basit Raza (COMSATS Institute of Information Technology, Pakistan)
Information Science Reference • copyright 2016 • 330pp • H/C (ISBN: 9781522504481)
• US $195.00 (our price)

Network Security Attacks and Countermeasures
Dileep Kumar G. (Adama Science and Technology University, Ethiopia) Manoj Kumar Singh (Adama Science and Technology University, Ethiopia) and M.K. Jayanthi (King Khalid University, Saudi Arabia)
Information Science Reference • copyright 2016 • 357pp • H/C (ISBN: 9781466687615)
• US $205.00 (our price)

Next Generation Wireless Network Security and Privacy
Kamaljit I. Lakhtaria (Gujarat University, India)
Information Science Reference • copyright 2015 • 372pp • H/C (ISBN: 9781466686878)
• US $205.00 (our price)

www.igi-global.com

701 E. Chocolate Ave., Hershey, PA 17033
Order online at www.igi-global.com or call 717-533-8845 x100
To place a standing order for titles released in this series,
contact: cust@igi-global.com
Mon-Fri 8:00 am - 5:00 pm (est) or fax 24 hours a day 717-533-8661

Table of Contents

Detailed Table of Contents

Chapter 1

John Gammack, Zayed University, UAE
Andrew Marrington, Zayed University, UAE

Wearable technology collectively describes some of the most exciting emerging technologies, encompassing smart gadgets, garments, jewelry, and other devices worn on the user's body. In recent years, high profile wearable devices such as the Google Glass, Apple Watch, and FitBit have captured both the public imagination and headlines. Wearable technology has the potential to change the world even more profoundly than other mobile technologies. The appearance of such high profile wearable devices in the end-consumer market has also lead to serious consideration of the implications of such technologies, previously limited to the pages of science fiction. The implications for security and privacy of individuals and organizations, and the potential dangers to both society and the economy, must be considered and addressed in order for wearable technology to successfully deliver upon its many promises. Through addressing such concerns, the pathway to a "wearable future" can be unlocked, and users can adopt wearable technology with confidence.

Chapter 2

Sarra Berrahal, University of Carthage, Tunisia
Nourredine Boudriga, University of Carthage, Tunisia

Advancements in wearable and integrated sensing devices have given tremendous opportunities to enable advanced remote applications including sensing, monitoring, and tracking systems and states. Accordingly, wearable systems can be utilized to provide social and economic well-being for individuals by assisting them in the performance of their daily duties and for organizations by keeping their employees anytime, anywhere connected and by enhancing their productivity. However, wearable devices are, mainly, wireless in nature, which make them exposed to several types of security attacks that may threaten the life of individuals and the security of organizations. This chapter brings a comprehensive study on the benefits of wearable technologies and their related security and privacy issues, discusses the major policies that can be used to mitigate the risk posed by wearable technologies and the proposed techniques to assist users' safety in hazardous workplaces; and discusses the digital investigation of security incidents on wearable technologies.

Chapter 3

Joseph Ricci, University of New Haven, USA
Ibrahim Baggili, University of New Haven, USA
Frank Breitinger, University of New Haven, USA

There is no doubt that the form factor of devices continues to shrink as evidenced by smartphones and most recently smartwatches. The adoption rate of small computing devices is staggering and needs stronger attention from the cybersecurity and digital forensics communities. In this chapter, we dissect smartwatches. We first present a historical roadmap of smartwatches. We then explore the smartwatch marketplace and outline existing smartwatch hardware, operating systems and software. Next we elaborate on the uses of smartwatches and then discuss the security and forensic implications of smartwatches by reviewing the relevant literature. Lastly, we outline future research directions in smartwatch security and forensics.

Chapter 4

Mingzhong Wang, University of the Sunshine Coast, Australia
Don Kerr, University of the Sunshine Coast, Australia

With the features of mobility, reality augmentation, and context sensitivity, wearable devices are widely deployed into various domains. However, the sensitivity of collected data makes security and privacy protection one of the first priority in the advancement of wearable technologies. This chapter provides a study on encryption-based confidentiality protection for data storage systems in wearable platforms. The chapter first conducts a review to storage solutions in consumer wearable products and explores a two-tier, local flash memory and remote cloud storage, storage system in wearable platforms. Then encryption-based confidentiality protection and implementation methods for both flash memory and remote cloud storage are summarized. According to the interaction and integration of these two components, a categorization of confidential storage systems in wearable platforms is proposed. In addition, the benefits and selection criteria for each category are also discussed.

Chapter 5

In this chapter the security challenges raised by wearable technologies concerning the authenticity of information and subjects are discussed. Following a conceptualization of the capabilities of wearable technology, an authenticity analysis framework for wearable devices is presented. This framework includes graphic classification classes of authenticity risks in wearable devices that are expected to improve the awareness of users on the risks of using those devices, so that they can moderate their behaviors and take into account the inclusion of controls aimed to protect authenticity. Building on the results of the application of the framework to a list of wearable devices, a solution is presented to mitigate the risk for authenticity based on digital signatures.

Chapter 6

This chapter identifies concerns about, and the managerial implications of, data privacy issues related to wearables and the IoT; it also offers some enterprise solutions to the complex concerns arising from the aggregation of the massive amounts of data derived from wearables and IoT devices. Consumer and employee privacy concerns are elucidated, as are the problems facing managers as data management and security become an important part of business operations. The author provides insight into how companies are currently managing data as well as some issues related to data security and privacy. A number of suggestions for improving the approach to data protection and addressing concerns about privacy are included. This chapter also examines trending issues in the areas of data protection and the IoT, and contains thought-provoking discussion questions pertaining to business, wearables/IoT data, and privacy issues.

When considering the use of mobile or wearable health technologies to collect health data, a majority of users state security and privacy of their data is a primary concern. With users being connected 24/7, there is a higher risk today of data theft or the misappropriate use of health data. Furthermore, data ownership is often a misunderstood topic in wearable technology, with many users unaware who owns the data collected by a device, what that data can be used for and who can receive that data. Many countries are reviewing privacy governance in an attempt to clarify data privacy and ownership. But is it too late? This chapter explores the concepts of security and privacy of data from mobile and wearable technology, with specific examples, and the implications for the future.

Chapter 8

Marc L. Resnick, Bentley University, USA
Alina M. Chircu, Bentley University, USA

Today, innovation in and with Information and Communication Technology (ICT) is accelerating as consumers, companies and governments become users and designers of myriad ICT solutions whose ethical implications are not yet well understood. This chapter contributes to the growing body of research on ethical implications of one popular emerging ICT - wearable devices and associated technologies. Ethical challenges stemming from the extensive prevalence and comprehensiveness of wearable devices are related not only to the device design and use but also to the device-supported data collection and analysis and the creation of derivative products and services. Drawing from theories of ICT ethics, this chapter identifies the major ethical challenges posed by wearable devices and provides several guidelines on how these challenges can be addressed through ethically-informed design interventions.

Chapter 9

Roba Abbas, University of Wollongong, Australia
Katina Michael, University of Wollongong, Australia
M. G. Michael, University of Wollongong, Australia

Location-Based Services (LBS) provide value-added solutions to users based on location or position information and other contextual data. They enable the collection of GPS data logs or location chronicles, and may be deployed on a range of devices, many of which presently come in the form of commercially available product solutions with corresponding applications. This chapter presents the outcomes of an observational study of LBS users, which was designed to gauge user perspectives in relation to LBS socio-ethical dilemmas. The focus is on the outcomes of a spatial analysis exercise, which resulted in the development of a series of scenarios (in map format) that demonstrate varying LBS usability contexts. The scenarios range across various risk levels, and can be used as further input into consultative practices that are centered on the socio-ethical implications of LBS usage. Additionally, the results of the LBS observational study can be utilized to inform the need for LBS regulation. Future research directions are proposed, allowing for the study to be extended to wider contexts.

Chapter 10

Katina Michael, University of Wollongong, Australia
Deniz Gokyer, University of Wollongong, Australia
Samer Abbas, University of Wollongong, Australia

This chapter presents a set of scenarios involving the GoPro wearable Point of View (PoV) camera. The scenarios are meant to stimulate discussion about acceptable usage contexts with a focus on security and privacy. The chapter provides a wide array of examples of how overt wearable technologies are perceived and how they might/might not be welcomed into society. While the scenario is based at the University of Wollongong campus in Australia, the main implications derived from the fictitious events are useful in drawing out the predicted pros and cons of the technology. The scenarios are interpreted and the main thematic issues are drawn out and discussed. An in depth analysis takes place around the social implications, the moral and ethical problems associated with such technology, and possible future developments with respect to wearable devices.

Chapter 11

Michelle C. Antero, Zayed University, UAE

This chapter briefly introduces some historical and contemporary context before proposing a model course syllabus to implement a course in Management of Security Issues in Wearable Technology. The course syllabus is developed in line with the IS2010 curriculum recommended by the peak bodies (ACM and AIS) for a degree in Information Systems, Computer Information Systems or Management Information Systems. The design further follows the guidelines developed by the Accreditation Board of Engineering and Technology (ABET) that advocates that Course Learning Outcomes (CLOs) be developed for the list of topics covered by the material. In addition, the syllabus provides a basis for enterprise training relevant to managers and security specialists. The chapter also provides some general pedagogical guidelines on how each topic can be discussed and activities appropriate to the learners. It also uses Gluga et al.'s (2013) assessment criteria, based on Bloom's (1956) taxonomy to measure the depth of knowledge.

Chapter 12

Don Kerr, University of the Sunshine Coast, Australia
John Gammack, Zayed University, UAE

This chapter provides a contemporary example of how data from wearable devices can be used for "big data" type research. It then asked the question of data policies for the use of data generated by wearable devices. This is followed by an overview of the chapters in the book and how they fit within the general theme of the book. In addition, each chapter is categorised into whether it is social research or more technical type research. The chapter also includes concluding suggestions on the possible future research agenda for privacy and security within the subject domain of the use of wearables. In addition, insights into the future of wearables in relation to ethical considerations, privacy, security and data ownership is also given.

Preface

Wearable technologies are devices typically equipped with sensors and some form of network connectivity which can be worn about the body. Wearables can take many forms; they can be glasses, activity bands, watches, jewelry, clothing, or other accessories, or they could even potentially be located even "closer" to the user – as in the case of implantables or ingestibles! Since the first enthusiasts created their own wearable computers in the 1980s and 1990s out of custom hardware and software (Mann, 1997), the progressive miniaturization of computer components, the emergence of Bluetooth, and in more recent times the popularization of the cloud (used for off-device processing and storage alike) have together facilitated the emergence of consumer wearables (Starner, 2014). The appearance of a mainstream consumer market for wearable technologies in recent years heralds the arrival of what was once a science fiction future, where everyday life is augmented by the intimate presence of wearable devices designed to provide real-time information about the wearer and the world around them.

Yet as devotees of the genre would know, in science fiction the difference between utopia and dystopia is often only a matter of degree. The same wearable devices which, through monitoring their wearers and the world around them, enrich everyday life through providing information relevant to the geo-physical context of the wearer, may also provide a platform for privacy intrusion and attacks on the personal information security of the wearer. The information collected by the sensors of a wearable device could include information of the most intensely personal nature, such as our conversations with our friends and loved ones, or even small physiological indicators of our emotional state. When correlated with data collected from other sensors and other wearables, a person's wearable devices may (inadvertently or otherwise) allow an unauthorized observer to monitor their movements, personal interactions, health, and many other things.

The emergence of these wearable devices together with the ease of photographing and distributing private of confidential information has significant implications for our society and our businesses. The narrowed physical gap between person and technology implies the presence and potential use of wearable technologies during almost every human activity, including both intimate and illicit activities and every-thing between. The near-universal reach of modern smartphones has already ushered in an era of ubiquitous computing and a new culture of photosharing, leading to security and privacy concerns both for individuals and for businesses. As wearable technologies accelerate these developments, law, policy and individual behaviors must adapt. If wearable technologies are to thrive in the consumer market and live up to their promise of enhancing day-to-day life, then the potential security and privacy threats to individuals and organizations posed by these devices must be overcome.

This book, entitled *Managing Security Issues and the Hidden Dangers of Wear-able Technologies*, discusses positive and negative aspects of emerging wearable technologies both conceptually and empirically, alongside the implications for society, industry, government, and individual citizens. Managing the security, pri-vacy, and socio-ethical issues arising from wearable technologies is not simply a technical task – it also requires policies (both at the organization and government levels), and genuine societal reflection and debate on ethical norms and appropriate wearable usage. This book is intended to inform policy making, risk assessment, and academic research. Its target audience includes information security managers and analysts, information technology managers, students studying the security and privacy issues associated with wearables, and researchers.

ORGANIZATION OF THE BOOK

This book is organized into twelve chapters. Balance and diversity were editorial priorities in the selection of chapters for the book. A brief description of each of the chapters follows:

Chapter 1 introduces both the potential positive impact of wearables and the eponymous hidden dangers of wearable technologies. The chapter sets the scene for the rest of the book, introducing wearables to the reader and then broadly describing some of the threats to information security, privacy, and to society at large posed by poorly designed security mechanisms in wearable devices.

Chapter 2 expands on the threats mentioned in the introductory chapter, by exploring the risk associated with wearable technology both to individuals and to large organizations. The chapter discusses potential attacks on wearable devices, securing wearable devices, security data privacy for data collected by wearables, and the digital investigation of wearable devices.

Chapter 3 looks in detail at the security, privacy and digital forensics issues related to a particular sub-type of wearable technology - namely, the smartwatch. Digital forensics and information security and privacy are related, but have some competing interests; information security and privacy pertains to preserving the confidentiality of the data stored on the device, whereas digital forensics often involves compromising security measures in order to provide the court with better quality information. Flaws in smartwatch security, therefore, can be exploited to better facilitate digital forensics.

Chapter 4 provides a study on encryption-based protection for confidentiality of data stored on wearable platforms. Many wearable platforms consist not only of the wearable device itself but also incorporate cloud services, to which the wearable device connects via an Internet connection (either its own or one provided by a paired smartphone). With so much data being sent from the device to the cloud service provider, it is essential to ensure data confidentiality through proper encryption protocols, ensuring the confidentiality of data while it is processed, transmitted, and stored.

Chapter 5 addresses the challenging issue of authenticity. The issue of impersonation is a difficult one, especially as many wearables exist as a kind of intermediary between the user and the world around them. The chapter also provides a framework for the assessment of authenticity issues concerning wearable devices.

Chapter 6 discusses the potential impact of wearable devices on society and the economy. It includes a call to industry to collectively consider self-regulation rather than relying upon the government to do so.

Chapter 7 examines security, privacy, trust and ownership issues surrounding wearables in the health domain. The health domain has long experience dealing with wearables than the broader consumer market. The chapter poses the question "Is it the owner of the data's responsibility to ensure the privacy of the data, and if so, who is the owner of the raw data?" – a question which is more complicated than it at first appears because much depends on the context in which the data was collected.

Chapter 8 examines some of the hidden dangers of wearable devices, by considering wearables from the perspective of ICT ethics. After identifying the ethical pitfalls of wearable devices, the chapter shows how wearable manufacturers and policy-makers can remediate the ethical difficulties.

Chapter 9 discusses the potential misuse spatial data such as that collected by location-based services, which are integral to many wearable devices and other mobile technology (such as smartphones). The chapter builds on an earlier observational study of location-based services to illustrate user perspectives around the technology.

Chapter 10 explores social reactions to users of wearable devices, through a number of socio-ethical scenarios involving a student attending university wearing a wearable device (a head-mounted video camera). Each scenario showcases different social reactions to sousveillance (person-to-person surveillance using a portable camera or other surveillance device).

Chapter 11 is a model course syllabus, intended for use by instructors as a basis for building a special topic course in security and privacy issues of wearable technologies. The chapter proposes a set of course learning outcomes for a course in wearables security, and relates those to standard reference curricula in Information Technology and Information Systems. The chapter also provides an additional reading list which would be of interest to all readers who wanted to continue to explore the topics raised in this book after they finish reading it, whether they are students or not.

Chapter 12 is a conclusion, which discusses the themes arising from the previous chapters, and lays out some suggestions for future research. The chapter concludes the book on a positive note, expressing the hope that readers do not think that only a dystopia is inevitable. Through addressing the security, privacy, and socio-ethical concerns surrounding wearable devices, we can minimize potential harm and maximize the potential benefit from wearable technology.

USING THIS BOOK

If you are a manager or a policy maker, this book will help inform you about the wearables landscape and the security, privacy, and socio-ethical issues which require your attention. Chapters 1, 2, 6, 7, 8, 9, and 10 examine the security and privacy issues which confront individuals, businesses, and government, and the social and ethical issues which confront our society more broadly in the wearables era.

If you are an information security professional, this book will help you understand the threat environment and consider appropriate policy settings and risk controls to avoid or mitigate the risks arising from the rise of wearables in your organization. Chapters 1, 2, 3, 5, 6, and 8 are particularly relevant to information security managers and other information security professionals in industry.

If you are a faculty member preparing a special topic course on the security issues of wearable devices, this book can both help you prepare that course and serve as a required or recommended reading text for your students. Although all chapters will be relevant to you, Chapter 11 is an excellent starting point to help you design a course which suits the needs of your students and institution. Each chapter offers discussion points and questions relevant to essay and project-based investigations.

If you are a student, each chapter in the book covers a different topic or theme within the broader topic of the security issues and hidden dangers of wearable devices. Although you should start with chapter 1 and finish with Chapter 12, it is possible to read the book in any order. To continue to explore the themes in this book, the additional readings in chapter 11 are highly recommended.

If you are a researcher, there will no doubt be chapters in this book which are more relevant to your research than others. If you are in search of a new direction for your research within the topic of wearable technology, then chapter 12's discussion of the future of wearables and future directions of research is an ideal launching pad. In addition, each chapter offers discussion points and unresolved areas to inspire research questions.

REFERENCES

Mann, S. (1997, February). Wearable computing: A first step toward personal imaging. *Computer, 30*(2), 25–32. doi:10.1109/2.566147

Starner, T. (2014, October-December). How wearables worked their way into the mainstream. *IEEE Pervasive Computing / IEEE Computer Society [and] IEEE Communications Society, 13*(4), 10–15. doi:10.1109/MPRV.2014.66

Chapter 1
The Promise and Perils of Wearable Technologies

John Gammack
Zayed University, UAE

Andrew Marrington
Zayed University, UAE

ABSTRACT

Wearable technology collectively describes some of the most exciting emerging technologies, encompassing smart gadgets, garments, jewelry, and other devices worn on the user's body. In recent years, high profile wearable devices such as the Google Glass, Apple Watch, and FitBit have captured both the public imagination and headlines. Wearable technology has the potential to change the world even more profoundly than other mobile technologies. The appearance of such high profile wearable devices in the end-consumer market has also lead to serious consideration of the implications of such technologies, previously limited to the pages of science fiction. The implications for security and privacy of individuals and organizations, and the potential dangers to both society and the economy, must be considered and addressed in order for wearable technology to successfully deliver upon its many promises. Through addressing such concerns, the pathway to a "wearable future" can be unlocked, and users can adopt wearable technology with confidence.

DOI: 10.4018/978-1-5225-1016-1.ch001

INTRODUCTION

The purpose of this chapter is to introduce the field of wearable technology, and to provide a general background for the later chapters in this book. Often referred to simply as wearables, wearable technology, by definition, means a smart gadget or garment worn on an individual's body. This term includes smart watches, smart eyewear, smart jewelry, and wristbands for fitness tracking, as well as clothing or accessories enhanced to sense, record and transmit personal information. The field of wearables is one of the most exciting technologies to emerge in recent times, and is forecasted to continue to grow well into the future, with increased adoption and the continuing innovation of new devices and applications.

Wearable technology also includes *implantables*: devices that are surgically placed within the body, perhaps for medical monitoring but with the potential for identification, tracking and alerting applications. Other arguably wearable technology includes smartphones, from which many of today's users are effectively inseparable, and which are frequently the communication link between a wearable gadget and the wider Internet. Just as smartphones have become ubiquitous and have engendered a reconfiguration of organizational and societal practice, the advent of wearables promises to evolve this trend towards a new normality.

Whilst the growth of wearables continues as their positive benefits become realized, their "hidden dangers" are less often considered. The developers and adopters of wearable technologies will have more success and satisfaction if implicit issues of privacy, security, and safety are known, addressed and managed. Many of these overlap with social and technical issues related to individual smartphone use, including user identity, tracking or stalking, but also bring new problems in an enterprise context, where corporate data and other information can become vulnerable to underhanded or insecure leakage. There are many implications of smart wearables, which will require policy and legislative revisions.

In this chapter we overview the emerging space of wearables and raise some of the general concerns raised by their potential widespread adoption, for individuals, for organizations and for society. The subsequent chapters expand on several of these issues, both conceptually and empirically, suggesting not only practical recommendations but also emerging issues for research or debate as our understanding develops.

THE WEARABLES SPACE

Market and Growth

The market for wearable technologies has continued to grow significantly in recent years. An estimated 112 million devices are expected to be shipped annually in a market worth $19 billion US by 2018, more than double the size of the 2016 market (Statista, 2016). Other sources project even higher figures: one often-quoted estimate (cited in Ballve, 2013) is for 485 million devices by 2018, and whether such estimates prove conservative or bullish, all agree that the market will be huge.

Major players are involved in this space, suggesting well-funded innovation and marketing will continue, and devices will be closely integrated with dominant platforms and their evolution. Apple's Watch, Google's Glass, and Microsoft's Band[1] represent three wearable categories by major tech firms: many other firms, small and large, also offer branded products in these categories. Although lessons learned from the initial version of Google Glass mean that this device is not commercially available, it is likely to re-emerge in some form in the future, since Google has an ongoing project in this area. Whilst apps, pricing, digital ecosystem integration, style and battery life were some key variables governing consumer decisions, the players involved can be expected to address these (SDL Customer Journey Analytics, 2015), and shape the market. Indeed, one reason why market size estimates vary is arguably due to the privacy concerns with the Google prototype launched in 2013, and with the lack of immediately obvious added value beyond pager-level notification from the original Apple Watch.

The market space includes consumer and enterprise segments, offering various devices useful in both personal and workplace life, discussed further below. Smartwatches are already outselling Swiss watches (Strategy Analytics, 2016) and the expanding capabilities of fitness bands from glorified pedometers towards, for example, stress, sleep and heart rate trackers of medical value shows just some areas of the growth potential.

Such a range and scale implies wearables will have the ubiquitous presence already being shown by smartphone adoption, and will foster a proliferation of new apps along with a reconfiguration both of work and social processes. This potential, however, brings new dangers, as well as new forms of well-known dangers associated with security and privacy on the Internet. New risks include commercial risks associated with changing fashions and physical dangers due to body proximity, such as radiation or fiber allergies. Knowles (2014) observes that as wearables become mainstream the "attack surfaces" multiply – impacting BYOD policies and enterprise IT infrastructure. Knowles also notes that devices with smaller displays will inevitably omit details that could indicate a phishing or other cyber-attack attempt.

Accordingly, since the growth of wearables seems inevitable, it is appropriate briefly to consider the range of emerging wearable categories, before considering the technologies involved, and the hidden dangers these imply.

Categories of Wearable Technology

Wearables covers a range of product categories, from watches, eyewear and wristbands, to various forms of smart clothing. Invisibles (e.g. worn under clothes) and implantables (embedded under the skin) are also categories of wearable technology. Whilst prototype and early to market versions of these have been around for a few years, mainstreaming is happening, particularly for wrist-worn devices, which themselves continue to evolve greater functionality and features.

Other categories are not yet commonplace but are beginning to emerge, such as tattoos, and hearables—i.e. smart headphones or earpieces supporting numerous applications. In areas such as medicine, specialized (rather than necessarily mass-market) devices continue to be developed, such as Google's project to develop smart contact lenses to analyze tears for specific biomarkers (see USPTO, 2015). Subject to meeting safety, accuracy and commercial production requirements, development of such specialized wearables can be expected to continue.

One such specialized wearable category is "ingestibles", smart pills that travel through the digestive system, providing, via a stick on patch to a smartphone, data useful (for example) in monitoring individual medical reactions. The US Food and Drug Administration in 2012 approved such a pill, and pill-based cameras are anticipated to obviate, for example, colonoscopies (Sherbit, 2015a). Although the nature of such data is intimately private, its ownership and subsequent use is vulnerable, perhaps by insurance companies setting specific premiums, or refusing compensation due to a failure fully to comply with a dosage regime. With "medical surveillance" generating big data, and precision medicine potentially identifying individuals through unique DNA information, privacy compromise is a real threat in the absence of new and compelling safeguards. Given the potential of collecting and selling genomic information to "unscrupulous" pharma companies, major ethical questions also surround such developments (Sherbit, 2015b).

Ingestibles, implantables or "embeddables" are based inside the body, and can be used, for example, in heart or glucose monitoring applications. This "permanently worn" category has advantages with seniors or others who might be forgetful about their monitoring or dosing regimes. These effectively categorize their wearers as cyborgs, which is likely to meet social resistance, certainly as discretionary fashion, but may well increasingly become "mandated" as medical practice finds them useful in practice. In non- medical domains, the potential dangers with this category include biocompatibility, which can cause infection, cost and patient acceptance. If such devices are able to securely, reliably and unobtrusively monitor medically relevant readings, it is likely that this category will also grow.

Vulnerabilities in the wireless technology required for implantables is, however, the major concern: Glisson et al. (2015) demonstrated the "killing" of a medical mannequin by wirelessly breaching its security and altering pacemaker settings. Insulin pumps or other embedded devices could likewise become compromised, by accident or design, not to mention the long-term dangers associated with inaccurate medical school training due to hacked settings, as these researchers also note.

Jewelry is another wearables category, less fashion sensitive than clothing, but, unlike implantables or workplace garments with embedded devices, easily removable. Beyond watches, the dominant subcategory, developments in bracelets, necklaces and rings are also growing this part of the market. Ringly's products (ringly.com) provide a good example of the category. A normal looking ring with a semi-precious stone provides subtle alerts through light or vibration, and is integrated with numerous apps, both iOS and Android, identified as particularly relevant to its market. Payment apps, smart home integration and more are expected to follow but remaining within a strong design philosophy around simplicity and "making the technology disappear" (Charara, 2015).

One danger, however, with inconspicuous or unobtrusive technology is its potential use in corporate espionage, or (for example) casino signaling applications. Wearable cameras, including those supporting video streaming or Bluetooth have similarly small optical components, and can enable clandestine filming. Designed as attachable or in the form of jewelry, these devices again raise privacy and confidentiality concerns.

With all of these categories there are social implications, and while legal frameworks generally provide for data protection, privacy rights and respect for confidentiality, new technologies usually force development of new or amended laws. In the category of smart clothing, the person as a social or professional being is emphasized, and beyond the materials technologies involved, there are social issues around fashion and self-presentation that imply different types of risk.

Duval et al. (2009) note the lack of a coherent vision for smart clothing, and that humanistic needs must be understood as determinants of adoption. They consider human needs against Maslow's hierarchy of needs (Maslow, 1943), and across the human lifecycle, where the natural decline of the body raises specific issues, and smart clothes imply related solutions.

Humans, increasingly, often seek to resist the appearance of old age, and the implication of belonging less to the able-bodied world of independent adults. Some may not wish, for example, to wear "fall-detecting" pendants or garments, and resent interfaces that are not appropriately designed for older or feebler bodies, or that otherwise convey a perception of infirmity. Apart from ensuring basic safety and physiological needs, such as not warming the body too much, higher-level human needs are also implicated with smart clothing, again potentially affecting uptake. Duval et al (2009:184) suggest a possible loss of self-esteem due to "intelligent garments replacing" naturally human functions, but suggest design attention and more knowledge of these issues will help in the development of smart clothes.

The Technologies of Wearables

Many of the issues and technologies applicable in wearables are also applicable to smartphones, and can draw on our existing understanding of those. Indeed, as personal area network devices they often connect to the wider Internet through familiar smartphones using the Bluetooth communications standard. Bluetooth is a global and unlicensed protocol specified for a short-range radio frequency. Being designed for low power consumption, it allows data from (say) a fitness band to upload to an associated laptop, or messages from a phone to be notified to a smartwatch.

Bluetooth with paired devices is reasonably secure but requiring a proprietary device pairing was seen by potential consumers as a limitation of the Apple watch, which "doesn't work properly without an iPhone" (SDL, 2015). Other wearables are standalone or cross-platform, and Apple risks the commercial danger of alienating potential consumers not willing to be locked into their ecosystem, a situation which echoes that of Sony VCRs and the Betamax format in the 1980s. On the other hand, a 2016 study of 8 leading wearables showed that all but Apple's watch was a "privacy nightmare". If not paired with, and connected to, a mobile device, a Bluetooth identifier emitted by the devices enabled various vulnerabilities including long-term location tracking, third party data changes and record faking, compromising legal or medical applications (Open Effect, 2016).

Bluetooth is a radio standard, and operates wirelessly in the range of radiofrequencies. Wireless technology is used with implantables and wearable patches and many wearable applications use RFID (Radio Frequency Identification) or Near Field Communications (NFC) tags. Electronic garage door openers, cashless payments or contactless inventory updates are in common use among many applications for short range NFC. NFC, despite being on most Android devices, has some security issues, potentially enabling eavesdropping, data modification or credit thefts (Vila and Rodriguez, 2014).

Another related danger concerns physical health. The body absorbs energy from electromagnetic radiation, which cellphones emit, along with heat, e.g. to the ear and head. The extent to which such near field radiofrequency radiation is carcinogenic remains debatable, but it represents a legitimate fear for body-proximate technologies.

Other technologies come from developments in augmented and virtual reality. Both head-mounted or glove devices can detect motion, speed, hand or eye gestures, and detailed eye gaze, and have enterprise applications in medicine, surgery, firefighting, police work and other fields, as well as in consumer grade games and apps (Kress, 2015).

Sensors increasingly have sophisticated functionality, and in the case of wearable sensors for medical applications, these need to be non-allergenic, comfortable and not restrictive, non-toxic and reliably calibrated to standards and shifting baselines (Coyle et al, 2010). When chemical or biological sensors are involved in monitoring environmental or body samples, the complexity of ensuring reliable measures increases. As the Internet of Things continues to emerge, more and more sensor functionality in networks of limited security can be expected.

A third common technology used in smartphones and wearables is the accelerometer, which is widely used in many applications where it is relevant sensitively to detect direction, orientation and speed of motion. This technology however brings associated dangers, such as being able to identify a person's movements and activities, and even their location while driving (Murphy, 2016): "By using the accelerometer and knowing their start point, one could theoretically find out the person's path, speed at every point during the drive, and end destination". In addition, Aviv et al. (2012) found that tapping in a smartphone PIN causes slight changes in phone orientation, allowing effective guessing of likely PINs using the accelerometer data (the sensors broadcast such data, typically without requiring permission). Passwords can similarly be inferred from smartphone accelerometer data (Owusu, 2012) and keylogging nearby keyboards using smartphone accelerometer data has also been shown to be possible (Marquardt et al, 2011). These examples illustrate technologies relevant to wearables, and imply serious potential security and privacy breaches.

A technology specific to wearables is the materials used in smart clothing, which is a subject of continuing research and development. Issues include the temperature range of the wearer's body and the moisture caused by sweat, whose level varies by individual metabolism, gender and ambient conditions. A Finnish team has developed a smart clothing technology that adjusts temperature to desired levels, with applications such as distance running, post-surgery or firefighting. (VTT, 2016). Likewise, particularly in medical or workplace situations, properties of materials such as breathability, stiffness, stretchability, and durability are relevant considerations. Performance sportswear has been around for some time, and collaborations between big players such as Nike and Apple promise continuing innovations and developments.

In high fashion, the world's first "cognitive dress" premiered at the Costume Institute's 2016 Met Gala red carpet event, and was designed to reflect the sentiments tweeted about the event. One hundred and fifty LED flowers on the dress lit up in various colors, coded to reflect the trending sentiments in real time, as interpreted by IBM's Watson artificial intelligence system (Brady, 2016).

Other projects on conceptual fashion include Tally, a tail that wags in response to its wearer's heartbeat, and Shippo, a tail that responds to mood as indicated by neural waves, detected by a sensor inside a beret (Neuroware, n.d.), though at the time of writing these are not in mass production.

Some other conceptual designs, however, are already commercially available. Directly relevant to the issue of privacy, a theme discussed further in this volume, are garments designed for a world of increased surveillance. The privacy gift shop (Privacygiftshop.com, n.d.) offers counter surveillance "stealthware" designs, including hoodies, burqas and hijabs that shield against the thermal imaging used in drone based surveillance[2].

Although such innovations are largely conceptual at the moment, more mainstream fashion considerations suggest new commercial dangers to do with smart clothing. Traditional fashion variables such as aesthetics, materials washability, and comfort will, in general, constrain designs, and styles that inevitably become dated, or are not individually made to bespoke sizes, mean tricky calculations around manufacturing quantities, target markets and price points.

McCann (2015) observes that older "baby boomer" markets, for example, may not accept clothes with unsuitable interfaces, such as small displays, or being hard to fasten, and that "little has been done" to ensure appropriateness to the culture and changing physical needs of this market.

One approach to this problem for consumer, rather than workplace wearables, is "invisibles", worn under the clothes as stick-on strips, smart insoles, or smart buttons that do not make major fashion statements. Even smart (temporary) tattoos such as L'Oréal's patch for measuring UV exposure (McHugh, 2016) are becoming possible, logically leading towards implantables as a future for (especially) medical or military applications.

The promise of the technologies is clear, and the extension of functionality towards e.g. wearable payments, advanced biometrics or augmented reality applications can be expected to continue. The dangers accompanying these go beyond traditional personal or enterprise data privacy, reliability and security, authentication and identity theft, to encompass physical and commercial dangers also. And, as we shall see, there are other, significant social consequences as well.

ISSUES AND CONCERNS

Privacy

In information security, privacy is distinguished from confidentiality in that while confidentiality is about preventing unauthorized disclosure of information, privacy is about the terms under which one discloses information to another party, and what one permits that other party to do with the information. Users of health and fitness wearable devices such as those produced by FitBit, for example, use wearable technologies to monitor their health. The data collected by such devices is generally stored in a public cloud, with authorized access to an individual user's data governed by the user's account settings. A user might want to share their progress in their attempts to lose weight and exercise more with a group of friends on a similar quest, for example, and therefore permit members of that group to view the data collected by their wearable device. The data, however, remains in the cloud, under the custodianship of the manufacturer of the wearable device. Whether through a change in policy or through a corporate acquisition, the user's health and fitness data could one day be shared with, for example, a health insurer, or another party with a vested financial interest in the user's health. The result could be higher insurance premiums for reasons totally opaque to the user (Hammond, 2015). The user permitted their wearable device to collect health and fitness information about them for the purpose of sharing with friends and family, but the information could be ultimately used for purposes other than those which the user intended and to which they knowingly consented.

The use of data collected by wearables for purposes other than those to which the user knowingly consented by large corporates or governments is not the only privacy risk which arises from wearables. As Internet-connected devices with a variety of sensors to monitor both the wearer and the world around the wearer, wearable devices could impinge on the privacy of the wearer and those the wearer meets, allowing for remote monitoring. Wearables without an Internet connection may still impinge on the privacy of the wearer and others through the misuse of recordings made with that device. Wearing a GoPro head-mounted video camera, for example, may provoke fearful or even angry reactions from people around the wearer, even if the camera is not recording (Gokyer & Michael, this volume). Such reactions may be more pronounced because a wearable can monitor passively, with no apparent action required on the part of the user.

Contrast this with smartphones and tablets, which are ubiquitous and are equipped with video cameras, but which require the user to hold them up and point them at the target of their recording. With the wearable, the user's presence with the device is a warning of potential privacy impingement to those in the vicinity, whereas the smartphone is non-threatening until it is raised and pointed at somebody. We note, however, that early camera-equipped mobile phones elicited similar privacy concerns – namely, that they made it easier for cameras to be "smuggled in" to situations where a mobile phone was acceptable but a camera was not (such as a locker room). Mobile phone manufacturers responded by adding indicators that a phone was being used to take photographs, in the form of artificial camera noises and/or red indicator lights, which helped mitigate such concerns by making the new more familiar, but for the most part those privacy concerns faded as mobile phone use increased – the public became more familiar with the technology and more accepting of the privacy implications.

Wearable technologies hold many promises, connecting the cyber world to the physical in combinations that may profoundly change both. As they continue to evolve, privacy solutions will need to be engineered, so that consumers can embrace the wearable future without giving up their privacy and personal security. Privacy engineering focuses on systematically addressing privacy issues as they arise through the whole of the lifecycle of a socio-technical system; it is an emerging field of research which moves beyond narrow technical solutions to privacy to consider socio-technical systems (like wearable technologies) holistically, in social, legal, organizational, and technical contexts (Gürses & del Alamo, 2016). Formal privacy engineering of wearable technologies may prove an "enabler" to help developers of wearable technologies to overcome user reticence about their devices arising from privacy concerns. In the future, superior privacy engineering could be a competitive advantage in the wearable space.

Information Security

Since the introduction of laptop computers, the corporate sector has dealt with expanded threats to information security posed by the mobility of computing devices. A computing device which can be moved between trusted and untrusted networks with their user is both more exposed to risk itself and is a potential vulnerability for the trusted network. The advent of the smartphone accelerated the adoption of "Bring Your Own Device" (BYOD) policies, whereby employees could bring their own computing device to their workplace and join it to the corporate network. On the one hand this is enormously convenient for the company, which realizes significant productivity gains as employees are more likely to work outside of paid hours if they can work on their mobile device, and more convenient for the employee, who is spared the inconvenience of carrying two devices (one company-provided, one personal). On the other hand, such devices are significant security risks for the company whose data is blended with the employee's personal data on the device's storage, and may be exposed if the device is lost or otherwise compromised (Disterer & Kleiner, 2013).

Wearable devices are the next frontier for corporate BYOD policies and procedures. We posit that the majority of wearable devices will be personal as opposed to company property, and that many will connect with corporate networks either directly or indirectly. For example, a smart watch will synchronize its calendar to an employee's electronic calendar, whether through a connection facilitated by the employee's smartphone, or directly through the corporate network itself. BYOD policies will need to be revisited not only to consider wearable devices as new technologies, but also to consider the implications of their proliferation on smartphones, tablets and other devices already governed by existing policies, policies written before the non-wearable device in question became a "gateway" for wearable devices.

Like other mobile technologies, wearable devices are a potential platform for data exfiltration. In addition, their design tends to be focused on functionality and miniaturization, with security a secondary concern, particularly at lower price points (Hammond, 2015), and consequently the wearable devices themselves become a new vulnerability for the information security both of the individual user, and of the user's employer. These issues must be carefully weighed and considered by policy makers as they consider how wearable devices will interact with the corporate network.

Physical and Social Risks

Apart from privacy and security dangers there are various other issues specific to wearables that make them risky, and concern the personal and social body. Physical dangers such as allergies and radiation near the body have been noted, but fashion changes and perceptions of wearers in social contexts may imply they will not be so readily accepted as smartphones and tablets in social life.

One of the lessons learned from Google Glass was that its wearers were often perceived as geeks, secretly filming social life and uploading to the Internet. In countries such as the UAE, photographing without permission is a crime, as is uploading or posting identifiable individuals without their explicit permission. In other countries too, Glass wearers have been ejected from cafes and advised by Google not to be "creepy or rude, (aka, a "Glasshole")" (Google, n.d.) and there is disquiet about surreptitious photography, or conversation recording, where unguarded remarks may not remain private.

As was quickly realized from the learning exercise, a design overhaul to improve the image before commercial production was needed, and in 2015 Google partnered with the Italian design group Luxottica, who specialize in leading edge fashion, luxury and sport eyewear design. For mass-market consumer acceptance, chic rather than geek is imperative, and this is likely to significantly affect adoption.

Research on potential customers' perceived value of wearables has shown that users are less concerned with the risks in assessing overall benefit, than with the upside benefits. In informing their intention to adopt, users are more likely to consider the social image around the fashion or style aspects, and the usefulness and enjoyment to be gained (Yang et al., 2016). This propensity in itself suggests that, as with other aspects of technology security, many users either do not know or may not care about best practice protection or potential risks.

Focusing on healthcare wearables, Gao et al., (2015) found that privacy and health considerations, as well as technology features influenced decision-making on adoption. However, they also found a difference between users of medical devices and the more casual users of fitness wearables. As with the potential eyewear adoption, social and enjoyment factors played a role for potential consumers, along with usable functionality. Privacy and vulnerability risks also affected potential adoption for these users. If the perceived benefits exceed the risks, it is reasonable to expect widespread adoption. Other than mass-market clothes or devices, many niche markets are likely to emerge for wearables in professional or specialized applications. Nonetheless, it is a commercial risk if these do not meet industry and user requirements, and studies will be required to ensure these are suitable to purpose.

For medical device users in Gao et al's (2015) study the concerns were mainly about self-efficacy, ease of use, and perceived threats to health, particularly vulnerability and severity. Similarly, for surgeons, the use of smart eyewear, for instance, is not a fashion choice. Instead, it is a practical enhancement to their professional activity, allows them access to information in a hands-free manner. If such applications add significant value to existing professional practices, it implies lower risk commercial opportunities.

Practical usefulness was confirmed in an unpublished study by Hassanain (2014), who looked at the existing and potential use of Google Glass in the UAE. He found that a majority of doctors, police and oil workers were positive about the technology based on existing uses and application during the explorer period, and in a survey of fifty doctors, teachers and high school students, examined the prospects for wider adoption. Most respondents (70%) were excited about the technology, but were equally concerned with security and privacy implications.

The UAE is an enthusiastic adopter of high technology, and in general (64%) agreed that the country would adapt to smart eyewear just as it easily had done with laptops and smartphones. A substantial minority (26%) was skeptical, however, since privacy is a traditional value, legally enshrined, and smart eyewear presents a threat to this. Whilst 36% thought existing UAE law provided protection, (since the functionality is similar to smartphones, which are endemic in the UAE), the majority still thought the law might need to change before smart eyewear would be appropriate. Although limited, this study suggests that social and cultural factors may also affect adoption decisions, and that specific markets may have to disable or redesign certain functionalities.

Nonetheless, it is highly likely that devices such as a revised Glass product will be used by authorized professionals, such as the police, military, customs agents and doctors, as indeed is already happening in some cases. Other applications actively being explored currently include contactless payments using biometric security data via (authenticated) wristbands (Sacco, 2015). While these suggest future applications in retail and banking professions, they raise other forms of hidden dangers that will require still further research and development. In general, the immense potential of these technologies present many opportunities and challenges for enterprises as well as for consumers.

CONCLUSION

This chapter has briefly introduced some aspects of the current space of wearable computing, highlighting not only the potential of these, but also some of the inherent risks that may affect their adoption unless addressed. Some studies are beginning to emerge, even as the field changes and grows rapidly. Many more studies will be required before we understand the impacts of this emerging technology, at technical, personal, enterprise, social and cultural levels. In the remainder of the book several of the themes introduced here are explored in more detail, both conceptually and empirically, with practical implications for potential users of wearables, security managers of enterprises and policy makers alike. For academics an indicative syllabus and set of readings is identified, suitable for an academic or as a basis for training courses. Researchers in the field will likewise find many points for further debate and research within and at the end of each chapter, which are brought together thematically at the end of the book.

REFERENCES

Aviv, A. J., Sapp, B., Blaze, M., & Smith, J. M. (2012) Practicality of Accelerometer Side-Channel on Smartphones.*Proceedings of the 28th Annual Computer Security Applications Conference (ACSAC'12)*. Orlando, FL: ACM.

Ballve, M. (2013). Wearable Gadgets Are Still Not Getting The Attention They Deserve: Here's Why They Will Create A Massive New Market. *Business Insider*. Retrieved from http://www.businessinsider.com/wearable-devices-create-a-new-market-2013-8

Brady, S. (2016). *IBM Watson x Marchesa Twitter Dress Lights Up the Met Gala Red Carpet.* Retrieved from http://www.brandchannel.com/2016/05/02/ibm-watson-met-gala-050216/

Charara, S. (2015). *Ringly CEO: Keep smart jewellery simple with no screens or steps.* Retrieved from http://www.wareable.com/meet-the-boss/ringly-ceo-christina-mercando-smart-jewellery-2016

Coyle, S., Benito-Lopez, F., Byrne, R., & Diamond, D. (2010). On-Body Chemical Sensors for Monitoring Sweat. In A. Lay-Ekuakille (Ed.), *Wearable and Autonomous Biomedical Devices and Systems for Smart Environments*. Berlin: Springer-Verlag. doi:10.1007/978-3-642-15687-8_9

Disterer, G., & Kleiner, C. (2013). BYOD Bring Your Own Device. *Procedia Technology*, *9*, 43–53. doi:10.1016/j.protcy.2013.12.005

Duval, S., Hoareau, C., & Hashizume, H. (2009). Humanistic Needs as Seeds in Smart Clothing in Cho, G. (Ed) Smart Clothing Technology and Applications (pp. 153–188). Boca Raton, FL: CRC Press. doi:10.1201/9781420088533-c7

Gao, Y., Li, H., & Luo, Y. (2015). An empirical study of wearable technology acceptance in healthcare. *Industrial Management & Data Systems*, *115*(9), 1704–1723.

Glisson, W. B., Andel, T., McDonald, T., Jacobs, M., Campbell, M., & Mayr, J. (2015). *Compromising a Medical Mannequin.* Retrieved from http://arxiv.org/pdf/1509.00065

Google. (n.d.). *Glass Explorers*. Retrieved from https://sites.google.com/site/glass-comms/glass-explorers

Gürses, S., & del Alamo, J. M. (2016, March/April). Privacy Engineering: Shaping an Emerging Field of Research and Practice. *IEEE Security and Privacy*, *14*(2), 40–46. doi:10.1109/MSP.2016.37

Hammond, T. (2015, October 8). *The dark side of wearables: How they're secretly jeopardizing your security and privacy*. Retrieved from http://www.techrepublic.com/article/the-dark-side-of-wearables-how-theyre-secretly-jeopardizing-your-security-and-privacy/

Hasanain, A. (2014). *Eyewear and challenges to existing privacy paradigms and laws*. (Unpublished Masters Thesis). Zayed University, Abu Dhabi, UAE.

Knowles, R. (2014). *The wearables revolution is coming – security professionals must be ready*. Retrieved from http://www.techradar.com/news/world-of-tech/future-tech/the-wearables-revolution-is-coming-security-professionals-must-be-ready-1227542

Kress, B. (2015). Optics for Smart Glasses, Smart Eyewear, Augmented Reality, and Virtual Reality Headsets. In W. Barfield (Ed.), *Fundamentals of Wearable Computers and Augmented Reality* (2nd ed.). Boca Raton, FL: CRC Press. doi:10.1201/b18703-8

Marquardt, P., Verma, A., Carter, H., & Traynor, P. (2011) (sp)iPhone: Decoding Vibrations From Nearby Keyboards Using Mobile Phone Accelerometers. In *Proceedings of ACM Conference on Computer and Communications Security, CCS, 2011.* Chicago, IL: ACM. doi:10.1145/2046707.2046771

McCann, J. (2009). End-user based design of innovative smart clothing. In J. McCann & D. Bryson (Eds.), *Smart clothes and wearable technology*. Boca Raton, FL: CRC Press/Woodhead Publishing Limited. doi:10.1533/9781845695668.1.45

McHugh, M. (2016). *How L'Oreal Built a UV-Measuring Temporary Tattoo*. Retrieved from http://www.wired.com/2016/01/how-loreal-built-a-uv-measuring-temporary-tattoo/

Neurowear. (n.d.). *Projects / shippo*. Retrieved from http://www.neurowear.com/projects_detail/shippo.html

Open Effect. (2016). *Every Step You Fake: A Comparative Analysis of Fitness Tracker Privacy and Security Ver.0.3*. Retrieved from https://openeffect.ca/reports/Every_Step_You_Fake.pdf

Owusu, E. (n.d.). ACCessory: password inference using accelerometers on smartphones. *Proceedings of the Twelfth Workshop on Mobile Computing Systems & Applications*. New York, NY: ACM. doi:10.1145/2162081.2162095

Privacy Gift Shop. (n.d.). *Stealth Wear*. Retrieved from https://privacygiftshop.com/collections/stealth-wear

Sacco, A. (2015, August). Nymi Band uses your heartbeat to secure mobile payments. *CIO Digital Magazine*. Retrieved from http://www.cio.com/article/2969293/wearable-technology/nymi-band-uses-your-heartbeat-to-secure-mobile-payments.html

SDL Customer Journey Analytics. (2015). *Are wearables here to stay?* Retrieved from http://www.sdl.com/Images/SDL_wp_Wearables_SI_A4_hires_tcm94-84978.pdf

Sherbit. (2015a). *The Future of Wearables: Ingestible Sensors*. Retrieved from https://www.sherbit.io/the-future-of-wearables-ingestible-sensors/

Sherbit. (2015b). *iDNA: Why Apple (and Google) Want Your Genetic Information*. Retrieved from https://www.sherbit.io/apple-wants-your-dna/

Statista. (2016). *Facts and statistics on Wearable Technology*. Retrieved from http://www.statista.com/topics/1556/wearable-technology/

Strategy Analytics. (2016). *Global Smartwatch Shipments Overtake Swiss Watch Shipments in Q4 2015*. Retrieved from http://tinyurl.com/zma78ek

USPTO. (2015). *United States Patent Application Publication US 2015/0061837 A1 Reader Communication with Contact Lens Sensors and Display Device*. Retrieved from http://pdfaiw.uspto.gov/.aiw?PageNum=0&docid=20150061837

Vila, P., & Rodriguez, R. J. (2015). Relay Attacks in EMV Contactless Cards with Android OTS Devices.Hack in the Box 2015, Amsterdam.

VTT. (2016). *Smart clothing of the future will automatically adjust itself according to the wearer's actual needs*. Retrieved from http://www.vttresearch.com/media/news/smart-clothing-of-the-future

Yang, H., Yu, Zo, & Choi. (2016). User acceptance of wearable devices. *Telemat. Inf.*, *33*(2), 256-269.

KEY TERMS AND DEFINITIONS

Accelerometer: A small device that senses motion and measures acceleration forces. Commonly found in smartphones.

Bluetooth: A global and unlicensed protocol specified for a short-range radio frequency. Used to transmit between devices in a personal space area.

BYOD: Bring Your Own Device. A policy allowing or encouraging employees to bring their own personally owned technology to use in the workplace. Related terms include BYOT (Technology) BYOP (Phone) and so on.

Glasshole: An individual who behaves in a rude or creepy way while using Google Glass.

Hearables: Smart in-ear headphones with communication and other functionality similar to fitness bands.

Implantables: (Also called embeddables), smart devices embedded under the skins or within the wearer's body. Traditional examples are heart pacemakers or chips for tracking pets.

Ingestibles: "Smart pills" that are swallowed, typically to sense and report specific medical data.

Internet of Things (IoT): Interconnected objects, devices, vehicles, buildings that can exchange information, and be controlled remotely, over the Internet.

Invisibles: Smart devices worn under clothing, or otherwise not obvious, such as insoles or buttons.

Smart (Eyewear): (Glasses) with enhanced functionality, such as Internet connectivity. Watches, wristbands and other body-worn items may also be prefixed by "smart" to denote this.

Smart Watch or Smartwatch: A wristwatch with advanced computer based functionality, similar to that of smartphones, and/or sensing capability.

Wearable: Any external or internal body-worn object with an embedded sensor or computer that can be connected to a network.

Wearables: A synonym for wearable computers or wearable technology in general.

ENDNOTES

[1]   All trademarks used throughout this book are the property of their respective owners. No endorsement of any organization or product is implied.

[2]   We are grateful to Ona Thornquist for drawing our attention to these examples.

Chapter 2
The Risks of Wearable Technologies to Individuals and Organizations

Sarra Berrahal
University of Carthage, Tunisia

Nourredine Boudriga
University of Carthage, Tunisia

ABSTRACT

Advancements in wearable and integrated sensing devices have given tremendous opportunities to enable advanced remote applications including sensing, monitoring, and tracking systems and states. Accordingly, wearable systems can be utilized to provide social and economic well-being for individuals by assisting them in the performance of their daily duties and for organizations by keeping their employees anytime, anywhere connected and by enhancing their productivity. However, wearable devices are, mainly, wireless in nature, which make them exposed to several types of security attacks that may threaten the life of individuals and the security of organizations. This chapter brings a comprehensive study on the benefits of wearable technologies and their related security and privacy issues, discusses the major policies that can be used to mitigate the risk posed by wearable technologies and the proposed techniques to assist users' safety in hazardous workplaces; and discusses the digital investigation of security incidents on wearable technologies.

DOI: 10.4018/978-1-5225-1016-1.ch002

PROMISES AND CHALLENGES OF WEARABLE TECHNOLOGIES TO INDIVIDUALS AND ORGANIZATIONS

The recent technological advancements in wearable systems have provided an unprecedented opportunity for enabling advanced sensing purposes without constraining the user's activities. Such purposes comprise ubiquitous real-time monitoring, tracking, and controlling systems. The term "wearable" refers to miniaturized computing devices that are incorporated into items of clothing and accessories and can be comfortably attached to or worn on the body to automate or enhance personal activities (Sultan, 2015). Indeed, individuals (at home or workplace) can be equipped with a useful set of smart, multi-functional, independent sensor nodes which are able to form a connected network. They can be of different types, including physiological and environmental wearable sensors. Particular classes of wearable sensors include body sensors for healthcare (e.g., heart rate detectors and temperature sensors), speed and motion sensors (e.g., GPS, compasses, and accelerometers), multimedia sensors for environmental monitoring (e.g., video sensors, audio sensors and voice-to-text recognition sensors), and sensors for road safety and intelligent traffic management.

Wearable sensors are in charge of detecting, collecting, and transmitting data to a main node (or system) that will provide a highly optimized processing (e.g., data aggregation, prioritization, and scheduling) (Berrahal & Boudriga, 2014). The motivation for the development of wearable systems is enhanced by the remarkable benefits that could be provided for efficiently monitoring individuals as well as improving an organization's productivity, which will be highlighted in the following two paragraphs.

For individuals, wearable systems can be a helpful way to monitor and track individuals' health statuses in real-time by measuring their biological signs such as body temperature, blood saturation, and oxygen level. In particular, a wearable system on a patient can send alerts to caregivers reporting on the occurrence (and even prior to the occurrence) of health deterioration, such as a heart attack. A wearable system assists physicians and health care professionals in the early detection of diseases, in intervention to improve a patient's comfort, in providing a wide range of advanced healthcare services for people with various degrees of cognitive and physical disabilities such as remote real-time health monitoring, and in accessing to medical data at minimal cost (Darwish & Hassanien, 2011). In addition to the observation of life signs, the opportunity of tracking human behavior and environmental metrics related to hazard phenomena might reduce the risk of mistakes and avoid lethal consequences. Moreover, wearable systems allow greater autonomy of mobility. This allows workers in complex and hazardous workplaces to identify signs and handle any danger. Therefore, a set of sensors can be carried by firefighters or attached to their uniforms to supervise their life signs and manage risks associated to their surrounding environment during the accomplishment of their duties.

In organizations, the potential benefits of wearable technologies include, but are not limited to, the increase of employee productivity, the enhancement of efficiency in solving issues faster, and the growth of overall organizational effectiveness. Wearable systems can keep remote workers connected to their offices and workmates while improving their safety in critical missions. The rapid deployment, self-organization and fault tolerance features of the wearable technology make it a very promising technique that can be considered as a part of monitoring systems in organizations with high-risk roles like the fire department, border surveillance, and remote healthcare to provide workers' safety. In particular, the deployment of a wearable system in medical environment has significant advantages over the traditional systems by providing better health treatment, improving a patient's quality of life, and optimizing the workload of medical staff (Ullah *et al*, 2012).

Therefore, instead of scheduling measured face-to-face meetings, health institutions may provide to monitor patients' health parameters thanks to the use of wearable technologies which operate remotely, continuously, and in real time. In addition, the collected information may be shared among and accessed by various networked users including the patient, doctors and nurses. Besides, the hands-free nature of many wearable devices facilitates the work of health professionals, especially those working in sterile environments. For example, in an operating room where hand washing is required, a surgeon can use smart glasses to continuously receive information and real-time consultation when a second opinion is needed throughout surgery without needing to use their hands. Wearable systems with video and audio capability will enable training and collaboration opportunities for professionals. Thus, users can connect to other professionals, creating the opportunity for real-time collaboration with other organizations to take pictures and record video, to increase productivity by solving issues faster, and to improve operation outcomes. With new devices on hand, small businesses are free to try them out and find the best ways to work with them.

This chapter intends to focus on the security and privacy issues of wearable technology and brings a comprehensive study on risks affecting individuals as well as organizations. Mainly, the vulnerabilities presented by wearable technology include malware (e.g., viruses, and rootkits), and attacks attributed to unsecured wireless connections (e.g., sniffing and man-in-the-middle attacks). In this context, a literature review of the major research works related to the management of risks on wearable technologies is proposed and the following objectives are addressed:

1. Identifying and classifying the major attacks targeting wearable technologies and their impact on wearable devices and information collection quality;
2. Discussing the major policies and procedures that can be used to mitigate the risk posed by wearable technologies and to reinforce data privacy; and

3.   Investigating incidents based on wearable technologies and describing some techniques for the provision of individual safety in hazardous environments.

ATTACKS TARGETING WEARABLE TECHNOLOGIES

Since wearable devices and their applications are, mainly, wireless in nature, they are exposed to several types of security attacks that may induce serious problems and influence both the life of individuals and the security of organizations using wearable systems. In general, these attacks are associated with social, economic, political, and cultural conflicts. An attacker is guided by two main motives, namely mission inference and data benefit (Antonopoulos, Voros, Hey, Anastasolpoulou, & Bideaux, 2015). While the former intents to damage the wearable device and make it inoperable, the latter aims to gain access to the sensitive and confidential data being collected and monitored to affect data privacy.

Impacts on Wearable Devices: Mission Inference

Although, the provision of advanced, unobtrusive, cost effective, and continuous sensing and monitoring, wearable technologies (e.g., sensors) remain devices with little external security features, which make them prone to physical tempering and in consequence increases their vulnerabilities (Al Ameen & Kawak, 2011). These vulnerabilities can be exploited to execute attacks that affect wearable device availability, and consequently the life of system users and an organization's credibility. In the following, three main types of attacks on wearable devices are described.

- **Unauthorized Access to the Wearable Devices:** The wearable devices should be effectively interoperable to guarantee the success of the application supported by wearable devices. In addition, the safety of individuals as well as organizations is compromised when unauthorized parties are able to gain illegal access to their wearable devices. Such an attack is known as a "sinkhole attack", where the attacker tries to attract all the traffic through a compromised node. Therefore, when a wearable device is compromised, the attacker may have access to manipulate information on that device, which then jeopardizes the wearer's physical safety. Since organizations such as hospitals use wearable systems to track users' habits and behaviors and to collect health information, failing to effectively protect such sensitive data could lead to negative attention such as the occurrence of digital crime.

- **Attacking the Wearable Device Availability:** Keeping a wearable system available for its intended use is a crucial requirement that should be provided in applications with high-critical roles. However, attacks such as denial-of-service (DoS) try to bring down the performance of the deployed network by preventing authorized access to network resources or by delaying time critical operations, which may have serious consequences to the health and well-being of individuals. DoS attacks can drain the device's battery by performing an energy-hungry program by repetitively sending request messages to access the wearable device, forcing it to reply to every request until it is inoperable. As wearable devices have limited storage capacity, a buffer overflow attack is another form of DoS that can be launched to exhaust the device's memory in order to prevent it from responding to data collected from sensors.

- **False Data Injection on the Wearable Device:** Wearable devices such as sensors for human activity monitoring enable the record of personal information, including the current location and health status of the user and several residential details. In addition, if deployed in hazardous environment such as borderlines or densely populated areas, wearable devices can be captured and compromised by an attacker in order to gain access to the entire system. The attacker aims to intercept personal data, inject malicious and false sensor reports on the deployed devices, as well as launch denial of service attacks in order to compromise the trustworthiness of the communicated information and, in consequence, undermine the system's capacity to detect valid events. This will unavoidably increase the possibilities to make false decision and even cause lethal consequences on individuals as well as organizations in the case of critical applications such as health monitoring, border surveillance, and environmental monitoring.

Impact on Data Collection: Threats to Data Privacy

Collecting personal and sensitive information can be defined as a double edged sword for individuals and organizations. On the one hand, managing personal health related information enables individuals (e.g., patients, firefighters, soldiers, and employees) to be continuously monitored, tracked, and assisted in their daily activities, which enhances their safety. On the other hand, a set of possible attacks may be launched to exploit any private information owned by these users to put them on risks by causing mental, physical, social, or economic problems. Such attacks can be categorized into two broad areas: private data theft threats, and private data misuse threats that arise from an individual that is trying to exploit the disclosed data beyond its intended use.

A private data theft attack can be defined as a security incident that emerges from inappropriate access to sensitive, protected and confidential data (e.g., the user's identity, location coordinates, device ID, pictures, and video) by internal agents abusing their privileges or by external attackers exploiting the security vulnerability in the targeted system. The success of such an attack enables the execution of frequent scenarios that involve private data misuse, ones that try to mistreat the stolen private data by abusing, disseminating, and leaking it. What's more, these often introduce weaknesses in a system. Motives behind such an attack could be both of economic or non-economic nature. For example, for some organizations such as the insurers, private data theft attacks may have economic value, while some other organizations (such as a healthcare institution) may have non-economic motives.

The attacks targeting the misuse of private information owned by a given organization can be frequent and may, each time they are launched, generate a misuse which causes a direct or indirect financial loss (Miaoui, Boudriga, & Abaoub, 2015). Such an attack can be conducted in order to:

1. Disseminate the stolen private data of a given organization (e.g., customers' credential information, and employees' personal data) in order to damage the organization's reputation and to affect negatively its market value and the trust level of its customers (Miaoui, Boudriga, & Abaoub, 2015). In addition, dissemination of private data may affect the dignity of individuals and, in consequence, result in embarrassment, and discrimination harm. In healthcare application, for example, an attacker who gains privileged access to a health monitoring application may be able to extract sensitive information, including identification information, health records, therapy specification, and history of recommended treatments. The extracted information may be diffused to outsiders for profit, to take revenge on a given person (e.g., celebrity and politician), or to render the organization (i.e., the clinical organization) untrusted.
2. Use the identification information and security credentials (e.g., user accounts' password) stolen from the compromised wearable system of the victim's organization in order to damage the information systems of its partners, by exploiting the mutual trust between them. The attacker uses the collected credentials to compromise the user's device and all data on it. Such an attack may be associated to military or industrial espionage scenarios.
3. Misuse the stolen private data to incorrectly send or receive inappropriate data in order to weaken the whole wearable system and affect the data integrity in such an attack is affected. For example, the breach of customer identification and credit card numbers in a banking company may be conducted in order to commit illegal financial transactions on behalf of these customers. In addition, the stolen identification information of first responders during a surveillance

mission (i.e., soldiers, police officers, firefighters) may be used by an attacker to inject false data. This increases the rate of undetected intrusions. This may lead to life threatening situations. A misuse of private data may occur not only from outside of the information flow chain but also from users who are legally privileged to access the information system. In particular, an employer having access to medical records of employees may deny promotion or, worse, terminate employee employment. In addition, organizations may incur financial losses as a result of malpractices and unnecessary services.

4. Leakage of footprint data in the information system of the victim (individual or organization) may allow attackers to identify the vulnerabilities in the related information system in order to harm it. The adversary can use the collected information to associate a message with a unique transmitter, and then uses multiple phases of inference to deduce the location and the type of wearable devices. Once this is known, various private activities associated to individuals and organizations can be inferred. Therefore, leakage of footprint data may be conducted to determine the daily living activities and to provide data for longitudinal studies, which poses opportunities to violate privacy and to conduct criminal and terrorist attacks using wearables.

In practice, the successful execution of a private data theft attack does not involve a systematic execution of data misuse attack; nonetheless, it associates an additional threat on the owner (i.e., the individual or the organization) of the stolen data. Such a threat can be perceived as the probability that the same or another malicious user misuses the stolen information. In the following, three types of private data misuse attacks are presented.

- **Eavesdropping Attacks:** The eavesdropping process refers to the hearing of a private conversation over a confidential communication in an unauthorized way (Venkatraman, Daniel, & Murugaboopathi, 2013). The eavesdropped information device remains the same within the wearable; nonetheless, its privacy is compromised. The captured data is transferred to the attacker by some means for further illegal processing. When the exchanged messages are not encrypted, they can be analyzed by an attacker in order to extract sensitive information, including the identification information, a physiological metric related to the patient's health status, a therapy specification, and a history of recommended treatments. In addition, eavesdropping attacks may lead to life threatening situations by allowing criminally minded people and institutions to eavesdrop on the user's geographical location (Al Ameen, Liu, & Kwak, 2012).

- **Fingerprint and Timing-Based Snooping (FATS) Attack:** This attack can be executed in many residential environments and smart buildings (homes, enterprises, and safety departments) by eavesdropping on the sensor's radio (even when all of the transmissions are encrypted) in order to collect and assemble the timestamps and fingerprints of all messages generated by the wearable devices. The collected fingerprints are then used to associate the messages with a unique transmitter and execute multiple phases of inference to extract the location and the type of sensor (Srinivasan, Stankovic, & Whitehouse, 2008a). Such an attack allows the attacker to exploit and process the set of stolen information to enable a generation of new insights about how individuals live, work, eat, travel, study, and sleep (Srinivasan, Stankovic, & Whitehouse, 2008b).

- **Jamming Attack:** Since the communication medium between wearable devices is radio-based, jamming activities are always possible (Saleem, Ullah, & kwak, 2011). During such an attack, the attacker creates electromagnetic interference in the operational frequencies of the network and in proximity to the targeted devices to corrupt the transmitted message. The attacker can also cut off the link among the connected wearable devices using continuous radio signal transmissions to block the access of authorized users to a particular frequency channel (Venkatraman, Daniel, & Murugaboopathi, 2013). In particular, a jamming attack would prevent the medical wearable device from collecting reading and critical events from sensors, and consequently, actions such as delivering the adequate therapy, alarming, or reacting appropriately are not enabled.

SECURING WEARABLE TECHNOLOGIES

In wearable-based applications, where various sensor devices are embedded on the human body to monitor sensitive information, a centralized control device can be applied for data transmission from in and out of the network. Security measures including data encryption, user authentication, data integrity checks and similar processes can be used to control the exchanged traffic and reinforce security against several malicious attacks and data breaches. This section is intended to discuss the major techniques that can be applied to secure wearable technologies. For this, four major security services can be distinguished:

- **Data Encryption Service:** One of the most commonly techniques used in order to provide confidentiality of data against eavesdropping attacks. This means that critical data, including keys and user identities, should be encrypted to avoid that it is not disclosed during transmission. Sensitive data can be characterized from the kind and type of protocol being used (i.e. symmetric or asymmetric cryptography, mutual authentication, identity or nonce based encryption) (Malik, 2012). Ensuring data confidentiality means that the data can only be accessed and retrieved by only those entities (individuals or organizations) that are authorized for this purpose. Although the provision of data confidentiality may overcome the problem of data leakage, it is not useful against false data injection attacks.

- **Data Integrity Service:** An efficient method against data modification attacks. It entails two main functions, namely data integrity and data origin authentication. Through the provision of data integrity, the receiver can be assured that the data has not been altered or tampered. Data integrity can be provided using Message Authentication Code (MAC), where the sender and receiver share a secret key (Malik, 2012). On the other hand, data origin authentication provisioning proves to the receiver that the received data has been originated by the specified source (i.e., wearable system).

- **Authentication Service:** An efficient technique that needs to be implemented in wearable systems to avoid and minimize impersonation attacks. Each individual carrying a wearable monitoring system and taking part in the communication should be authenticated prior to being allowed to access to the shared resources (Malik, 2012). However, symmetric authentication techniques are not practical and recommended for a multi-party communication scenario (necessitates strong trust assumptions). The mutual authentication and one-way authentication techniques can be used to provide authentication based on trust requirements.

- **Freshness Protection Service:** Aims to guarantee that the received data collections are recent and that previous received messages have not been replayed. Since confidentiality and authentication services may not be useful against replaying the old frames eavesdropped by an attacker, data freshness becomes an evident service to provide, especially in wearables, sensor-based networks that use shared resources and operations (Al Ameen, Liu, & Kwak, 2012). To ensure data freshness, nonce (i.e., a randomly generated number) or a time token (i.e., time dependent counter) can be attached to the data (Malik, 2012). Consequently, messages having old time tokens and an aforementioned nonce are rejected, which guarantees the achievement of data freshness by only approving recent data.

Security measures in wearable technologies should be applied in three main levels - namely, administrative, operational (physical), and technical.

- *Security measures at administrative level* should be implemented in order to manage the wearable system and check the security breaches by the administrator system. To this end, a well-defined user hierarchy in conjunction with strong authentication measures can be useful to prevent security breaches at this level (Al Ameen, Liu, & Kwak, 2012). The security measures should also grant the access to the private collected data only to authorized users, according to different types of privileges.
- *Security measures at operational level are required to be implemented* since the wearable devices may be vulnerable to human-induced and natural incidents. Human-induced incidents take the form of attacks on system availability such as DoS attacks. Natural incidents may take different forms, including the possible destruction of sensors under harsh conditions, the degradation after an operational time period of systems' conditions due to energy exhaustion of the limited power of sensors, and the malfunctioning of sensors, as they may be sensitive to the direct effects of the environment surrounding them (e.g., fire, vegetation, wear, and weather). Such a problem may lead to the malfunction of the wearable system and may induce serious problems to the overall system operation and to human life. Therefore, a careful designing of devices is an essential requirement in order to make them temper proof (Al Ameen, Liu, & Kwak, 2012).
- *Security measures need also to be applied at Technical Level.* In general, wearable systems are based on a server/client architecture where the data generated by all clients equipped with wearable devices is sent to central servers, where it will be stored and processed. Therefore, security measures should be applied at both the server side and end-user side to ensure safe transmission and exchange of information.

SECURING DATA PRIVACY

Privacy is among the major concerns in wearable systems with regard to public safety applications, including healthcare, military and firefighting. This is because the wearable devices are in charge of collecting critical information such as the health records of patients, the locations of military personnel, and the private information related to a specific mission. Privacy issues arise from many reasons including personal beliefs, cultural and social environments, and other general public and private causes. In addition, wirelessly sending out sensitive data from a wearable device can generate serious threats to the privacy of an individual as well as organizations.

Compared to traditional security and authentication techniques, the biometrics-based technology offers numerous advantages in terms of reliably and capability of detecting pretender users based on distinctive behavioral (e.g., signature) or physiological (e.g., fingerprints, retina, face) characteristics (Ramli, Ahmad, Abdollah, & Dutkiewicz, 2013). The usage of biometrics in securing a healthcare application has multiple advantages. It facilitates patient admission, offers an easy access to patients' medical records, eliminates duplicate and redundant medical records, establishes uniform method of authentication, identifies unconscious or compromised patients, and detects the misuse of medical services.

Fingerprint biometrics provide the needed security measure to ensure authorized and appropriately authenticated users to access the network. Researchers (Chen et al, 2008) describe an authentication solution that uses the fingerprint technology in order to secure and protect personal medical records against unauthorized users. Leonard, Pons, & Asfour (2009) propose a framework that uses four types of biometric identifiers (i.e. fingerprint, iris, retina, DNA) to distinctively identify patients using their complete electronic health record. Hembroff & Muftic (2010) integrate fingerprint biometrics in the smart card as an authentication measure in order to decrease the possibility of conducting impersonation attacks. The fingerprint-based technique is practical in order to authenticate the users' access to the health-related information stored in patients' medical smart cards.

Additional potential biometric modalities have been researched within the health care industry based on bio-signals. The work presented in Irum, Ali, Khan, & Abbas (2013) supports the use of biometric measurements and proposes a hybrid technique that supports both plug-and-play capability and some pre-deployment of keys in order to strengthen the security among Wireless Body Area Networks (WBANs). The proposed technique considers two main levels of security measures, which are intra-WBAN and inter-WBAN secure communications. In the first level, the sensor nodes are in charge of measuring physiological values (PVs) of the human body. The keys are then automatically calculated among the sensor nodes using the measured PVs. The proposed technique, during intra-WBAN communication, has a linear time complexity for feature generation from electrocardiogram (EKG) signals. The second level considers the securing of inter-WBAN communications (performed via their personal servers (PSs)) and is entirely based on preloading of keys. The generation of keys is achieved with the help of biometrics of any PS (key generator), which is in charge of generating a key pool using its biometric values and then transmitting it to the entire network. A key refreshment mechanism schedule is provided where each medical station assigns any PS the responsibility of refreshing the key. In Wang (2011), ECG signal is employed in a data authentication approach to reduce the overhead of key exchange process. The ECG biometric signal is used as a security scheme to provide secure communication inside the WBAN. In their approach, sensors within a BAN also employ the biometric authentication to differentiate which person they belong to.

Other researchers (Ellouze, Allouche, Ben Ahmed, Rekhis, & Boudriga, 2013) propose a novel solution for securing cardiac Implementable Medical devices (IMDs) against unauthorized access, battery depletion, and denial of service attacks. In this solution, new components have been introduced to the architecture of an IMD in order to perform Radio Frequency (RF) energy harvesting. The latter is implemented as a mechanism to enforce secure key generation and to design a powerless mutual authentication protocol. A technique for dynamic biometric keys extraction from electrocardiogram signals collected at both sides (the programmer and the IMD) is also used in order to allow a secure access to the IMD devices in both, regular and emergency situations.

In Park, Basaran, Park, & Son (2014), an energy-efficient privacy protection for smart home environments using behavioral semantics is proposed. It uses the concept of semantic similarity where a selected group of sensor nodes are in charge of generating fake data, which are semantically similar to the real phenomena that is being monitored. These fake activities together form an activity cloak that hides the actual observed private activities. However, generating fake data from all of the sensors may result in excessive dissipation of precious energy without any additional benefit. In addition, the distribution of private activities throughout the day is commonly similar in residential environments, and this fact can be exploited by the adversary. Therefore, the attack does not start with zero information and with some additional knowledge, such as the job of the residents, it can considerably reduce the number of possibilities. In this context, the method described in Park, Basaran, Park, & Son (2014) aims to hide the real phenomena by cloaking it with additional activities that have a high probability of occurrence in order to significantly reduce the energy overhead of privacy protection.

INVESTIGATING WEARABLE TECHNOLOGIES BASED INCIDENTS

The threats associated with the unexpected increase in the number of security attacks and the sophistication of intrusion techniques made it impossible to prevent effectively and completely the attacks on wearable devices, regardless of the undertaken security measures. Indeed, security measures are not always sufficient to avoid and stop every attack. Such a weakness points up the need for conducting and developing an efficient incident investigation plan in order to, efficiently, react to security incidents (Rekhis, 2007). The investigation can be defined as the process of detecting attacks and appropriately collecting and analyzing the digital evidence in order to report the incident and carry out audits to avoid future attacks (Rekhis & Boudriga, 2011). The digital evidence can be defined as *any information stored or transmitted using a computer that support or refute a theory of how an offence occurred or that address critical elements of the alibi such as intent or alibi* (Casey, 2004). Nowadays, digital evidence may be crucial in criminal investigation since many crimes are committed completely through wearable technologies such as identity and data privacy theft, murder, economic fraud, or terrorism.

Digital Investigation Phases

Three phases constitute the digital investigation process. They are:

- **The Preparation Phase:** It entails the preparation of a specific set of investigation tactics as well as a set of forensic toolkits, defining tools and hardware to be used. The set of investigation tactics focuses on the description of the several features of the system that will be investigated using the best standards and available technical resources such as details of vulnerabilities and attacks. To identify the affected system resources, a system baseline that takes a snapshot about important features (e.g., configuration, system processes, and checksums) has to be performed. The snapshot is then compared to the snapshot that has been taken during the investigation process. Such a comparison should be made in order to provide some useful information to allow the detection of the occurrence of security incidents as well as the identification of its cause, source, and scope.

- **The Data Collection Phase:** It involves the collection and secure recording of evidence using standardized and accepted procedures. The evidence collection should be made in such a way that a trade-off between its cost and its usefulness is established (i.e., a maximized usefulness and a minimized cost), regardless the objective and scope of the investigation. Any investigation should be quickly implemented, especially in high availability systems (e.g., in healthcare systems where mobile patients are always connected via their wearable and implanted medical devices to the medical server) so that the safe state of the compromised system is reestablished. On the other hand and due to speed worry, investigators should be cautious about missing or losing valuable data. A plan is developed to collect and acquire data that ranges from volatile data to a sector-by sector copying of disk content (Brannon & Song, 2008). Chain of custody is a widely used procedure during digital forensic investigation. CoC represents a log file where records related to each action taken on the collected evidence is listed. Such a file will serve as a proof to demonstrate investigation's credibility.

- **The Data Analysis Phase:** It aims at inspecting all significant information and correctly reconstruct fragments of data to determine the causes and the effects of the occurred incident. However, unlike the two previously mentioned phases that can be partially automated, data analysis has few elements that should be performed mechanically. In addition, data analysis encounters some difficulties regarding the minimization of the amount of data to be analyzed. The data analysis is, generally, followed by a reporting phase. The latter involves writing a report that outlines the analysis process as well as the pertinent evidences recuperated from the overall investigation.

Requirements for an Efficient Digital Investigation for Wearables

The ad-hoc nature of wearable networks makes them vulnerable to various security threats. In addition, their deployment in hazardous and unattended areas and their physical interaction with environment lead to additional vulnerability and increase the likelihood of being attacked. However, merely detecting these attacks is often insufficient to efficiently react against the conducted incident (e.g., criminal activities). Wearable devices collect, over an operational period, a wealth of data about their users' identities, their health information, and their habits and behavior. Such information can be very valuable in a course of an investigation since it can provide a source for profiling the user habits and behavior. Therefore, digital investigation is a crucial process that should be carried out in order to study and analyze traces left behind on wearable systems. An efficient system for digital investigation of lethal attacks on wearable devices should fulfill the following requirements.

- **The Deployment of a Set of Observers:** The communication in a wearable system should be observed by a set of investigator nodes, called "observers". The latter should be able to cover, monitor, and secure the communication between wearable devices (e.g., sensors) within their coverage area. Compared to the wearable sensors, the network of observers is composed of a set of resource-rich devices that are equipped with enhanced collection, storing, processing, and transmission capabilities. Therefore, during investigations, the observers are assumed to perform several types of operations, including the collection of information regarding the network topology in the covered area and the identity of the nodes whose behavior is suspicious, the sniffing of datagrams sent by covered sensors and the routing paths they followed, the securing of digital evidences generation and forwarding to the base station (BS), and the exchange of evidences with other observers. The network of observers can be also configured to wake-up additional or unreachable devices, if necessary.

- **The Generation of a Set of Accurate and Reliable Copies of Evidence:** The wearable device should generate and made available for investigation a set of accurate and reliable copies of evidences. Ellouze, Rekhis, Allouche, & Boudriga (2014) have discussed that at least three types of evidence that should be available by a medical device. The first type includes traces related to the collected EMG data over a sufficient period of time preceding the patient's death. This information could allow the identification of the cause and time of the patient's health deterioration. The second type refers to traces related to the medical device responses each time an emergency situation is detected (e.g., fibrillation in case of an IMD), which would allow the identification of inappropriate responses. The third type of traces is associated to sensitive activities that have been undertaken by remote users including authentication and reconfiguration of therapy parameters. The recognition of such sensitive activities will be helpful for the identification of potential malicious attacks that produced inappropriate responses.

- **The Need for a Cooperative Investigation (between Technical Investigator and Medical Experts):** Because the main purpose of a wearable device is the collection of health-related parameters of its user, digital investigations should take into consideration two types of evidence -- namely, technical evidence and medical evidence. The former provides a history of the set of sensitive events that occurred on the device configuration or triggered by the connected users (e.g., unsuccessful and successful attempts of remote access, and alteration of the therapy settings). The latter is a set of findings derived by pathologists and medical experts during the examination of the victim and the investigation of the carried medical device (e.g., the patient's electromyogram (EMG), and the set of responses and the therapy delivery undertaken by the device over time). Therefore, without the approval of a medical expert, a technical investigator is unable to solely demonstrate that a lethal attack conducted on the wearable medical device is the source of the patient's death. On the other side, a forensic pathologist is unable to prove that a patient death (induced by an inappropriate response) can always be associated to a criminal modification of the medical device settings (Ellouze, Rekhis, Allouche, & Boudriga, 2014). To address such a problem, technical investigators can assist pathologists in proving the occurrence of malicious incidents using the collected evidences. Consequently, an efficient digital investigation system of security attacks on wearable medical devices should implement a cooperative investigation approach that merges the inferences derived by technical investigators and the inferences generated by medical experts in the same framework.

CASE STUDY

This section focuses on the description of a case study related to a postmortem investigation on a cardiac implantable medical (IMD) device that was discussed in Ellouze, Allouche, Ben Ahmed, Rekhis, & Boudriga (2014). The researchers provided a three-step methodology of investigation that implies the correlation between conclusions derived from both technical and medical investigations, which we will discuss below.

The first step entails the conducting of a medical investigation that uses the medical evidence collected by pathologists from the IMD during investigation. A set of invariants are defined at this step in order to provide a description of anomalies and irregularities that can be detected by a physician on an EMG and the related set of unpredicted responses of the IMD. A set of inference rules describing an inference engine have been formulated to highpoint causal relations between the different types of arrhythmia and IMD reactions. The proposed inference engine is executed in backward chaining, starting from the event of heart death, in order to allow medical investigators (i.e., pathologists) to program the generation of possible medical scenarios that illustrates and describes the evolution of the patient's health status till he died. A second step consists of a technical investigation, during which the IMD device is technically examined by a physician in order to reconstruct attack scenarios, according to the collected technical evidence. The initial system state of the IMD is described by technical investigators. Such a description is based on an investigation library that contains a description of all simple attacks targeting IMDs and the sequence of action performed by the device in response to the detected incident. At this stage the technical investigator remains unable to prove and confirm that the derived attacks are the cause of the patient's death. The third step focuses on the correlation of the reconstructed scenarios taken from medical and technical investigations in order to prove that one of the attacks conducted on an IMD device and described during the technical scenarios, producing t least one of the generated potential medical scenarios. The correlation between medical and technique scenarios is important to validate the generated medical scenarios since some events could be unobserved by the IMD.

Description of the Conducted Scenario

- **The Criminal Attack Scenario:** After the performance of a successful authentication of himself to an IMD using the acquired credentials, the attacker succeeds in gaining access to all data collected and stored within the medical device. The attacker is, therefore, able to read the health status of the patient by examining health-related data. The criminal attack scenario considers that the attacker at this stage aims to misconfigure the IMD device and to make it unable to efficiently detect, identify, and respond to arrhythmia. To do so, the attacker proceeds by the modification of the therapy settings by changing the thresholds related to the detection of some arrhythmia. After that, the attacker will be disconnected.

- **The Medical Incident:** Due to any normal physiological situations (e.g., stress, fright, and anger), the patient gets a Sinus-Tachycardia (ST), a few hours after the criminal attack. However, since the IMD is now a misconfigured device, such an event is detected as a Ventricular Fibrillation (VF). In this case, the IMD reacts by a significant electric shock. Inappropriately identifying the occurred event every time the same arrhythmia happens, the IMD will generate the same electric shock response (five other electric shocks). The last electric shock, among the delivered ones, led to the occurrence of a real VF event. The IMD device may be unable to respond to such VF because the maximum number of electric shocks that can be delivered within a predefined period of time, has been reached (6 is the maximum number of electric shocks set by physicians). During the resultant deactivation period, a real VFs can happen without being responded by the IMD, which consequently may lead to the patient's death. Such a scenario is illustrated in Figure 1.

Figure 1. A typical example of an attack scenario on the IMD

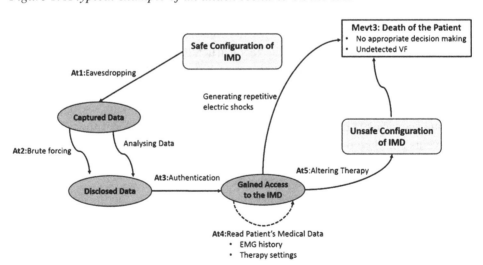

Postmortem Analysis

During the postmortem investigation process, a set of techniques, including a medical inference mechanism, inferring medical scenarios, technical investigation, and correlating potential scenarios, are utilized.

- **The Collection of Medical and Technical Evidence:** The technical evidences collected from the IMD device shown three events, which are time-stamped and described in the following according to their order of appearance: Tevt1) The opening of a session after a successful authentication with the delivery of session identity and user id; Tevt2) The update of therapy settings values; Tevt3) The session closing with the provision of session identity.
- **The Collection of EMG History and Traces of IMD Responses:** The medical evidence collection illustrated a set of events that are associated to significant arrhythmia and IMD responses. These events are described in the following according to their order of appearance: Mevt1) The occurrence of six successive episodes of Sinus-Tachycardia (ST), each ST is directly followed by a delivery of a therapy appropriate for VF; Mevt2) The delivery of a number of VFs instances. The intensity of these VFs grew from an instance to another. However, none of these VFs is followed by an IMD response; and Mevt3) The occurrence of a heart death.
- **The Generation of Potential Medical Scenarios:** Based of the collected medical evidence and the set of inference rules described in Ellouze, Allouche, Ben Ahmed, Rekhis, & Boudriga (2014), one potential medical scenario can be generated as follows: Starting with a heart death event (Mevt3), rule (3) that states that the occurrence of a VF, to which the IMD does responds inappropriately or not respond, leads to the occurrence of a heart death can be executed in regressive chaining, since the premises of the rule correspond to the medical event Mevt2. Then, Rule (1), which uses the same premises provided by Rule 3, but with the generation of a consecutive VF instead of heart death, is executed in backward chaining several times (a number of times equal to the instances of VF in event Mevt2). Finally, Rule (12) that states the occurrence of repetitive ST, each one being followed a wrong response of the IMD, which leads to the occurrence of a VF. Its consequence is a VF and its premises are provided by the event Mevt1. Finally, the conclusion derived from the inference system corresponds to a medical scenario in the form of

(Mevt1, Mevt2, Mevt3).

- **The Generation of Technical Attack Scenarios:** Using the traces collected from the IMD log and based on the investigation library that describes a set of simple attacks threatening IMDs, two main possible technical attack scenarios are identified:

The attacker conducts an eavesdropping attack (At1) to capture the credentials exchanged through messages, which use weak and lightweight encryption due to energy constraints. Therefore, by brute-forcing these credentials (At2), the attacker succeeds to authenticate himself to the IMD device. After that, a session is opened by the IMD (At3). At this stage, the attacker is able to visualize and read the collected medical data (At4) including EMG history and therapy settings. At the end, the attacker misconfigures the IMD by altering the therapy settings (At5) and then disconnects (At6).

The attacker intercepts the exchanged traffic between the IMD device and the programmer (At7), at the time when a physician was consulting the configuration state of the IMD. After the interception action, the attacker replays the access request (At8). Replaying the access request causes the opening of an IMD session (At3). At this stage, the attacker reads the stored medical data (At4), alters the therapy settings (At5), and then disconnects (At6) (as in the previous scenario).

The actions At1, At2, At7, and At8 are not included in the collected evidences since they target network resources, and therefore are not unobservable by the IMD device. At4 is also not included in the collected evidences because it is a legitimate action that does not appear to be sensitive. Consequently, the observable event is in the form of (At3, At5, At6), which corresponds to events Tevt1, Tevt2, and Tevt3 available in the collected technical evidence.

- **The Correlation of the Derived Technical and Medical Scenarios:** Two causes, respectively, affect correlations which confirm that the medical scenario was caused by each one of the possible technical attack scenarios. Consequently, the patient's death can result from a lethal and criminal attack conducted on the IMD device. The first correlation is between a misconfiguration action of the IMD device by modifying therapy settings (At5) and an inappropriate IMD response provided by the event (Mevt1). The second correlation is between therapy settings alteration (At5) and the absence of IMD response provided by event (Mevt2).

TECHNIQUES FOR INDIVIDUAL SAFETY
IN HAZARDOUS ENVIRONMENTS

Human intervention in a hazardous environment is, generally, risky, tedious, error-prone, costly, and time-consuming. In this context, it is envisioned that wearable technologies such as WBANs and wearable sensors can be utilized by safety providers (e.g., firefighting departments, police agencies, border patrols, and hospitals) to overcome such a problem and to enable real-time surveillance. In addition, some WBAN-based systems have been designed to provide continuous health monitoring of people suffering from chronic diseases or health disorders including diabetes, Parkinson's disease, and Alzheimer's disease, for instance. While some techniques focused on posture detection and human behavior tracking (e.g., tracking user's location), others make use of physiological and environmental sensor devices in order to identify irregular health conditions.

In the following, some techniques and approaches that were proposed in the literature to assist the safety of individuals working in hazardous environments are presented. In particular, we consider two main applications; namely firefighting and health monitoring.

Wearable Firefighting Systems: Assisted Indoor Navigation

The LifeNet project described in Klann (2007) provides the functionality of traditional lifelines and support firefighters' navigation in indoor environments. It is composed of a set of deployed sensor nodes that provide both relative positioning and a wearable system. The latter manages some specific data collected from the sensor network to help a navigational guidance using a head-mounted display transported by the firefighters. Each sensor node acts as a waypoint to guide the firefighter when he navigates in the area of the incident. After being deployed, the LifeNet sensors collect environmental information (e.g., the temperature and the air quality) around firefighters and also on whether they have been moving (Klann, 2009). These sensors will also help firefighters in building escape routes.

Scholz & Decker (2010) described another navigation system, called the Landmarke project, in which a set of nodes called "Landmarke nodes" is deployed either in an automatic way or completely by the firefighters themselves to provide navigational assistance. These Landmarke nodes act as waypoints with special capabilities to find the closest exit, to find a lost firefighter, to tag important places, or to collect information regarding the progress of the firefighting mission. They allow recognizing areas under very harsh conditions and enabling navigation under circumstances in which this would be normally not possible. The firefighters are also equipped with a set of wearable sensors in the form of a body area network (BAN). The latter acts as interactive clothes, to call the attention of firefighters and allow them to interact with the set of deployed landmarks. Wearable sensors carried by the firefighters and the landmarks exchange information, building a layer of information that provides a perception of the environment.

In Berrahal & Boudriga (2015), the authors propose a smart navigation approach for firefighters working in indoor environments. The designed approach is based on the use of wireless body area networks (WBANs) carried by firefighters and on a novel concept of graph called Temporal Mobile Weighted Graph (TMWG), where information regarding the firefighters' health and their surrounding environment are collected every time slot. In addition, based on the management of histories of collections, the hazard is assessed and predicted using a library of estimation models. Problems such as setting up real-time techniques that can predict the isolation moments of firefighters and predict the occurrence of damage aggravation are addressed. Besides, the proposed firefighting system employs a cooperative communication model between WBANs, either via same or different teams, to overcome significant connectivity troubles (e.g., path loss problems), which can be inevitably experienced in hazardous indoor environment. The proposed approach allows the assistance of firefighters' mobility safety (using appropriate sensors), while analyzing and assessing the risk and the errors associated to their locations.

Wearable Health Monitoring Systems

In Patel (2010) a home-monitoring system is developed in order to monitor patients with Parkinson's disease and other medical conditions. The proposed system is based on a wireless wearable sensors network that collect a set of physical information from people that experience severe motor fluctuations. To relay the collected data to a remote clinical site, a web-based health monitoring application is designed. On the other hand, in order to guarantee both data availability and data security of the health monitoring system, a well-provisioned centralized portal server offers a reliable and secure central location for synchronizing real-time data delivery and multimedia services.

Singh (2014) focused on the use of a handheld tele-electrocardiogram (ECG) system in order to identify heart conditions of underserved population in rural areas. In such an environment, the doctor per patient ratio is low and the access to health care organizations is generally difficult. Therefore, a clinical validation has been conducted by considering handheld tele-ECG as a screening tool for evaluation of cardiac diseases in the rural population. ECG was obtained in 450 individuals (mean age 31.49 ± 20.058) residing in the periphery of Chandigarh, India, from April 2011 to March 2013, using the handheld tele-ECG machine. The data were then transmitted to physicians in Postgraduate Institute of Medical Education and Research (PGIMER), Chandigarh, for their expert opinion. ECG was interpreted as normal in 70% individuals. Left ventricular hypertrophy (9.3%) was the commonest abnormality, followed closely by old myocardial infarction (5.3%).

In Kakria, Tripathi, & Kitipawang (2015) a real-time health monitoring system for remote patients with heart disease is described. The system integrates wearable sensors and Smartphone, considering the cost minimization, the ease of use of the application, the security of collected and transmitted data as well as data accuracy. The conceptualized system provides a web interface for two-way communication between the medical staff and the monitored patients. The wearable system is used in order to collect patient's physiological information, which is then transmitted wirelessly (using Bluetooth low energy technology) to a smartphone. The latter transmit the received data via Wi-Fi or 3G to a web interface. In addition, emergency alerts are generated by the designed system by comparing patient's data with a set of predefined values. The transmission of such alerts will enable doctors to identify when a patient's health status should be investigated.

Another technique, one that focuses on the deployment of WBAN-based systems for healthcare purposes at home, has been proposed in Otto, Jovanov, & Milenkovic (2011). A prototype has been built using sensors devices including a heart and a motion sensor and a home health server application. Accordingly, a multi-tiered architecture is considered. The first tier consists of a set of tiny and smart wireless devices that are strategically deployed on the human body in order to collect, process, and store user information. Then, using wireless communication, the set of sensors transmit directly the collected data to a WBAN gateway. The latter offers time synchronization services by periodically transmitting beacon messages and forwarding messages to either a home server or a medical server. In the case where the user is out of the communication range of the WBAN gateway, the collected data is automatically buffered locally in the sensor nodes. These data can be transmitted when the WBAN communication is reestablished.

In Javaid, Faisal, Khan, Nayab, & Zahid (2013), a Wireless Body Area Sensor Networks (WBASN) for measuring fatigue of soldiers was proposed. It includes three sensors attached to the soldier's body to monitor specific parameters such as body temperature, blood glucose levels, and heart rate. Therefore, the collected data is sent to the Base Station (BS). In Akram(2015), a FAtigue MEasurement (FAME) protocol is proposed for soldiers and soccer players using in-vivo sensors in the form of WBASNs. This work intended the previous technique and introduced a composite parameter to measure fatigue by setting a threshold value for each sensor. On the basis of the defined threshold, whenever any threshold was exceeded, the soldiers or players are confirmed to be in a state of fatigue. In addition, a vibration pad is used to provide relaxation services for tired muscles.

CONCLUSION

In this chapter we studied security and privacy issues of the wearable technology and we provided a comprehensive study on risks affecting individuals as well as organizations. To this end, we started the manuscript by bringing a description of the major challenges of wearable technologies on individuals as well as organizations. In addition, we identified and classified the major attacks targeting wearable technologies and their impact on wearable devices and information collection quality. Attacks on wearable devices include performing an authorized access to the wearable device, affecting device availability, and conducting false data injection. Attacks on information collection aims to allow the attacker exploiting any private information owned by users of the wearable system in order to implement either data theft or misuse. This would put individuals and organizations on risks by causing mental, physical, social, and economic problems. Eavesdropping, FATS, and Jamming are among the major attacks that may be conducted to implement private data misuse. In addition, we discussed the major policies and procedures that can be used to mitigate the risk posed by wearable technologies and to reinforce data privacy. Since security measures are not always sufficient to avoid and stop every attack conducted on the wearable system, we discussed the need for implementing investigation approaches and we described the requirements that should be fulfilled to achieve an efficient investigation. A typical example of postmortem investigation on a cardiac implanted medical device is described to explain how technical and medical investigation can interoperate to help identifying the cause of death of a patient and take the appropriate actions to strengthen the security of the implanted device against future attacks. Finally, we described some WBAN-based systems that have been proposed in the literature to assist individuals working in hazardous environment by enhancing their protection through the use of a set of wearable sensor nodes strategically attached to their clothes, body, or equipment.

PERSPECTIVES ON WEARABLE TECHNOLOGIES

The advancements on wearable sensing technologies are drastically revolutionizing our daily life, by participating as a major system in the provision of public safety security by efficiently monitoring the health statuses of patients as well as individuals working in hazardous environments. In addition, they offer economic well-being for organizations by improving their productivity. To develop an efficient wearable system. the following perspectives have to be addressed and discussed.

- **The Setting Up of Warning Systems for Risk Aggravation:** A wearable system must integrate risk awareness capabilities in order to be able to identify the situation and risks associated to the environment where it is deployed. For example, the communications of wireless devices in clinical healthcare environment could cause a significant rise in the electromagnetic interference with critical medical systems (e.g., wearable sensors attached to patients). Delaying urgent data transmission, as well as data loss, are among the major consequences of inter-device interference that can lead to the death of the monitored patient due to remaining undiagnosed and untreated for a period of time (e.g., VF). Therefore, to mitigate potential risks of interference between wireless devices and wearable medical equipment in close vicinity, an interference-awareness system may be deployed on the patients, doctors, nurses, healthcare structures, and even ambulances to support the generation of alerts in case of interference. The deployment of such a system in an organization (equipped with wearable sensors that collect sensitive information associated to its activity as well as employees) may be also useful to detect wireless devices with data collection capabilities and to generate alerts, if necessary.
- **The Implementation of Multiple Types of Investigation Tools:** A postmortem digital investigation consists on implementing a reactive investigation of attacks on a wearable device (after the attack was) in order to collect any stored information and digital traces left behind by the attacker to investigate how and when the malicious action was performed. However, with the sophistication and the increase of the number of lethal attacks on wearable sensors, another type of digital investigation, called either "proactive" or "online investigation", should be implemented. The latter is required to deal with data volatility and dynamicity, since the attacker may be able to hide and even erase any traces on the wearable system. By being proactive, the investigation is ready for incidents and allows wearable system to better handle attacks by performing data collection, detecting suspicious events, analyzing evidence, and reporting an incident before its completion. An on-line investigation can be performed in organizations such as banks as an investigation-business related approach that determines and predicts the occurrence of new attacks using the collected evidences.
- **Developing Guidelines for Use and Interception of Wearable Devices in Organizations:** Wearable systems are deployed everywhere in hospitals, factories, airports, and enterprises. Therefore, the establishment of access rules

that authorize or deny the acceptance of new wearable devices is required to minimize the risk of attacks and inter-device interference. In addition, since an authorized wearable system may be compromised, the setting up of a warning system that detects suspicious behaviors and actions performed by an accepted user should be considered.

QUESTIONS

Although the unprecedented opportunities provided by wearable technologies to improve the overall quality of our daily lives and economic well-being apply to a wide range of fields, including environmental surveillance, health care assistance, and human behavior tracking. At the same time, it's essential to be mindful of the consequences and risks of these devices. We should note that the benefits provided by wearable systems must be balanced with the security, safety, and privacy concerns of the user. Based on the topics discussed along this chapter, the following questions can be expressed and investigated in order to properly use wearable technologies:

- What is the type and nature of evidence that can be included in the postmortem investigation described in the case study section?
- What causes the set of evidence to be lost or missed during the investigation? And what security measure should be taken to avoid such a problem?
- What makes the implementation of wearable technologies in hazardous and harsh environment into a challenging task? And what are the major security issues that can threaten the appropriate functioning of the worn system?
- What are the major requirements that should be satisfied by the WBAN-based system to additionally guarantee of data security and integrity? Is there any dependency between the guarantee of data security and the provision of quality of service (QoS) by the generated heterogeneous traffic?

REFERENCES

Akram, S., Javaid, N., Ahmad, A., Khan, Z. A., Imran, M., Guizani, M., & Ilahi, M. et al. (2015). A Fatigue Measuring Protocol for Wireless Body Area Sensor Networks. *Journal of Medical Systems*, *39*(12), 1–15. doi:10.1007/s10916-015-0338-8 PMID:26490151

Al Ameen, M., & Kwak, K. (2011). Social Issues in Wireless Sensor Networks with Healthcare Perspective. *The International Arab Journal of Information Technology*, *8*(1), 52–58.

Al Ameen, M., Liu, J., & Kwak, K. (2012). Security and Privacy Issues in Wireless Sensor Networks for Healthcare Applications. *Journal of Medical Systems*, *36*(1), 93–101. doi:10.1007/s10916-010-9449-4 PMID:20703745

Antonopoulos, C. P., Voros, N. S., Hey, S., Anastasolpoulou, P., & Bideaux, A. (2015). Secure and Efficient WSN Communication Infrastructure. In Cyberphysical Systems for Epilepsy and Related Brain Disorders (pp. 163-188). Berlin: Springer International. doi:10.1007/978-3-319-20049-1_9

Berrahal, S., & Boudriga, N. (2014). A Smart QoS- based Traffic Management for WBANs. In *Proceedings of the 14th International Symposium on Communications and Information Technologies (ISCIT 2014)*. doi:10.1109/ISCIT.2014.7011892

Berrahal, S., Boudriga, N., & Chammem, M. (2015). WBAN-Assisted Navigation for Firefighters in Indoor Environments. *Ad Hoc & Sensor Wireless Networks Journal*, *28*(5).

Brannon, S. K., & Song, T. (2008). Computer Forensics: Digital Forensic Analysis Methodology. *Computer Forensics Journal*, *56*(1), 1–8.

Buergy, C., & Kenn, H. (2013). Wearable systems for industrial augmented reality applications. In *Proceedings of the 2013 ACM conference on Pervasive and ubiquitous computing adjunct publication*. doi:10.1145/2494091.2499568

Casey, E. (2004). *Digital Evidence and Computer Crime* (2nd ed.). Academic Press.

Chan, M., Estève, D., Fourniols, J. Y., Escriba, C., & Campo, E. (2012). Smart wearable systems: Current status and future challenges. *Artificial Intelligence in Medicine*, *56*(3), 137–156. doi:10.1016/j.artmed.2012.09.003 PMID:23122689

Darwish, A., & Hassanien, A. E. (2011). Wearable and implantable wireless sensor network solutions for healthcare monitoring. *Sensors (Basel, Switzerland)*, *11*(6), 5561–5595. doi:10.3390/s110605561 PMID:22163914

Ellouze, N., Allouche, M., Ben Ahmed, H., Rekhis, S., & Boudriga, N. (2013). Securing Implantable Cardiac Medical Devices: Use of Radio Frequency Energy Harvesting. In *Proceedings of the International Workshop on Trustworthy Embedded Devices (TrustED 2013) in conjunction with CCS 2013*. Berlin, Germany: ACM. Doi:10.1145/2517300.2517307

Ellouze, N., Allouche, M., Ben Ahmed, H., Rekhis, S., & Boudriga, N. (2014). Security of implantable medical devices: Limits, requirements, and proposals. *Security and Communication Networks, 7*(12), 2475–2491. doi:10.1002/sec.939

Irum, S., Ali, A., Khan, F. A., & Abbas, H. (2013). A hybrid security mechanism for intra-WBAN and inter-WBAN communications. *International Journal of Distributed Sensor Networks*.

Kakria, P., Tripathi, N. K., & Kitipawang, P. (2015, December). A Real-Time Health Monitoring System for Remote Cardiac Patients Using Smartphone and Wearable Sensors. *International Journal of Telemedicine and Applications*. PMID:26788055

Klann, M. (2009). Tactical Navigation Support for Firefighters: The LifeNet Ad-Hoc Sensor-Network and Wearable System. In *Proceedings of Mobile Response: 2nd International Workshop on Mobile Information Technology for Emergency Response*. Berlin: Springer.

Klann, M., Riedel, T., Gellersen, H., Fischer, C., Oppenheim, M., Lukowicz, P., . . . Visser, O. (2007). Lifenet: an ad-hoc sensor network and wearable system to provide firefighters with navigation support. In Proceedings Of UbiComp: Demos Extended Abstracts.

Malik, M. Y. (2012). An Outline of Security in Wireless Sensor Networks: Threats, Countermeasures and Implementations. In N. Zaman, K. Ragab, & A. Abdullah (Eds.), Wireless Sensor Networks and Energy Efficiency: Protocols, Routing and Management (pp. 507-527). Hershey, PA: Information Science Reference. doi:10.4018/978-1-4666-0101-7.ch024

Miaoui, Y., Boudriga, N., & Abaoub, E. (2015). Economics of Privacy: A Model for Protecting Against Cyber Data Disclosure Attacks. In *Proceedings of the 3rd Information Systems International Conference*. doi:10.1016/j.procs.2015.12.165

Otto, C. A., Jovanov, E., & Milenkovic, A. (2006). A WBAN-based System for Health Monitoring at Home. In *Proceedings of the 3rd IEEE-EMBS International Summer School and Symposium on Medical Devices and Biosensors*. MIT. doi:10.1109/ISSMDBS.2006.360087

Patel, S., Chen, B. R., Buckley, T., Rednic, R., McClure, D., Tarsy, D., & Bonato, P. et al. (2010, August). Home monitoring of patients with Parkinson's disease via wearable technology and a web-based application. In *Proceedings of the 32nd Annual International Conference of the IEEE EMBS*.

Ramli, S. N., Ahmad, R., Abdollah, M. F., & Dutkiewicz, E. (2013). A biometric-based security for data authentication in Wireless Body Area Network (WBAN). *Advanced Communication Technology (ICACT), 2013 15th International Conference on.*

Rekhis, S. (2007). *Theoretical Aspects of Digital Investigation of Security Incidents.* (Doctoral Dissertation). Available from CN&S research lab. (CNAS-2008-103)

Rekhis, S., & Boudriga, N. (2011). Logic-based approach for digital forensic investigation in communication Networks. *Computers & Security, 30*(6), 376–396. doi:10.1016/j.cose.2011.02.002

Saleem, S., Ullah, S., & Kwak, K. S. (2011). A study of IEEE 802.15. 4 security framework for wireless body area networks. *Sensors (Basel, Switzerland), 11*(2), 1383–1395. doi:10.3390/s110201383 PMID:22319358

Scholz, M., & Decker, T. R. (2010). A flexible architecture for a robust indoor navigation support device for firefighters. In *Proceedings of the 7th International Conference On Networked Sensing Systems (INSS2010).* doi:10.1109/INSS.2010.5573554

Scholz, M., Reidel, T., & Decker, C. (2010). A flexible architecture for a robust indoor navigation support device for firefighters. In *Proceedings of the 7th International Conference On Networked Sensing Systems (INSS2010).* doi:10.1109/INSS.2010.5573554

Srinivasan, V., Stankovic, J., & Whitehouse, K. (2008a). Protecting your Daily In-Home Activity Information from a Wireless Snooping Attack. In *Proceedings of the 10th International Conference on Ubiquitous Computing UbiComp'08.* doi:10.1145/1409635.1409663

Srinivasan, V. Stankovic, J. & Whitehouse. K. (2008b). A fingerprint and timing-based snooping attack on residential sensor systems. *ACM SIGBED, 5*(1).

Sultan, N. (2015). Reflective thoughts on the potential and challenges of wearable technology for healthcare provision and medical education. *International Journal of Information Management, 35*(5), 521–526. doi:10.1016/j.ijinfomgt.2015.04.010

Thomaz, E., Parnami, A., Bidwell, J., Essa, I., & Abowd, G. D. (2013, September). Technological approaches for addressing privacy concerns when recognizing eating behaviors with wearable cameras. In *Proceedings of the 2013 ACM international joint conference on Pervasive and ubiquitous computing* (pp. 739-748). New York, NY: ACM. doi:10.1145/2493432.2493509

Ullah, S., Higgins, H., Braem, B., Latre, B., Blondia, C., Moerman, I., & Kwak, K. et al. (2012). A Comprehensive Survey of Wireless Body Area Networks. *Journal of Medical Systems*, *36*(3), 1065–1094. doi:10.1007/s10916-010-9571-3 PMID:20721685

Venkatraman, K., Vijay Daniel, J., & Murugaboopathi, G. (2013). Various Attacks in Wireless Sensor Network: Survey.[IJSCE]. *International Journal of Soft Computing and Engineering*, *3*(1), 208–211.

Wang, W., Wang, H., Hempel, M., Peng, D., Sharif, H., & Chen, H. H. (2011). Secure stochastic ECG signals based on Gaussian mixture model for e-healthcare systems. *IEEE Systems Journal*, *5*(4), 564–573. doi:10.1109/JSYST.2011.2165597

Zheng, Y.-L., Ding, X. R., Poon, C. C. Y., Lo, B. P. L., Zhang, H., Zhou, X.-L., & Zhang, Y.-T. et al. (2014). Unobtrusive Sensing and Wearable Devices for Health Informatics. *IEEE Transactions on Bio-Medical Engineering*, *61*(5), 1538–1554. doi:10.1109/TBME.2014.2309951 PMID:24759283

KEY TERMS AND DEFINITIONS

Attack: An attempt to gain unauthorized access to a service, a resource or information, or the attempt to compromise availability, integrity, or confidentiality of a given system.

Data Encryption: The process of converting plain text into encrypted symbols and characters to illegal from understanding the real message.

Digital Forensics: Consist of collecting and analyzing digital data.

Eavesdropping Attacks: The process of secretly overhearing a private conversation over a confidential communication in an unauthorized way.

Private Data Theft: The action of copying, transmitting, viewing, and stealing protected, sensitive, or confidential data.

Risk: Identified when the collected measurements regarding the monitored hazard deteriorate, in a short period of time, and reach a threshold value predefined by the system.

Wearable Systems: Portable electronic devices that can be embedded on the human body (unobtrusively) as an accessory (e.g., smart watches) or as part of the clothing.

Chapter 3
Watch What You Wear:
Smartwatches and
Sluggish Security

Joseph Ricci
University of New Haven, USA

Ibrahim Baggili
University of New Haven, USA

Frank Breitinger
University of New Haven, USA

ABSTRACT

There is no doubt that the form factor of devices continues to shrink as evidenced by smartphones and most recently smartwatches. The adoption rate of small computing devices is staggering and needs stronger attention from the cybersecurity and digital forensics communities. In this chapter, we dissect smartwatches. We first present a historical roadmap of smartwatches. We then explore the smartwatch marketplace and outline existing smartwatch hardware, operating systems and software. Next we elaborate on the uses of smartwatches and then discuss the security and forensic implications of smartwatches by reviewing the relevant literature. Lastly, we outline future research directions in smartwatch security and forensics.

DOI: 10.4018/978-1-5225-1016-1.ch003

INTRODUCTION

Smartwatches have recently become a novel consumer product especially with the release of the Apple Watch, which has certainly galvanized the wearable-tech market. eMarketer, an independent market research company expects smartwatches will lure consumers away from fitness trackers - which is currently the most popular wearable device (eMarketer, 2015). Smartwatches process a variety of personal data, different from data processed by current smartphones, making the study of smartwatches from the security and forensics perspectives important.

Since the advent of smartphones, law enforcement, criminals, and organizations have been able to collect a plethora of personal data about their consumers allowing service providers and device manufacturers to profile their users. Smartphones can collect data such as shopping preferences, Global Positioning System (GPS) coordinates, weight, gender, and age just to name a few examples. Undoubtedly, people have become personally and emotionally attached to these devices (Thorsteinsson & Page, 2015). Notwithstanding, we have now entered the era of smartwatches as device factor continues to decrease in size. Now that smartwatches such as the Samsung Gear 2 Neo, LG G, and Apple Watch have a flourishing adoption rate and employ many of the similar capabilities as smartphones, one may ask the question *What additional personal data are these smart devices able to collect and how safe is that data during transit and storage?* We posit that smartwatches will become fully integrated personal digital assistants that not only will receive notifications from a one's smartphone but also monitor one's health.

Research on smartwatch security is sparse, which is why it is important to understand their functionality and their vulnerabilities. The security of data that is stored and transmitted from and to a smartwatch suggests that encryption is important to protect data from prying eyes. Identifying potential challenges may make users aware of the likely risks from using smartwatches and may assist in preventing sensitive data from being leaked. While we observe the size of smart devices shrinking over time, it is not difficult to imagine the possibility for smartwatches replacing smartphones one day.

In this chapter, we first outline the history of smartwatches, and the current smartwatch marketplace in an effort to familiarize the reader with this technology. Next, existing smartwatch hardware, operating systems and software are delineated to provide insight into how one could implement methods and technologies in smartwatch security and forensics. We then follow that with the uses of smartwatches to provide an understanding of how they operate. Then, the security implications of smartwatches are discussed, followed by a review of the preliminary forensic analysis research on smartwatches; exemplifying how one may forensically obtain digital evidence from them. Finally, future research directions related to smartwatch security and forensics is discussed.

THE ROAD TO SMARTWATCHES (HISTORY)

The advancement in digital technology typically targets two challenges:

1.   **Performance:** Everything should be *faster and better*;
2.   **Form Factor:** We continuously aim for building more compact devices.

The size of the digital computer has continued to shrink from the reprogrammable digital Electronic Numerical Integrator And Computer (ENIAC) that occupied an entire room, to the desktop, to the mobile smartphone which can fit in one's pocket. Paralleled with the decrease in size was the escalation in processing power and storage – instead of a few kilobytes of memory and a single core with a few hertz, we now have multi-cores and terabytes of memory.

Narrowing our focus to watches, we identify a similar trend. Many attempts to create a functional smartwatch were made between 1972 and 2013, with limited results. The earliest model of a computerized wristwatch was the Pulsar, launched in April 1972, which was the first ever wristwatch capable of storing data (Edwards, 2012). Even though the amount of data it could store was limited, one may view this as the preliminary step towards smartwatches as we know them today. Over time, manufacturers such as Sony, Casio, and Timex created digital wristwatches; devices that have a digital time display while providing extra features such as timers, a stopwatch and calendars. Additionally, some watches were capable of running full operating systems such as the GNU/Linux wristwatch by Steve Mann – it also had the ability to be used as a video phone but the problem was that it required the use of a body-worn computer system as a base station, making it completely dependent on another device (Mann, 2001). Such early devices were limited and "clunky" compared to the smartwatches available today.

In 2013, the size and cost of hardware matured to the point where it finally became possible to integrate into watches and add additional sensors/features such as a heart rate monitor, pedometer, GPS, accelerometer, etc. The Samsung Galaxy Gear 2 is an example of such a smart watch, and is depicted in Figure 1. We posit that this innovation projected the smartwatch as desirable product. Given the recent advances in smartwatch technology, we argue for the necessity in examining their market penetration rate.

Figure 1. Samsung Galaxy gear 2[1]

SMARTWATCH MARKET

Market researcher Strategy Analytics stated that in 2014, device makers including Samsung, LG, Motorola and Pebble shipped a total of only 4.6 million smartwatches worldwide, and while it is forecasted to jump to 28.1 million in 2015, that is still a blip compared to the number of smartphones shipped (Walton, 2015). It is however important to note that reports have predicted that 91.6 million smartwatches will be sold by the year 2018 (Danova, 2014). The forecasted growth is shown in Figure 2.

Apple is anticipated to take control over half of the smartwatch market with its Apple Watch by shipping about 19 million of its 2015 launched smartwatches; re-

Figure 2. Projected smartwatch annual sales according to cited data from Lamkin, 2015.

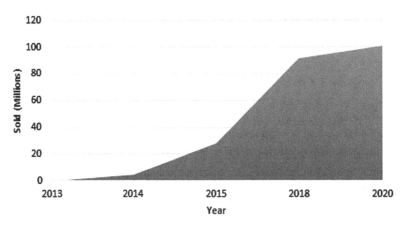

sulting in an estimated 56% of the market share (Lamkin, 2015). Currently, the majority of smartwatches on the market are Apple Watches followed by Samsung and other smartwatch companies such as Microsoft, Motorola, Pebble, etc. (Gibbs, 2015).

The smartwatch market is expected to mature, making them possibly the most popular wearable technology in the near future. With consumers becoming more comfortable using wearable technology, smartwatches could potentially pave the way for other wearable devices. It can be overwhelming to stay abreast with the pace of smartwatch technology, so examining them now while at their infancy will provide greater comprehension of the technology and its budding impact. As smartwatch technology gains more traction, advances in hardware, operating systems, and software are expected to evolve in order to provide seamlessly integrated and powerful devices to consumers.

SMARTWATCH HARDWARE, OPERATING SYSTEMS, AND SOFTWARE

Despite multiple vendors implementing proprietary hardware and operating systems, generally, most smartwatches are similar. On the other hand, software that can be found on smartwatches is limited, but applications are growing in numbers. We discuss smartwatch hardware, operating systems and software in the sections that follow.

Hardware

A smartwatch contains a processor with one, two or even four cores (e.g., Samsung Galaxy Gear, Samsung Gear 2, and LG Watch Urbane) enabling multitasking. Processor speeds vary widely from only a few hundred Megahertz to 1.2 Gigahertz (e.g. LG G Watch, Asus ZenWatch, Samsung Gear Live). The leading companies in the smartwatch market emphasize smartwatch speed and efficiency. This allows for significant variations in smartwatch performance.

Currently, the majority of smartwatches on the market have about 512 Kilobytes of RAM and anywhere from 4 Megabytes (Pebble Watch) to 32 Gigabytes (Exetech XS3) of flash storage in total, including the operating system. The Apple Watch has 512 Kilobytes of RAM and a maximum of 8 Gigabytes of storage, including a 2 Gigabyte cap for music (Neild, 2015). Similar to personal computers, laptops and smartphones, where we have seen evidence of Moore's Law, the digital storage size and processing speed of the smartwatch surpasses its predecessor each year, and may approximately double annually (Moore, 1965). Many smartwatches pack a plethora of microchips, as shown in Figure 3, onto a circuit board in order to provide func-

Figure 3. Moto 360 - a Motorola smartwatch circuit board[2]

tionality comparable to a smartphone. Most, but not all, smartwatches currently rely on a smartphone to perform tasks with regards to data processing and connectivity to the Internet. Most smartwatches now come prepackaged with various sensors.

Sensors

The size of a smartwatch is in the tens of millimeters; some are bulkier than others. There are numerous small sensors and circuits that fit into a smartwatch such as an ambient light sensor, pedometer, heart rate monitor, WiFi antenna, Bluetooth, speaker, microphone, cellular antenna, GPS, touchscreen, accelerometer, flash storage, and gyroscope to name a few. We expect the number and variety of sensors fitted to smartwatches will continue to expand over time. Each sensor performs a specific task that enhances the functionality of the smartwatch (Valdes & Chandler, 2005), such as:

- **Ambient Light Sensor:** When exposed to a certain degree of light, this sensor will adjust the display screens brightness autonomously.
- **Pedometer:** Detects and records the number of steps a person takes, adding health functionality to smartwatches.
- **Magnetometer:** Used for improved accuracy in motion tracking, can be used as a compass.
- **Heart Rate Monitor:** Measures an individual's heart rate.
- **Accelerometer:** Measures the acceleration that the smartwatch moves.
- **Gyroscope:** Determines orientation by measuring rotation.

- **Global Positioning System (GPS):** Determines the location of an individual based on longitudinal and latitudinal coordinates.
- **Compass:** Compliment the GPS to determine cardinal geographic directions.

One may envisage from this list of sensors the amount and variety of data that may be collected with a smartwatch– which begs the question of examining the privacy implications of such devices. With that said, smartwatches still face some hardware limitations which we discuss in the section that follows.

Current Hardware Limitations of Most Smartwatches

As described in the previous section, most smartwatches lack the ability to independently access a mobile network because they do not integrate the necessary hardware. The form factor of a smartwatch is so small, making it difficult to add auxiliary hardware – but that is quickly changing. This is why many smartwatches on the market use Bluetooth to act as a bridge for communicating with other smart devices (e.g. smartphone) that are able to access mobile telecommunication networks. This allows the smartwatch to sync contacts, calendar, weather, and other personal data with service providers and device manufacturers.

One smartwatch thus far has been able to overcome this challenge but at the cost of larger form factor. The LG Watch Urbane 2nd Edition, "Doesn't need your phone to connect to the Internet. It does that through a built-in radio, which can connect to LTE and 3G, or to your phone via Bluetooth and WiFi if you for some reason still want to connect your watch to your phone like our forefathers did" (Pierce, 2015). It is one of the first smartwatches that does not require a smartphone to access the Internet. The downside of this watch is that it is bulkier than its counterparts. Capabilities like direct Internet connectivity provide smartwatches more independence, making them akin to smartphones.

Smartwatch Operating Systems

Currently, Android Wear and Tizen are the operating systems which ship with the most different smartwatch models, used by 7 (Android Wear) and 5 (Tizen) different devices in the market. Apple's Watch OS may hold a larger market share, in terms of number of users, due to the commercial success of the Apple Watch. The variety of operating systems found in smartwatches requires service and technology providers to develop multiple patches for different operating systems and calls for security researchers to learn how to acquire and protect data based on the implementations of these different operating systems. Table 1 shows the number of smartwatch models which ship with each different operating system at the time of writing.

Table 1. Smartwatch operating systems

Operating System	Number of Watches
Android Wear	7
Tizen	5
Pebble	2
WebOS	2
ELF OS	2
Android 4.0	1
Watch OS	1
MicroC/OS-II	1
Qcom OS	1
Firefox OS	1
Open Source Watch	1

Since smartwatches are expected to become a popular commodity, especially with the release of the Apple Watch, companies in the fashion industry will become interested in developing their own smartwatch (Covill, 2015). This is a valid assumption because current fashion houses such as Fossil, Michael Kors, and Armani, as well as traditional watchmakers, like Casio and Rolex, have taken an interest in developing their own smartwatches. These companies will have to either pick or create an operating system, which could add to the already growing list of smartwatch operating systems. This has implications for digital forensics; potentially making it difficult to successfully navigate an operating system and retrieve data for use in investigation.

Understanding how an operating system works has always been important for forensic investigators and criminals alike. An operating system manages user input, outputs data, handles files and directories on storage devices, implements system security, and controls hardware. With this in mind, an individual who has basic knowledge of how different operating systems work may be able to explore and manipulate how one can retrieve and hide data. Whether the smartwatch's operating system is open or closed source is also significant from the perspectives of security, privacy and forensics. Open source operating systems are supported by a community of developers that collaborate to develop and/or improve code. Such operating systems may benefit from more robust security (since their code is potentially subject to broader scrutiny), and may be preferable from the perspective of a forensic examination too (since the structure of acquired data is likely better documented). The Open Source Watch is an open source smartwatch project that includes the operating system and 3D printing schematics for anyone to freely use and modify (DoNothingBox LLC, 2013). Closed source operating systems are proprietary and are generally tied to a particular vendor's hardware platform.

Application Software

Smartwatches have the ability to run applications and play digital media such as music and the radio, and simultaneously stream the sound to Bluetooth headphones (Saha, 2015). Many smartwatches have touchscreens allowing users to access functions like a calculator, thermometer, compass and more. Smartwatches are capable of performing many tasks and as technology gets better they could potentially perform the same tasks as smartphones. With their hardware improvements, developers are designing applications specifically for smartwatches. They are able to provide unique data about a person given their size and where they reside - on a person's wrist. This allows for more intimate data collection, while also presenting a user-friendly interface for human-computer interaction.

At the time of writing this chapter, thousands of applications were already available for smartwatches. Currently, the Apple Watch (which runs Watch OS) has over 6,000 applications (Hein, 2015). Android Wear OS and Tizen OS have over 4,000 Android Wear applications (Temple & Naziri, 2015). It is important to note that many of these applications have the ability to send data to the cloud for processing and then present useful information to a user in real time.

SMARTWATCH USES

Smartwatches can be considered smart because they possess the ability to communicate with other devices around them as well as interact with their users. Furthermore, smartwatches can store a reasonable amount of data, and process data in real time and present it when it is relevant to or requested by the user (e.g., heart rate, smartphone notifications, etc.), and can be used independently of a smartphone. Compared to regular digital watches, smartwatches possess the ability to use different communication technologies such as Bluetooth, WiFi, Long-Term Evolution (LTE), etc. and the ability to sync with another device providing real time intelligence, such as alerts from a smartphone for text messages, e-mails, phone calls, social media, etc. Upon receiving a notification, the smartwatch vibrates, making the notification much more immediate (and harder to ignore). Many anticipate that smartwatches will play a critical role in the Internet of Things (IoT).

The Role of Smartwatches in IoT

IoT describes commonplace items that are connected to the Internet (e.g. connected smart coffee maker or a connected smart television). Typically, these devices can communicate with other smart devices, such as a smartwatch, that can allow a user to remotely configure, for example, a coffee machine to make coffee in the morning, or to check the status of a washing machine.

With IoT's continuous growth, adoption and integration into our everyday lives, smartwatches have developed the ability to interact and communicate with other IoT devices. In fact, smartwatches themselves are regarded as IoT devices. Notifications from the devices in one's home can report whether or not the lights were left on or if the laundry is done and all of that data can be sent to a smartwatch – typically worn by users at all times (especially if the smartwatch is water resistant).

Smart locks can communicate with one's smartphone or smartwatch to grant a person access into their home, office, or hotel rooms (if the hotel supports the technology) by using Bluetooth or WiFi and their respective software applications. Smart locks, such as the August lock and Danalock, can unlock doors as one approaches them (Chang, 2013). Not only do they lock and unlock based on an individual's proximity, some models can even take pictures of those entering a home. This technology can be used to identify and keep a timeline of the people coming and go from a home.

Smartwatches can also turn smart light bulbs on or off upon entering or exiting a room, such as the Philips Hue (Philips, 2015). An individual can dim the light bulbs, set a wake up time, and even change the colors of the lights to match a movie that could be playing at home. They also allow a person to set timers when an individual is not home in an attempt to deter criminals.

Another role that smartwatches play in IoT is the ability to communicate with vehicles. For example, Ford created an application to allow the smartwatch to receive and send data to/from a Ford electric vehicle for locking/unlocking a car, reading the vehicle's mileage summary, last trip summary, vehicle location, and other information (Ford Motor Company, 2015). Any IoT device conceived in the future may have the ability to communicate with a smartwatch, which in itself is a good reason to be concerned about smartwatch security.

Smartwatches Help You Make Payments

Outside the scope of the home, smartwatches can now also be used to make payments. Being able to pay for items using a smartphone is not new, but having to take out a smartphone, unlock it, open an app, and then having to wait until the payment has been accepted may be less convenient than using a smartwatch for the same task. Samsung and Apple have incorporated a Near Field Communication (NFC) chip into their smartwatches to allow for payments (Torres, 2015). This makes paying for items much easier because all that is needed is to hold the smartwatch near an NFC reader. This means that criminals interested in stealing money may one day target smartwatches, since they will serve as digital wallets.

Health Monitoring

Smartwatches embody all of the sensors adopted by fitness trackers and more. A fitness tracker (e.g., Jawbone Up24, Nike Fuelband, Fitbit Force) is worn like a smartwatch except it is limited to obtaining and processing data related to your health. Like fitness trackers, smartwatches can influence the wearer's actions by providing them feedback on health and fitness and suggestions on how to optimize health results.

Since the smartwatch can be worn at all times of the day, it can continuously monitor the wearer's health. With the ability to monitor an individual's health, a smartwatch can offer a beneficial tool for doctors to monitor the health of their patients. An added incentive for keeping smartwatches on at all times is that they can monitor the wearer while they sleep. This can provide data that can be aggregated and statistically analyzed. Sleep statistics can identify sleep patterns and help individuals set goals to improve the quality and quantity of sleep (Hawkins, 2015).

Water Sports

For individuals who are interested in water activities such as diving and swimming, smartwatches such as the Swimmo or Runtastic Orbit are available. Such smartwatches provide real time data to track distance, calories burned, heart rate, swimming pace, and duration of swimming. These devices have the functionality of a typical smartwatch but are water resistant and are designed with swimmers in mind, allowing them to dive up to 100 meters.

With all of these current and potential smartwatch uses, one can quickly see that they can store and transmit personal data, and interact with systems that affect our daily lives, from fun and games, to banking and health. This data has security, privacy and forensic implications. It is imperative, the, to explore both the security as well as the forensics of smartwatches.

SMALL FORM FACTOR SECURITY AND FORENSICS

Smartwatches have many convenient applications for their users. With this convenience, however, comes security and forensic implications. Nevertheless, all smartwatches may contain data, which can leak sensitive things about a person, or perhaps be used as a form of digital evidence in a digital investigation.

Security Risks from Small Form Factor

The decrease in the size of the form factor of computers has allowed them to become portable and light enough to carry around. At the same time, digital devices have become more or less interchangeable for many purposes. For instance, e-mails can be checked on a smartphone, tablet or laptop. This makes portable devices a target for theft because their size and portability makes them easy to steal, and the wealth of sensitive data they typically contain.

Security and Laptops

Companies will often provide laptops to their employees to enable them to perform work equally well in the office or at home. Often, depending on the organization, these laptops contain customer information or other valuable data making them a worthwhile target to criminals. A report by the Ponemon Institute, sponsored by Intel, conducted a study on 329 participating private and public sector organizations located in the United States. The findings on the number of laptops lost were astronomical – over a 12 month period 86,455 laptops were reported lost or missing (Ponemon, 2009). In another Ponemon Institute report, they concluded that the cost per stolen laptop was $49,246 (Ponemon, 2010). It is easy to see why laptops are high-value targets for criminals. Smartphones are now slowly replacing laptops for work on the go.

Security and Smartphones

Since smartphones have become ubiquitous, companies have begun to issue them to their employees or allow employees to bring their own device and implement a smartphone security policy since they present the same challenges as laptops but are available to criminals in a much smaller form factor. In a survey of Information Technology (IT) practitioners about endpoint security, 75% of respondents noted mobile devices such as smartphones represent the greatest potential security risk, followed by the increase in the risk associated with third party applications (Karlovsky, 2014). Smartphones contain data such as e-mails, passwords, locations, photos, videos, and so on, which are all valuable to criminals as they can provide useful and actionable private data.

There are many accounts that detail the value and severity of smartphone thefts, such as the 2014 "Mustafa Organization" crime ring. As reported by Paul McEnroe from Star Tribune "Members of this organization hired criminals to steal smartphones, then they would sell smartphones on the black market to buyers in the Middle East and China, making close to $4 million selling these phones over the past eight years. Each smartphone sold anywhere between $500 and $1000" (McEnore, 2014). An article by Consumer Reports indicated that in 2014 over 2.1 million Americans had their smartphones stolen, exposing a huge amount of personal data (Deitrick, 2015). As the number of thefts continues to rise, it is imperative that consumers take protective measures to ensure that both their devices and data do not fall into the wrong hands. With that said, smartwatches are even smaller in size than smartphones, and due to the symbiotic relationship many smartwatches have with smartphones, much of what has been said about smartphone risk applies equally to smartwatches.

Security, Forensics, and Smartwatches

The significance of the form factor of a device to the security of the device is obvious; the smaller and more portable devices are, the easier it is to physically steal or misplace them. However, the paradoxical security challenge of these devices being so small is that their size is not just an advantage to criminals, but also a hindrance for a forensic analyst, who seeks to extract the storage media and acquire a forensic image of the device to analyze the content for use in a criminal investigation. Smartwatches contain flash memory in the form of microchips soldered onto a circuit board. The process of having to physically extract the flash memory is tedious and leaves very little room for error. A small mistake may destroy evidence, or make it impossible to return the smartwatch in good working order.

At the time of writing this chapter there was a scarcity of scholarly research on the security and exploitation of smartwatches. Every time there is new technology, there is always going to be the need to examine security design decisions. In the case of smartwatches, we know that they collect sensitive personal data. In the sections that follow, we describe the few main research studies conducted in the realm of smartwatch security and forensics.

HP Fortify: Smartwatch Security Assessment Report

In a report by HP on IoT Security, one topic was evaluating the security of the top 10 current smartwatches (Smith & Miessler, 2015). All of the tested smartwatches were proven to have security vulnerabilities – operating systems tested included Android and iOS. These vulnerabilities included authentication and authorization problems, insecure connections to the cloud and mobile interfaces, and improper configuration and implementation of Secure Socket Layer / Transport Layer Security (SSL/TLS). During their research they tested all the device features a typical user would use such as activity and health monitoring, messaging, email, scheduling and weather. One of the many security flaws detected included a Domain Name Server (DNS) service being used on one of the watches allowing an adversary to use it as part of a DNS amplification attack. According to the United States Computer Emergency Readiness Team (US-CERT), a DNS amplification attack is a popular form of Distributed Denial of Service (DDoS), in which attackers use publically accessible open DNS servers to flood a target system with DNS response traffic (United States Computer Emergency Response Team, 2013). This means that an attacker can use a spoofed IP address that causes the DNS to send packets to requested IP address.

All of the smartwatches that included cloud connectivity employed weak password policies, allowing the researchers to read data that should be encrypted. In 90% of the tested watches, the smartwatch communication could be intercepted. Half of the devices did not offer a screen lock, which is a simple yet effective deterrent to criminals. Smartwatches which included a mobile application with authentication allowed unrestricted account enumeration - in other words it was easy for researchers to identify usernames as a result of the authentication mechanisms the smartwatches used. A combination of account enumeration, weak passwords, and lack of account lockout meant that 30% of the watches and their applications were vulnerable to account harvesting. All the researchers needed to do in order to collect this data was constantly prompt an application for password recovery and in return that application would unwittingly validate the user's account. The other way to obtain this data was to perform an initial configuration of an application and account creation.

There was a lack of transport encryption, which is critical for ensuring that data being transmitted to multiple locations in the cloud is private. All of the tested watches utilized SSL/TLS, but 40% of them either employed weak ciphers or proprietary transport encryption versions or were susceptible to a Padding Oracle On Downgraded Legacy Encryption (POODLE) attack. A POODLE attack exploits a publicly-disclosed vulnerability in SSL v3.0. This vulnerability is the result of a design flaw in SSL v3.0, does not affect TLS and is limited to SSL 3.0, which is widely considered an obsolete protocol (Oracle, 2015). The report further explained that to conduct a man-in-the-middle attack would be effortless due to the weak encryption methods used in current smartwatch implementations.

The report also pinpointed that there were software and firmware vulnerabilities in the tested smartwatches. Seven of the tested devices would transmit firmware updates without encryption and without encrypting the update files. Fortunately, all of these vital updates included a digital signature of some type, making it difficult for anyone to try to maliciously manipulate the software and firmware updates.

Keystroke Detection

A compromised smartwatch may pose additional security threats even to devices not on the same network as the smartwatch. Researchers were able to detect keystrokes on a physical keyboard by using an application they developed for a Samsung Gear Live smartwatch (Wang, Tsung-Te, & Choudhury, 2015). They achieved this by using some of the sensors commonly found on smartphones and smartwatches. On the smartwatch, the sensors were able to pick up subtle wrist movements, something not feasible with smartphones.

There are many types of sensors that can collect a plethora of data, but the two sensors that the researchers were particularly interested in were the accelerometer and gyroscope. The application was made to mimic a pedometer. Once the application obtained the required permissions, the application could launch a side-channel attack – an exploit that collects data from other parts of the smartwatch such as the gyroscope and accelerometer. In this attack, the application could derive data that was being typed on a keyboard such as passwords, e-mails, search queries, and so on.

To establish a baseline, two of the researchers typed 500 words each on a keyboard while wearing the smartwatch on their left wrist. Then, they collected the data from the accelerometer and gyroscope to use as training data, and processed the different steps it took to type each word, including keypress detection, hand-motion tracking, character point cloud computation, and Bayesian modeling and inference.

In greater detail, to determine which key was pressed, the researchers relied on the accelerometer in the smartwatch and a recording camera to record which keys were being pressed. By keeping their fingers rested on the home row, they were able to determine which finger moves and which character it presses by interpreting the positive and negative X (hand moves left and right), Y (hand moves up and down the keyboard), and Z (hand moves down to indicate key pressed) coordinates produced by the accelerometer. They were able to discern that the highest positive displacement happened when pressing the number keys at the top of the keyboard and the lowest negative displacement happened on the last row of the keyboard. While conducting this part of the study, it was recognized which keys were used the least (1, t, r, 4, 5) and which caused strong overlap ("asdf", "zxcv", and "q23"). Overlap is assumed to mean that the fingers move over these keys the most. They also noticed that keys pressed with the right hand recorded very little movement in the left, which was to be expected.

On the cloud server side, the researchers (posing as attackers) created an offline reference file. This was done by typing every character on a computer keyboard multiple times. The reference file was run through a program that computes a Character Point Cloud (CPC), giving the researchers the exact coordinates for each key on the keyboard. For example, an attacker would type on a keyboard while wearing a smartwatch to record the coordinates and just use the keyboard to indicate which keys were pressed, thus providing exact details on which coordinates correspond with which keys. The purpose of the CPC is to provide a comparison to the coordinates that comes from a user's smartwatch. This gives the cloud service the ability to calculate which keys the user is most probably pressing when the cloud service receives a given set of coordinates from the compromised smartwatch. The quality of this probabilistic matching could be improved with multiple training sets from multiple users – which it could be assumed that a practical CPC implementation would include. The offline file is processed by the server and passes through a keystroke detection module which detects the timing of each keystroke by analyzing the Z axis and creates a 2D map. The keystroke detection module then outputs this data in a useful fashion by creating a set of tuples <$location_i$, $time_i$> (the subscript i represents iteration). $Location_i$ records the location of where the finger was and the $time_i$ records the time the finger was pressed down.

All of the data collected from the user's application is then sent to a program on the cloud server called the Unlabeled Point Cloud (UPC). The UPC determines where the coordinates are and when the keys were pressed, but it does not have absolute certainty which key was pressed (hence, unlabeled). At this point the UPC and CPC are forwarded to a Cloud Fitting Module (CFM), which determines the possible keystrokes collected by the UPC, and references the CPC to provide the best keystroke fit.

After the CPC and UPC are computed and compared, the data that was processed in the CFM is passed onto a Bayesian Inference Module (BIM). Bayesian Inference is based on Bayes theorem which is a statistical method to determine the probability that an event will occur given that a separate event already occurred. This module takes the data from the CFM, UPC, and words from a dictionary. For example, the BIM will compare a word from the dictionary to the keystrokes entered by the user. Since there is already a comparison made by the CFM, the BIM can take the comparison data and determine which keystrokes were most likely pressed. Once the BIM has processed the possible typed words, it lists the word and the probability that it is the intended word the individual had entered. Table 2 shows an example; the actual sentence is revealed at the bottom of the Table.

Table 2. After the researchers typed a sentence, BIM returned a probability chart as shown. The words in each column are ranked in decreasing order of probability.

Rank	W1	W2	W3	W4	W5	W6	W7	W8
1.	motor	pistol	profound	technology	angel	those	that	disappear
2.	monitor	list	journalism	remaining	spray	today	tight	discourse
3.	them	but	originally	telephone	super	third	tightly	secondary
4.	the	lost	original	meanwhile	fire	through	thirty	adviser
5.	then	most	profile	headline	shore	towel	truth	discover

Wang, Tsung-Te, & Choudhury, 2015.
Note: The sentence written by the researchers is: "The most profound technology are those that disappear".

This keylogging research illustrates that it is practical to, in effect, "install" a keylogger on a computer without installing malicious software or hardware on the computer, but rather by compromising the smartwatch of the computer's user. This research should remind users to be wary of the applications that they download due to the type of data the sensors can provide.

Preliminary Forensic Analysis

Recent preliminary work illustrated a mechanism for forensically acquiring data from smartwatches (Baggili, Oduro, Anthony, Breitinger, & McGee, 2015). The purpose of the study was to attempt to identify and crack the security mechanisms of two different smartwatches in order to learn how they store, manage, and share user data, add to help determine how to allow an investigator to forensically image the watches. The research was conducted to provide law enforcement and other agencies a methodical approach for smartwatch forensics.

The study incorporates two parts, the first focused on data that could be possibly acquired from a smartphone synced with the watches, and the second concentrated on data that could be acquired directly from the smartwatches. In both parts of the study, the researchers followed guidelines for forensically examining artifacts as recommended by National Institute of Standards and Technology (NIST) (Kent, Chevalier, Grance, & Dang, 2006).

The researchers utilized a Samsung Galaxy S4 Active smartphone, Cellebrite UFED 4 PC (used to acquire a physical image from the phone), .XRY Logical (used to acquire logical images from both smartphones for redundancy and comparison), Cellebrite Physical Analyzer (used to analyze the physical image), LG G smartwatch, Samsung Gear 2 Neo smartwatch, and Autopsy (an open source forensic image analyzer).

The smartwatches employed were designed to integrate with a smartphone via Bluetooth. The researchers conducted multiple tasks on the smartphone and smartwatch to create data which would be harvested later. These tasks included setting calendar events, sending an e-mail, tracking footsteps, utilizing voice recognition on the smartwatch to tell weather, checking the wearer's heart rate with the smartwatch, and using the voice recorder on the smartwatch.

Once the scenario data was created, the researchers acquired physical forensic images (exact copy of the smartphones storage) from the smartphone using the Cellebrite UFED 4PC tool. The UFED 4PC is a software-based mobile forensic tool used to perform forensic acquisition and analysis of a mobile device. The smartphone had to be manually put into 'download mode' to connect to the tool. In an effort to ensure the data was not altered during the copy, the researchers ran a SHA256 hashing algorithm prior to and after imaging the device to maintain integrity of the data. After verifying that the copies were identical the researchers proceeded to make a logical image for comparative purposes using .XRY.

After the data was acquired they ran it through the Cellebrite Physical Analyzer (another forensic software-tool used to analyze the acquired images), which was used to examine the data that was found on the smartphone. The tool parsed the files from the image and created a summary of the recovered files. It was able to extract the calendar, call log, contacts, email, etc.

Once the researchers acquired data from the smartphone, they attempted to identify if any data was left on the phone from the Samsung Gear 2 Neo. The goal here was to identify if any of the simulated data was placed onto the smartphone from this smartwatch. They were able to find many forensic artifacts on the smartphone that contained data about the smartwatch such as timestamps of when the smartwatch was last updated, what type of smartwatch was paired to the phone (including model number), system photos and icons, and the voice memo recorded on the smartwatch, all of which was recovered from the phone's forensic image. It was also noted they were able to identify when the Galaxy Gear Manager application was first downloaded onto the smartphone.

After obtaining data about the Samsung Gear 2 Neo from the smartphone, the researchers began to search for data about the LG G smartwatch. In order for the LG G smartwatch to work on the smartphone, they had to install the Android Wear application on the smartphone. The primary objective was to identify if the pedometer data on the smartwatch was recorded on the smartphone. Their results were fruitless, revealing no useful data on the smartphone from the LG G smartwatch.

Prior to this research there had been no preliminary forensic analysis for smartwatches. This presented challenges for the researchers and forced them to develop a methodology specifically for the forensic examination of smartwatches. They referenced online hacking and modder communities to assist them in designing a methodology for forensically obtaining a forensic image. Both of the tested smart-watches had to be placed in a debug mode and it was necessary to use the Android Debug Bridge (ADB) and Smart Development Bridge (SDB). ADB acts as a bridge from a computer to an Android device allowing for users to modify the device's software from a computer's command line interface. SDB performs a similar function to ADB for devices which use the Tizen operating system.

The first watch to be forensically imaged and analyzed was the Samsung Gear 2 Neo, which utilizes the Tizen operating system. This specific smartwatch does not have WiFi capabilities, only Bluetooth, meaning that the only way to forensically obtain an image was over a USB connection. There were requirements before starting the imaging process. The first step was to gain root access to the smartwatch so that the researchers could gain access to the watch's filesystem. The next step was to reset the smartwatch and put it into a download mode (similar to the smartphone). Then the read-only memory (ROM) on this device had to be flashed (giving root access to the smartwatch), requiring the need for a utility software development tool called Odin to perform the flashing. Once the flashing process was completed the researchers could then access the smartwatch using SDB and turned on root access to elevate their permissions, giving them the ability to image the device.

It was immediately identified that the smartwatch memory was broken into multiple partitions, each serving a unique purpose. One of the partitions was referenced to be the most relevant to an investigator, which was the user partition, *mmcblk0p14*. After the partitions were determined, another tool was required to transfer the image of the partition to the workstation. Disk dump (dd) was preloaded with the Tizen operating system, which is a tool used to make bit to bit copy of a storage device. Another tool used was netcat, which was bundled into Toybox, a package that contains a series of Linux command utilities. This package had to be pushed onto the smartwatch and once pushed and permissions were set, the researchers were able to make the smartwatch listen for a connection. Then the researchers were able to send a command using ADB from the workstation to start the dd imaging process. The smartwatch dumped the data from the partition onto the workstation, providing a physical image for them to work with. They used a popular open source forensic tool called Autopsy to analyze the data and found messages, health/fitness data, e-mail, and contacts/address book as shown in Table 3.

The LG G watch runs the Android Wear operating system and was connected to the workstation in the same manner as the Samsung Gear 2 Neo. They could not follow the exact same methodology to obtain data forensically from the smartwatch since flashing the device actually deleted data on it - making the process intrusive. However, they still wanted to examine what data could be acquired from the device, even after the data was deleted.

Table 3. Summary of findings for Samsung Gear 2 Neo Smartwatch

Location	File Name	Purpose
apps.com.samsung.message.data.dbspace	.msg-consumer-server.db	Messages
apps.com.samsung.shealth	.shealth.db	Health/Fitness Data
apps.com.samsung.wemail.data.dbspace	.wemail.db	E-mail
dbspace	.contacts-svc.db	Contacts/Address book

Baggili, Oduro, Anthony, Breitinger, & McGee, 2015.

Table 4. Summary of findings for LG G Smartwatch

Location	File Name	Purpose
data.com.android.providers.calendar.databases	calendar.db	Events/Notifications
data.com.android.providers.contacts.databases	contacts2.db	Contacts/Address book
data.com.google.android.apps.fitness.databases	pedometer.db	Health/Fitness Data

Baggili, Oduro, Anthony, Breitinger, & McGee, 2015.

They began by enabling the ADB Debug mode on the smartwatch, downloaded the appropriate drivers onto the workstation for the smartwatch, and connected the smartwatch to the workstation via a USB cable. Then they used the LG G Watch Restore Tools and ADB device commands to verify connectivity. Once established, they were able to perform the factory reset and performed the initial setup. This required them to re-establish connection to the smartwatch from the workstation. Then to be able to gain root access the researchers installed SuperSU, a zip file that grants root access to the smartwatch.

The imaging method was similar to the Samsung Gear 2 Neo smartwatch by using netcat from the Toybox[3] package and the dd tool to acquire data from the smartwatch to the workstation. They copied the Toybox package to a dev directory and changed its permissions in order to allow it to execute. In a similar fashion, they listed all of the partitions and identified which partition contained the user data, in this case it was located in *mmcblk0p21*. Then, with the physical image, the researchers were able to load it to Autopsy and were able to identify data even after the smartwatch had been reset, the results of their findings are in Table 4.

After recording their findings, it was also noted that none of the data on the smartwatches were encrypted. Their research could prove to be valuable to examiners trying to collect data from smartwatches by using their methods, especially since this type of research has never been done before.

Corporate Policy Concerns

With the vulnerabilities that a smartwatch presents, it is paramount for organizations to implement reasonable security policies that consider smartwatches. These devices currently raise a wide array of security concerns and organizations counteract those by implementing policies. In general, there are two approaches that corporations implement for mobile devices:

1. Bring Your Own Device (BYOD), and
2. Providing mobile devices to employees.

In a BYOD policy, the company allows its employees to use personal devices to connect to the corporate network and access company resources. This provides benefits to the company such as not having to install and maintain an infrastructure for enterprise mobile solutions and may save money because organizations do not have to purchase the devices and pay for their associated service charges.

As technology advances, organizational policy, procedures and regulations are usually poorly planned and implemented or not implemented quick enough to address the dependency on the latest technology (Utter & Rea, 2015). When new technology is released and gains traction, it often takes large organizations time to research and develop an appropriate policy response to possible risks associated with that technology. BYOD has risks linked to applications being installed by end users that may compromise the corporate Information Technology infrastructure and data (Wood, 2012). There are many risks associated with BYOD because of this exact reason, but of course there are ways to counter these risks.

Corporations that provide mobile devices can increase the security of their corporate networks because their IT departments can implement default policies and security settings which mitigate security vulnerabilities. Providing employees with mobile devices has large costs associated both with capital expenditure for the purchase of the devices, replacing lost/stolen/obsolete devices, and providing on-going support for such devices.

There are advantages to both policies but with the vulnerabilities already identified on modern smartphones, it may be a safer for companies to implement a provided device policy for smartwatches. Once smartwatch security improves, it may be wise then for companies to implement a BYOD policy.

FUTURE RESEARCH DIRECTIONS

Since smartwatches are physically attached to an individual they can become significantly more personal and provide unique data especially with respect to health. An article by Horizon Magazine has shown that the smartwatch in combination with other wearable technology can help diagnose depression (Pearse, 2015). Researchers are trialing smartwatch-style wearable technology for diagnosing mental health conditions accurately and objectively and they anticipate that real-time monitoring of the data could help prevent suicide.

Although this initially sounds like a fantastic tool to help doctors diagnose mental illness, it raises security concerns. As discussed above with respect to capturing keystrokes via compromised smartwatches, it was easy for researchers to collect data from a smartwatch and send it to the cloud. Malicious applications may collect health information for consumer profiling – of course, this is may produce a violation of Health Insurance Portability and Accountability Act (HIPAA) – so more research needs to be conducted on how smartwatches need to be used without violating health regulations.

As smartwatches become more integrated into society, research should be conducted to identify the psychological effect that smartwatches and other wearable technology may have on people. Smartwatches offer interaction with many devices (e.g. cars and smartphones), which could present an unintentional vulnerability. Which raises another potentially interesting research topic, could it be feasible to create a universal security platform for all smartwatches? If so, how would it be integrated into the current smartwatch ecosystem? As identified in the preliminary forensics section, smartwatches have much data to offer a forensic analyst, but the full extent of other types of data on smartwatches has yet to be revealed, and the impact smartwatch forensic data may have on an investigation is still unknown.

CONCLUSION

The miniaturization of computer technology has come a long way from enormous early computers like ENIAC to the smartwatches we have today. Being able to provide convenient and relevant data to users makes smartwatches attractive consumers. The smartwatch presents many challenges since it is a new technology. The lack of security and the ease of access to the device storage is unnerving, making its users vulnerable to cyber attacks. These attacks may leak personal-sensitive data about an individual, such as their e-mails, contacts, messages, finances and health information. The addressed challenges in this chapter are of concern to anyone that wishes to adopt smartwatches, whilst providing them with the ability to understand the risks associated with using a smartwatch. As the technology matures, stronger security measures should be implemented, providing better privacy and safety, making the smartwatch a more resilient piece of wearable technology.

REFERENCES

Baggili, I., Oduro, J., Anthony, K., Breitinger, F., & McGee, G. (2015, August). Watch What You Wear: Preliminary Forensic Analysis of Smart Watches. *Availability, Reliability and Security (ARES), 2015 10th International Conference*, (pp. 303-311).

Chang, A. (2013, June 19). *Smart Locks: Wired*. Retrieved from Wired: http://www.wired.com/2013/06/smart-locks/

Covill, M. (2015, May 22). *Watches2U Will Smartwatches Become Future*. Retrieved from TechnologyTell: http://www.technologytell.com/apple/150314/watches2u-will-smartwatches-become-future/

Danova, T. (2014, April 29). *global-smartwatch-sales-set-to-explode-2014-3*. Retrieved from Business Insider: http://www.businessinsider.com/global-smartwatch-sales-set-to-explode-2014-3

Deitrick, C. (2015, June 11). *Consumer Reports*. Retrieved 10 4, 2015, from Consumer Reports: http://www.consumerreports.org/cro/news/2015/06/smartphone-thefts-on-the-decline/index.htm

DoNothingBox LLC. (2013). *Open Source Watch*. Retrieved from http://oswatch.org

Edwards, B. (2012, April 15). *Story: Slideshow: PC Mag Digital Group*. Retrieved from PC Mag Digital Group: http://www.pcmag.com/slideshow/story/296609/the-digital-watch-a-brief-history/2

eMarketer. (2015, June 11). *Putting Smart Watch Adoption in Perspective: eMarketer*. Retrieved from eMarketer: http://www.emarketer.com/Article/Putting-Smart-Watch-Adoption-Perspective/1012595#sthash.RzZiBqXh.dpuf

Ford Motor Company. (2015, September 17). *Media Center: Ford*. Retrieved from Ford: https://media.ford.com/content/fordmedia/fna/us/en/news/2015/09/17/new-ford-smart-watch-apps.html

Gibbs, S. (2015, August 28). *Technology: The Guardian*. Retrieved from The Guardian: http://www.theguardian.com/technology/2015/aug/28/apple-watch-smartwatch-sales-analysis

Hawkins, S. (2015, March 20). *How Smart Watches Can Help Improve Your Health: Intermountain Health Care*. Retrieved from Intermountain Health Care: https://intermountainhealthcare.org/blogs/2015/03/how-smart-watches-can-help-improve-your-health/

Hein, B. (2015, June 9). *Apple Watch Now Has Over 6000 Apps: Cult of Mac*. Retrieved from Cult of Mac: http://www.cultofmac.com/325765/apple-watch-now-has-over-6000-apps/

Karlovsky, B. (2014, May 07). *Smartphones represent the greatest IT security risk to business: Good Mobility Index*. Retrieved from PC Advisor: http://www.pcadvisor.co.uk/news/enterprise/smartphones-represent-the-greatest-it-security-risk-to-business-good-mobility-index-3515300/

Kent, K., Chevalier, S., Grance, T., & Dang, H. (2006). *Guide to integrating forensic techniques into incident response*. NIST Special Publication, 800-886.

Lamkin, P. (2015, May 11). *Tech: Forbes*. Retrieved from Forbes: http://www.forbes.com/sites/paullamkin/2015/05/11/101-million-smartwatch-shipments-by-2020-with-apple-and-google-leading-the-way/

Mann, S. (2001, July 1). A GNU/Linux Wristwatch Videophone. *Linux Journal*.

McEnore, P. (2014, August 12). *Feds bust wordwide smartphone theft ring based in Twin Cities*. Retrieved from Star Tribune: http://www.startribune.com/feds-bust-worldwide-smartphone-theft-ring-based-in-twin-cities/270960821/

Moore, G. (1965). Moore's law. *Electronics Magazine*. Retrieved from http://www.extremetech.com/extreme/210872-extremetech-explains-what-is-moores-law

Neild, D. (2015, September 16). *Apple Watch Vs. Samsung Gear S2 Comparison*. Retrieved from Gizmag: http://www.gizmag.com/apple-watch-vs-samsung-gear-s2-comparison/39399/

Oracle. (2015, April). *Oracle Technology Network: Topics: Security*. Retrieved from Oracle.com: http://www.oracle.com/technetwork/topics/security/poodlecve-2014-3566-2339408.html

Pearse, D. (2015, August 25). *Wearable Sensors Help Diagnose Depression: Article: Horizon Magazine*. Retrieved from Horizon Magazine: http://horizon-magazine.eu/article/wearable-sensors-help-diagnose-depression_en.html

Philips. (2015). *What Hue Does: About Hue: Meet Hue*. Retrieved from Meet Hue: http://www2.meethue.com/en-us/about-hue/what-hue-does/

Pierce, D. (2015, September 30). *LG Watch Urbane Cellular Connected: Wired.* Retrieved from Wired: http://www.wired.com/2015/09/lg-watch-urbane-cellular-connected/

Ponemon, L. (2009, February 9). *The Cost of a Lost Laptop.* Ponemon Institute LLC. Retrieved from Intel.com: https://www-ssl.intel.com/content/dam/doc/white-paper/enterprise-security-the-cost-of-a-lost-laptop-paper.pdf

Ponemon, L. (2010). *Missing a Laptop? Join the Billion-Dollar Club.* Ponemon Institute.

Saha, A. (2015, March 12). *10 Reasons to Buy a Smartwatch: techgyd.* Retrieved from techGYD: http://www.techgyd.com/10-reasons-to-buy-a-smartwatch/15144/

Smith, C., & Miessler, D. (2015, August). *Website.* Retrieved from http://go.saas.hp.com/fod/internet-of-things

Temple, R., & Naziri, J. (2015, July 28). *Best Android Smartwatch apps 2015: Wearables: News: techradar.* Retrieved from techradar: http://www.techradar.com/us/news/wearables/best-android-wear-smartwatch-apps-2015-1281065

Thorsteinsson, G., & Page, T. (2015, January 21). How attached to our smart phones are we? *International Journal of Mobile Learning and Organisation, 8,* 201 - 215. Retrieved from Science Daily: www.sciencedaily.com/releases/2015/01/150121083646.htm

Torres, J. (2015, June 8). *Samsungs Next Smartwatch Will Have NFC For Samsung Pay: Slash Gear.* Retrieved from Slash Gear: http://www.slashgear.com/samsungs-next-smartwatch-will-have-nfc-for-samsung-pay-08387154/

United States Computer Emergency Response Team. (2013, July 22). *DNS Amplification Attacks: Alert (TA13-088A): US-CERT.* Retrieved from US-CERT: https://www.us-cert.gov/ncas/alerts/TA13-088A

Utter, C. J., & Rea, A. (2015). The "Bring Your Own Device" Conundrum for Organizations and Investigators: An Examination of the Policy and Legal Concerns in the Policy and Legal Concerns in Light of Investigatory Challenges. *The Journal of Digital Forensics, Security and Law,* 57 - 72.

Valdes, R., & Chandler, N. (2005, April 13). *Clocks Watches: Gadgets: How Stuff Works.* Retrieved from How Stuff Works: http://electronics.howstuffworks.com/gadgets/clocks-watches/smart-watch.htm

Walton, Z. (2015, November 06). *Wearables: WTVOX.* Retrieved from WTVox: https://wtvox.com/wearables/researchers-able-to-hack-smartwatches/

Wang, H., Tsung-Te, L. T., & Choudhury, R. R. (2015, September). MoLe: Motion Leaks through Smartwatch Sensors. *Annual International Conference on Mobile Computing and Networking*. Paris: Association for Computing Machinery's Special Interest Group on Mobility of Systems, Users, Data, and Computing. doi:10.1145/2789168.2790121

Wood, A. (2012, June 22). *News: TechTarget*. Retrieved from TechTarget: http://searchmobilecomputing.techtarget.com/news/2240158544/Web-apps-easier-for-IT-to-secure-but-BYOD-users-go-native

KEY TERMS AND DEFINITIONS

Accelerometer: A small device that senses motion and measures acceleration forces. Commonly found in smartphones.

Bluetooth: A global and unlicensed protocol specified for a short-range radio frequency. Used to transmit between devices in a personal space area.

BYOD: Bring Your Own Device. A policy allowing or encouraging employees to bring their own personally owned technology to use in the workplace. Related terms include BYOT (Technology) BYOP (Phone) and so on.

Internet of Things (IoT): Interconnected objects, devices, vehicles, buildings that can exchange information, and be controlled remotely, over the Internet.

Policy: An enforceable set of organizational rules and principles used to aid decision-making that have penalties for non-compliance, such as the termination of an employee's contract with an employer.

Smart (Eyewear): (Glasses) with enhanced functionality, such as Internet connectivity. Watches, wristbands and other body-worn items may also be prefixed by "smart" to denote this.

Smart Watch or Smartwatch: A wristwatch with advanced computer based functionality, similar to that of smartphones, and/or sensing capability.

Wearable: Any external or internal body-worn object with an embedded sensor or computer that can be connected to a network.

ENDNOTES

[1] Image modified from the original photograph by Kārlis Dambrāns, © 2013, used with permission under the Creative Commons Attribution 2.0 Generic license (https://creativecommons.org/licenses/by/2.0/). Original image available online: https://www.flickr.com/photos/janitors/10289879613/

2   © 2016, iFixit. Used with permission.

3   http://www.landley.net/toybox/about.html Last accessed 2015-11-07.

Chapter 4
Confidential Data Storage Systems for Wearable Platforms

Mingzhong Wang
University of the Sunshine Coast, Australia

Don Kerr
University of the Sunshine Coast, Australia

ABSTRACT

With the features of mobility, reality augmentation, and context sensitivity, wearable devices are widely deployed into various domains. However, the sensitivity of collected data makes security and privacy protection one of the first priority in the advancement of wearable technologies. This chapter provides a study on encryption-based confidentiality protection for data storage systems in wearable platforms. The chapter first conducts a review to storage solutions in consumer wearable products and explores a two-tier, local flash memory and remote cloud storage, storage system in wearable platforms. Then encryption-based confidentiality protection and implementation methods for both flash memory and remote cloud storage are summarized. According to the interaction and integration of these two components, a categorization of confidential storage systems in wearable platforms is proposed. In addition, the benefits and selection criteria for each category are also discussed.

DOI: 10.4018/978-1-5225-1016-1.ch004

INTRODUCTION

With the ever-increasing computational power along with decreasing cost, micro-processor chips in tiny sizes are becoming wearable. That is, they can be embedded into clothes, personal accessories, and even bodies (Mann, 1997). With the development of wearable technologies, a new computing paradigm is emerging. In comparison with traditional computers, which are machines separated from their users, wearable devices are attached to our bodies, extending the limitation of our bodies with various capabilities of sensing, communicating, and computing (Roggen, Magnenat, Waibel, & Troster, 2011).

With the features of mobility, reality augmentation, and context sensitivity, wearable devices can be applied in various domains, including military and medical monitoring and emergency response (Billinghurst & Starner, 1999). In recent years, the popularity of wristbands, smart watches, and the buzz around Google Glass signaled the success and wide acceptance of wearable technologies.

Although wearable devices come in various sizes, shapes, and capacities, they are generally designed to perform data collecting and processing tasks. In essence, they are a tiny version of connected computers. Since wearable devices are directly attached to human bodies, the data gathered, such as health measurements and GPS locations, are usually highly linked to users' privacy. For example, activity trackers and smart watches can measure users' heart rates, precise steps, sleeping quality, and sometimes locations. The leakage of these data enables unauthorized parties to assess and predict the lifestyle and health conditions of the users. Insurance companies may use these data to increase health premiums, or even to cancel a policy. The risk and fear of exposure of these sensitive data is one of the major inhibitors to the adoption of wearable technologies (Al Ameen, Liu, & Kwak, 2012).

The flow of data in wearable technologies involves the stages of data sensing, local processing, local storage, and transmission to remote server or storage. Security or privacy breaches generally occur in the storage and transmission stages. However, traditional security and privacy preserving solutions cannot be applied directly to all categories of wearable devices with varied hardware capacity, including processors, RAM, power supply, and communication rage (di Pietro & Mancini, 2003). Especially, due to the size and weight constraints, the battery capacity in wearable devices becomes a major restriction from providing rich functionality (Huang, Badam, Chandra, & Nightingale, 2015).

Solutions for secure communications between wearable devices and storage server have been widely studied (Al Ameen et al., 2012; di Pietro & Mancini, 2003; Starner, 2001). However, limited literature can be found for the research on secure and confidential storage management in wearable platforms. Therefore, this chapter provides a thorough review on existing storage solutions for wearable devices, and discusses possible mechanisms to provide confidentiality protection for their storage systems. The objectives of this chapter are to:

- Review and compare the storage solutions for popular consumer wearable devices in the market,
- Explain the features of two key storage components in wearable platforms: flash memory which is widely used as local storage media, and cloud storage which is applied as final data destination,
- Summarize the application of encryption into flash memory and cloud storage to support confidentiality, and
- Discuss four categories of confidential storage systems, including NLNC (non-confidential local and non-confidential cloud storage), NLCC (non-confidential local and confidential cloud storage), CLCC (confidential local and confidential cloud storage), and CLNC (confidential local and non-confidential cloud storage), to accompany different application scenarios in wearable platforms.

The chapter is organized as follows. A literature review on data security and privacy protection in wearable technologies is provided first. Then a data storage architecture in wearable platforms is introduced, and various commercial productions are analyzed accordingly. After two key components, local flash memory and remote cloud storage, of the storage systems are identified, these are considered in detail. The next step looks at the research in terms of encryption-based confidentiality protection for both flash memory and remote cloud storage. Since local and cloud storage are applied in combination in practice as a confidential storage system in wearable platforms, a categorization is proposed. The benefits and selection criteria for each category are discussed. Finally, the implementation techniques for confidential flash storage are discussed.

BACKGROUND

Data security and privacy are two indispensable requirements for trustworthy wearable applications. Data security refers to protecting data from corruption and unauthorized access, while data privacy requires that data can only be collected and used according to the agreed purposes.

Since wearable devices operate in open wireless environment, their data are prone to various threats, including eavesdropping, modification, and injection. Threats, from the device point of view, can be summarized into two categories: data storage and data access (Li, Wenjing, & Kui, 2010). Potential threats include device compromise and network attacks. This chapter focuses on the security and privacy issues related to data storage.

Confidentiality, integrity, and availability are three key requirements for data storage security and privacy (Kesh & Ratnasingam, 2007). Storage confidentiality means no one except authorized users can access data from the storage even if the device is compromised. Storage integrity stands for the protection of data storage from unauthorized modifications. And storage availability refers to that data must be retrievable for authorized parties from the storage when it is needed. Encryption is an important technology to achieve these features (Diesburg, Meyers, Lary, & Wang, 2008). This chapter focuses on confidentiality protection.

The inherent nature of resource constraint in wearable devices prevents them from storing all data locally. The collected data have to be distributed to other locations if data persistence is required. Most research in this field focused on solutions for secure distributed data storage (Chessa & Maestrini, 2003; Li et al., 2010; Subramanian, Yang, & Zhang, 2007; Wang, Ren, Yu, & Lou, 2011; Zhou & Huang, 2013). They proposed the peer-to-peer organization of mobile devices or sensors to enable the share of storage pool among devices. The topics of study include data access control, key management, and device interoperability. However, our review of commercial wearable devices finds that most of them are not designed to share their storage or other resources with others. In fact, pairing a wearable device with a powerful intermediate system, such as smart phones or computers, is a more common solution.

Our review also finds that most commercial wearable products utilize cloud storage as the final data persistence solution. In this way, the wearable technologies benefit from the features of scalability, economy, and availability in cloud computing. Security of cloud storage has been extensively studied in the research community (Brodkin, 2008; Kamara & Lauter, 2010; Neumann, 2014; Wei et al., 2014).

Although there are many studies about confidential sensor storage and cloud storage respectively, their interaction and integration as a whole storage solution for wearable platforms have not been systematically investigated. This chapter provides such an effort and insight into the integration of local and cloud storage.

STORAGE IN CONSUMER WEARABLE DEVICES

As computing gadgets, wearable devices continuously collect data from their sensors. No matter whether the sensed data get processed or not, they need to be stored, either locally or remotely. In other words, they have to be accompanied with some data storage mechanisms to have sensed or processed data stored.

Figure 1. Data storage architecture in wearable platforms

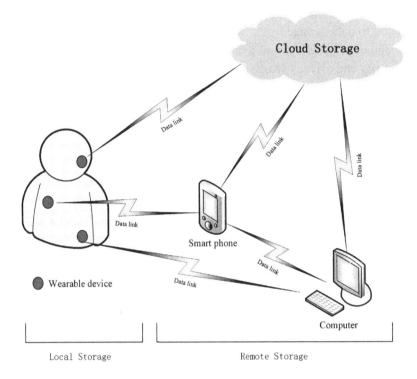

In general, the storage systems for wearable platforms consist of two parts: local storage and remote backup. Figure 1 illustrates the data storage architecture commonly used in commercial wearable technologies.

It is a two-tier storage model consisting of local and remote storage. Local storage is embedded into wearable devices, while remote storage can be a smart phone, a computer, or a cloud solution.

After a wearable device collects some data from sensors, it has three choices:

- Upload the data directly to a remote storage without local saving.
- Save the data locally, with the data uploading as an optional operation.
- Save the data as a local cache, and upload them to a remote storage regularly when there is a connection available.

The adoption of the first option requires stable and continuous connections between the wearable device and the remote system. However, it is not practical because these devices are frequently away from smart phones or computers. Moreover, to maintain a data link connection all the time increases power consumption dramatically.

Table 1. Configuration for Google Glass Explorer version 2

Item	Feature
Processor (CPU)	Texas Instruments OMAP 4430 1.2 GHz Dual
Operating System	Android 4.4
Display	Prism projector 640×360 pixel
RAM	2 GB
Network	Wi-Fi (802.11b/g), Bluetooth
Storage	16 GB flash memory
Battery	570 mAh

Google Glass (Google Inc.) applies the second option. Table 1 shows the key parameters for Google Glass Explorer version 2. Google Glass has considerably powerful hardware configurations as a smart phone at the cost of US$1500. Therefore, it operates as a smartphone to store all data locally, and supports data synchronization according to user configurations and specific applications. According to the application setting, data can be uploaded to a smart phone, a computer, or a cloud.

The hardware configurations for smart watches vary significantly. Table 2 compares three popular smart watch products in the market, including Apple Watch (38mm) (Apple Inc., 2015), Samsung Galaxy Gear S (Samsung Electronics, 2015), and Pebble Time (Pebble Technology).

Although hardware configurations can be as superior as Apple Watch and Gear S, almost all smart watches need to be paired with smart phones for long-term data storage. The general data synchronization routine can be summarized as follows:

Table 2. Comparison of smart watches: Apple Watch (38mm) vs. Samsung Galaxy Gear S vs. Pebble Time

Item	Apple Watch (38mm)	Samsung Galaxy Gear S	Pebble Time
Processor (CPU)	Apple S1 520 MHz	Dual-Core 1 GHz	Cortex-M4 100 MHz
Operating System	WatchOS 2	Tizen	Pebble OS
Display	272×340 pixels	360×480 pixels	144×168 pixel
RAM	512 MB	512 MB	256 KB
Network	Wi-Fi (802.11 b/g/n), Bluetooth, NFC	Wi-Fi (802.11 b/g/n), 3G, Bluetooth	Bluetooth
Storage	8 GB flash memory	4 GB flash memory	16 MB flash memory
Battery	205 mAh	300 mAh	130 mAh

Step 1: Pairing the watch and the phone via Bluetooth.

Step 2: Install watch applications on the phone.

Step 3: Watch collects data and stores them locally.

Step 4: If the paired devices are connected by Bluetooth or in the same Wi-Fi net-work, stored data are synchronized automatically to the paired phone.

Once the data arrive at the smart phone, further storage to a computer or a cloud depends on the application settings. Although some smart watches have a Wi-Fi module, they do not allow applications to upload data to a cloud directly. The reason may be the high power consumption of Wi-Fi connection.

Another popular category of consumer wearable technologies is activity tracker, which is a dedicated electronic device to monitor and collect fitness-related metrics, including walking or running distance and steps, calorie consumption, heartbeat, and quality of sleep.

Representative tracker products in the market include Fitbit Charge (Fitbit Inc., 2015), Jawbone UP24 (Jawbone), and Nike+ FuelBand SE (Nike Inc., 2013). There is no official release of their hardware configurations. However, they are capable of keeping collected data locally for a period. For example, Fitbit Charge holds detailed minute-by-minute information for the most recent 7 days, and 30 days of daily summaries. In comparison, Jawbone UP24 can store up to nine months of movement and sleep data.

Since these activity trackers have limited storage and processing capacity, they need to be paired, either via Bluetooth or USB wire, with a smart phone or a computer, to share the Internet connection, and data are in fact synchronized to cloud storage.

In summary, although wearable devices have distinct size, shape, and capacity, the general solution for data storage consists of local non-volatile flash memory and remote cloud.

Flash Memory

In comparison with disk systems, flash memory provides significant performance advantages and power savings, making it a popular storage solution for embedded devices. As the drop of price and rise of capacity, it also becomes popular in storage solutions for laptops, desktops, and data centers.

Flash memory contains no magnetic or optical component, but an electronic chip which can electrically update the data in it. It was invented as an advancement from EEPROM (electrically erasable programmable read-only memory) by Toshiba in 1984.

There are two distinct categories, NAND and NOR, of flash memory. They are named according to the method by which the flash cells are organized. Since NOR flash supports random access, it is ideal to be used as random access memory. In comparison, NAND flash must be treated as blocks and is best suited for persistent storage (Leventhal, 2008).

A NAND flash chip is organized as a set of blocks. Each block is made up of 64 or 128 pages. The size of a page is typically 512, 2048, or 4096 bytes. A few bytes are attached to each page to be used as an error correcting code (ECC) checksum (Grupp et al., 2009).

A NAND flash device has three types of operations: read, program (write), and erase. Since NAND manages data in blocks, the erase operation works on entire blocks and sets all the bits in the block to 1. A write operation updates entire pages at once and can only change the bits from 1 to 0 (Grupp et al., 2009; Mittal & Vetter, 2015). Therefore, if a bit needs to be changed from 0 to 1, an erase operation is first performed to change all bits in the block to 1, and then write operations are executed to set necessary bits back to 0. Most NAND devices can endure 100,000 program-erase cycles.

To improve update performance and prolong the lifespan of NAND devices, wear leveling is applied. Supported by either the drive controller or file systems, wear leveling remaps write operations to some spare pages to avoid repeated erase-program operations to the same location in case of new page update requests.

Cloud Storage

Wearable devices are mobile in nature, and suffer from the inherent problems of resource constraints. An intuitive solution is to offload storage and computation to cloud computing platforms. Cloud computing "is a model for enabling ubiquitous, convenient, on-demand network access to a shared pool of configurable computing resources (e.g., networks, servers, storage, applications, and services) that can be rapidly provisioned and released with minimal management effort or service provider interaction". (Mell & Grance, 2011, p2)

Cloud storage provides data storage service for users via the Internet. Service providers utilize virtualization technologies to build a logical storage pool from various storage units or disks. Users buy or lease storage capacity from the pool according to their needs. As with electricity, water, and gas, storage is offered as a utility and you only pay for what you use.

Cloud-based storage plays an indispensable role in the storage solutions in wearable platforms. Even though a wearable device has limited storage capacity, all historical data can be stored in servers for future reference. Moreover, users do not need to worry about data management and maintenance, such as data availability and protection, on their own computers. As well, no matter where users are, as long as there is an Internet connection, they have immediate access to storage services via web service interfaces.

There are three approaches to offer Cloud storage to wearable devices (Fernando, Loke, & Rahayu, 2013):

- **Remote Cloud Storage:** The wearable devices connect to remote storage server via cellular or Wi-Fi network directly. This resembles the general usage of Dropbox or Google Drive on desktop computers.
- **Sensor Cloud Storage:** Wearable devices are not only storage consumers, but also storage providers. They collaborate with each other to form a wireless ad hoc network, which operates in a peer-to-peer architecture. This approach enables the possibility of doing collective sensing.
- **Cloudlet:** In cases where wearable devices have limited processing and communication capacity, a middle tier, or cloudlet, can be introduced to connect the wearable devices and the cloud. A cloudlet can be a desktop or a laptop whose compute cycles, storage resources, and communication capacities can be leveraged by nearby mobile devices (Mahadev, Bahl, Caceres, & Davies, 2009).

Remote cloud storage is not appropriate for most wearable devices nowadays because of high requirements on networking capability. However, if the price and size of commodity hardware keep on dropping along with the improvement of performance, more and more wearable devices will be equipped with Wi-Fi, 3G, or 4G network modules for direct access to remote cloud storage services.

Sensor cloud storage is not a practical option for most wearable devices because of their limited storage capacity. Moreover, saving data to or retrieving data from another device involves abundant network transmissions, which are power-hungry operations. As it is an ad hoc network, the high network and security management overhead should also be considered. However, this solution offers an alternative to organize and optimize the storage capacity of all devices.

Configurations using cloudlets are the de facto solutions for wearable devices. Most wearable devices require a pairing with a smartphone, which is used as the cloudlet for storage and bandwidth. It is up to the system designer whether the cloudlet is the final storage or it is just a transit point to remote cloud storage. Most activity trackers, such as Fitbit Charge and Jawbone UP24, use smart phones as a gateway to their remote cloud storage. Although there are many security and privacy concerns about Cloud storage (Kamara & Lauter, 2010; Neumann, 2014), consumers of commercial products in general have no choice but to trust the storage service provided by vendors.

CONFIDENTIAL DISK AND CLOUD STORAGE

Cryptography Background

If a computer can be physically isolated or disconnected from the outside world, the confidentiality of its data can be preserved. However, in an interconnected world, complete isolation is hard to achieve.

The most widely-used mechanism to achieve data confidentiality is through encryption (Diesburg et al., 2008). Encryption is the process that encodes messages or data to an unrecognizable or "encrypted" form, so that only authorized parties can access messages after decryption.

The encryption process can be represented as a function $c = E(k, m)$. m is the original plaintext, and c is the ciphertext which is the encrypted or encoded form of m. c is unreadable by a human or computer. k is a secret key which is used during the encryption process E.

The decryption process is used to recover the plaintext from the ciphertext. It can also be represented as a function $m = D(k', c)$.

There are two types of encryption.

- **Symmetric Key Encryption:** The sender and receiver share the same key. That is, $k = k'$.
- **Asymmetric (Public) Key Encryption:** The encryption (public) key, k, is published for anyone to use and encrypt messages. The receiver uses a different decryption (private) key, k', to recover the plaintext. RSA (the Rivest-Shamir-Adleman cryptosystem) is in this category.

The Data Encryption Standard (DES), Triple-DES (3DES), and the Advanced Encryption Standard (AES) are common symmetric key encryption algorithms. They take a block of n-length bits as input, and generate a block of n-length bits as the output. A key in DES is 56 bits and a block is 64 bits. Because of the short key, brute-force enumeration can be used to break the key with modern computation power in a short time. For example, a machine called the "DES Cracker" could find a DES key in 56 hours in 1998.

AES was designed to replace DES in 2001. Although the block size in AES is 128 bits, various key sizes of 128, 192, and 256 bits are supported.

The most important part of encryption is the distribution and protection of keys since the encryption function is assumed to be publicly available.

Since symmetric key encryption uses the same key for both encryption and decryption, it can achieve higher data throughput. The algorithm is in general easier to implement, and uses less processing power. However, both the sender and the receiver need to maintain the secrecy of the key. That is, a key management component, which introduces memory and communication overhead, should be included in the design. A secure channel should also be applied to initialize the key before any data communication.

Conversely, public key encryption only needs to keep the private key secret, and avoids the overhead of key management. However, the performance of the most popular public key encryption is several orders of magnitude slower than the best known symmetric key counterparts (Menezes, Van Oorschot, & Vanstone, 1996).

Confidential Disk Storage with Encryption

Although encryption process incurs overhead and latency in data processing and key management, it can provide a satisfiable solution for secure data management. For data persistence, since data need to go through several layers before they reach the physical media (Figure 2), additional concerns about encryption-based confidential data storage should be addressed (Diesburg et al., 2008).

Figure 2. Storage data path

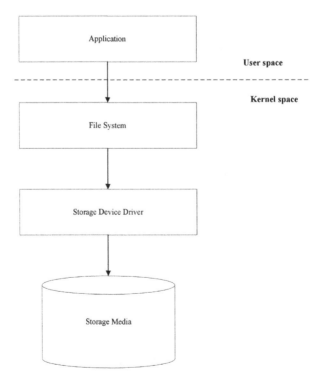

- **Single Generic Data Type:** Since encrypted and non-encrypted data are in general not differentiable along the storage data path, plaintext data may be cached.
- **Poor Consistency Guarantees:** Assume that data are always encrypted. During the editing of a file, there are two copies available: a newer and un-saved version of an encrypted file in memory, and an older version on the disk. Hibernation operation of the system may lead to different versions of encrypted data on disks.
- **Information Hiding:** The file system may save an updated file to different sectors in the physical media without erasing its previous occupation. Therefore, multiple copies with similar content will reside in the disk. Although the user can only view the latest version, attackers can retrieve older file versions.

Multiple versions of ciphertext blocks may frequently co-exist on the storage device. Since most wearable devices use NAND memory as storage media, and wear leveling is commonly applied to avoid expensive erase-program operations, information hiding becomes a more prominent problem. For example, Diesburg et al. (2008) carried out an experiment to demonstrate the plaintext recovery from multiple versions of a file encrypted with 128-bit AES in OFB mode with the same initialization vector and key. The experiment is based on *jffs2* (Journaling Flash File System version 2), which is tailored to provide wear leveling and performance optimizations for flash devices, and operates directly on the flash chips.

Confidential Cloud Storage

If a private cloud is deployed, the infrastructure is located on site and the users have full control over the hardware, applications, and data. Therefore, customized access control rules can be deployed and disk encryption can be applied to achieve confidentiality.

However, if a public cloud, such as Amazon S3, Google Storage, and Dropbox, is used to avoid the building and maintenance cost, users need to build security and privacy protection over the public cloud service to ensure that the cloud storage provider cannot read (confidentiality) or modify (integrity) any part of user data. Encryption is the major tool to achieve this task (Kamara & Lauter, 2010; Neumann, 2014; Wei et al., 2014). Data encryption is generally conducted at the user side before uploading to the cloud.

The naïve solution is to encrypt all data and generate digital signatures before sending them to the cloud. Although it preserves confidentiality and integrity, data integrity verifications need to retrieve all data from the server for signatures generation, which is expensive and undesirable. Moreover, search over the data is not well supported. Users have to store the index locally, or retrieve and decrypt all data to search locally. Addressing these issues, a variety of techniques were developed specifically for secure cloud storage.

When preparing data for storage in the cloud, the data processor begins by indexing it and encrypting it with a symmetric encryption scheme (e.g., AES) under a unique key. It then encrypts the index using a searchable encryption scheme and encrypts the unique key with an attribute-based encryption scheme under an appropriate policy. Finally, it encodes the encrypted data and index in such a way that the data verifier can later verify their integrity using a proof of storage. (Kamara & Lauter, 2010)

If the creator and consumer of the encrypted data belong to the same user group, symmetric key encryption can be applied because of higher efficiency. However, if they are not in the same user group, public key encryption should be used.

TWO-LAYER CONFIDENTIAL STORAGE SYSTEMS

Wearable platforms have four choices in implementing confidential storage systems after applying confidential support to two levels, local and cloud, of storage for wearable devices. Figure 3 illustrates the relationship between these four categories.

Figure 3. Categories of confidential storage systems in wearable platforms

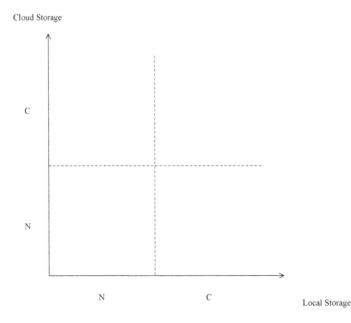

C stands for confidential storage, and *N* stands for non-confidential support for the storage. It should be noted that this discussion focuses on storage component, but not the communication channel between the device and the cloud.

There is no one-size-fits-all solution, and different combination of confidential or non-confidential local and cloud storage should be compared before the final decision in storage design. In general, confidential local storage can guarantee data security and privacy, but it demands more computation and memory resources, which may not be possible in wearable environment. Confidential cloud storage can prevent users' data from the monitoring and misuse of service providers, but it gives up the benefits of cloud-based data processing. With confidential cloud storage, users need to retrieve their data back and perform analysis locally.

NLNC Storage System

NLNC stands for non-confidential local and non-confidential cloud storage. This solution provides no confidentiality guarantee in data storage. However, due to the resource constraints of wearable devices, this may become the only option.

In general, if a device has very limited computational and memory capacity, it also has limited storage capacity. That is, it can only record personal data for a short period. Even if local data are compromised, there is a high probability that attackers cannot gather enough information to invade users' privacy. However, if highly sensitive data are collected, then this approach is not suitable.

Non-confidential cloud storage enables the utilization of cloud computing resources to analyze historical data. To apply this approach, it is assumed that service providers are trustworthy. They will not only not violate your privacy, but also have the capability to protect your data from unauthorized access. Authentication and access control technologies are usually applied.

NLCC Storage System

NLCC stands for non-confidential local and confidential cloud storage. If wearable devices have limited resources to do local encryption, but cloud storage is not trustworthy, an intermediate system, such as a cloudlet, a smart phone, or a local computer, needs to be introduced to provide encryption service to users' data.

Data are stored in plaintext in wearable devices and then synchronized to an intermediate system before they are uploaded into the cloud storage. The intermediate system carries out data encryption, and then uploads encrypted data into the cloud. In this way, user's privacy and confidentiality are protected against cloud providers.

However, since cloud providers have no access to original data, all data processing requirements need to be implemented locally, and related data need to be downloaded each time.

CLCC Storage System

CLCC stands for confidential local and confidential cloud storage. If wearable devices are configured with more powerful hardware, they become capable of local encryption. The encrypted local data can be directly uploaded into the cloud storage without any modification to achieve confidential cloud storage. This provides complete confidentiality protection for users' data. However, all data processing tasks completely rely on local resources.

Apple Watch falls into this category. Users' activity data on Apple Watch are encrypted with keys protected by users' passcode. The data are also store in encrypted format in iCloud (Apple Inc.). Although Samsung Galaxy Gear watch has similar hardware configuration as Apple Watch, its data are not protected by encryption (Page, 2015).

CLNC Storage System

CLNC stands for confidential local and non-confidential cloud storage. Although the approach of confidential local and confidential cloud storage provides complete protection over users' data, it cannot benefit from the full power of cloud computing. Therefore, most commercial products, including Fitbit and Jawbone, apply confidential local but non-confidential cloud solution.

In this solution, data collected are stored in encrypted format. Thereafter, there are two choices. One choice is to decrypt data at an intermediate system before they are uploaded to the cloud. Therefore, users own and manage keys for encryption and decryption. The other choice is to upload encrypted data directly to the cloud storage where data are decrypted and saved. In this design, cloud service providers own the decryption keys. Users in general have no control or access to their data except downloading them from the service provider.

Confidential Flash Storage Implementation

As shown in Figure 2, there are several layers between the data collection and the physical storage. Therefore, confidential protection or encryption can be implemented at different levels (Bagci, Pourmirza, Raza, Roedig, & Voigt, 2012; Diesburg & Wang, 2010).

- **Hardware-Based Confidential Storage:** Encryption functionality is implemented by hardware. Since encryption is embedded into devices, it is not flexible about the key management or encryption mechanisms. However, it provides superior performance. An example solution is a secure flash drive. Encryption mechanisms are provided on the flash drive firmware. Therefore, encryptions are transparent to other parts of the system.

- **Software-Based Confidential Storage:** Encryption functionality is implemented by software. Since it requires no specialized hardware, it offers an economic solution for storage encryption. In addition, it supports flexibility of implementation and management. Diesburg and Wang (2010) proposed the following categories with regards to software-based solutions.

  - **Encryption Programs:** They reside in user space and employ cryptographic operations at a fine granularity. They can be flexibly installed and managed as plugins into the system. However, application-level solutions can only provide a limited level of confidentiality. Before files are encrypted, temporary plaintext files may be created and cached by the file systems or operations systems.

  - **User-Space File Systems:** A virtual user-space file system can be built without modifying any kernel module or code. Encryption is conducted at this level before data are forwarded to an underlying legacy file system in the kernel space. Various encryption algorithms can be used and temporary files are placed in encrypted directories. However, the directory structure and file metadata information are still revealed in user-space file systems.

  - **Stackable File Systems:** Kernel functionality is extended by inserting an extra cryptographic file system layer by intercepting system calls. Stackable file systems can run inside the kernel and can operate on top of any other file system without requiring other user-level processes or daemons to run. They share the same drawbacks of user-space file systems, but perform better since they avoid back-and-forth system calls between the user space and kernel.

  - **Disk-Based File Systems:** They operate at a lower level of abstraction than stackable file systems. They have full control over all directories and file metadata and operations.

  - **Block-Based Solutions:** They are implemented to encrypt and decrypt large chunks of data at the level of a partition or disk, which is below any file system. They are transparent to the user and to the file system. Encryption must be performed over the entire disk on all types of data, swap and temporary files, and keys.

SOLUTIONS AND RECOMMENDATIONS

In this chapter, we identified a two-tier storage system for wearable platforms, which include local flash memory and remote cloud storage. Therefore, if data confidentiality is required, the encryption-based protection needs to be implemented at either or both layers according to the user requirements and system resources.

Encrypted Flash Memory

For flash memories that are embedded into wearable devices, encryption mechanisms can be built into flash drive firmware if budget allows. This hardware-based solution provides better performance and the protection is transparent to other components of the device. The drawback is inflexibility of key management.

In contrast, software-based solutions for confidential storage can be adopted. Block-based solutions are recommended because they provide best performance, security protection, and system transparency in all software-based solutions. However, they require modification to core codes of operation systems' kernel, which is error-prone and risky. Disk-based file systems are also recommended because they support full control over all directories and file metadata and operations. If directory structure and file metadata are not sensitive, user-space file systems are recommended because they are easier to implement without modifying any kernel module or code. If only partial data need encryption, independent encryption programs are suggested.

Encrypted Cloud Storage

If confidentiality protection is required on the cloud side, a private cloud storage is recommended because it provides users with full control over the hardware, applications, and data. With well-designed access control mechanisms, disk encryption may not be necessary, which improves the overall system performance.

However, in some cases, public cloud services are utilized to avoid building and maintenance costs. In this case, storage encryption should be applied to avoid potential monitoring and abuse from service providers. Unfortunately, encrypted cloud storage gives up the benefits of cloud-based data processing. Moreover, users have to retrieve historical data from the cloud and perform analysis locally.

An intermediate system, such as smart phones and computers, plays an important role regarding the data transmission between local and cloud storage. Encryption or decryption functions may need to be implemented in the intermediate system in each combination of local and cloud storage.

- **Non-Confidential Local and Non-Confidential Cloud Storage:** This solution provides no confidentiality protection in data storage. However, due to the resource constraints of wearable devices, this may become the only option.
- **Non-Confidential Local and Confidential Cloud Storage:** If wearable devices have limited resources to do local encryption, but cloud storage is not trustworthy, the intermediate system can be used to encrypt users' data before uploading to the cloud.
- **Confidential Local and Confidential Cloud Storage:** If wearable devices are configured with more powerful hardware, they become capable of local encryption. The encrypted local data can be directly uploaded into the cloud storage without any modification to achieve confidential cloud storage. This provides complete confidentiality protection for users' data.
- **Confidential Local and Non-Confidential Cloud Storage:** Data are stored in plaintext in the cloud even though they are encrypted in wearable devices. Most commercial products apply this model because they provide not only cloud storage, but also advanced data processing and analysis services. The decryption can be implemented by either intermediate systems or cloud services.

FUTURE RESEARCH DIRECTIONS

This chapter has focused on the security requirement of confidentiality, without discussing the integration and availability of data storage. However, these are also important for a practical data storage system, and should be studied in combination with encryption-based confidentiality solutions.

Hardware and software based secure flash memory implementation is another direction for future research. The focus should be put on the efficiency and flexibility of encryption processing and key management.

For secure cloud storage, there are at least two interesting fields of study. One is data processing in encrypted format, such as searchable encryption schemes. Another is the proof of storage to show that cloud providers do not modify users' data.

For intermediate systems connecting wearable devices and cloud storage, secure communications and synchronizations for cloudlets or smart phones are another focus. In particular, the security of temporary storage in intermediate systems should also be considered.

Moreover, with ongoing advancement in commodity hardware, such as the decrease of size and price and increases in performance, more wearable devices in the near future may be equipped with Wi-Fi, 3G, or 4G network module for direct access to remote cloud storage services. The effectiveness of data security solutions may become especially important then.

As the number of wearable devices per person increases, it may become possible to build a local ad hoc sensor or mobile cloud system. The security and privacy protection in this setting is also an interesting topic.

CONCLUSION

Although wearable technologies have the potential to improve our life quality, security and privacy concerns become an important factor that could prevent its wide adoption by the public. Data storage is responsible for the long-term persistence of users' data, thus becoming an important part in data processing life cycle for wearable devices. This chapter provided a study on encryption-based confidentiality protection for data storage systems in wearable platforms.

We first conducted a review of storage solutions in consumer wearable products and explored a two-tier, (local flash memory and remote cloud storage) storage system in wearable platforms. Subsequently, encryption-based confidentiality protection mechanisms for flash memory and cloud storage respectively were discussed. In addition, the hardware- and software-based implementation techniques for confidential flash storage were introduced.

Since local and cloud storage are applied in combination in practice as a confidential storage system in wearable platforms, a categorization, with four possibilities, was proposed according to the considerations of interaction and integration. The benefits and selection criteria for each category were also discussed. Practitioners would compare and select from NLNC (non-confidential local and non-confidential cloud storage), NLCC (non-confidential local and confidential cloud storage), CLCC (confidential local and confidential cloud storage), or CLNC (confidential local and non-confidential cloud storage) as suits their needs most.

In the future, more wearable devices may be equipped with Wi-Fi or 4G network modules for direct access to remote cloud storage services due to the continuing advancement in commodity hardware. However, the proposed four categories of confidential storage systems would still remain applicable by shifting the functionality of intermediate systems into wearable devices.

Finally, solutions, recommendations, and emerging research topics were suggested.

DISCUSSION POINTS

- With more and more private data collected continuously, should we allow their storage in plaintext with cloud service providers?
- Data encryption consumes constrained computation, memory, and battery capacity of wearable devices. If data collected are sequences of numbers, such as activity logs and heart rates, without any personal detail, should these data also be encrypted for local storage?
- With ever-increasing hardware capacities, should wearable devices be designed to connect to the Internet directly without a pairing device?
- How can data confidentiality in an intermediate system, such as a smart phone or a desktop computer be protected?
- For some commercial wearable products, users cannot obtain their data until data are stored into the companies' cloud servers. That is, users have no control over what kind of data should be uploaded, and they cannot verify what the true contents of the data are. However, this is one of the most popular storage models in the market. Discuss the reasons for this situation, and give your suggestions.
- Does the prevalence of wearable technologies mark the end of privacy?
- As more and more wearable devices are attached to users, is it a good idea to connect them to build a "wearable cloud"?
- Discuss the relationship between wearable technologies and Internet of Things (IoT). Can security and privacy protection mechanisms in IoT be applied directly into wearable technologies?
- What should be the core features of operating systems and file systems for wearable technologies with varying hardware capacity?

QUESTIONS

- What are the benefits of using flash memory in wearable devices?
- What is an intermediate system in wearable storage systems? Explain why they are widely applied in wearable technology.
- What are cloudlets? What are the differences between cloudlets, smartphones, and computers?
- Do an Internet search on power consumption levels of computation, Wi-Fi, and Bluetooth communications. Explain the reasons that most wearable devices provide only Bluetooth connections. Discuss the impact of data encryption on battery life.

- The data communications between wearable devices and other platforms are in general encrypted. If data storage is also required to be encrypted, can we just do data encryption once to reduce computation cost?
- What are NLNC, NLCC, CLCC, and CLNC storage systems?
- Identify some applications of CLNC storage systems, and briefly describe the data processing stages in the system.
- What is a searchable encryption scheme and how does it work?

REFERENCES

Al Ameen, M., Liu, J., & Kwak, K. (2012). Security and Privacy Issues in Wireless Sensor Networks for Healthcare Applications. *Journal of Medical Systems*, *36*(1), 93–101. doi:10.1007/s10916-010-9449-4 PMID:20703745

Apple Inc. (2015). *Apple Watch User Guide. Version 1.0.* Retrieved from https://manuals.info.apple.com/MANUALS/1000/MA1708/en_US/apple_watch_user_guide.pdf

Apple Inc. (n.d.). *Privacy*. Retrieved from http://www.apple.com/au/privacy/approach-to-privacy/

Bagci, I., Pourmirza, M., Raza, S., Roedig, U., & Voigt, T. (2012). *Codo: confidential data storage for wireless sensor networks.* Paper presented at the IEEE 9th International Conference on Mobile Adhoc and Sensor Systems (MASS), Las Vegas, NV.

Billinghurst, M., & Starner, T. (1999). Wearable devices: New ways to manage information. *Computer*, *32*(1), 57–64. doi:10.1109/2.738305

Brodkin, J. (2008). *Gartner: Seven cloud-computing security risks.* Retrieved from http://www.infoworld.com/article/2652198/security/gartner--seven-cloud-computing-security-risks.html

Chessa, S., & Maestrini, P. (2003). *Dependable and secure data storage and retrieval in mobile, wireless networks.* Paper presented at the International Conference on Dependable Systems and Networks.

di Pietro, R., & Mancini, L. V. (2003). Security and Privacy Issues of Handheld and Wearable Wireless Devices. *Communications of the ACM*, *46*(9), 75–79. doi:10.1145/903893.903897

Diesburg, S. M., Meyers, C. R., Lary, D. M., & Wang, A.-I. A. (2008). *When cryptography meets storage.* Paper presented at the 4th ACM international workshop on Storage security and survivability, Alexandria, VA. Retrieved from http://dl.acm.org/citation.cfm?doid=1456469.1456472

Diesburg, S. M., & Wang, A.-I. A. (2010). A survey of confidential data storage and deletion methods. *ACM Computing Surveys*, *43*(1), 1–37. doi:10.1145/1824795.1824797

Fernando, N., Loke, S. W., & Rahayu, W. (2013). Mobile cloud computing: A survey. *Future Generation Computer Systems*, *29*(1), 84–106. doi:10.1016/j.future.2012.05.023

Fitbit Inc. (2015). *Fitbit Charge Product Manual. Version 1.1.* Retrieved from https://staticcs.fitbit.com/content/assets/help/manuals/manual_charge_en_US.pdf

Google Inc. (n.d.). *GLASS FAQ.* Retrieved from https://sites.google.com/site/glasscomms/faqs

Grupp, L. M., Caulfield, A. M., Coburn, J., Swanson, S., Yaakobi, E., Siegel, P. H., & Wolf, J. K. (2009). *Characterizing flash memory: Anomalies, observations, and applications.* Paper presented at the 42nd Annual IEEE/ACM International Symposium on Microarchitecture.

Huang, J., Badam, A., Chandra, R., & Nightingale, E. B. (2015). *WearDrive: Fast and Energy-Efficient Storage for Wearables.* Paper presented at the 2015 USENIX Annual Technical Conference (USENIX ATC 15), Santa Clara, CA. Retrieved from https://www.usenix.org/conference/atc15/technical-session/presentation/huang-jian

Jawbone. (n.d.). *Jawbone UP24 Support.* Retrieved from https://help.jawbone.com/up24

Kamara, S., & Lauter, K. (2010). Cryptographic Cloud Storage. In R. Sion, R. Curtmola, S. Dietrich, A. Kiayias, J. Miret, K. Sako, & F. Sebé (Eds.), Financial Cryptography and Data Security (Vol. 6054, pp. 136-149). Springer Berlin Heidelberg. doi:10.1007/978-3-642-14992-4_13

Kesh, S., & Ratnasingam, P. (2007). A knowledge architecture for IT security. *Communications of the ACM*, *50*(7), 103–108. doi:10.1145/1272516.1272521

Leventhal, A. (2008). Flash storage memory. *Communications of the ACM*, *51*(7), 47–51. doi:10.1145/1364782.1364796

Li, M., Wenjing, L., & Kui, R. (2010). Data security and privacy in wireless body area networks. *Wireless Communications, IEEE*, *17*(1), 51–58. doi:10.1109/MWC.2010.5416350

Mahadev, S., Bahl, P., Caceres, R., & Davies, N. (2009). The Case for VM-Based Cloudlets in Mobile Computing. *Pervasive Computing, IEEE*, *8*(4), 14–23. doi:10.1109/MPRV.2009.82

Mann, S. (1997). Wearable computing: A first step toward personal imaging. *Computer*, *30*(2), 25–32. doi:10.1109/2.566147

Mell, P. M., & Grance, T. (2011). *SP 800-145. The NIST Definition of Cloud Computing*. Retrieved from http://nvlpubs.nist.gov/nistpubs/Legacy/SP/nistspecialpublication800-145.pdf

Menezes, A. J., Van Oorschot, P. C., & Vanstone, S. A. (1996). *Handbook of applied cryptography*. CRC Press. doi:10.1201/9781439821916

Mittal, S., & Vetter, J. S. (2015). A Survey of Software Techniques for Using Non-Volatile Memories for Storage and Main Memory Systems. *Parallel and Distributed Systems, IEEE Transactions on,* (99). doi:10.1109/TPDS.2015.2442980

Neumann, P. G. (2014). Risks and myths of cloud computing and cloud storage. *Communications of the ACM*, *57*(10), 25–27. doi:10.1145/2661049

Nike Inc. (2013). *Nike+ FuelBand SE User's Guide*. Retrieved from https://support-en-us.nikeplus.com/ci/fattach/get/853467/1406073309/

Page, C. (2015). *Samsung and LG smartwatches leave sensitive data open to hackers*. Retrieved from http://www.v3.co.uk/v3-uk/news/2413018/samsung-and-lg-smartwatches-leave-sensitive-data-open-to-hackers

Pebble Technology. (n.d.). *Pebble Help Center*. Retrieved from http://help.getpebble.com/?b_id=8309

Roggen, D., Magnenat, S., Waibel, M., & Troster, G. (2011). Wearable Computing. *Robotics & Automation Magazine, IEEE*, *18*(2), 83–95. doi:10.1109/MRA.2011.940992

Samsung Electronics. (2015). *Gear S User Manual. Rev.1.4*. Retrieved from http://downloadcenter.samsung.com/content/UM/201501/20150109141014529/SM-R750_UM_EU_Tizen_Eng_Rev.1.4_150106.pdf

Starner, T. (2001). The Challenges of Wearable Computing: Part 2. *IEEE Micro*, *21*(4), 54–67. doi:10.1109/40.946683

Subramanian, N., Yang, C., & Zhang, W. (2007). Securing distributed data storage and retrieval in sensor networks. *Pervasive and Mobile Computing*, *3*(6), 659–676. doi:10.1016/j.pmcj.2007.06.002

Wang, Q., Ren, K., Yu, S., & Lou, W. (2011). Dependable and Secure Sensor Data Storage with Dynamic Integrity Assurance. *ACM Transactions on Sensor Networks*, *8*(1), 1–24. doi:10.1145/1993042.1993051

Wei, L., Zhu, H., Cao, Z., Dong, X., Jia, W., Chen, Y., & Vasilakos, A. V. (2014). Security and privacy for storage and computation in cloud computing. *Information Sciences*, *258*, 371–386. doi:10.1016/j.ins.2013.04.028

Zhou, Z., & Huang, D. (2013). *Efficient and secure data storage operations for mobile cloud computing*. Paper presented at the 8th International Conference on Network and Service Management, Las Vegas, NV.

KEY TERMS AND DEFINITIONS

CLNC Storage System: Data are stored in ciphertext in local storage, but in plaintext in cloud storage.

Cloudlet: Decentralized and widely dispersed Internet infrastructure components whose compute cycles and storage resources can be leveraged by nearby mobile computers.

NLCC Storage System: Data are stored in plaintext in local storage, but in ciphertext in cloud storage.

Sensor Cloud: Wireless sensors pool and share their computing, network, and storage resources.

Storage Availability: Data must be retrievable for authorized parties from the storage when it is needed.

Storage Confidentiality: No one except authorized users can access data from the storage even if the device is compromised.

Storage Data Path: A sequence of processing stages for data storage from user-space applications to physical storage media.

Storage Integrity: The protection of data storage from unauthorized modifications.

Chapter 5
Authenticity Challenges of Wearable Technologies

Filipe da Costa
University of Minho, Portugal

Filipe de Sá-Soares
University of Minho, Portugal

ABSTRACT

In this chapter the security challenges raised by wearable technologies concerning the authenticity of information and subjects are discussed. Following a conceptualization of the capabilities of wearable technology, an authenticity analysis framework for wearable devices is presented. This framework includes graphic classification classes of authenticity risks in wearable devices that are expected to improve the awareness of users on the risks of using those devices, so that they can moderate their behaviors and take into account the inclusion of controls aimed to protect authenticity. Building on the results of the application of the framework to a list of wearable devices, a solution is presented to mitigate the risk for authenticity based on digital signatures.

INTRODUCTION

For a long time information security management has been based on the CIA triad, the acronym denoting the principles[1] of Confidentiality, Integrity, and Availability. Over time, the sufficiency and appropriateness of these three cornerstone principles of information security have been challenged by several authors. In 1998, Parker

DOI: 10.4018/978-1-5225-1016-1.ch005

complemented them with three new principles, namely Ownership, Authenticity, and Utility (Parker, 1998). The arrival of the new millennium with the need for organizations to adopt more agile and flat structures led Dhillon and Backhouse (2000) to argue for the inclusion of four people-related principles, known under the RITE acronym, meaning Responsibility, Integrity, Trust, and Ethicality. More recently, Teixeira and de Sá-Soares (2013) proposed a revised framework composed of thirteen information security principles and five sub-principles.

In a sense, these sets of information security principles convey worldviews concerning the theory and practice of information security. But new technology may alter our worldviews. An illustrative case is the emergence and evolution of wearable technologies and mobile computing devices offering us true information systems in our pocket, on our wrist, or through our glasses. These technologies are being equipped with ever-stronger information acquisition, storage, processing, display, and communication capabilities. By adopting and using wearable technologies in our daily activities, we are on the verge of a revolution that brings the potential to change the way we live, think, feel, and act.

What challenges will this new era bring us? What will be the impact of wearable technologies on our current accepted information security principles? Will we need to revamp them? Will we be forced to add new principles? Or will we even have to abandon principles once taken as a mainstay?

Wearcams connected to the Internet and sharing images in real time pose new challenges to confidentiality. Wearable GPS (Global Positioning System) devices (as simple as most common cell phones) shrink the frontiers of personal privacy. Losing our smartphone puts us out of sync with the world and makes us unavailable to others. These all exemplify issues that wearable technologies may raise to information security principles. But among the principles, we are particularly interested in the impacts of wearable technologies on *authenticity*, here defined as "Information is in accordance with a particular reality, and its genuineness and validity are verifiable, or an individual, entity or process is who it claims to be" (Teixeira & de Sá-Soares, 2013). This interest in authenticity stems from the fact that, in a scenario where all people are connected, not directly, but through their devices or wearable technology, it is crucial to develop mechanisms to ensure that information received is real and that the subjects we interact with are who they claim to be.

Wearable technologies may be conceived as cognitive prostheses that expand our human capabilities. Increased volumes of information; virtual and augmented reality; sensors feeding us real time news, opinions, restaurant suggestions, and likes from friends; apps a fingertip away, all extend what we know, and shape what we do or choose. Radio-Frequency IDentification (RFID) tags make now possible the Internet of Things (IoT). In fact, in an "all connected" society, wearable technologies make possible the Internet of People (IoP). Will we exchange wearable technologies or are one's own wearable technologies so personal that without them one will feel naked? It will not take much for wearable technologies to become blended with the body, in a morphing process of technology and human tissue (e.g. implantables), giving rise to bionic entities and redefining our identity, raising many new questions.

How will we assure that the information we receive through our wearable technologies is in accordance with reality? How will we verify the genuineness and validity of that information? Rather, will that even be possible? How can we be sure that an individual, entity or process that digitally addresses us is whom it claims to be? How can we ascertain who we really are? Will we know who we really will be? How do we prove that we are authentic? Will the machines we wear become autonomous and when they are capable of self-programming will look at us, as we look now at things, as other devices? Can these devices impersonate us? How much control will we have over our wearable technologies? Will we be aware of providing our information to third parties without any guarantee about which information is really shared? Will we measure up with our wearable devices in terms of intelligence? Will we inherit the bugs of the devices we wear? Will the Nokia slogan "Connecting people" in the future make no sense? Maybe we will know the interface for people, not the persons.

Against this background, this chapter begins by reviewing the concepts of authenticity and wearable technology. Then, it presents the "wearable ecosystem" and its underlying dangers, discussing how current and foreseeable wearable technologies may impact on the authenticity of information and subjects. Thereafter, it suggests a classification system to help users to be aware of the risks of wearable devices on authenticity and to assist them managing such risks. As a proposal for future research, a hierarchical scheme for digital signatures is proposed to mitigate the risks of authenticity for information and subjects when immersed in the wearable ecosystem.

BACKGROUND

To better understand the authenticity challenges posed by wearable technology, this section defines and discusses the key concepts involved, namely Authenticity and Wearable Technology.

Authenticity

Explicitly suggested by Parker (1998) as an information security principle, in this chapter the word *authenticity* is used to express the quality of information that is "in accordance with a particular reality, and its genuineness and validity are verifiable, or that an individual, entity, or process is who it claims to be" (Teixeira & de Sá-Soares, 2013, p32).

Just as a modern server uses its digital certificate to prove its authenticity, employing it to authenticate its messages, in the Middle Ages kings had personal seals, which were used to seal the important communications of their kingdoms. Seals prevented the message from being read by others without the knowledge of the intended receiver, thus ensuring the message's confidentiality. The recipient could also verify the message's integrity and authenticity. If the seal remained intact, the message received would be the one the sender wrote, i.e., it will not have been subjected to any modification, and so maintained its integrity. In this case, the proof of a message's authenticity rested on the fact that the seal was unique and not transferable.

Even though the concepts of integrity and authenticity have resemblance, they should not be confused, as explained by Parker (1998): we may assure that a certain message is faithful, but it may not be authentic, e.g., due to misappropriation of its author's identity, or if a user enters false information into a computer system it may have violated authenticity, but as long as the information remains unaltered, it has integrity. Thus, it is crucial to rigorously define each security principle, in order to clarify and contrast meanings and to effectively plan their compliance.

Decomposing the adopted definition of authenticity, we can immediately separate this principle in its main components, namely by dividing the definition into three key parts, two of which refer to information and the third to individuals, entities and processes. Hence,

- **Information Has to Be in Accordance with a Particular Reality:** Reality is understood as the context in which the information is produced. For information to be authentic it must be conform to its reality. Moreover, the verification of information's genuineness and validity depends on that context: the same information in different contexts may be evaluated differently in terms of authenticity, and,
- **The Genuineness and Validity of Information Are Verifiable:** The genuineness of information alludes to its original state, as opposed to the possibility of being a fabrication or imitation. The use of the word validity refers to situations of information being worthy of acceptance as legitimate to meet a certain goal and of being free of misrepresentation. These proprieties or states of information need to be verified, i.e., to be able of being tested (confirmed or falsified) by such means as experiment or observation, in order to conclude about its authenticity; or
- **An Individual, Entity, or Process Is Who It Claims to Be:** This third component presents a major challenge. Firstly, we need to identify and define the subject in question, i.e., to what, or to whom, we want to prove its authenticity. After this identification, it is required to prove if the subject is authentic,

101

i.e., that the subject actually corresponds to whom it claims to be. The word "subject" arises here in its broadest sense and may represent an individual, entity, or process responsible for certain actions.

To improve the understanding of this concept, it is relevant to identify other information security principles to which authenticity relates. Besides the proximity to integrity, authenticity has a relationship with the security principle of *traceability*. In the realm of information security, we employ the word traceability to signify that "actions relevant to information security are observable and imputable to their authors" (Teixeira & de Sá-Soares, 2013). If one cannot guarantee the principle of authenticity, one cannot guarantee the principle of traceability. In other words, the violation of authenticity implies the violation of traceability: it is not possible to prove the authorship nor the sequence of a set of performed actions if the information or the subjects involved are not authentic.

A concept that is often confused with authenticity is authentication, being in some cases considered or at least assumed as synonyms or indistinguishable (cf. Ben Aissa et al., 2009 and Liu et al., 2012). However, we cannot regard them as synonymous, since they belong to entirely different classes in the domain of information security: while authenticity should be regarded as a principle of security, authentication is a security control intended to assure that a claimed feature of an entity is correct (ISO/IEC, 2014). In the realm of this discussion, authentication is a security process that conducts the test of authenticity of a subject. Another security process related to the proof of authenticity of an entity is identification. While in identification a security control plays an active role aiming to identify an entity, for example, via biometric devices, in authentication a security control plays a more passive role – the entity firstly claims to have a certain identity and afterwards the security control aims to confirm the identity of the entity, for example, through a login procedure (username/password). It is common to characterize authentication as a 1:1 process (check if an entity is who it claims to be – a one to one match) and identification as an n:1 process (among a set of n possible entities, find the one whose identity is being claimed).

Importance of Authenticity

We live in a society dominated by the continuous exchange of information, a 24/7 news cycle, posts on the wall of our social network, and many other forms and media. However, given the ease of today's communication, we must take into account the quality of information that reaches us, especially if it is authentic. Certainly, not all information that reaches us is reliable – it might have been handled or the source might not be credible. Therefore, we must seek to ensure that information is in accordance with our reality and that it is genuine, so as not to allow that a fictional or even a false reality is being projected upon us. Hence, it becomes increasingly important to be equipped with mechanisms that allow us to make this validation and selection. Since cybercrime is a growing phenomenon (Zingerle & Kronman, 2013), computer forensics assumes greater prominence. In the realm of these investigations, authenticity plays a crucial role, in that in any dispute, legal or judicial, it is important to confirm that the information stored in our devices, purportedly resulting from our actions, is authentic (Zhao et al., 2012). In forensic investigations, that information may be used as a basis for profiling (Marrington et al., 2007), allowing the tracking of our actions and places visited. In case the authenticity of the information source is compromised, we may face problems ordering the events, resulting in severe inconsistencies in the timeline of facts. This issue can be a major problem during the evidence validation process (Marrington et al., 2011).

Indeed, the information collected can only be used as evidence if its authenticity is guaranteed, as well as the authenticity of its source and the processes involved in its production or transmission; otherwise, one cannot ensure the non-repudiation of certain actions. If on the one hand, without this guarantee, someone or some entity or process can impersonate another and thereby incriminate it – in this case the accused would be punished unfairly, on the other hand, a criminal aware of this lack of guarantee can propose the elimination of proof – in this case the accused escapes unpunished for a crime that was eventually perpetrated.

In health systems, intelligent transport systems, government applications, and other critical areas where the exchange of information is crucial, ensuring authenticity of information as well as of its origin is essential. When remotely monitoring a patient's physical activity, ensuring correctness and authenticity of the received data is imperative. This applies not only to the fidelity of the monitoring process, but also to prevention mechanisms for fraud in case treatments are, for instance, financed by health insurance contracts (Alshurafa et al., 2014). For intelligent transportation systems, the authenticity of information and of its source is very important, since invalid information may result in serious traffic accidents and human losses (Zhao et al., 2012). On the electronic government front, as an illustration, South Korea adopted SecureGov, a framework of multiple security mechanisms to prevent illegal use and leakage of information, to prevent illegal modification of information, and to ensure the authenticity of the user and delivered information (Choi et al., 2014).

Threats to Authenticity

Following the adopted definition for authenticity, the threats to authenticity can be grouped into two main groups: those that endanger the authenticity of information and those that endanger the authenticity of subjects. Although one may find various examples of threats against authenticity, some paradigmatic cases will suffice to illustrate attacks on authenticity.

Despite the constant efforts to ensure the authenticity of information, through such controls such as the use of encryption, digital signatures, checksums, and transactions confirmation, these mechanisms are also the target of counterfeiting attempts, some of them successful. The success of these attacks can be explained, at least in part, by the encryption flaws made public and by the growing of private computing power. Indeed, given the evolution of technology and its increased dissemination and ease of access, it is becoming less complicated to bring together technological means with considerable capacity at reasonable cost to exploit those flaws (Pearce et al., 2013).

The authenticity of a subject may be put into question in case of impersonation, i.e., when a subject impersonates another, without being noticed. As an example of impersonation we have the 2011 Norway attacks. The attacks of July 22, 2011, in Norway, consisted of an explosion in the area of government buildings in the capital, Oslo, and a shooting that occurred a few hours later on the island of Utøya. The shooter, dressed with a police uniform (Hager, 2011), joined people on the island on the pretext of clarifying the attacks in Oslo, justifying its presence on the island as being a routine check after the bombing in Oslo (El País, 2011). In this scenario, the information "issued" by the shooter was in line with the reality, as there was an attack in Oslo to government buildings and the campsite on the island had been organized by the Norwegian Labor Party, so the presence of the police was seen as ordinary. So, this information is authentic and its genuineness and validity could be verified. However, its source is not authentic, since it is not who it claims to be. People on the island authenticate the subject through something he had with him, the police uniform.

A similar situation may happen in computer systems. For example, in terminals that access different platforms and services via a Single Sign-On (SSO) authentication policy, the threat of user impersonation is also present. Indeed, Mayer et al. (2014) documented five systems that have been the target of successful SSO attacks. In these cases, the authentication process was considered successful, i.e., the subjects were allowed access by the system, however, they were not authentic – although authenticated they were not really who they claimed to be. Moreover, the subject authenticated by the system may be authentic, but at a later time the subject using the system (already authenticated) may not remain the same, it may change to a different subject, who may not have authorization to use the system. This requires the system to periodically verify the current user's authenticity, for instance, by checking if the user is who it claimed to be by analyzing its key stroke dynamics (Monrose & Rubin, 2000).

Wearable Technology

Since the beginning of human civilization, the desire to create utensils and tools has been present in our mind. Humanity aims to increase its (particularly sensory) capacity by developing tools as items of clothing or as accessories. These artefacts, such as watches, glasses or others embedded in clothes, that expand human capabilities, were named by Rodrigo (1988) as external cognitive prostheses.

Wearable technology and devices have emerged with the intrinsic human wish for possession and use of such devices and with the evolution of technology, in particular ubiquitous computing, i.e., computer systems that cooperate with each other transparently to the user (Cirilo, 2008). These devices, some very sophisticated in terms of technology, features and computing power, have different functions employed in different areas such as health, entertainment, fitness, production, among many others, and are becoming increasingly common in our daily routines.

Thus, we define wearable device as an artifact – i.e. something made or given shape by man, such as a tool (Collins, 2015) – that can be used as an external prosthesis in order to extend the cognitive and sensory ability of the person who uses it.

Evolution of Wearable Devices

The first known wearable device were the eyeglasses (Rhodes, n.d.), produced in Italy around 1285-1289 (Glasseshistory, n.d.). However, historical evidence points to the first wearable devices involving some technology as being the Nuremberg egg, a type of "clock-watch", ornamental small spring-driven clocks made to be worn around the neck, produced in Nuremberg in the mid-to-late 16th century (1510) (Dohrn-van Rossum,1996, p122; Fanthorpe & Fanthorpe, 2007, p25) and to the Abacus ring created in Qing Dynasty in China, a silver ring decorated with a functional abacus, a sort of calculator that allowed performance of some mathematical operations, dated around 1700 (Chinaculture.org, 2010; Zolfagharifard, 2014). In the years 1980-90, Casio launched and produced the Casio CMD-30B, a wristwatch with keyboard, calculator, TV remote control and the capacity of information storage (CASIO, n.d.). In the 90's, the Internet and mobile phones began to be part of firms' and ordinary individuals' daily lives. In May 1998, Bluetooth was launched by Ericsson with a participation of Nokia, IBM and Toshiba (Karlsson & Lugn, n.d.). Nokia subsequently launched mobile phones with sales records over almost the whole world (Stinson, 2015).

Haunted with the so-called millennium bug, the year 2000 arrived and with it the era of mobility. Devices that hitherto had no network connection began to come equipped with wireless networking systems via Bluetooth, WAP, GPRS, or Wi-Fi. All the devices were now (able to be) networked.

In 2010, Nike launched the Nike+Sportsbands, a bracelet that by using motion sensors gives important information about training. Since then, there have been many other fitness gadgets featuring GPS functionalities and data synchronization with other devices such as mobile phones. It has become common to share in social networks our travelled paths, whether it is running or riding a bicycle.

Most devices are now "smart", having the ability to collect information about who we are, where we are and what we do. Our devices are able to communicate with other devices and have processing capabilities that turn them into pocket computers. Since 2013, the appearance of smart wearable devices has become more evident: eyewear (e.g. Google Glass), lifelogging cameras (e.g. Narrative Clip) and smartwatches (e.g. Apple's SmartWatch) illustrate this evolution.

Today, in the era of IoT, we have actual computers that fit in the palm of our hand, and whose complexity makes us think about the future. We can easily imagine a smart hand or foot or a Bluetooth shoelace that tightens itself. From the simple analogue watch and glasses, going through Casio CMD-30B, perhaps the most famous of all, to smartwatches, the evolution of such devices has been extraordinary, as well as the technology that supports them, such as nanotechnology, wireless communication systems, new textiles fibers, among many others.

There are many practical applications of today's wearable technology, in numerous areas, and in many cases using devices and earlier technology. For example, RFID tags have seen their applicability increase with the advent of these new devices. Another example is FedEx that has equipped many of its delivery vehicles with hands-free ignition and the vehicle security control system that is activated by an RFID bracelet that the driver has on his arm (Schell, n.d.). Many sensors are now used in clothing that enable us to remotely monitor the vital signs of outpatients (Hurford, 2009).

Wearable devices are also widely used in medicine and in different scenarios. In cases of Lennox-Gastaut syndrome, a childhood severe encephalopathy, the Vagus Nerve Stimulation (VNS) is a less invasive treatment to control epileptic seizures (Jobst, 2010). Wearable devices, such as bracelets, watches or glasses, can also contribute to a better social interaction for those who have limitations in communicating or socializing, as in the case of autistic individuals (Kirkham & Greenhalgh, 2015).

Given the usefulness and potential of wearable devices, in particular smartwatches, NASA challenged developers to design an app for astronauts to use when they are in space (Geier, 2005). We will not know what the future holds, but certainly this stimulating and exciting evolution will continue.

Icons

There are different types of wearable devices that by their functionality and usage stand out from the rest. Below are presented some of those devices, considered here as icons[2].

- **Google Glass (Google):** Despite the project's "discontinuation" in January 2015, the existing prototype of these glasses has Wi-Fi, video/photo camera, sound system, and display. It is an augmented reality device that responds to commands in natural language. It allows us to surf the Internet or to see useful information about the place we are during a walk without the use of keyboards or other extra devices, such as a smartphone. Google Glass may be connected to other devices.
- **Narrative Clip (Narrative):** Designed to be attached to clothing, this camera can be used as a decorative accessory and shoots two photos per minute automatically, thus helping to create a kind of logging of the places one has been to. It comes with internal storage capacity, GPS and it can synchronize photos with applications by Wi-Fi and Bluetooth LE. Photographs are captured with the local reference and date of origin, in order to enable research and may also be shared in social networks.
- **Motorola Moto 360 (Motorola):** This is a smartwatch equipped with Google Android operating system, thereby enabling the development, installation and use of applications similarly to what happens with a smartphone. This watch comes equipped with GPS, Wi-Fi, motion sensor, camera and integrated sound system. It even allows viewing and making videos.
- **Mi Band (Xiaomi):** Equipped with motion sensors, this bracelet indicates to the user the number of steps traveled over a day/night. After synchronization provided by a smartphone application, the user may have an estimate of the calories consumed during a certain period of time.
- **Chameleon 4V+ (Weldline/Air Liquide):** This is a protection mask for welders. Like a helmet, it is placed on the head and, thanks to its display controlled by sensors sensitive to light and to stronger radiation that can cause injury to the human eye, darkens at the time of welding and lightens right away. Its functioning is similar to sunglasses, but the color of the lens varies according to the light and radiation to which it is subjected to.
- **Genesis-Artificial Pancreas (Pancreum):** This device intends to function as an artificial pancreas, by reading the glucose level in blood. It allows the monitoring of the readings through an application available for smartphone. It can automatically inject insulin if necessary.

The brief review of these icons suggestively illustrates the range of areas where such devices can operate and the versatility of their applications.

Types and Categories of Wearable Devices

There are several types of wearable devices. Depending on its working method and technology employed they can be grouped by types. Table 1 shows major types of wearable devices following the work by Hurford (2009).

Based on the Innovation World Cup categories organized by Wearable Technologies Conference (WTC, n.d.), these devices can also be grouped into categories according to their core market sector, as illustrated in Table 2.

Taking into consideration the types and categories of wearable devices shown in Table 1 and Table 2, respectively, the wearable devices previously considered icons may be ranked as displayed in Table 3.

In a classification system based on categories and types, to classify according to category is a simple task; however, it is difficult to fit each device in only one type. For example, the smartwatch "Moto 360" or "Google Glass" can be put into four different types, namely as "smart computer", "data acquisition & sensors", "location & position", and "display". Another example is the "artificial pancreas", which may assume the types "medical device" and "data acquisition & sensors". Many of the wearable devices have a wide range of features, thus limiting some wearable devices classification systems and hampering more specific analysis, such as the identification of wearable devices authenticity risk levels. These limitations led the authors to propose an authenticity analysis framework for wearable devices, which is described in the next section.

AUTHENTICITY ANALYSIS FRAMEWORK
FOR WEARABLE DEVICES

In order to classify wearable devices in terms of authenticity, it is useful to first define and understand their environment, herein termed as the Wearable Ecosystem.

The Wearable Ecosystem

Communication is certainly a vital function for all living beings, humankind being no exception. Over the years a lot has changed, moving from simple communication between people – Human-to-Human (H2H) – to other forms of communication, especially at a distance, such as mail, telephone or Internet.

Authenticity Challenges of Wearable Technologies

Table 1. Wearable devices types

Type	Description	Examples
Smart Computer	There are now devices that according to their computational capabilities for data collection, processing, storage, and communication are pocket computers. Many of these devices, equipped with operating systems such as Android, are programmable. This has made the development of applications for such devices increasingly common and popular.	Moto 360 (Motorola)
Controls & Switches	There are situations where it is essential to have our hands free, but today we have a range of devices, all with their checks and controls which makes that increasingly difficult. One way to make them more user-friendly may involve the centralization of those commands in our clothes or accessories.	Fibretronic Smartlife Technology
Data Acquisition & Sensors	In many everyday activities, it is important to know our health status, for example, the vital signs in outpatients or the fatigue when we drive. Wearable devices can help to identify our vital signs and health status (Uddin et al., 2015).	Vivago WristCare PROMeTHEUS project (European Union)
Location & Position	The widespread use of GPS features allowed many of our devices to identify and retrieve our location in real time. Not being dependent on terrestrial antenna systems, wearable GPS devices are extremely useful in rescue missions of people lost in more isolated or hostile environments that require quick action.	Interactive Wear AG (Know Where Jacket) NavJacket (O'Neill)
Display	A display provides information in various ways and in various formats such as plain text, image, video, or sound. Through it, we can watch videos, listen to music, identify the state and understand better the environment in which we find ourselves. However, its handling during certain activities can be very dangerous or impossible and therefore, the solution will certainly involve its presence in displays embedded in our clothing or in objects such as glasses or helmets.	Google Glass
Lighting Systems	Handling lanterns and other lighting systems may be dangerous or limited in our day-to-day life or work. The inclusion of lighting systems in our clothes or accessories is a solution.	Philips Lumalive
Medical Devices	In extreme sports or occupations with most risk of hypothermia, in particular, it is important to keep the body warm. New textile fibers and the existence of wearable devices capable of detecting and regulating the temperature can be an important combination in rescue people. Such devices can also be crucial to outpatients or in the event of regular medication necessity. In patients with Type I diabetes, for example, who need to monitor blood glucose and if necessary self-inject insulin, wearable devices may be an important help to improve their living conditions.	WarmX Therm-ic Genesis – Artificial Pancreas (Pancreum)
Power	Energy is one of the major challenges of wearable devices. The miniature form factor that is essential for these systems leaves little space to accommodate energy storage (Williamson et al., 2015). There are already some proposals to solve the problem. Backpacks, or even clothes, embedded with solar panels can now be used for charging other devices and smartphones (Hurford, 2009).	Zegna solar powered jacket (Ermenegildo Zegna)

Inspired by Hurford (2009).

Table 2. Wearable devices categories

Category	Description	Examples
Sports & Fitness	In professional sports and other physical activities, training optimization is crucial. In order to accomplish it, monitoring becomes essential. These days, the sharing in social networks of workouts and routes traveled is increasingly popular and simple. The use of wearable monitoring and sharing devices that are noninvasive is becoming popular (Milosevic & Farella, 2015).	Adidas 1 Nike+ iPod
Healthcare & Wellness	In many treatments of chronic diseases, wearable devices have taken a very important role. They can be used to monitor vital signs or as automatic medication delivery systems. This type of device, by not being invasive, is very useful and important in improving the quality of life of those who use them.	Smartlife technology
Security & Prevention	The number of wearable devices available for the safety of its users, and even for the prevention of accidents at work or otherwise, is potentially countless. In the metallurgical sector, for example, it is common to see the welders in masks that look like astronauts helmets with viewers equipped with sensors and special liquid crystals that, depending on light intensity (during the welding process), are more or less opaque, avoiding eye injuries.	NavJacket (O'Neill)
Gaming & Lifestyle	With the evolution of technology, ubiquitous computing and augmented reality, we all seek new experiences, even during our daily tasks. Many of them assume the form of wearable devices.	Mp3blue jacket (Rosner) Google Glass Mi Band

Adapted from (WTC, n.d.).

Table 3. Icon wearable devices classified by category and type

Type	Categories			
	Sports and Fitness	Healthcare and Wellness	Security and Prevention	Gaming and Lifestyle
Smart Computer				Moto 360
Controls & Switches				
Data acquisition & Sensors	Mi Band		Chameleon 4V+	Narrative Clip
Location & Position				
Display				Google Glass
Lighting System				
Medical Devices		Artificial Pancreas		
Power				

There are numerous forms and architectures for human communication systems, from mail to email. With the increasing use of mobile phones, the Short Message Service (SMS) and the Multimedia Messaging Service (MMS) have become increasingly important data transmission mechanisms.

With the evolution of technology as well as the wearable computing capabilities and networks, including Wi-Fi, it is possible to have these devices networked, acting as networked nodes, and performing functions of clients or servers (peer-to-peer).

Given the nature of wearable technology, these isolated or connected devices, in an M2M (Machine-to-Machine) scheme, can be considered, in terms of communication, as external frontiers of the person who uses them with its environment, thereby defining an interface between the holder and the outside.

As its user interface, these devices can define two types of communication. In an interaction between two persons, subject A equipped with device Ia (interface a) and subject B equipped with device Ib (interface b) can establish the following kinds of communications, in a notation *à la* Unified Modeling Language (UML) and with Cn indicating the time sequence of communication:

- **Interface-to-Human (I2H):** The communication begins in A but the message is issued by A's interface (Ia) directly to subject B (Figure 1a). When B responds to A (Figure 1b) the response will be received and delivered by A's interface. Subject A will receive B's message directly from A's interface, and not from B.
- **Interface-to-Interface (I2I):** A message from A is sent via A's interface (Ia) that communicates with subject B via its interface (Ib), and vice versa (Figure 2). The communication can occur in both directions, but each subject only communicates directly with his own interface.

Figure 1. Interface-to-Human communication scenarios

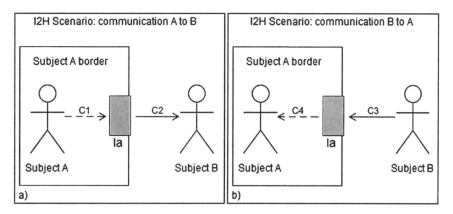

Figure 2. Interface-to-Interface communication scenario

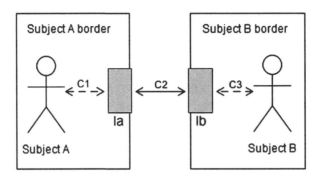

In both scenarios, I2H and I2I, there is no direct contact between subjects: all communications are mediated. Whereas in I2H scenario this mediation is partial, since subject B is not using his interface, and communicates directly with A's interface (connection represented by C3 in Figure 1b), for B there is no border notion. In I2I scenario, the communications of A to B and of B to A are completely mediated, i.e., no subject sends a message to outside his border, directly. Each one communicates to the outside using its interfaces.

As members of this Wearable Ecosystem, people can "wear" network interfaces making them nodes of a new network where people and things are all connected. The intra- and interconnections between people, people as wearable devices users, people's devices and third parties' devices forms a new mesh, expanding their communications network and defining a new paradigm in personal and interpersonal communications. This new giant mesh may be called by the emerging term "Internet of People" (IoP), as illustrated in Figure 3.

Based on natural ecosystem definition – a system formed by the interaction of a community of organisms with its environment (ecosystem, n.d.), a Wearable Ecosystem could be defined as a system formed by organisms: the humans – as users - and their wearable devices – as artefacts. In this ecosystem all interactions are mediated by artefacts.

This new ecosystem presents new challenges to civilization as a whole. Taking into account the development of machine automation over the last three centuries, Davenport and Kirby (2015) organized that evolution into three eras:

- **Era One (19th Century):** Machines take away the dirty and dangerous – industrial equipment, from looms to the cotton gin, relieves humans of onerous manual labor;

Figure 3. Internet of People

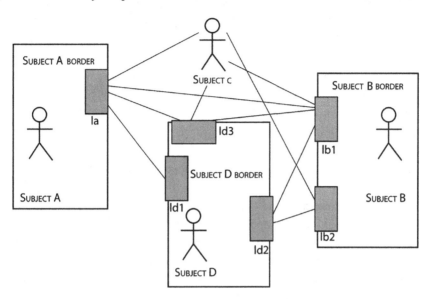

- **Era Two (20th Century):** Machines take away the dull – automated interfaces, from airline kiosks to call centers, relieve humans of routine service transactions and clerical chores;
- **Era Three (21st Century):** Machines take away decisions – intelligent systems, from airfare pricing to IBM's Watson, make better choices than humans, reliably and fast.

In Era Three of machine automation evolution, wearable devices are in a privileged position compared to any other machine, given their proximity to their users. These devices can collect users' behaviors, reactions and routines more accurately than any other machine, because they do it in a transparent and non-invasive way, that is, without the user being conditioned (Xu et al., 2008). This proximity, combined with their ability to collect and process data, makes these devices able to feed and teach their smart systems, including decision-making systems.

With all the information these devices can collect and the advances in artificial intelligence (AI), we may have, at some point, wearable interfaces that assuming the role of a person's external interface can easily pretend to be that person and be able to pass the Turing test.

The Turing test (Turing, 1950) assesses the ability of a machine to demonstrate intelligence capabilities equivalent to a human, or to be indistinguishable from a human. With the evolution of wearable interfaces, especially in terms of their computational capability and artificial intelligence capacity, they may imitate their user, making "going through the user", as *their* interface with another subject or interface.

Should the Turing test be changed? So far this test uses two types of players: the man and the machine. In terms of test, we have the duel between human mind and machine. With the presence of wearable intelligent interfaces, we now have three types of possible players:

- A human (as a being, standalone);
- The machine (standalone);
- A hybrid human-machine (a human equipped with its artefacts).

In the hybrid human-machine scenario, where machine represents the set of wearable interfaces holding the capability of communication controlled by AI algorithms, it may not be possible to distinguish what belongs to the human and to his or her devices. Will intelligent wearable interfaces be able to pass the Turing test and so impersonate a human? If so, we may consider a new kind of impersonation, thus putting at risk the guarantee of its authenticity: it is not an individual who is impersonating another, but it is one of their features that is impersonating him or her.

Nowadays, it is often hard to ensure authenticity despite the existing controls. Even in peer-to-peer connections, attacks such as "man-in-the-middle" (MITM) are sometimes successful, despite the existing mechanisms, such as the use of digital signatures and public/private keys.

The privileged position of wearable devices in relation to their users makes it easy for them to intrude in the communications they mediate, pursuing attacks such as MITM, particularly in communications identified with C2 and C3 in Figures 4 and 5. This privileged position, and the access to their users' personal informa-

Figure 4. Potential attacks (identified by bolt signal) under I2H communications

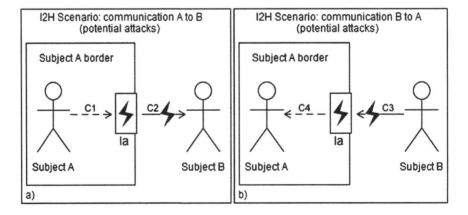

Figure 5. Potential attacks (identified by bolt signal) under I2I communications

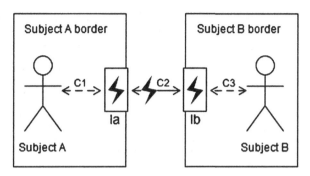

tion – allowing them to set a profile of their users and thus behave similarly – can also allow them to go through one, or more, real actors in communication (i.e., via impersonation). In this scenario, it might make sense to also consider a new type of attack, namely *interface-as-a-person.*

In face of impersonation by a wearable device (such as those shown by Ia and Ib in Figures 4 and 5), manipulation of reality may take place, that is, information coming from the outside, or sent to the outside, may be manipulated in a way to induce its receptor to a "virtualized" and perhaps fallacious reality. All these new ways of interaction pose severe challenges to the authenticity of information and subjects.

The Framework for Analysis

In order to be able to determine the authenticity risk of a wearable device, taking into consideration its capabilities and features, the authors propose a classification framework based on a scale of 1 (2^0) to 4095 (2^{12}-1) points, in which the value 1 is the lowest authenticity risk level of a device and 4095 the highest possible value for that risk.

The rating system (cf. Table 4) is a system based in binary 12 bits (1 + 11 bits), in which each bit indicates whether a feature is present or not in the device under study. This classification system is based in a table with the most important features of devices sorted by their degrees of risk of not ensuring the authenticity principle in descending order, from left to right (11 bits). Hence, the most problematic features to authenticity, for example, the computational capabilities, occupy the most significant bits (to the left). The functionalities conveying less risk, such as simply reading data, are located in the lower bits (to the right). The 12th bit (n = 11), the most significant, is a special bit and it intends to identify whether the device is critical in the context in which it operates.

Table 4. Rating system used in the framework

Group/Feature		($n=$)	Description
Internal Information Manipulation	Read	0	The first bit ($n=0$) is used to classify devices, such as sensors, that have the functionality for reading certain information, for example, ambient and body temperature sensors, that represent less danger to the guarantee of information authenticity. In this case, a violation of information's authenticity is limited to hardware error.
	Write	1	Devices such as displays or indicators, which show different types of information in human friendly format, have a low risk, but higher than the previous ones, since the representation of information must be careful so as not to compromise information or its understanding.
	Storage	2	The evolution of technology and the miniaturization of electronic components enable information storage units in extremely small devices. Therefore, devices with storage capacity are becoming increasingly common. However, this kind of functionality represents, in terms of internal information manipulation group, the feature with the greatest potential risk to the authenticity of information since it is needed to ensure two authenticity related concerns: the stored information is authentic and uncorrupted, and the reading process presents authentic information.
Information Collection	Sound/Image/ Video	3	Wearable devices can easily obtain and collect information about their users, activities and environment. Today, it is common to find devices that take pictures, make videos or determine their location, read and identify fingerprints and monitor vital signs. Thereby, the group "information collection" is the second in terms of risk potential, and can be divided into three sub-groups according to the kind of information they can collect: biometrics, location or sound/image/video. Due to its nature, biometric information is the most relevant in terms of potential risk, followed by devices with GPS functionality. Comparatively, the sound/image/video recording feature is considered having the lowest risk level.
	GPS	4	
	Biometrics	5	
Connection	Sync (via proprietary application)	6	The pairing or networking capability of these devices with other devices is increasingly recurrent. Given that they may be associated with important information about their users and the environment in which they operate, this capability represents a very high risk for ensuring the authenticity of the information sent or received. If the connection is only to enable synchronization, using a proprietary application provided, then this risk is the lowest of this group. The autonomous functionality of receiving and sending information is the most serious, since in this case the device is available on the network. In the case of a networked system, it may become under attack and thus starting to behave in an unexpected or undesired way, for example, being the target of malware attacks.
	Receive	7	
	Send	8	

continued on following page

Table 4. Continued

Group/Feature		(*n=*)	Description
Smart Computing	Process	9	The processing capacity of existing wearable devices is compatible with any smartphone or even a personal computer, enabling them to manipulate information by applying algorithms with some complexity.
	Programmable	10	The computing capabilities found in many devices allow the installation of new applications, popularly dubbed as apps, through platforms offered by entities responsible for their operating system, or through external platforms that may have no quality control or validation systems. In many cases, it is available an Integrated Development Environment (IDE) for the development of applications, even by the user. Sometimes, the knowledge required for the development of those applications is not very high, as it is possible to program in a very high level, via drag and drop editors, and despite the platforms validation of some software quality aspects available in "apps stores", often the responsibility for the use of the information that is given in the application is dependent on its developer. So, this feature is the one that represents the greater potential risk to the guarantee of authenticity.
Critical Function		11	The 12th bit (*n=*11), the most significant, is a special bit used to identify whether the device is critical in the context in which it operates. Based on the classification system in types and categories presented above, it is natural for this bit to be 1 for the devices with the following categories: "Healthcare & Wellness" and "Security & Prevention. However, it is not expected to be always like that so it should be analyzed case by case.

The authenticity risk level – $R_{authenticity}$ – for a specific wearable device can be determined by computing Equation 1:

$$R_{authenticity}\left(device\right) = \sum_{n=0}^{11}\left(2b_n\right)^n \tag{1}$$

where b_n represents the value (zero or one) of the bit at position n (0-11).

The use of binary representation and the above formula allows two devices to have the same classification, if and only if, they have the same functions, so the comparison between devices is linear.

As an example, Figure 6 shows the classification for two non-critical devices $\left(b_{11} = 0\right)$, using the suggested rating system. The first is a temperature sensor and the second is a smartwatch.

Of the two non-critical devices used for illustration, the one with a lower risk level is the sensor because information that can be collected is just the temperature and it has no critical role. The smartwatch, in spite of not playing a critical role, has

Figure 6. Non-critical wearable device classification examples

	Smart Computing		Connection			Information Collection			Internal Information Manipulation			Authenticity Risk Level
	Critical Function	Programmable	Process	Send	Receive	Sync (via app)	GPS	Image/Video	Sound	Storage	Write	Read	
(n=)	11	10	9	8	7	6	5	4	3	2	1	0	
Temp. Sensor	0	0	0	0	0	0	0	0	0	0	0	1	1
Smart-watch	0	1	1	1	1	1	1	1	1	1	1	1	2047

a higher risk level because it has access to a large set of its user's information that can manipulate and disseminate without intervention or even the knowledge of its user.

Simplifying the classification system and its scale, the risk can be translated into the 12 classes, in human friendly format, depicted in Figure 7. To promote the intuitive understanding about the classes range, code levels, from D^+ to A^-, are employed (colors can also be used to flag classes – red for the higher levels of risk and green for lower levels, with orange and yellow being used in the intermediate classes). The most significant non-zero bit of the rating of a device defines the device's risk class.

The classification level main classes (A to D) have the following heuristic meanings:

Figure 7. Authenticity risk classification levels

	Smart Computing		Connection			Information Collection			Internal Information Manipulation		
	Critical Function	Programmable	Process	Send	Receive	Sync (via app)	Biometrics	GPS	Sound/Image/Video	Storage	Write	Read
(n=)	11	10	9	8	7	6	5	4	3	2	1	0
Classification level class:		D	D⁻	C⁺	C	C⁻	B⁺	B	B⁻	A⁺	A	A⁻

Figure 8. Icons classification

	Critical Function	Smart Computing		Connection			Information Collection			Internal Information Manipulation			Authenticity risk level and class
		Programmable	Process	Send	Receive	Sync (via app)	Biometrics	GPS	Sound/Image/Video	Storage	Write	Read	
(n=)	11	10	9	8	7	6	5	4	3	2	1	0	
Artificial Pancreas	1	0	1	0	0	1	1	0	0	1	1	1	D⁺ 2663
Moto 360	0	1	1	1	1	1	0	1	1	1	1	1	D 2015
Mi Band	0	0	0	0	0	1	1	0	0	1	0	1	C⁻ 101
Chameleon 4V+	1	0	0	0	0	0	0	0	0	0	1	1	D⁺ 2051
Narrative Clip	0	1	1	0	0	1	0	1	1	1	1	1	D 1631
	0	1	1	1	1	0	0	1	1	1	1	1	D

A=Attention;
B=Be careful;
C=Caution;
D=Danger (or even Death).

Icon Devices Analyses

Based on the simplified classification system, Figure 8 shows the authenticity risk level and class for the wearable devices previously presented as "icons".

Of the icon wearable devices presented, the simplest is the welding mask (Chameleon 4V+), given that in terms of technology only has light sensors and a display that controls the brightness that comes to the user. However, it plays a critical role given the protection it provides to its users, therefore, assuring that the components of this device (hardware) are authentic is very important, otherwise it may compromise its operation, which means, as a result, that its class is D⁺. Also rated as D⁺, even though it has a risk value higher than the first, is the artificial pancreas, given its vital role as well as the technology it employs. In this case, the risk is not only related to its hardware but also to its firmware and software.

The smartwatch (Moto 360), the smart glasses (Google Glass) and the camera (Narrative Clip) are the most popular of the list, and possibly the most used due to their features and similar manner of use. They have an operating system and enable their programming though the installation of applications. In this classification system they have class D. In spite of not playing a critical role, they have access to a large set of their users' information that they can manipulate and disseminate without intervention or even knowledge of their users.

The device with the lowest risk level is the fitness bracelet (Mi Band) because, despite being close to its user 24 hours per day, the information that can be collected is very limited (e.g., it is confined to the movements and the cardiac activity of the wearer). Information diffusion is also limited, since the device only communicates with other devices (not wearable) through a provided application. In this case, the risk can be considerable if the application that allows synchronization and information collection does not comply with an appropriate level of security.

Preventive Factor

Based on the ratings of the devices analyzed, we observe that, regardless of the context (critical or not) in which they operate, most wearable devices are in class D, i.e., the highest level of risk for authenticity. If we associate to this high potential risk their privileged position in relation to their users, the information they have access to and their computational and communication capabilities, we conclude these types of devices may pose a real threat to authenticity. Therefore, preventive measures should be defined in order to mitigate their potential risk.

Considering that the application of preventive measures targets a particular feature of the device (corresponding to the index n), which allows the reduction of the potential risk of the device, and that may be defined by the P_n coefficient, its impact can then be included in authenticity risk calculation formula shown previously in Equation 1, as given by Equation 2:

$$R_{authenticity}\left(device\right) = round\left(\sum_{n=0}^{11} \frac{1}{P_n}\left(2b_n\right)^n\right) \tag{2}$$

where b_n represents the bit value (zero or one) in the position n (0-11) and P_n the value of the preventive coefficient correspondent to n. The preventive coefficient is a heuristic value and can take values from $\mathbb{N}$, i.e., all natural numbers (1,2,3, …). The value 1 for P_n coefficient means that no preventive action was applied.

As an example, considering a critical sensor, if we use two sensors in parallel (using the mean value as final value) the estimate preventive coefficient could be 2 for the correspondent index ($n=11$). For the read feature ($n=0$) if we use sensors with different serial numbers the probability of failure of both sensors may be reduced, in this case the estimated preventive coefficient could be 2.

Certainly, it may not be feasible to remove features from these kind of devices or to completely eliminate the risk for authenticity. However, it may be possible to mitigate this risk. The preventive factor arises in this framework as a mechanism to represent the risk reduction for authenticity associated with each feature of the device (based on its respective preventive coefficient) and, concomitantly, to reflect this risk mitigation in the device's authenticity risk value. This way, if a wearable device was designed and developed to promote authenticity, the rating system of the proposed framework will take it into account, distinguishing the risk level of the device from other devices with similar features but lack of preventive mechanisms.

SOLUTIONS AND RECOMMENDATIONS

Based on the result of the classification system and its application, one recommendation and a possible solution are proposed to mitigate the risk for authenticity on wearable devices.

The classification system may be used as a mechanism to inform end users about the risks that are present when using a specific device. By including the respective class in the device's package, this information can be used as an element of choice between devices.

A possible control to mitigate the risk for authenticity on these devices is Hierarchical Digital Signatures.

Digital signatures can provide the assurance and evidence of the identity and provenance of the author, i.e., the signatory (Saxena and Chaudhari, 2012). However, given the possible types of communication that may occur in the presence of increasingly sophisticated wearable devices, as previously discussed and outlined in Figures 4 and 5, the inclusion of the traditional digital signature, as we know it, may not be sufficient.

These devices can impersonate their users by sending messages to themselves or by manipulating users' messages. It is argued that to ensure authenticity of the authorship of each of the exchanged messages, they must be digitally signed with the signature of the authentic author. A message sent by a device (even on the advice of its user) must be signed with its signature, and never with the user's signature.

Incidentally, a device should not sign by its user (or owner) in order to prevent impersonation attacks. Signing a device must guarantee the identification of his authorship and of its user. In this respect what is proposed is a new hierarchical scheme for digital signatures. The hierarchy of digital signatures may be represented in a diagram of signatures and their extensions (cf. Figure 9) in a similar manner as a class diagram, from object oriented programming paradigms.

Figure 9. Proposed signatures hierarchy

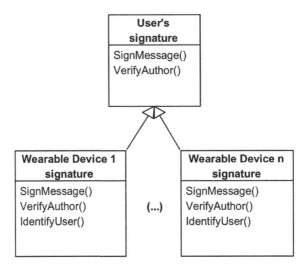

This new scheme allows the receiver of a message to identify the author through its signature and if it was intermediated by any interface, identifying which interface was used and who owns it. The human author cannot repudiate the authorship of a particular message, if it was initially signed with its signature.

In order to illustrate how this mechanism works, it is necessary to recall the communication scenario of Figure 4. In the scenario presented in Figure 4a, subject A starts a communication to subject B; this communication will be mediated by Ia. The message is then signed by subject A and transmitted to A's interface. This interface will sign the message with its digital signature (this signature is actually an extension to the signature of its user). Subject B receives the message and can verify the authorship of the source (in this case Ia) as well as that it is an intermediated communication by an interface, since there is information about a user (subject A). These two levels of message signature prevent impersonation, i.e., the IaaP attack, and ensure the authorship of the original author (subject A), and the interfaces that mediate the communication (Ia). In the scenario illustrated in Figure 4b, subject B in response to subject A (communication C3) uses its own signature to sign the message and to send it to subject A, however, this communication will be mediated by A's interface (Ia). Interface Ia receives and displays a message to the subject who is using it. This subject A can then validate the authorship of the message and verify there are no intermediaries (subject B has no interface), ensuring this way the authenticity of the message and its authorship.

This new mechanism will bring new challenges to manufacturers of this type of device, as it will be necessary to develop a security kernel responsible for this new feature.

One possible solution would be to implement a Reference Monitor (cf. Rushby, 1981). A reference monitor will be the most critical part of this new security kernel, controlling access to objects and acting as a mediator of transactions with the system. This component must be:

- Tamper-proof (it cannot be modified nor avoided),
- Always invoked (single point through which all requests for access must go) and
- Small enough to be subject to analysis and testing, making it possible to ensure its completeness.

In this case, the reference monitor can be conceived as a digital signatures manager, storing the digital signatures of device and owner, and ensuring their authenticity in terms of source and use.

FUTURE RESEARCH DIRECTIONS

The focus of this work is on the challenges of wearable technologies from the point of view of authenticity as a security principle. The proposed classification system is applicable for classifying the risk for authenticity of information and subjects. Subsequent research work could extend the analysis to other security principles, for instance integrity or availability of information. The hierarchical architecture for digital signatures could also be evaluated from the point of view of other security principles.

It will also be interesting to involve and consult people, as users of these technologies. A survey could help to understand their level of knowledge on this topic, and to identify their awareness about the risks underlying these technologies. Based on their opinions as users or future users of these technologies, it would be important to validate the utility of the classification system proposed in this chapter, in order to identify possible requirements, changes or new directions to follow, so that it may be an aid in creating a culture of security. Finally, it would be interesting to try to conduct work aimed to normalize the scale for rating the preventive factor, so that its current heuristic nature could be replaced by a systematic quality.

CONCLUSION

From the evolution of wearable devices, not only have new devices resulted with many new features that may be important aids in our activities, but also a number of new challenges to the information security field, such as the ones concerning the assurance of authenticity.

Given the capabilities integrated in wearable devices, and their wide range of applications, it becomes necessary to take some precautions in their use. The framework presented in this chapter intends to alert and sensitize users of this technology to the potential risks and dangers to which they may be subjected, providing them with a classification tool for evaluating and comparing this type of devices. It is not intended to call into question the usefulness of this technology, but to make their potential users aware of the associated authenticity risks and of the effectiveness of preventive measures that may mitigate the corresponding dangers.

Based on usage scenarios of wearable devices, potential attacks that can be carried out, putting into question the authenticity of the information involved or the authenticity of the sender of the message have been discussed. In order to promote the authenticity, both of information and subjects involved in the interactions, a mechanism of hierarchical digital signatures was suggested.

Certainly, the evolution of these devices will not stop here and new challenges will emerge, an expected situation that requires, from now on, the management of wearable technologies security issues.

DISCUSSION POINTS

- Considering the definition of authenticity adopted in this chapter, authentic information does not cease being authentic just because the person who transmitted it is not authentic. In legal disputes, should information from these sources be accepted as evidence?
- Would it be possible and useful to employ a graphic class classification system for the risks to information authenticity in user manuals of wearable devices, in order to educate some less careful users of the risks to which they are exposed in terms of information authenticity?
- If the evolution of wearable interfaces, namely in increased computational capability and artificial intelligence capacity, enables them to imitate their user, representing that user as its interface with another subject or interface, should the Turing Test be extended?
- Will wearable devices ever be capable of simulating their users (human)?
- Which are the rules for, and roles of, users of these kinds of devices?

- Will wearable devices be capable of imitating another human being, inducing their users to believe in a fabricated reality?
- Regarding the "Wearable Ecosystem" concept, how may authenticity risk be mitigated in this new ecosystem?
- Will we exchange wearable technologies or will one's wearable technologies be so personal that without them one would feel as if naked?

QUESTIONS

- Given the expected development of wearable technology, wearable devices may undertake a more active role in their relationship with the user, as suggested with the ecosystem presented in this chapter. What kind of security controls may be developed and used to mitigate the risk for information authenticity?
- How can we verify the genuineness and validity of that information?
- What can be understood by a "Wearable Ecosystem"?
- What are the key components of a "Wearable Ecosystem"?
- Which kind of mediated communications can be found in a "Wearable Ecosystem"? List the problems that can arise in this type of communication, focusing on the authenticity of information and subject.
- On the Wearable Ecosystem like the one presented by the authors in Interface-to-Human (I2H) or Interface-to-Interface (I2I) communications, will attacks such as man-in-the-middle and interface-as-a-person be the only kind to occur?
- Might a user of a wearable device be obliged to reject the authorship of a certain communication or its content, attributing it or the manipulation of its content to a wearable device?
- Is the hierarchical system of digital signatures enough to mitigate the risks of information authenticity *per se*?
- Can the classification system for authenticity risk presented in this chapter help raise the awareness of users of wearable devices on the risks of authenticity, as a tool for user education?

REFERENCES

Alshurafa, N., Eastwood, J. A., Pourhomayoun, M., Nyamathi, S., Bao, L., Mortazavi, B., & Sarrafzadeh, M. (2014, June). *Anti-cheating: Detecting self-inflicted and impersonator cheaters for remote health monitoring systems with wearable sensors.* Paper presented at 11th International Conference on Wearable and Implantable Body Sensor Networks (BSN), Zurich, Switzerland. doi:10.1109/BSN.2014.38

Ben Aissa, A., Abercrombie, R. K., Sheldon, F. T., & Mili, A. (2009, April). Quantifying security threats and their impact. In *Proceedings of the 5th Annual Workshop on Cyber Security and Information Intelligence Research: Cyber Security and Information Intelligence Challenges and Strategies* (p. 26). ACM.

Casio. (n.d.). *Operation Guide 1138 1173 Casio* [PDF document]. Retrieved from Casio Support Online Web site: http://support.casio.com/storage/en/manual/pdf/EN/009/qw1173.pdf

Chinaculture.org. (2010). *The Story of the Chinese Abacus: The Abacus with Chinkang Beads.* Retrieved from http://www.chinaculture.org/classics/2010-04/20/content_383263_4.htm

Choi, J. J. U., Ae Chun, S., & Cho, J. W. (2014, June). Smart SecureGov: mobile government security framework. In *Proceedings of the 15th Annual International Conference on Digital Government Research* (pp. 91-99). ACM.

Cirilo, C. (2008). *Computação Ubíqua: definição, princípios etecnologias.* Retrieved from: http://www.academia.edu/1733697/Computacao_Ubiqua_definicao_principios_e_tecnologias

Collins. (2015). *Collins English Dictionary – Complete and Unabridged.* Retrieved October 8 2015 from http://www.thefreedictionary.com/artifact

Davenport, T. H. & Kirby, J. (2015, June). Beyond Automation – Strategies for remaining gainfully employed in as era of very smart machines, *Harvard Business Review*.

Dhillon, G., & Backhouse, J. (2000). Technical opinion: Information system security management in the new millennium. *Communications of the ACM, 43*(7), 125–128. doi:10.1145/341852.341877

Dohrn-van Rossum, G. (1996). *History of the Hour: Clocks and Modern Temporal Orders* (T. Dunlap, Trans.). Chicago, IL: The University of Chicago Press.

Ecosystem. (n.d.). *American Heritage® Dictionary of the English Language, Fifth Edition.* Retrieved October 11 2015 from http://www.thefreedictionary.com/ecosystem

Fanthorpe, L., & Fanthorpe, P. (2007). *Mysteries and Secrets of Time* (Vol. 11). Dundurn Press Toronto.

Geier, B. (2005, August 12). NASA wants you to make a smartwatch app for astronauts. *Fortune*. Retrieved from http://fortune.com

Glasseshistory. (n.d.). *History of Eyeglasses and Sunglasses*. Retrieved from http://www.glasseshistory.com/

Hager, E. B. (2011, July 22). Explosions in Norway. *The New York Times*. Retrieved from http://www.nytimes.com

Hurford, R. D. (2009). Types of smart clothes and wearable technology. In J. McCann & D. Bryson (Eds.), *Smart clothes and wearable technology* (pp. 25–44). Cambridge: Woodhead Publishing. doi:10.1533/9781845695668.1.25

ISO/IEC. (2014). *ISO/IEC 27000 – Information technology – Security techniques – Information security management systems – Overview and vocabulary*. International Organization for Standardization/International Electrotechnical Commission.

Jobst, B. C. (2010). Electrical stimulation in epilepsy: Vagus nerve and brain stimulation. *Current Treatment Options in Neurology*, *12*(5), 443–453. doi:10.1007/s11940-010-0087-4 PMID:20842599

Karlsson, S., & Lugn, A. (n.d.). *The history of Bluetooth*. Retrieved from: http://www.ericssonhistory.com/changing-the-world/Anecdotes/The-history-of-Bluetooth-/

Kirkham, R., & Greenhalgh, C. (2015). Social Access vs. Privacy in Wearable Computing: A Case Study of Autism. *Pervasive Computing, IEEE*, *14*(1), 26–33. doi:10.1109/MPRV.2015.14

Liu, H., Saroiu, S., Wolman, A., & Raj, H. (2012, June). Software abstractions for trusted sensors. In *Proceedings of the 10th International Conference on Mobile Systems, Applications, and Services* (pp. 365-378). Ambleside, UK: ACM.

Lymberis, A. (2004). *Wearable ehealth systems for personalised health management: state of the art and future challenges* (Vol. 108). IOS press.

Marrington, A., Baggili, I., Mohay, G., & Clark, A. (2011). CAT Detect (Computer Activity Timeline Detection): A tool for detecting inconsistency in computer activity timelines. *Digital Investigation*, *8*, S52–S61. doi:10.1016/j.diin.2011.05.007

Marrington, A. D., Mohay, G. M., Clark, A. J., & Morarji, H. L. (2007) Event-based computer profiling for the forensic reconstruction of computer activity. In AusCERT Asia Pacific Information Technology Security Conference (AusCERT2007): Refereed R&D Stream.

Mayer, A., Niemietz, M., Mladenov, V., & Schwenk, J. (2014, November). Guardians of the Clouds: When Identity Providers Fail. In *Proceedings of the 6th edition of the ACM Workshop on Cloud Computing Security* (pp. 105-116). Scottsdale, AZ: ACM.

Milosevic, B., & Farella, E. (2015, May). Wearable Inertial Sensor for Jump Performance Analysis. In *Proceedings of the 2015 workshop on Wearable Systems and Applications* (pp. 15-20). ACM. doi:10.1145/2753509.2753512

Monrose, F., & Rubin, A. D. (2000). Keystroke dynamics as a biometric for authentication. *Future Generation Computer Systems*, *16*(4), 351–359. doi:10.1016/S0167-739X(99)00059-X

País, E. (2011, July 23). Horror en la isla de Utoya: "Debéis morir, debéis morir todos". *El País*. Retrieved from http://internacional.elpais.com

Parker, D. B. (1998). *Fighting computer crime: A new framework for protecting information*. John Wiley & Sons, Inc.

Pearce, M., Zeadally, S., & Hunt, R. (2013). Virtualization: Issues, security threats, and solutions. *ACM Computing Surveys*, *45*(2), 17. doi:10.1145/2431211.2431216

Rhodes, B. (n.d.). *A brief history of wearable computing*. Retrieved from http://www.media.mit.edu/wearables/lizzy/timeline.html

Rodrigo, M. A. (1988). Ser Y Conocer: Peculiaridades Informáticas de la Especie Humana. *Cuadernos Salamantinos de Filosofia*, *15*, 5–20.

Rushby, J. (1981). The Design and Verification of Secure Systems. *ACM Operating Systems Review*, *15*(5), 12–21. doi:10.1145/1067627.806586

Saxena, N., & Chaudhari, N. S. (2012, October). Secure encryption with digital signature approach for Short Message Service. In *2012 World Congress on Information and Communication Technologies (WICT)*, (pp. 803-806). IEEE. doi:10.1109/WICT.2012.6409184

Schell, D. (n.d.). *RFID Keyless Entry And Ignition System Speeds FedEx Couriers*. Retrieved from http://www.bsminfo.com/doc/rfid-keyless-entry-and-ignition-system-speeds-0001

Stinson, B. (2015, March 14). Nokia's 3310: the greatest phone of all time. *Techradar*. Retrieved from http://www.techradar.com

Teixeira, A., & de Sá-Soares, F. (2013). A Revised Framework of Information Security Principles. In S. M. Furnell, N. L. Clarke, & V. Katos (Eds.), *Proceedings of the European Information Security Multi-Conference EISMC 2013—IFIP Information Security Management Workshop*.

Turing, A. M. (1950). Computing Machinery and Intelligence. *Mind. New Series*, *59*(236), 433–460. doi:10.1093/mind/LIX.236.433

Uddin, M., Salem, A., Nam, I., & Nadeem, T. (2015, May). Wearable Sensing Framework for Human Activity Monitoring. In *Proceedings of the 2015 workshop on Wearable Systems and Applications* (pp. 21-26). ACM. doi:10.1145/2753509.2753513

Williamson, J., Liu, Q., Lu, F., Mohrman, W., Li, K., Dick, R., & Shang, L. (2015, January). Data sensing and analysis: Challenges for wearables. In *Design Automation Conference (ASP-DAC), 2015 20th Asia and South Pacific* (pp. 136-141). IEEE. doi:10.1109/ASPDAC.2015.7058994

WTc. (n.d.). *Innovation Worldcup Categories*. Retrieved from: http://www.wearable-technologies.com/innovation-worldcup/categories/

Xu, Y., Li, W. J., & Lee, K. K. (2008). *Intelligent wearable interfaces*. Hoboken, NJ: John Wiley & Sons. doi:10.1002/9780470222867

Zhao, M., Walker, J., & Wang, C. C. (2012, August). Security challenges for the intelligent transportation system. In *Proceedings of the First International Conference on Security of Internet of Things* (pp. 107-115). ACM. doi:10.1145/2490428.2490444

Zingerle, A., & Kronman, L. (2013). Humiliating Entertainment or Social Activism? Analyzing Scambaiting Strategies Against Online Advance Fee Fraud. *Cyberworlds (CW), 2013 International Conference on, Yokohama* (pp. 352-355).

Zolfagharifard, E. (2014, March 19). Is this the first wearable computer? 300-year-old Chinese abacus ring was used during the Qing Dynasty to help traders. *Daily Mail*. Retrieved from: http://www.dailymail.co.uk

KEY TERMS AND DEFINITIONS

Artifact: Something made or given shape by man, such as a tool that can be used as external prosthesis in order to extend the cognitive and sensory ability of the person who uses it.

Impersonate: Ability of a person, process or thing to assume a character or appearance of another one, normally for fraudulent proposes.

Interface: A wearable device that assumes, in a communication scenario, the bridge between a person (that is using this device) and the external entities.

Interface-as-a-Person (IaaP): The privileged position of the wearable devices in relation to their users, makes it easy for them to intrude in the communications they mediate, and combined with the access to their users' personal information – allowing them to set a profile of them and thus behave similarly – can also allow them to go through one, or more, real actors in communication.

Interface-to-Human (I2H): In a communication between subjects A and B, the communication begins in subject A but the message is issued by his/her interface directly to subject B. When B responds to A, the response will be delivered and received by A's interface. Subject A will receive B's message directly from A's interface, and not from B.

Interface-to-Interface (I2I): In a communication between subjects A and B, a message from A is sent via A's interface that communicates with subject B via its interface, and vice versa. The communication can occur in both directions, but each subject only communicates directly with his own interface.

Internet of People (IoP): A new network where people and things are all connected. Immersed in the "Wearable Ecosystem", people can "wear" network interfaces making them nodes of this new giant mesh.

Wearable Ecosystem: A system formed by organisms – the humans, as owners – and their wearable devices, as artefacts. In this ecosystem all communications are mediated by artefacts – as interfaces, assuming two schemas: I2H and I2I.

ENDNOTES

[1]   In this work we chose the word *principle* over alternatives, such as *property* or *requirement*, to refer to the concepts of confidentiality, integrity, availability, etc., in order to convey the sense of guiding foundation for the efforts to protect information and information–related assets.

[2]   The information about these devices was retrieved from respective project/ manufacturer official websites.

Chapter 6
Privacy Dangers of Wearables and the Internet of Things

Scott Amyx
Amyx McKinsey, USA

ABSTRACT

This chapter identifies concerns about, and the managerial implications of, data privacy issues related to wearables and the IoT; it also offers some enterprise solutions to the complex concerns arising from the aggregation of the massive amounts of data derived from wearables and IoT devices. Consumer and employee privacy concerns are elucidated, as are the problems facing managers as data management and security become an important part of business operations. The author provides insight into how companies are currently managing data as well as some issues related to data security and privacy. A number of suggestions for improving the approach to data protection and addressing concerns about privacy are included. This chapter also examines trending issues in the areas of data protection and the IoT, and contains thought-provoking discussion questions pertaining to business, wearables/IoT data, and privacy issues.

INTRODUCTION

Data privacy concerns are not new, but they are taking on an increased urgency as more wearable and Internet of Things (IoT) devices are used in commercial, public, and private settings. While companies may be partially addressing enterprise, con-

DOI: 10.4018/978-1-5225-1016-1.ch006

sumer, and employee concerns about data privacy and collection, it is difficult to be completely prepared for the ubiquity of connected sensors that will rapidly become part of everyday life. This lack of preparedness can be seen in the innumerable data breaches that have resulted in lost consumer confidence, damaged reputations, stolen confidential business insights, identity theft, and litigation.

Technological solutions, such as firewalls and antivirus software, provide only part of the solution to the challenge of successfully managing wearables and IoT data. A change in the approach to data security on devices and on corporate servers (or in the cloud) is foundational to success: privacy must be a priority, and enterprises that engage in positive privacy practices will offer a unique differentiation in the market. As argued below, companies that are serious about protecting data need to incorporate privacy into their business models, promote a culture of privacy in the workplace, empower a Chief Privacy Officer, become involved in standards-based consortiums, and develop an enhanced privacy policy that is easy to understand. All connected devices need to have software/encryption protections and enterprise storage of data needs to be secure and maintained.

BACKGROUND

The advent of the Internet of Things (IoT), sometimes referred to as the Internet of Everything (IoE), and wearables has had a tremendous impact on consumer and enterprise concerns about privacy. The IoT consists of any object that can be connected to a network, and wearables are clothing, jewelry, or accessories that can collect and transmit data about the wearer. The IoT is driven by M2M (machine to machine) telemetry, and although some consider these two terms to be interchangeable, there are important differences (see Polsonetti, 2015). In this work, the term IoT will be used to refer to objects, in or upon which sensors can be placed, and which allows them to connect to a network.

Benefits and Drawbacks

Wearables and the IoT come with a number of benefits and drawbacks. The benefits of these devices can be seen in the data they supply. Ubiquitous connected sensors and devices constantly recording, transmitting, and sending data create an enormous opportunity for businesses to generate detailed consumer profiles to improve marketing campaigns and engender increased revenue through targeted advertising. The data derived from IoT devices can also improve productivity in the workplace, as the monitoring of certain activities can give insight to management while enhancing innovation, cooperation, and safety practices at the individual and team levels. (For example, IoT sensors on equipment can indicate when a machine is being placed under great stress and may suffer a malfunction that endangers employees.) The utilization of data is beneficial on multiple levels: studies have shown that companies that are data-driven make more money than their counterparts, since more data yields increased insight and control (McAfee & Brynolfsson, 2012).

However, the ubiquity of the IoT and wearables creates serious privacy concerns, both for companies and for consumers. The theft of corporate secrets damages investment in R&D, brand image and corporate reputation, and revenue. The theft of an individual's data can not only harm the person, but it can also damage the company responsible for managing the data. For example, when Experian suffered a cyberattack that resulted in the data theft of 15 million T-Mobile customers, both companies had lawsuits filed against them (Larson, 2015).

The unfortunate truth facing most companies is that few wearables and IoT devices are secure. In fact, it is difficult to keep up with the evolving security needs of the technology, much less the protection of the massive quantities of data being gathered. Wearables and the IoT are therefore particularly large targets for data leaks or theft, and will continue to be so. This type of data is not confined merely to that given out by commercial fitness devices, such as name, location, step count, or heart rate. IoT devices and wearables are available for industrial, municipal, medical, and private use. Connected devices, such as those that monitor employee activities or those that regulate insulin pumps, broadcast a tremendous amount of data. The events described below show that a number of companies are not adequately addressing data privacy concerns; changes need to be made in order to preserve and promote corporate viability in the era of ubiquitous connected devices.

One industry study by Symantec (Symantec Security Response, 2014) showed that wearables data could be harvested by using a simple, commercially-available device (a Raspberry Pi computer). The data the researchers were able to collect did not have to be stolen from the devices, and the information that was collected included individual names, birthdays, passwords, and serial numbers. The researchers were able to monitor individuals based on the hardware addresses broadcasted by the IoT devices; indeed, the Symantec team also noted that 20% of the apps they reviewed did not make an attempt to hide or protect the data being collected, that is, they did not encrypt the data *at all*.

The enterprise management of consumer data in general must take into account the safety, perceptions, and abilities of the individuals providing the data. Managers need to be aware of the methods for managing the IoT and wearables in the workplace, and directly address the most effective means of utilizing them. The effects of poorly managing customer and enterprise data can be far-reaching. Since the impact of data security is so broad, complete end-to-end solutions are needed: suggestions for such solutions are described later in this chapter.

Consumer Privacy Concerns

Pew Research has shown that Americans are very concerned with privacy, and this concern took on a new fervor after Edward Snowden released government documents about the NSA's spy programs (Rainie & Madden, 2015). Hartman (2004) noted that over 90% of those surveyed about privacy issues want the government to legislate protections, even as a distrust of the government grows. Average citizens used to enjoy a degree of anonymity, but that is rapidly disappearing as data collection and aggregation increase.

Increasing disregard of an individual's privacy in the US is particularly troubling, as alarms are being raised about data abuse in the form of harassment for non-criminal issues; the public backlash that arose from the IRS misuse of tax information is one example of the snowballing concern over privacy (Goldfarb & Tumulty, 2013). In 2014, the Internal Revenue Service (IRS) disclosed that the agency had been targeting certain groups applying for tax-exemptions based on their perceived political affiliations. IRS workers were asked to flag certain keywords for non-profit organizations; a number of these key words were tied to perceived political views. It was also found that the IRS was also using donor lists from non-profits for audits (Judicial Watch, 2015).

Wearables and the IoT have a greater ability to collect even more detailed information about individuals, and this data can be combined with easily-obtainable identifying information to create a surprisingly in-depth picture of a single person's lifestyle, purchasing habits, belief systems, and social interactions. Indeed, Sweeney (2000) showed that only five pieces of information were actually required to uniquely identify approximately 87% of the population; pieces of information that can easily be obtained from a number of sources, including unsecured wearables and IoT devices.

Businesses that collect wearables and IoT data should be concerned about data privacy, since the last few years have been host to a large number of high-profile thefts of private data, including personal information, business emails and confidential information, and health and insurance records. Identity theft continues to be of particular concern to consumers (Finklea, 2014). The Bureau of Justice Statistics shows that ID theft is on the rise, and the cost of attempting to recover one's reputation is high (Bureau of Justice Statistics, 2011).

For businesses to get a better understanding of the best approach to privacy, it is important to view data security from the consumer's standpoint. Motti and Caine (2014) highlighted the particular concerns users had about wearable data privacy:

- **Infringing on the Privacy of Non-Users:** Wearable device data can be synced online with social networks, revealing information about others. In many cases, this information is being sent automatically.
- Confidential information may be displayed on screens, giving others access to non-public data.
- Consumers do not have control over who views their information.
- **Surveillance and Sousveillance:** Outside intrusion into daily life though monitoring can be particularly worrisome; these types of monitoring are often associated with malicious intent.
- Head-mounted devices that collect audio and video information can provide an incredibly broad range of extremely personal data about others. Advances in facial recognition software make this a particularly serious concern.
- Clandestine audio or video recording.
- **Right to Forget:** There are some events in life that are best left in the past or that consumers want to forget; data, however, can be stored for a very long time, so consumers are worried that they may be penalized for a past event or mistake.

These issues are being addressed in some fashion or to some degree by corporations that develop wearables and IoT devices, but there is little industry cohesion. No enterprise is completely addressing all of these customer needs. Data breaches and leaks damage corporate reputations and brand images (Ponemon, 2011), and potentially expose businesses to customer distrust, new legislative actions and possible lawsuits. All of these concerns are related to fear---fear that personal information will be revealed to those not originally granted access, that more information is being secretly gathered than was originally agreed upon, or that multiple sources of data are being aggregated to develop in-depth individual profiles for malicious purposes. Consumers, however, have good reason to fear.

Data Breaches and Consumer Confidence

Data breaches have an effect on consumer confidence, and ignoring this effect comes with significant risks. It is important to understand that the repetitive nature of data breaches has caused a shift in public sentiment. There is a significant backlash to the gathering of data, and companies that deal with the IoT and wearables need to understand its foundation.

For companies that create or utilize wearable or IoT devices, security needs to be end-to-end: the device needs to be secure (e.g., the design of the device should take into consideration a safety measure in case it is lost or stolen, such as password protection), the data transmissions need to be secure (encrypted), the company culture needs to promote privacy protections (e.g., privacy policies and the promotion of privacy in the workplace), and the storage methods (whether at the company itself or in the cloud) need to be secure. Unfortunately, few companies use an end-to-end approach for privacy management--- though to be fair, it is difficult to provide such an approach. For example, one of the first end-to-end solutions on the market was TRUSTe's, which was launched in November of 2014 (TRUSTe, 2014).

The 2013 release of top-secret records showed that the NSA, and other spy agencies, was gathering large quantities of information about regular citizens through the PRISM program (Greenwald, 2013). The government, however, was not the only bogeyman. The records also revealed that nine large companies were helping aggregate information about consumers. Microsoft, Yahoo, Google, Facebook, PalTalk, AOL, Skype, YouTube, and Apple were all implicated.

This shock was soon followed by the revelations about the Facebook psychology experiment, which it executed on its unknowing users in violation of the rules of research conduct. In 2014, it was revealed that Facebook was modifying the news feeds of some of its users (about 700,000 accounts). The company wanted to investigate the impact of social media on users' moods by manipulating the number of positive or negative items available for view. While there was a significant uproar over the company's experiment, Facebook did point to its "terms of service" agreement, indicating that the experiment was considered within the scope of its interactions with users (Goel, 2014). Some users, however, felt that the company had violated what is considered a basic tenet of academic research: the informed consent[1] of participants.

While there are few hard numbers on the backlash over the NSA issue, it has been reported that almost 50% of the Facebook users that left after the experiment quit due to privacy concerns (Woolaston, 2013).

Large data breaches at companies are particularly damaging to the public trust, and have resulted in significant damage to the corporations themselves. In 2013, Target, for example, admitted the loss of at least 70 million records on its website while Home Depot in 2014 confessed that at least 53 million email addresses from its databases had been stolen. UPS admitted a breach in 2014, as did numerous other companies including Neiman Marcus, Dairy Queen, Goodwill, Kmart, and Staples (Hardekopf, 2015).

Wearables and IoT devices are also increasingly pushing into the realm of medicine. These devices provide targeted but highly personal information about a patient's well-being and needs. Since these types of devices tend to be more invasive than a wellness product, there is a great need to provide extremely secure environments for the data. However, hospitals, like other companies, have experienced dangerous "data hemorrhages" that have resulted in the dissemination of millions of patient records containing highly personal information (Johnson, 2009). The US Department of Health and Human Services maintains a breach report on the numerous data issues found at healthcare service providers[2]. Recent examples of data breaches include attacks on Healthfirst's patient portal (affecting 5,300 patients) and UCLA Health (affecting 4.5 million people); employee carelessness and outright theft were also responsible for the dissemination of personal information (Jayanathi, 2015).

Wearables, IoT, and the Workplace

The temptation to use the IoT to monitor every facet of a business is attractive, especially when small productivity gains in a number of areas can result in additions to revenue, reduced time to value, and positive, lasting change (LaValle, Lesser, Shockley, Hopkins, & Krushwitz, 2010). Should managers watch employees more? There are important reasons to utilize wearables and IoT devices in the workplace. Fraud prevention, cutting down on wasted time ("cyber loafing", or using company time to surf the internet), and fending off potential lawsuits are all reasonable explanations for the expansion of employee monitoring. There are also safety, productivity, and revenue gains to be derived from increasing monitoring in the workplace.

Employees are getting used to the idea of some type of monitoring at work, although most of the monitoring may come in more conventional forms than wearables or IoT sensors (such as cameras, ID badges with chips for access, and specialized software). Hartman (1999) noted that over 20 million employees were subject to some type of digital monitoring as long ago as 1993, and that number has grown as businesses find new ways to use technology to enhance productivity.

Wearables or IoT sensors placed on the body might, however, draw a different reaction from workers, since the addition of such devices to a person might seem extremely intimate or invasive. The other downside to monitoring comes as a link to productivity gains. Martin and Freeman (2003) noted that studies indicated productivity gains from monitored workers were often linked to high stress and poor health outcomes for those workers; greater stress on individual health led to missed working days and higher incidents of work-related injuries, such as carpal tunnel syndrome. Workers who see the monitoring as micro-management or distrust will not feel valued and may take action against what is viewed as tyrannical oversight. This is no small problem in regards to corporate data security--- a majority of data breaches (about 59%) are the result of employee or insider actions from within the company. Unhappy, careless, or misinformed employees are frequently responsible for theft or data loss, as shown through a UK government-backed research study (Bradley & Vaizey, 2015).

Enterprise Perceptions

Numerous companies have failed to integrate privacy concerns into their overall operations. Part of the issue lies in business perceptions. Technology is frequently seen as the answer to solving data issues, but purely technological solutions cannot address all of the complications related to data management and storage. Another issue is that companies frequently only *react* to data breaches: they do not have adequate safeguards in place to begin with.

Popular myths among small business include the idea that they are too minor to attract notice or that only companies with online payment exposure are at risk., Bradley & Vaizey (2015) noted, however, that small companies are particularly interesting targets for data thieves because they frequently operate on a shoestring budget but may have access to vast quantities of unsecured consumer data. The same study showed that that the leadership at such firms often indicates that there is not enough money to tackle the security issues or do not know how to begin to address security issues dealing with privacy and data.

Large companies may have more secure technological systems in place to protect data, but these systems are not necessarily completely adequate. This can be seen in the case of JP Morgan Chase: the company did not utilize a "common" two-step authentication measure that led to a massive data heist (Goldstein & Perlroth, 2015). Large companies face the increased chance of a data breach since they make such inviting targets, not just to disgruntled employees or domestic hackers, but also to foreign thieves. FBI director James Comey once famously noted that: "There are two kinds of big companies in the United States. There are those who've been hacked by the Chinese and those who don't know they've been hacked by the Chinese" (Quoted in Cook, 2014).

Another common misperception is that technology can solve privacy issues. For example, many companies have invested in antivirus software, firewalls, and other technology-based solutions. Unfortunately, IT departments tend to be small, and protecting data does not simply involve stopping a malicious attack from the outside. Companies may provide some server-side data protection, but may not be equipped to protect the actual wearable device in the hands of the consumer, or the IoT device with the employee.

Many data breaches occur from inside companies themselves, but even without inside help, data theft can occur at any stage of the gathering, sending, or retrieving process for wearables and IoT devices. For example, CISCO routers were hacked with malicious software ("SYNful"), so the firewalls and antivirus protections at companies or organizations made little difference in the data harvesting; the data thefts had apparently been going on for at least a year and had affected government and private organizations on three continents (Auchard, 2015). As noted earlier, not all wearables and IoT devices make use of security functions on the actual device or during the transmission of the data.

While the majority of companies have privacy policies and may take some steps to protect data through technological methods, such as firewalls or antivirus software, few have a comprehensive approach that affects every level of the organization and sets privacy as a foundational, driving principle. A multi-pronged approach is therefore needed for developing more reliable systems for data protection.

ISSUES, CONTROVERSIES, AND PROBLEMS

Two significant challenges have collided with privacy concerns. It appears that some companies are not taking data security seriously. This is particularly dangerous in light of the fact that the IoT and wearables sector is exploding. Many companies have at least some technology solutions in place to protect server-side data, as well as privacy policies that limit enterprise exposure to consumer litigation. However, these solutions are not adequate to address the immense data collecting abilities and ubiquity of the IoT.

Privacy must be central to a company's policies and activities at every level. It is clear that companies (and government organizations, for that matter) are not providing adequate protections for the data to which they currently have access, so it is unlikely that any company is prepared for the heightened protections needed for the data derived from IoT devices and wearables. Data theft is on the rise, and enterprises that use or provide wearables or IoT devices need to lead with privacy in order to survive and thrive. A number of specific concerns arise from these two challenges.

Limited IT/Security Budgets

As margins tighten and companies are belt-tightening, it can become difficult to focus on something as ephemeral-sounding as security---after all, there is no direct return on Investment (ROI) for any particular security implementation. This way of thinking is particularly dangerous in the area of the IoT and wearables, since these devices will be collecting data on a massive scale. There needs to be a significant alteration in the approach to data security. As seen in Motti and Caine's (2014) research, data privacy is valued for a broad range of reasons, but all of the reasons are related to a basic understanding of human nature. Extremely-limited IT budgets are not benefitting the company's bottom line if they result in a breach that causes customer flight or a loss of corporate secrets.

Increased Use of Wearables and IoT Sensors

Statistics on wearables and the IoT show the incredible growth and projected market worth. For example, the value of the market in 2018 was projected to be almost double what it was in 2015, about $12.6 billion (Statista, 2015). Few other sectors can match such growth, especially in light of the sluggish economy and recovery after the GFC of 2008. CISCO estimated that over 50 billion connected devices will be online by 2025, each one adding to a mind-boggling collection of data that will be transmitted, stored, and analyzed by a global army of private companies and public organizations.

While it is not surprising that advanced nations, such as the US, UK, Australia, and South Korea are speeding towards massive IoT implementations, it might come as a shock that African nations and other less-developed counties are quickly becoming a new market for connected devices (Nyambura-Mwaura, 2015). Wearables and the IoT are global issues, and companies of all sizes need to address the privacy issues related to them before suffering corporate setbacks and government regulation.

ENTERPRISE SOLUTIONS TO PRIVACY CONCERNS

A significant problem linked to data breaches lies in corporate approaches to privacy. Some industry leaders are beginning to address these issues, but these few advocates and processes are not adequate in addressing the realities of ubiquitous computing.

Technology Solutions

Many businesses use common technological safeguards for data, such as antivirus software and firewalls. They are also utilizing different forms of encryption to ensure safety. For example, public key encryption is currently considered a particularly useful option for protecting data. Public key encryption uses two "keys": a public one and a private one. Public key encryption can be useful in creating safer transactions, but it is not foolproof. Multiple safeguards are required to effect a reasonable technological solution to data breaches. However, a purely technological approach is inadequate since most breaches are caused by insiders: securing data therefore requires an examination of human nature (Anderson, 2001).

Monitoring and Company Culture

Using workplace monitoring can provide productivity gains, but it needs to complement a solid corporate culture that shows a respect for employee privacy. There are companies successfully implementing monitoring systems, but it can be difficult to draw the line between helpful data collection and stressful micromanagement that leads to disgruntled employees. In addition, not all work lends itself well to monitoring, for example creative activities such as design, programming, research, or modeling.

Research has shown that monitoring can result in stressed, unhealthy or angry employees (Holman, Chisick, & Totterdell, 2002) unless proper feedback and a solid, respectful company culture exists (Chalykoff & Kochan, 1989). While constant or excessive monitoring can lead to a host of problems, targeted, anonymous monitoring that provides employees support and feedback has shown to be useful---an indicator that company culture is vital to the successful implementation of any project. Employees perform best when they feel that the business is concerned about their well-being as well as protecting the privacy of the employees. It can, however, be difficult to effectively create a culture of privacy in the workplace, and this leads to employees who are either misinformed or do not care about privacy. This is where corporate leadership could play a key role in firming up enterprise security.

Leadership sets the tone for the company culture, so getting employees to engage in a greater understanding and compliance with data security involves management that perceives value in the person. Seijts and Crim (2006) showed that employees "reward" leaders with better engagement in the workplace when leaders can "connect", or show how they value employees. This same study highlighted a key problem in dealing with employees: a staggering 54% of them simply show up and do their job, while 17% are actively disengaged. Since most data breaches occur from within the company, leadership needs to move to create a significantly different environment.

Privacy Policies

The implementation of updated privacy policies is probably one of the lowest cost options for targeting security issues. However, many of these existing policies are extensive and employ legal jargon; they are confusing or simply seemed targeted at protecting the enterprise at the cost of the consumer. Much of the language can be opaque and open to interpretation (Dehghantanha, Udzir, & Mahmod, 2010). On the other hand, it is better to have a policy than not. The Symantec researchers who showed that large amounts of personal data could simply be harvested with some inexpensive hardware were discouraged to find that 52% of the apps they investigated did not have a privacy policy (Symantec Response, 2014).

Spending More, but Not Enough

While limited IT budgets are a common lament for small and mid-sized companies as well as for startups, it does not mean that no money is being thrown at security issues. In fact, businesses are spending more money on IT security than ever before. Gartner reported that in 2014, more than $71.1 billion was spent by companies to protect their computer systems from attack and expected this to increase as companies begin to take security issues more seriously (Gartner 2014). It is doubtful that these companies are taking into consideration the upcoming wave of IoT devices and wearables.

How much money should be spent on security and privacy solutions? Finding the right amount to spend is not easy, but the funding issues for computer security probably have more to do with what is referred to as the "wait-and-see" approach to data breaches---one that has cost businesses and consumers billions (Gordon, Loeb, & Lucyshin, 2003). For example, Google stepped up its investment in the protection of user data, but only after it was revealed that the company participated in the US government's information dragnet (Timberg, 2013).

Dealing with Exposed Security Flaws

Individuals and security firms are beginning to act independently to reveal security flaws in consumer products. While this can be beneficial in uncovering serious data leaks before a crisis, not all companies are responding in an appropriate manner. Enterprises have been poorly managing data hacks by "white hat hackers". For example, in 2012, a team of University of Southern California researchers built an app that could control a Volkswagen vehicle's computer systems remotely---an extremely dangerous flaw in the system design. Volkswagen sued—and obtained—a two-year injunction that forced the researchers into silence (Solon, 2013).

Volkswagen's response to the security issue is not unique. White hat hackers do not steal data and are commonly acting in the public's interest, but habitually end up facing lawsuits or jail time for their work (Jackson Higgins, 2014). The Digital Millennium Copyright Act (DMCA) and the Computer Fraud and Abuse Act (CFAA) are often utilized to bring charges against white hat hackers instead of attacking and fixing the security problem.

Little can be gained from attempting to prevent tinkering with consumer products with legalese, either. GM, for example, issued a statement that indicated that consumers who purchase their vehicles are "leasing" the software in them, opening up any tampering with the system to corporate legal action (Bigelow, 2015). Using lawsuits to shut down those who highlight serious security flaws is counterproductive and dangerous. These types of approaches also damage corporate reputation and brand image, since the public will associate the enterprise with a lack of concern for the public good.

FALLOUT FROM SECURITY BREACHES

The "wait-and-see" attitude cannot survive in the age of wearables and the IoT---companies need to address security issues and lead with privacy. By tackling these issues head-on, it may be possible to avoid or diminish the problems associated with the fallout from security breaches and data theft. Failing to deal with privacy concerns now means that companies will have to deal with losses in areas like revenue, resources, and brand recognition, as discussed below.

Loss of Revenue and Resources

The most notable outcome of failing to focus on privacy or data security issues comes in the form of lost revenue and wasted resources. Some companies have had bank accounts hacked or credit cards stolen, just as consumers have. Others suffer from the loss of secret or proprietary information that could have led to market domination. One example of this loss is the data theft that occurred at US Steel. US Steel had developed a proprietary pipe for extraction, which would have positioned the company well to take advantage of the US fracking boom. However, there was a sudden influx of Chinese pipe into the market, and the pipe was amazingly like that provided by US Steel---except it was priced to undercut the American company's product. The issue was brought to the attention of the US government and charges were eventually laid against a team of Chinese hackers. However, as the hackers are all foreign nationals, little can be done to undo the damage or reclaim the lost revenue (Talbot, 2015).

US Steel is not the only company who has suffered at the hands of foreign "black hat hackers". Westinghouse Electric Co. (Westinghouse), U.S. subsidiaries of SolarWorld AG (SolarWorld Allegheny Technologies Inc. (ATI), the United Steel, Paper and Forestry, Rubber, Manufacturing, Energy, Allied Industrial and Service Workers International Union (USW), and Alcoa Inc., have all brought charges against data thieves to little effect (US Department of Justice, 2014).

Breaches at companies are common, and it is possible to perform damage assessments. It is almost impossible to know how much information has already been obtained from unsecured wearable devices---but it is likely a large amount, considering that many computer professionals are well-aware of the security deficiencies of wearables.

For example, wardriving is the act of driving around and noting wireless access points (which are either hardware or software that allow a company's wearable or IoT devices to connect to the internet)—and it is not illegal (Hurley, 2004). The instructions for setting up a simple system can be readily found in computer security books or websites. Many wardrivers are simply experimenting and mean no harm, but there is no way to ensure that every person who starts harvesting user data is harmless. If an individual working on her network certification can scoop up unencrypted wearables or IoT data, so can competitors.

Damage to Brand Recognition and Corporate Image

In a bustling global economy, brand image and corporate reputation provide an edge over competitors. However, when it appears that a company has a lax approach to data security or that the consumer is not of central concern, the enterprise image and reputation suffer damage---and it is not always clear how long the problem will persist in the mind of the consumer. The high-profile data losses at Target have cost the company its coveted place as a leading mid-market retailer: a serious loss considering that then US First Lady Michelle Obama herself gave the company a boost by publicly shopping there. When Target customers were first made aware of the data breach, the company's profits fell about 50% in the quarter immediately after the breach, and the quarter after that showed a further 30% decrease in profits (McGrath, 2014).

Costly Lawsuits and Legal Actions

The joke about America being the "land of the lawsuit" is not particularly amusing, especially since data privacy issues are resulting in more legal actions against companies. While suffering the loss of revenue and reputation are serious enterprise considerations, lawsuits are quickly becoming one way to punish companies that do not take care of data privacy. A list called the "Top 20 Government-imposed Data Privacy Fines Worldwide" collated by the International Association of Privacy Professionals, (IAPP, 2014) shows that Apple received fines totaling $32.5 million dollars, Google received fines of $22.5 million, and Cignet health $4.3 million. Government regulating bodies are getting more involved in legal actions as well. The US Federal Trade Commission (FTC) is now actively addressing complaints that corporations are not providing enough security for consumer data, or lack appropriate privacy protections. For example, mobile device/app maker HTC failed to protect data and was successfully sued by the FTC on behalf of the public (FTC, 2013).

Increased Business Regulation and Legislation

Governments are beginning to broach privacy issues. Europe's Right-to-Forget laws, originally created to allow a second chance for convicted criminals who had served their sentences, were foundational to legal cases against Google; the company lost a key lawsuit from a man who wanted his past mistakes stripped from the search engine's results. Other suits are beginning to gain momentum as governments wrestle with managing the "right to know" with the "right to forget". These legal actions are only the beginning trickle of a tsunami of problems, and increased government oversight is fast becoming a popular topic among consumers.

Increasing government regulation is costly and intrusive, with the potential to severely limit consumer and enterprise protections from unwanted or unmerited red tape or legal actions. Doing business in a global economy means that foreign regulation is as important as domestic. For example, European data privacy concerns are already enshrined in treaties and in its proposed constitution: For example the Data Protection Directive 95/46/EC(European Commission, 1995) and Article II-68 (Protection of Personal Data: see Fuster, 2014). Business leaders also need to be aware of domestic legislation that is currently in the works to address the data privacy issues experienced by consumers. For example, a US senate subcommittee report, " (US Senate, 2014) that investigated online advertising and data usage clearly indicated that the senators felt companies are not responsibly providing data protections for consumers. One of the recommendations of the subcommittee was that

... the FTC should consider issuing comprehensive regulations to prohibit deceptive and unfair online advertising practices that facilitate or fail to take reasonable steps to prevent malware, invasive cookies, and inappropriate data collection delivered to Internet consumers through online advertisements. (p. 9)

What would be considered deceptive or unfair? What would the subcommittee consider "reasonable steps"? Would these issues be settled by how much money a company spends on security, or would there be a list of regulations requiring compliance? While it may not be clear exactly where the lines are drawn for advertising security, it is clear that the subcommittee is interested in increasing regulation. Stringent regulation creates difficult hurdles for businesses to overcome. Currently, there is no single set of federal guidelines concerning data privacy, but states and regulators have a broad range of rules.

The US National Association of Manufacturers (NAM) reported that regulations in the manufacturing sector alone cost about $20,000 a year per employee, and about $10,000 per employee in other sectors. Small businesses were suffering from these costs and were shouldering a heavier burden than larger, more established companies----they were responsible for a cost of about $35,000 a year per employee. The report showed that this cost tallies to about $2.028 trillion for businesses, and is comparable to about 20% of the average company's payroll (NAM, 2014). Additional regulation, especially that added to a small or mid-sized company, could be catastrophic.

SOLUTIONS AND RECOMMENDATIONS

The clearest path towards effectively managing data privacy concerns is to deal with them directly and to consider privacy as one of the key aspects of doing business. Privacy should be a part of the leadership directives, the company culture, the brand image and reputation, and should be implemented throughout the organization's technological approach. Protecting privacy differentiates a company in an evolving market. Moving past compliance to leadership is increasingly becoming important.

Privacy as a Foundation

Privacy should be a foundational tenet of every enterprise, especially as wearables and the IoT advance into every aspect of life. Leadership needs to develop a comprehensive approach and strategy for implementing privacy at every level of the enterprise. Business plans need to incorporate privacy, and mission statements should make it clear that the consumer, employee, and corporate data are being managed safely with a high regard for confidentiality. Since managers and other corporate officials set the tone for privacy management, top-level policy must prioritize data security, safety, and a concern for the individuals involved, both employees and customers.

It is important to see data protection in light of market differentiation: customers are more likely to appreciate an enterprise's product and services if they feel safe using them. Driving privacy commitments through *visible* leadership is one way that leadership can promote a respect for data security and privacy. Targeted employee monitoring solutions can be used in the workplace, with reasonable limits for data use. It is here that particular approaches such as data anonymization can play a simple yet effective role. Data anonymization involves collecting data that is stripped of identifying markers. For example, it can be used in an entire department in order to harvest useful information that can guide safety and productivity decisions without targeting a particular individual.

Company culture can make or break privacy policies and security implementations. Employees are always acting as representatives for the corporate brand as long as they are employed by the company. While non-disclosure agreements (NDAs) and other agreements attempt to prohibit employee divulgence of corporate information, the ubiquity of anonymous chat rooms and social media sites guarantee that not every worker will worry about dismissal for a disclosure. Showing employees the seriousness of data protection and then modeling the behavior creates employee-ambassadors that spread the word about a company's commitment. Company culture should incorporate the ideas of security and privacy. This includes promoting the idea that there are real people behind the data and that these individuals can suffer harm if privacy protections are not implemented or executed well. Promoting a culture of understanding is fundamental to success and getting employees to empathize with those whose data they manage is key to driving a positive culture. Leaks that occur from carelessness can be addressed through policies on data handling and through encouraging employees through incentive programs.

Involving customers in data privacy is important as well. Engaging customers through targeted communications, advertising, and conversations with company representatives can help bolster privacy and security. Customers that engage with the company on issues of privacy can then garner a better understanding of their own role in protecting their data. They also become exposed to the corporate approach to their data privacy, and this enhances the corporate image. For example, Disney uses a wristband with customer data on it that allows for access to its parks and attractions; the consumer knows what information is being gathered upfront. The company has noted that the wristbands are popular and have resulted in increased attendance (Palmeri, 2016).

Chief Privacy Officer (CPO)

A major recommendation is to create, and empower, a Chief Privacy Officer. Creating a position and a department that focus on privacy issues and data security concerns reveals a real commitment to protect consumers. The creation of the department enhances the corporate management of data security and privacy in three ways: the department can solely focus on security needs, it shows employees how valued privacy is, and it creates a positive view of the company in the eyes of the public. The department can also work with the IT department to make sure that the software and hardware concerns are being addressed in a timely manner. The CPO can manage continuing education so that employees are always current about privacy and security needs and concerns.

Privacy by Design Framework

A strong commitment to implanting secure measures at every stage of data management or transmission is vital. Implementing privacy into the corporate vision and business plan will help managers set reasonable targets for ongoing security updates and costs. One framework that is particularly useful is Privacy By Design, developed by Dr. Ann Cavoukian, who was one of the Information and Privacy Commissioners of Ontario. The framework stresses seven key supports[3]:

1. Proactive not reactive; preventative not remedial,
2. Privacy as the default setting,
3. Privacy embedded into design,

4. Full functionality – positive-sum, not zero-sum,
5. End-to-end security,
6. Visibility and transparency – keep it open,
7. Respect for user privacy – keep it user-centric.

Clearly, this framework addresses the privacy concerns raised by Motti and Caine. By implementing a proactive, end-to-end strategy to protect data, it is possible to reduce the number of areas where data breaches occur.

Industry Self-Regulation

The best way to ensure data security and the standardization of protocols is to work with others in the same industry. Companies involved in the IoT and wearables are uniquely positioned to have a powerful impact on the direction of privacy standards. A number of industry organizations already exist that support standardization, protection, and advancement of secure devices and sensors. By supporting and becoming involved in these consortiums, businesses can ensure that they are not only in compliance with the law, but also that they are truly affording their customers the best in data security: belonging to, and taking an active part in, a consortium also enhances a company's brand image and reputation as a leader in data security issues.

Some of the better-known consortiums are:

- The AllSeen Alliance (allseenalliance.org) is one of the largest groups, and its framework is based on AllJoyn (an open source project created by Qualcomm Innovation Center, Inc.). Its members include companies like Microsoft, Qualcomm, Sony, ADT, AT& T, Cisco, Honeywell, and Haier.
- The Open Interconnect Consortium (openinterconnect.org) is dedicated to the principles of open source standardization. Its board of directors includes representatives from Samsung, Intel, Cisco, and GE.
- Industrial Internet Consortium (industrialinternetconsortium.org) is another non-profit consortium that targets the framework and direction for IoT devices. It was started by industry leaders AT&T, Cisco, GE, IBM, and Intel, and its membership includes hundreds of companies.
- OASIS (oasis-open.org) is supported by Microsoft and IBM, with sponsorships from a broad range of companies, including Adobe, Boeing, the US Department of Defense, Verisign, and Nokia.
- The Eclipse Foundation (eclipse.org) is working on creating a framework for the IoT. Google, IBM, Red Hat, Oracle, and SAP are all members.

Privacy Policies

In order to get the most out of privacy policies, the policies need to be easy to understand and include several levels that clarify or add detail about the enterprise's and consumer's rights and responsibilities. Privacy policies need to address some of the most difficult questions posed about IoT and wearable data. The policies should explain exactly what types of data are being gathered from devices and indicate the reasons for the data collection. How the data will be used, who will have access to it, and how long it will be stored all need to be included in the policy. Corporate privacy policies should be designed with opting out as the initial customer choice. Making privacy policies clear can be challenging, but it can be done.

A drill-down approach to content is best: the policy is first explained in simple, succinct language. Additional paragraphs can provide greater detail or legal terminology. One example of a customer-focused policy comes from Facebook. Facebook's Privacy Checkup tool is simple to understand and allows a granular level of privacy settings.

Managing Data Breaches

Data breaches will eventually happen on large and small scales. Corporate policy needs to address these issues with clearly defined steps and protocols. For in-house data security issues, the problem needs to be identified and fixed as soon as possible. For leaks of enterprise or consumer data outside of the organization, the company needs to have a public method for notifying the public, apologizing for the breach, explaining the situation, as well as its severity and expected outcomes. The steps the company is taking to remedy the problem should also be included.

Consumers may no longer want their data stored on a company's systems, but that may not be possible. Offering to remove identifying consumer data is one option, or creating a policy with a reasonable time limit for the data erasure is another. The nature of the data should be taken into consideration, as well. For example, if the database is storing personal health data along with a consumer's address and identifying information, the enterprise has the responsibility to consider the customer's privacy over the enterprise use of the data. Non-user data that appears in the database should be deleted; devices should not gather non-user data.

Employee Work-Related Data

Employee data collected while on the job may be anonymized, but what happens to that data when the employee leaves the company? Employees are concerned that data collected about them at work will be used against them for future employment.

One option is to view employee data as having the same tenure as the employee. Employee data should be considered to be on loan for the duration of the employment; after an employee leaves or is terminated, the data must be erased as well.

DATA STORAGE

Data storage and management must take into consideration a variety of solutions. Data anonymization, which is the stripping or encrypting of identifying data, makes the storage of that data safer. Data minimization refers to only gathering and using exactly the type of data needed for a wearable or IoT device to effectively provide the service it needs to. For example, if a health wristband needs to show how many steps a user has taken, does it also need to collect the user's location? The data should then be removed after it has served its purpose.

Data Vaults and Private Clouds

Two secure storage approaches are currently garnering attention: the data vault, which is a kind of architecture that allows for the owner's control of the data, and the private cloud, which is set up behind the company's firewall and allows for enterprise control of data. Data vaults would allow for the maximum in user control while still permitting companies to take advantage of certain types of information; of course, these types of storage options would significantly reduce the amount of data that may be available to businesses. One business that is successfully using data vaults is . Consumers are able to manage access to data such as insurance information, prescriptions, and other types of healthcare data (Singer, 2012).

Businesses that find value in the cloud may want to go with their own private cloud, since it offers the same types of ease-of-use and services as a typical cloud service. Fujitsu notably uses a private cloud to allow for better data management. The company has 170,000 employees, and expects significant cost savings from adopting a private cloud (Fujitsu, 2012).

Local Data Storage and Home Automation Hubs

Local data storage in wearables and connected homes can deliver the benefits of the cloud, but do not transmit data over an Internet connection. Users of local data storage can securely access and manage their information, so these options operate in a somewhat similar fashion to a data vault---outside access would be limited to those the owner allows. Some wearable and IoT devices can also provide local storage solutions. One example of this type of wearable is the ReVault smartwatch: it allows for auto-synchronization across all of the user's devices while safely storing all private information.

IoT devices in the home provide a particularly tricky field for data collection, but newer technologies, such as the home automation system, are creating value for consumers and businesses. A home automation system stores and manages data within the home environment, such as data about energy usage or temperature regulation; this data collection can include data gathered from wearables. More on this emerging technology can be found elsewhere (e.g. LaMarche, Cheney, Roth, & Sachs, 2012; Samsung, 2016).

FUTURE RESEARCH DIRECTIONS

The possibilities for research in the areas of enterprise privacy approaches, data collection and aggregation, and wearables and the IoT are limitless, but there are a few key areas that are quickly evolving into viable fields of interest.

- Increasing litigation and consumer demands may curb or even result in the cessation of data collection for some enterprises. Who will determine the limits of the rights/responsibilities related to personal data?
- Emerging trends in data security include increasing attacks from both foreign domestic hackers on small and mid-sized businesses that utilize or sell wearables or IoT devices. Domestic wearables data breaches are likely to be the domain of local data thieves and corporate saboteurs for the near future due to the ease of data harvesting in public areas. How can companies address multiple threats, and how can they handle these situations when litigation may not be an option?
- Companies will need to face the increasing chance of both cyber terrorism and actual physical acts of terrorism. This type of aggression is already occurring in the US military: soldiers' family information gleaned from social or government sites has been used by foreign nationals to threaten military families in the US (Fantz, 2015). How will companies approach overall security for their customers and employees?
- Open source solutions will increasingly be used to provide enhanced security for small and mid-sized companies. What approaches can businesses use to engage open source solutions?
- What newer methods of data analysis can help limit the amount of data gathered and stored? These methods need to focus on and revise assumptions of consumer behavior in order to create better models and profiles.

- Greater government involvement is inevitable, as well as a push for global standards and protocols for data protection and consumer privacy rights. How can enterprises take the lead in effectively managing government involvement?

CONCLUSION

This chapter examined the challenges facing managers in regard to the increasing amounts of data derived from wearables and IoT devices. It offered insight into some of the questions concerning data rights, privacy, and solutions. Decision-makers and leaders need to make data security and privacy a foundational part of their business plan in order to protect enterprise and consumer data, enhance brand image and reputation, prevent lawsuits, and promote freedom from excessive legislation.

The IoT and wearables allow for massive amounts of data aggregation, but consumers are increasingly wary of the storage and use of this data. Past data breaches have proven that consumer fears about data misuse and abuse are well-founded. Companies that sell or use wearables or IoT devices will face data security issues at some point in their lifespan, regardless of the size or nature of the business. With this in mind, enterprises need to engage privacy directly through concerted leadership directives. They also need to design and implement a corporate culture that values privacy and the people involved, create a privacy officer position (or department), establish clearly-defined policies that provide for security, and methods for addressing breaches. Businesses need to get involved in consortiums and use data storage solutions that give the most protection to consumer, employee, and enterprise data.

DISCUSSION POINTS

Consumer Privacy

Consumers are willing to turn over some types of data when they see value in the return. However, the return on that data is typically temporary, while the aggregated data from devices can be stored permanently. What types of policies can be developed to help consumers understand the trade-offs? How can a company show its commitment to privacy? How should a company manage privacy issues in light of a lawsuit?

People in advanced countries are becoming acclimated to the idea of extensive monitoring and data collection. How will that affect enterprise data security? Should consumers have the right to demand access to enterprise databases if it is believed it would be in the public interest? Is a constantly-monitored consumer the best kind of customer, or do people who know they are being watched behave differently than those who don't know they are being watched?

Employee Privacy

Monitoring some work activities can cut costs and boost productivity. Could monitoring be damaging creative problem solving, since thinking about a solution is rarely quantifiable? Will employee monitoring affect the quality of applicants that apply for positions at a company? Will monitoring encourage employee fraud, either through skirting the tracking of the device or direct tampering?

Collecting employee data can give insights into corporate functioning, but it also creates a profile of an individual worker. How can employees be protected from the creation of a detailed personal profile? Should they be? How much control should enterprises have over employee data? What happens to a company when employee data gathered from monitoring becomes public knowledge?

Enterprise Security

Most data breaches occur due to employee behavior, either through a misuse or malicious use of protections or policy. How might a company's policies currently address issues related to malicious use of data? Are there levels of malicious use that are managed in different ways? How do successful enterprises work to impede misuse of data through accident or carelessness? How effective are policies in addressing employee use of data?

Cost is a motivating concern in all data privacy issues, but it is extremely difficult to quantify data security's return on investment (ROI). How should companies determine security budgets? Should these budgets be explained at all levels of the organization? How much information should employees have about security issues? Would costs affect consumer perceptions of the company?

QUESTIONS

- How should managers approach data management/privacy?
- How will their approach affect the enterprise and consumer?
- Do companies really need to spend a lot on security, or does the size of the company (or type of data gathered) affect its likelihood of getting hacked?
- Wearable owners may be sharing their data, and that of others, unwittingly. Should companies have the right to track all wearable data?

- Who owns this data?
- What happens when a customer no longer uses the product?
- What are corporate responsibilities for the data privacy?
- How can these issues be managed in social, private, and work contexts?
- How can managers deal with employee rights and wearables?
- How long will data be stored, and what rights do companies and users have?
- What rights do other individuals have?
- How does location disclosure affect others? How does it relate to tracking or protecting others?
- How can companies head off data privacy issues and protect their image?

REFERENCES

Anderson, R. (2001). Why information security is hard - an economic perspective. *Seventeenth Annual Computer Security Applications Conference*. DOI: doi:10.1109/ACSAC.2001.991552

Auchard, E. (2015, September 16). Cisco router break-ins bypass cyber defenses. *Reuters*. Retrieved from http://www.bbc.com/news/technology-28602997

Bigelow, P. (2015, May 20). General Motors says it owns your car's software. *Autoblog*. Retrieved from https://www.gov.uk/government/news/cyber-security-myths-putting-a-third-of-sme-revenue-at-risk

Bureau of Justice Statistics. (2011, November 30). *Identity Theft Reported by Households Rose 33 Percent from 2005 to2010*. Retrieved from http://www.bjs.gov/content/pub/press/itrh0510pr.cfm

Chalykoff, J., & Kochan, T. (2006). Computer-Aided Monitoring: Its Influence On Employee Job Satisfaction And Turnover. *Personnel Psychology*, *42*(4), 807-834. 10.1111/j.1744-6570.1989.tb00676.x

Cook, J. (2014, October 6). FBI Director: China Has Hacked Every Big US Company. *Business Insider*. Retrieved from http://www.businessinsider.com/fbi-director-china-has-hacked-every-big-us-company-2014-10

Cyr, B., Horn, W., Miao, D., & Specter, M. (2014). *Security Analysis of Wearable Fitness Devices (Fitbit)*. Massachusetts Institute of Technology. Retrieved from https://courses.csail.mit.edu/6.857/2014/files/17-cyrbritt-webbhorn-specter-dmiao-hacking-fitbit.pdf

Dehghantanha, A., Udzir, N. I., & Mahmod, R. (2010). Towards a Pervasive Formal Privacy Language. In *Advanced Information Networking and Applications Workshops (WAINA), 2010 IEEE 24th International Conference* (pp. 1085-1091). DOI: doi:10.1109/WAINA.2010.26

European Commission. (1995). *Directive 95/46/EC of the European Parliament and of the Council.* Retrieved from http://eur-lex.europa.eu/legal-content/en/TXT/?uri=CELEX:31995L0046

Fantz, A. (2015, March 23). As ISIS threats online persist, military families rethink online lives. *CNN.* Retrieved from http://www.cnn.com/2015/03/23/us/online-threat-isis-us-troops

Federal Trade Commission. (2013, July 2). *Enforcement Case Proceedings in the Matter of HTC America Inc.* Retrieved from https://www.ftc.gov/enforcement/cases-proceedings/122-3049/htc-america-inc-matter

Finklea, K. (2014, January 16). Identity Theft: Trends and Issues. *Congressional Research Service.* Retrieved from https://www.fas.org/sgp/crs/misc/R40599.pdf

Fujitsu Limited. (2012, January 19). *Fujitsu Uses Private Cloud for Communications Platform to Integrate Global Communications.* Retrieved from http://www.fujitsu.com/global/about/resources/news/press-releases/2012/0119-02.html

Fuster, G. G. (2014). *The Emergence of Personal Data Protection as a Fundamental Right of the EU.* Cham, Switzerland: Springer International. doi:10.1007/978-3-319-05023-2

Gartner. (2014). *Gartner Says Worldwide Information Security Spending Will Grow Almost 8 Percent in 2014 as Organizations Become More Threat-Aware.* Retrieved from http://www.gartner.com/newsroom/id/2828722

Goel, V. (2014, June 29). Facebook Tinkers with Users' Emotions in News Feed Experiment, Stirring Outcry. *New York Times.* Retrieved from http://www.nytimes.com/2014/06/30/technology/facebook-tinkers-with-users-emotions-in-news-feed-experiment-stirring-outcry.html?_r=0

Goldfarb, Z., & Tumulty, K. (2013, May 10). IRS admits targeting conservatives for tax scrutiny in 2012 election. *The Washington Post.* Retrieved from http://www.washingtonpost.com/business/economy/irs-admits-targeting-conservatives-for-tax-scrutiny-in-2012-election/2013/05/10/3b6a0ada-b987-11e2-92f3-f291801936b8_story.html

Goldstein, M., & Perlroth, N. (2015, March 15). Authorities Closing In on Hackers Who Stole Data From JPMorgan Chase. *The New York Times*. Retrieved from http://www.nytimes.com/2015/03/16/business/dealbook/authorities-closing-in-on-hackers-who-stole-data-from-jpmorgan-chase.html

Gordon, L. A., Loeb, M. P., & Lucyshin, W. (2003). Information Security Expenditures and Real Options: A Wait-and-See Approach. *Computer Security Journal*, *19*, 2. Retrieved from http://papers.ssrn.com/sol3/papers.cfm?abstract_id=1375460

Greenwald, G. (2013, June 6). NSA collecting phone records of millions of Verizon customers daily. *The Guardian*. Retrieved from http://www.theguardian.com/world/2013/jun/06/nsa-phone-records-verizon-court-order

Hardekopf, B. (2015, January 13). The Big Data Breaches of 2014. *Forbes*. Retrieved from http://www.forbes.com/sites/moneybuilder/2015/01/13/the-big-data-breaches-of-2014/

Hartman, L. P. & Bucci, G. (1999). The Economic and Ethical Implications of New Technology on Privacy in the Workplace. *Business and Society Review*. DOI: 10.1111/0045-3609.00021

Holman, D., Chisick, C., & Totterdell, P. (2002). The Effects of Performance Monitoring on Emotional Labor and Well-Being in Call Centers. *Motivation and Emotion*, *26*(1), 57-81. Retrieved from http://link.springer.com/article/10.1023/A:1015194108376

Hurley, C. (2004). *WarDriving: Drive, Detect, Defend: A Guide to Wireless Security*. Rockland, MD: Syngress Publishing.

Jackson Higgins, K. (2014, October 21). White Hat Hackers Fight For Legal Reform. *Dark Reading (Information Week)*. Retrieved from http://www.darkreading.com/white-hat-hackers-fight-for-legal-reform/d/d-id/1316838

Jayanathi, A. (2015, September 1). 19 latest healthcare data breaches. *Becker's Health IT & CIO Review*. Retrieved from http://www.beckershospitalreview.com/healthcare-information-technology/19-latest-healthcare-data-breaches.html

Johnson, M. E. (2009). Data Hemorrhages in the Health-Care Sector. In R. Dingledine & P. Golle (Eds.), Lecture Notes in Computer Science: Vol. 5628. *Financial Cryptography and Data Security* (pp. 71–89). doi:10.1007/978-3-642-03549-4_5

Judicial Watch. (2015, July 22). *New Documents Show IRS Used Donor Lists to Target Audits*. Retrieved from http://www.judicialwatch.org/press-room/press-releases/judicial-watch-new-irs-documents-used-donor-lists-to-target-audits

LaMarche, J., Cheney, K., Roth, K., & Sachs, O. (2012). *Home Energy Management: Products & Trends*. Fraunhofer Center for Sustainable Energy Systems Marco Pritoni, Western Cooling Efficiency Center. Retrieved from http://cdn2.hubspot.net/hub/55819/docs/lamarcheetal_2012_aceee.pdf

Larson, E. (2015, October 7). T-Mobile, Experian Sued Over Data Hack Affecting 15 Million. *Bloomberg*. Retrieved from http://www.bloomberg.com/news/articles/2015-10-07/t-mobile-experian-sued-over-hack-on-15-million-customers

LaValle, S., Lesser, E., Shockley, R., Hopkins, M. S., & Krushwitz, N. (2010). Big Data, Analytics and the Path From Insights to Value. *Sloan Review, Winter Research Feature*. Retrieved from http://sloanreview.mit.edu/article/big-data-analytics-and-the-path-from-insights-to-value

Martin, K. & Freeman, R. E. (2003). Some Problems with Employee Monitoring. *Journal of Business Ethics*, *43*(4), 353-361.

McAfee, A., & Brynolfsson, E. (2012, October). Big Data: The Management Revolution. *Harvard Business Review*. Retrieved from https://hbr.org/2012/10/big-data-the-management-revolution/ar

McGrath, M. (2014, February 26). Target Profit Falls 46% On Credit Card Breach And The Hits Could Keep On Coming. *Forbes*. Retrieved from http://www.forbes.com/sites/maggiemcgrath/2014/02/26/target-profit-falls-46-on-credit-card-breach-and-says-the-hits-could-keep-on-coming/

Motti, V. G., & Caine, K. (2014). Users' Privacy Concerns About Wearables: impact of form factor, sensors and type of data collected [PDF]. *Financial Cryptography and Data Security Proceedings*. Retrieved from http://fc15.ifca.ai/preproceedings/wearable/paper_2.pdf

Nyambura-Mwaura, H. (2014, November 6). Africa fast off blocks in adopting Internet of Things - industry group. *Reuters*. Retrieved from http://www.reuters.com/article/2014/11/06/africa-tech-idUSL6N0SW5O920141106

Palmeri, C. (2016, January 10). Why Disney Won't Be Taking Magic Wristbands to Its Chinese Park. *Bloomberg*. Retrieved from http://www.bloomberg.com/news/articles/2016-01-10/why-disney-won-t-be-taking-magic-wristbands-to-its-chinese-park

Polsonetti, C. (2015). Know the Difference Between IoT and M2M. *Automation World*. Retrieved from http://www.automationworld.com/cloud-computing/know-difference-between-iot-and-m2m

Ponemon Institute. (2011, November). *Reputation Impact of a Data Breach U.S. Study of Executives & Managers*. Retrieved from https://www.experian.com/assets/data-breach/white-papers/reputation-study.pdf

Rainie, L., & Madden, M. (2015, March). Americans' Privacy Strategies Post-Snowden [PDF]. *Pew Research*. Retrieved from http://www.pewinternet.org/files/2015/03/PI_AmericansPrivacyStrategies_0316151.pdf

Seijts, G., & Crim, D. (2006). What Engages Employees the Most, or the Ten Cs of Employee Engagement. *Ivey Business Journal*. Retrieved from http://iveybusinessjournal.com/publication/what-engages-employees-the-most-or-the-ten-cs-of-employee-engagement/

Shahnazarian, D., Hagemann, J., Aburto, M., & Rose, S. (2013). *Informed Consent in Human Subjects Research*. Office for the Protection of Research Subjects (OPRS), University of Southern California. Retrieved from oprs.usc.edu/files/2013/04/Informed-Consent-Booklet-4.4.13.pdf

Singer, S. (2012, December 8). Company envisions vaults for personal data. *New York Times*. Retrieved from http://www.nytimes.com/2012/12/09/business/company-envisions-vaults-for-personal-data.html

Solon, O. (2013, August 14). VW Has Spent Two Years Trying to Hide a Big Security Flaw. *Bloomberg Business Review*. Retrieved from http://www.statista.com/statistics/259372/wearable-device-market-value/

Sweeney, L. (2000). *Simple Demographics Often Identify People Uniquely*. Retrieved from http://dataprivacylab.org/projects/identifiability/paper1.pdf

Symantec Security Response. (2014, July 30). How safe is your quantified self? Tracking, monitoring, and wearable tech. *Symantec*. Retrieved from http://www.symantec.com/connect/blogs/how-safe-your-quantified-self-tracking-monitoring-and-wearable-tech

Talbot, D. (2015, June 10). Cyber-Espionage Nightmare. *MIT Review*. Retrieved from http://www.technologyreview.com/featuredstory/538201/cyber-espionage-nightmare/

Timberg, C. (2013, November 6). Google encrypts data amid backlash against NSA. *Washington Post*. Retrieved from http://www.washingtonpost.com/business/technology/google-encrypts-data-amid-backlash-against-nsa-spying/2013/09/06/9acc3c20-1722-11e3-a2ec-b47e45e6f8ef_story.html

TRUSTe. (2014, November). *Beta Program for TRUSTe Data Privacy Management Platform Commences at Full Capacity*. Retrieved from https://www.truste.com/about-truste/press-room/beta-program-truste-data-privacy-management-platform-commences-full-capacity/

US Department of Justice. (2014). U.*S. Charges Five Chinese Military Hackers for Cyber Espionage Against U.S. Corporations and a Labor Organization for Commercial Advantage*. Retrieved from http://www.justice.gov/opa/pr/us-charges-five-chinese-military-hackers-cyber-espionage-against-us-corporations-and-labor

US Senate. (2014). *Online Advertising and Hidden Hazards to Consumer Security and Data Privacy*. Retrieved from https://otalliance.org/system/files/files/resource/documents/report_-_online_advertising_hidden_hazards_to_consumer_security_date_privacy_may_15_20141.pdf

Woolaston, V. (2013). Facebook users are committing 'virtual identity suicide' in droves and quitting the site over privacy and addiction fears. *UK Daily Mail*. Retrieved from http://www.dailymail.co.uk/sciencetech/article-2423713/Facebook-users-committing-virtual-identity-suicide-quitting-site-droves-privacy-addiction-fears.html

ADDITIONAL READING

Martin, K. (2015). Understanding Privacy Online: Development of a Social Contract Approach to Privacy. *Journal of Business Ethics*. doi:10.1007/s10551-015-2565-9

Martin, K., & Freeman, R. (2013). The Separation of Technology and Ethics in Business Ethics. *Journal of Business Ethics*, *53*(4), 353–364http://link.springer.com/article/10.1023/B:BUSI.0000043492.42150.b6. RetrievedSeptember262015. doi:10.1023/B:BUSI.0000043492.42150.b6

Mun, M., Hao, S., Mishra, N., Shilton, K., Burke, J., Estrin, D., . . . Govindan, R. (2010). *Personal Data Vaults: A Locus of Control for Personal Data Streams*. Presented at ACM CoNEXT 2010, November 30 – December 3 2010, Philadelphia. Available from http://www.remap.ucla.edu/jburke/publications/Mun-et-al-2010-Personal-Data-Vaults.pdf

Pa Pa, Y., Suzuki, S., Yoshioka, K., Matsumoto, T., Kasama, T., & Rossow, C. (2015, August 10). IoTPOT: Analysing the Rise of IoT Compromises. Retrieved September 26, 2015, from https://www.usenix.org/system/files/conference/woot15/woot15-paper-pa.pdf

Ryan, M. (2013, August 13). Bluetooth: With low energy comes low security. Retrieved September 26, 2015, from https://www.usenix.org/conference/woot13/workshop-program/presentation/ryan

Shilton, K. (2009, November). Four Billion Little Brothers?: Privacy, Mobile Phones, and Ubiquitous Data Collection. *Communications of the ACM*. 52,11, (pp. 48-53). DOI: 10.1145/1592761.1592778

KEY TERMS AND DEFINITIONS

Black Hat Hacker: A professional software and/or hardware thief who works to infiltrate systems for malicious purposes.

Cloud: Also "the cloud", referring to cloud-based computer services, or internet-based computing services.

Data Vault: A type of secure data storage.

Home Automation Hub: A central device that manages all of the IoT sensors or wearable devices in a localized area, usually a home.

Internet of Things: Objects that have embedded sensors that can connect to a network.

M2M: Machine-to-machine technologies, a term that is used to refer to a system that allows wired and wireless devices or networks to communicate.

Open Source: Free (or inexpensive) source code that is made available to anyone to copy and use.

Right to Forget: A key component of the European privacy laws that allows user information to be removed from certain Internet pages, such as search pages.

Wearables: Any object or piece of clothing with an embedded sensor or computer that can be connected to a network.

White Hat Hacker: A software and/or hardware professional who purposely tests or infiltrates systems to expose flaws in the name of the public good.

ENDNOTES

[1]   For more on informed consent, see the publication by the Office for the Protection of Research Subjects (OPRS), USC. (Shahnazarian, Hagemann, Aburto, and Rose, 2013)

[2]   The report can be found at ocrportal.hhs.gov/ocr/breach/breach_report.jsf).

[3]   see privacybydesign.ca and http://www.ipc.on.ca/images/Resources/7founda tionalprinciples.pdf.

Chapter 7
Security, Privacy, and Ownership Issues with the Use of Wearable Health Technologies

Don Kerr
University of the Sunshine Coast, Australia

Kerryn Butler-Henderson
University of Tasmania, Australia

Tony Sahama
Queensland University of Technology, Australia

ABSTRACT

When considering the use of mobile or wearable health technologies to collect health data, a majority of users state security and privacy of their data is a primary concern. With users being connected 24/7, there is a higher risk today of data theft or the misappropriate use of health data. Furthermore, data ownership is often a misunderstood topic in wearable technology, with many users unaware who owns the data collected by a device, what that data can be used for and who can receive that data. Many countries are reviewing privacy governance in an attempt to clarify data privacy and ownership. But is it too late? This chapter explores the concepts of security and privacy of data from mobile and wearable technology, with specific examples, and the implications for the future.

DOI: 10.4018/978-1-5225-1016-1.ch007

INTRODUCTION

This chapter examines at the current state of play with respect to wearables and the issues that have gained a lot of press over recent years. The chapter is broken into three main sections: the first discusses the present situation and the concerns the public has with respect to security and wearable devices. The second section discusses ownership of the data and how that effects security. Questions asked in this section are related to who owns the data and who is responsible for any data breaches. The third section looks at the integrity of mobile health information. This includes the need for verification of results and trust that the personal information is safe and secure.

HISTORY OF WEARABLE TECHNOLOGY

Wearable health technology refers to technology devices that is worn by consumers to track, monitor, and gather information related to health and fitness. These can be worn around the wrist or ankle, may be clipped to the body, or worn around the neck. Wearable technologies include smart watches, sports watches, fitness trackers, smart clothing, smart jewellery, head-mounted displays and implantable technology and can be synced with a mobile device or computer. Using technologies such as GPS, accelerometers and gyroscopes, they can monitor the heart rate, temperature, perspiration, body fat composition, and muscle activity to provide information about the user's health, movement, speed, and distance.

By this definition, the first wearable technology could be tracked back 700 years ago to the first wearable glasses. In 1759, John Harrison developed the H4 longitude watch that was able to determine the longitude at sea. And the first reported hearing aid was in 1911, with Siemens & Halske releasing the Esha-Phonophor (a device for the hearing impaired) (McLellan, 2014).

Whilst there was the development of numerous wearable technologies over the years, the first wearable health technology that collected and relayed health information was the pedometer. Whilst the first accurate measurement of distance walked occurred in the 15th century by Leonardo da Vinci, it was not until the late 18th century, when Thomas Jefferson developed the first prototype of the pedometer (a manual system that allowed the user to count their steps). Today's pedometers contain a pendulum to more accurately detect movement and can capture and transmit data electronically. The first smart watch that incorporated this technology was the Garmin Forerunner, released in 2003 (McLellan, 2014).

The next wave in wearable technology was the release of the Fitbit in 2008, leading to a new revolution in wearable technologies designed to monitor, collect and disseminate information about movement and health. Today, wearable technologies can be divided into three distinct groups: Fitness trackers and complex devices for mobile devices and applications; smart accessories (smart phones, smart watches) requiring third party applications; and smart wearables directly connect to the Internet (Denecke et al, 2015). Health data can now be transmitted to the user, to healthcare providers, and share among communities and through social media.

However, this technology is still limited in the interpretation of results. Further development is required to develop software and algorithms to extract data points and markers that will inform health promotion, prevention and management, such as the ability to interpret image or vocal data. The other limitation is in privacy, security and ownership of the data collected by wearable technology, which is the focus of this chapter.

THE CURRENT SITUATION ACCORDING TO PUBLIC FORUMS

In a recent article Teena Maddox (2015) suggested that people wearing fitness bracelets are jeopardizing their security and privacy. In this TechRepublic article, Maddox suggested that fitness bracelets cannot only detect activity but also inactivity. As the data is then uploaded to the cloud, it is possible that this information could be stolen by a third party who on-sells information to a multitude of willing businesses. In her example, Maddox mentioned this happening to health insurance companies. Maddox (2015) suggests that proof of a lack of activity in many situations could lead to "steep increases in health insurance, or even a policy cancellation" (Maddox, 2015).

This may be an extreme example, and may well only apply to consumers who have, as Maddox suggests, a "good health" discount (Maddox, 2015). However, it does provide a good example of how potentially important the privacy of personal information is and that there is a case to be considered with respect to privacy and personal information being uploaded to the cloud. For example, Maddox (2015) also states that "by the end of 2015, there will be an estimated 200 million wearable devices on the market". By the end of 2018 she estimates this to increase to 780 million. It is suggested that this provides an excellent opportunity for hackers to steal data for profit.

In another example, Gratton (2015) suggests that self-tracking devices are collecting health and lifestyle information, and in some cases even location information, and can be subject to breaches in privacy. Gratton (2015) provided an example where Fitbit accidently shared "user's sexual activity data". Forbes/Tech exposed the problem and staff writer Kashmir Hill explained that Fitbit had always tried to maintain competition amongst members by making activity available to all in an open fashion (Hill, 2011). However, as all activity was made available, people could also track sexual activity. This is an obvious unintended consequence of making all activity data available, but it did lead to embarrassing situations for members, so much so that Fitbit has removed all identifying information from profiles for the time being and made the default for activity sharing as private for new users (Hill, 2011).

Maddox (2015) also suggests that because the market in fitness wearables is so competitive, companies such as Fitbit need to release new and innovative products to market very quickly. Under this scenario, privacy and security are usually the last thing that the manufacturer are concerned about. This can have adverse implications further down the track, with security issues becoming more concerning over the past few years. The unintended privacy issues as demonstrated on the Fitbit example above, is a classic example of rushed product releases and poorly though out policy frameworks.

SECURITY AND PRIVACY

So what is security and privacy when talking about our health data? Cohn (2006) succinctly distinguishes privacy, confidentiality and security in a letter to the Secretary, U.S. Department of Health and Human Services, as "Health information privacy is an individual's right to control the acquisition, uses, or disclosures of his or her identifiable health data. Confidentiality, which is closely related, refers to the obligations of those who receive information to respect the privacy interests of those to whom the data relate. Security is altogether different. It refers to physical, technological, or administrative safeguards or tools used to protect identifiable health data from unwarranted access or disclosure."

Given the above examples, do our mobile and wearable health technologies allow us to monitor a number of different physiological measures at the cost of our individual privacy? Many applications to capture this data specify by default that the owner authorises the company access to the data and in many cases, to provide that data to a third party. How many users are aware that they can change their privacy settings in their wearable technologies as easily as they do their Facebook account? And what legislation requires companies protect the health data? Many countries are reviewing privacy legislation in light of the issues arising since the evolution of the internet of things.

Security of health data may appear easier to achieve given it is more visible to the user. We can password protect our devices to prevent third party access, but this functionality typically does not exist with the applications used to support the capture of our health data on our mobile devices. With many mobile users neglecting to secure their devices, in the wrong hands the health data on these unlocked devices can be easily accessed.

OWNERSHIP

I hope each of us owns the facts of his or her life. – Ted Hughes, 1989

Ownership of the data is another consideration in privacy and security of mobile and wearable health technologies. Is it the owner of the data's responsibility to ensure the privacy of the data, and if so, who is the owner of the raw data: the person who enters the data (user) or the company that provides the hardware to capture the data (wearable tech company), the company that provides the software to manage the data (which may be a different company)? The inventor of the world wide web, Tim Berners-Lee, told the IPExpo Europe (Hern, 2014) in London's Excel Centre in 2014 "users should own their own data and be free to merge it with other sets as and when it could provide them useful insight…If you give [people] the ability to see how [data is] used and you ban its misuse then people are much more happy to open up to their data being used."

So why is ownership an important issue? Ownership implies a level of control over how and when the data is used. A majority of consumers report wanted to own or at least share ownership of the data with the company that produces the hardware and/or software that collects the data, to maintain that control (CITIT, 2014). Yet consumers are still confused as to who actually owns the data. A survey reported 54% or responders believe they own all their personal health data, 30% believe they share ownership with the company, and 4% believe the company owns the data (CITIT, 2014).

In short, typically the consumer does not 'own' the data captured by wearable health technologies (Piwek et al, 2016). Most companies require users to agree to a terms of use agreement before a user can access any software. These typically state that the company either fully owns or has full and complete rights to the data, including the right to repackage and sell datasets to others as long as they have been anonymized. Yet many users agree to these terms of use agreement without being fully aware that they are providing these rights to the company, and the above discussed survey shows the majority of users, despite these agreements, still believe they own the data. Many countries privacy laws don't cover data generated by wearable devices. While this presently is not a major barrier to the use of mobile and wearable health technologies, the public attitudes may influence future policy making in this area. This may include the development of new policies that govern the ownership of this type of data.

Another reason why data ownership is an important issue to consumers is because of privacy concerns. In another survey, over 90% of respondents stated the anonymity of the data was an important factor, with 57% stating they would share their data (i.e. for research purposes) on the condition that their privacy would be protected (Xu, 2011).

In 2009, the European Commission issued a Communication on the Internet of Things, a proposition that the development of technology will result in the connection of everyday devices with the ability to share data. COM (2009) highlighted the potential for problems, including privacy, data protection, and data ownership. The Commission argued that users must remain complete control of their personal data and consent should be fully informed, particular with regards to how and when the data would be used (European Parliament, 2015).

Whilst it has been suggested that companies do not want to empower consumers by allowing them access to their own data or that to do so will come at a cost to the consumer. Yet, this simple act of empowerment can engage consumers to the benefit of both the consumer and the company. Until what time policy is changed, the emphasis is on the consumer to claim ownership of their data and direct the companies with regards to privacy and transparency. However, such empowerment also brings responsibility. This includes taking steps to ensure the data is secure and reading in full any terms of use agreements.

PROTECTING HEALTH DATA

Health data is very personal. The users of health data are searching for the attributes of their data to be personal while demanding quality of care. Changing the attributes and sharing those attributes without ownership, leads to a perceived breach of privacy at a personal level. With technological maturity, users of health data varies, while the use of data brings mutual benefits (Burns & Johnson, 2015). Protection of health data relays individual behaviour and organisational accountability that has the ability of managing the information attributes. Similar to the physical assets protection mechanisms, taking additional precautions while managing personal health data electronically would support individual expectations that manage a breach of privacy. The practical question is, how are we going to achieve this? Perhaps, in the wake of wearable health technologies it is paramount to manage the intentional and internal misuse while reducing and managing external access. Subsequently, requesting the protection of data ownership might help this expectation however, provisions of data ownership require further investigation and research.

In contrast to any information system generally, health information systems hold multidimensional attributes and, demands additional care when information is processed. The computation, information management and processing steps require extra set of guidelines since health information is very personal. In a nutshell, health data is a product of health information exchange, sharing and repositioning effort (clinically) of the electronic health records between the public (e.g., the patients) and professionals (e.g., clinicians, healthcare service providers and healthcare authorities). These synergies have wider potential to improve healthcare by ensuring a high availability of information and lowering the healthcare services costs. Whilst, health information sharing has positive outcomes there are some areas that need attention. That is balancing competing requirements and interest between healthcare consumers (i.e. patients) and healthcare professionals. While consumers want control over who can access their information and how it is used, healthcare professionals desire easy access to as much information as required in order to make well-informed decisions and provide quality of care. In order to balance these requirements, the information accountability mechanism (Gajanayake, R Iannella, R & Sahama, T., 2011) would be a practicable solution however it is beyond the scope of this chapter.

OPTING OUT AND DELETING THE DATA STORED ON THE CLOUD

Deleting existing data stored in the cloud is not as easy as pressing a single delete button as Robert Sheldon describes in his blog (Sheldon, 2014). Sheldon explains that users with a Dropbox accounts for example need to access files for a multitude of devices and that Dropbox must automatically sync these files to the cloud servers. This syncing is an ongoing process. Sheldon further explains that Dropbox has a lot as stake with respect to delivering a reliable service. No provider wants to be thought of as having an unreliable service and therefore these companies build in redundancies in the form of backups in various locations. This means that customer data is usually across many data centres in various locations around the world. It therefore becomes fairly obvious to even the most naïve user that deleting files from such a complex process can, at best, be describes as problematic.

SOCIAL MEDIA AND THE WEARABLE TECHNOLOGY

With the increased use of social media, there has been an increase in the sharing of data from wearable technologies across social communities. This is particularly so with younger people, with social media being defined as their natural environment

(Denecke et al, 2015). Denecke and colleagues explain (2015, p. 138) that social media "represents a space for connection, identity exploration, a space to express ideas, sexual identities, feelings, problems, and also a space where we receive feedback from others". "Health subcultures" are emerging in the microblogging and social networking sites to encourage and provide accountability and encouragement between members (Chretien & Kind 2013). Members will share data outputs from their wearable health technologies amongst the community or on their (public) profile.

The major challenge when sharing health data on social media sites if maintaining user privacy. Privacy and data security has received increased attention with the increased use of social media, yet further education of users is required to improve information security. Members of communities sharing health data should be made aware of the level of security applied to their health data when joining a community. Increased awareness of the issues of security and privacy when sharing health data on social media sites will drive the need for improved legislation to enforce privacy requirements.

TRUST OF COMPASSION WITH THE ONLINE COMPANION

Whilst computing power becomes astronomical, information sharing over computer networks and distributed computer systems presents different sets of problems. These problems are dynamic, and there are no patterns or rules to follow. The data ownerships and custodianships are still debatable in such computer network systems; users tend to share information with passion, compassion, and without boundaries. These human behaviours are localising issues related to lack of understanding the vulnerabilities of the data and information that they are sharing. Furthermore, such human behaviour is sometimes costly emotionally, socially, economically and technically. These consequences are hard to rectify, establish the proof, adhere the trust and holding the person accountable.

In the social context, trust is driven by the persona where personal attributes, reputation, integrity and behaviours. Often, colleagues and referrals reassure these attributes and behaviours. This is also practicable and applicable with human computer interaction where shared information is the centre of the scenarios and effort. For instance, when you are encountered with a complex computer networks, which network nodes would you be trusting? How would you know the trusted nodes are identifiable? Technically and philosophically, by reducing number of network nodes should increase the level of trust. This is the obvious reaction to when you are in a web of complex networks. This tactical approach is correlated with human behaviour where by reducing number of network nodes to communicate with and thereby reducing the risk that will be imposed when sharing data (the unknown factor). This is a naturally human exercise to reduce the risk of being exposed and vulnerable. The veracity of tactical behaviour is such that human is tackling, when minimising the risk would be a practical solution when interacting with wider area networks (WAN).

With the exponential growth of computer networks used by generation-Y (Gen-Y) (Saliya and Sahama, 2010) over the last decade (estimated to be 38%), this natural tactical response would not be a practicable scenario to manage. There are ample evidences that Gen-Y is responsible for online vulnerabilities. However, this topic is out of the scope for this chapter. Consequently, when considering the online world, there are millions of web sites and pages around. Most of them are presented professionally, with some clarity and graphics with attractive marketing pitches. The risk is, how do we know such web sites and/or pages are trustworthy online links that are providing information repositories or resources? The enhancement of 'digital signature' concept is in which public and private keys are utilised for information exchange, authentications, and verifications purposes. This concept is also posing another challenge such that, how do we know that the public key on the web is trustworthy? As a interim solution, the 'digital certificate' and digital certificate authorities (CAs) involvement would be a way forward to secure the trusted authentication however, this approach will acquired higher annual fees hence is not cost effective.

The security of health information drives policies and quantifiable technical capabilities when measuring 'action' and 'reaction' of the human interactions. On the other hand, confidentiality is confounded with human behaviours resulting the 'action' of individual taking 'reaction' to such human behaviours. There should be a balance between these two personas.

TIME TO MARKET AND USER CONCERNS

There is a massive drive to get products on the market very quickly and there is evidence that many companies have taken shortcuts with respect to security. In recent research Lee, Lee, Egelman and Wagner (2016) conducted a survey of 1,782 Internet users in which they asked about data and the capabilities of wearable devices. The survey revealed that there was a great deal of concern about various aspects of data collection associated with the use of wearables. Respondents ages varied from 18 to 73 and 57.9% were male, 41.0% female with the remainder declining to state gender. The researchers believed the sample was a good representation of the US population.

The most concerning aspect according to the survey was video capture and the use of financial data. The survey results further expanded on this by concluding systems that detect sensitive objects in photos and videos are concerning for people who want their privacy. (Lee et al 2016). Other factors that caused concern in this study were GPS tracking, audio recordings. Exercise patterns, sleep patterns, medication schedules and disclosure of their home or work address. The authors conclude that "users' self-reported privacy preferences are correlated with how they may react, even with respect to situations that they are unfamiliar with". The further indicated that the results "may be used by system designers to create permissions and access control mechanisms that do not directly depend on users' inputs" (Lee et al 2016, page 9).

Recent court cases have indicated the level of concern about privacy issues such as unauthorised video capture. This used to be the preserve of paparazzi taking unauthorised photos or videos of celebrities, however with the increased use of wearable technologies and the ability of these to video record any situation, these privacy issues are now becoming more prevalent in the general public.

HEALTH APPLICATIONS AS AN EXAMPLE OF THE URGENT NEED FOR SECURITY IN COMMUNICATIONS

Health and Aging

To emphasise the need for quick action with respect to ensuring security in communications with wearable devices, we examined literature discussing future trends for wearable technology in the area of health and aging. Dr Kevin Doughty is the Director, international Centre for Usable Home Technology (iCUHTec) and is based at Caernarfon, Wales in the United Kingdom. Dr Doughty is a world expert in assistive technologies for aged care and he has a very upbeat view of the technology and how it can assist older people. These views are being actively promoted to the aged care community worldwide. When one of the authors of this chapter asked Dr Doughty about the security issues, he stated that it is a very real and acknowledged problem, however it must be overcome because of all the advantages wearable technology can offer in improving the lifestyle and independence of older people. Doughty and Appleby (2016) has outlined the following points with respect to future trends in wearables for older people:

- The benefits of wearable technologies have been established Doughty and Appleby (2016) and the following areas have been identified as useful applications in the aged care industry. These applications include:
  ○ Overcoming sensory impairments such as deafness and speech problems.
  ○ Clothing to monitor and provide treatment for incontinence and other physically impairments to normal daily functioning.

- ○ Wearables to assist older people recovering from surgery and who need rehabilitation. GPS tracking and electronic fence boundaries for people who have dementia.
- ○ Virtual reality headsets for armchair travel and other applications to make life more enjoyable.

Dr Doughty also concluded that "The application areas for wearable devices, which originally was restricted to monitoring of fitness and exercise (as a glorified pedometer!), has extended recently to areas of social care, rehabilitation and healthcare monitoring" (Doughty & Appleby, 2016, p. 8). However, he also warned that "The improved compliance and data quality that are possible through the use of new technologies are likely to rapidly change the way that telehealth services are configured and delivered. They will need to be more agile and demonstrate a greater understanding of patient acceptability. Choice will be essential, and this means that service providers will have to be more agnostic to equipment providers and to include clear guidance on how services help patients to achieve more meaningful outcomes" (Doughty & Appleby, 2016, p. 8).

These predictions by experts such as Dr Doughty make the areas of non-medical, wearable devices a very attractive alternative for patients on a budget. However, it is also problematic in that the devices are not approved by the medical authorities (that is they have not gone through a fully approved medical trial) and (more importantly with regard to this chapter) they do not provide secure communications to the outside world. This lack of security in communications can be particularly problematic with unauthorised access to personal data and this can lead to identity theft, fraud and possible elder abuse.

Integrity of Mobile Health Data

Data transmissions from the mobile and wearable devices are critical for timely and most appropriate medical intervention. Ubiquitous data transmission, for instance between sensors and wearable devices, among health providers require technological and human intervention for precision medical treatments. Receiving the patient's CT scans via text message while walking towards the hospital (Bratu, 2014) or receiving the discharge summary via a mobile application whilst off-site have important care mechanisms and timely decision making. However, the integrity of the information requires verification and trust. This information integrity is built upon the information security issues around the information sources that were generated. The data transmitted to a clinical decision maker should be compatible, interpretable and have good quality to receive accurate and timely clinical and/or medical decision-making. In order to establish this data integrity within the wearable health technologies, the following sections have been organised.

Time Variant Information

Improving quality of care is bound by contextual awareness, effectiveness of the situation and awareness of the care processes (Andrews, Sahama, & Gajanayake, 2014; Black, Sahama, & Gajanayake, 2014; Gajanayake, Iannella, & Sahama, 2014). Furthermore, availability of health data demands accurate and valid recording of the right person at the right time. The contextual awareness of data sources play a critical role in ubiquitous medical devices. While the information quality is significant for timely decision-making, information security issues are also rather critical. In comparison, when managing, authenticating and sharing health data, it is important to preserve the privacy and manage the risk of data being shared inadvertently. Every effort should be taken by the user to ensure the protection of the data that they are sharing. This posts another challenge as to where the responsibility occurs to make such assurances and, who should make calls in the first instance. Is it the information source included in the device? Where is it the ownership of the source that the data is generated from?

Geolocation Data

Onserve (2015) provides geolocation services and in their blog they indicate the positive aspects of geolocation and the benefits that both consumers and businesses can find from the technology. These benefits include

- Tailoring of marketing campaigns based on end-user preferences.
- Improved customer engagement and better business analytics capabilities.
- Helping in locating assets.

Another benefit of geolocation data can be in the area of aged care with patient suffering dementia having more freedom than they otherwise would because carers can track their location at all times. The security issues here could still relate to people other than carers hacking into the wearables data and also tracking the patient with possible malicious intent. The trade-off here is the health and well-being of the patient against the possible risks of unauthorised tracking. Of course the problem would be of a far less concern if security was tightened through encryption or the use of other technological solutions.

Insurance Fraud and Theft

Remote health monitoring approaches are becoming common practices in general healthcare services. Inadvertently, this exercise could be combatting to reduce healthcare costs. Extensive efforts have been made in both academia and in the industry sectors in the research and development of smart wearable systems (SWS) (Chan eta l., 2012). The SWS are miniature electronic devices, attached to the body of a person and clothing. Consequently, these SWS are producing positive, productive outcomes while negative and adverse outcomes are also reported. For example, Fitbit, Nike Fuelbands, Google Glass and Golden-I are influencing people's daily life at work, home and the recreational activities socially.

Wearable technologies have certainly helped solve insurance fraud and theft more easily with technology being able to not only determine the exact location of the stolen item but to also take a photo of the perpetrator. This can also have implications for health insurance companies with people with certain disabilities being able to be tracked, thus determining the level of disability. This could have ramifications with respect to fraudulent payments etc. We suspect that health insurance companies may be promoting the use of wearable activity bracelets in order to objectively determine the level of activity undertaken by their members. Although not lawful in some countries, the implications of this could be different premium pricing based on the physical activity of each member. Furthermore, the activities monitored by SWS can be used against counterfeit insurance claims and make the claimant responsible for such action. The odds are, the legal framework towards these scenarios is underdeveloped. However, evidence against the false claims would be reasonable and not unobtrusiveness (Alemdar and Ersoy, 2010).

Keeping Track of the Mobile Workforce

Much of the impetuous for tracking software comes from businesses wanting to keep track of their workforce. These benefits are obvious for the business but as stated in their blog "Is location important or intrusive?" (Onserve, 2015). Others question the motivation of manufactures of geolocation functionally on items such as fitness bracelets (Maddox, 2015; Zdnet, 2015). The example given earlier of companies' on-selling data is enough for some to opt out of using the technology and express real concerns about the privacy aspects of their use. In addition, the push by manufactures to market and sell the latest technology as quickly as possible provides us with an environment of reduced concern with respect to the privacy and security issues associated with geolocation functionality within the technology.

A final consideration is bring your own device (BYOD) in general. With mobile technology being used for a variety of personal and work purposes, the risks in data security and privacy are enormous. Consider how often we transfer information from our mobile device to another person. There is a risk for accidental transfer of personal health data, as much as the risk of a third person interception. Furthermore, with the increase use of BYOD in health, there is the potential for (unintentional) breaches in patient privacy when this data is shared with another.

HEALTHCARE INFORMATION TECHNOLOGY (HIT)

The health sector and health systems in general are complex with multi-dimensional data attributes. The attributes of the health data are ill defined until meaningful clinical decision-making takes place. The exponential growth of technological capabilities drive growth of the healthcare sector while vulnerabilities of information sharing go unnoticed. Healthcare information technology (HIT) takes a very clear position by its own rights to make these radical changes. An information technology enabled health ecosystem is the enterprise with hope, challenges and innovation.

An acceptable HIT system enables the managing of healthcare information systems with valid and innovative designs. It will support usability and interoperability by reducing the service cost and improving efficiencies by lowering errors that warrant the improvement of quality of life. We are a long way away in reaching this expectation. There are two major research areas that HIT needs to address. These are healthcare information integration and information accountability (Gajanayake, Iannella, & Sahama, 2011). While the information accountability mechanism is not discussed in this chapter, it is important that we describe the information integration issues in wearable health technologies. Consequently, it is important to understand that the information accountability mechanisms are a basis for the privacy principle where positive development towards economic value and business implications are under investigation (Article 29, 2010; Zimmermann & Cabinakova, 2015). Advancement of pervasive Information Technology and wearable health technologies stimulate organisation to embrace real-time information. This expectation triggers the synergies and demand of work ready home and mobile offices. The world around us is ubiquitous. Coffee shops with Wi-Fi while city centers are offering Wi-Fi services for free. The majority of the cities in developed and developing countries offering Wi-Fi with no cost or reasonable cost which is encouraging. Does this driving force ask the consumers to be mobile and ubiquitous? If so, what are the implications? Do these facilities make us work more smartly and efficiently?

EMPOWERING DATA USERS

The empowerment of consumers require realisation of data use and users (Burns & Johnson, 2015). Health data from the commodity perspective creates opportunities and value co-creation (Andrews et al., 2014). While the quality of life is driven by quality of care (Sahama and Liang, 2012), it is important to understand data integrity and information integration issues as an information user and/or consumer. This is a complex situation and has no precedence when the situations are in emergencies that might occur. That is, in this particular situation caring is the major goal rather than maintaining the privacy attributes or data ownership. While caring for better healthcare is acceptable and thereby improves the quality of life, the underlying principle behind this cure is data curation. There should be "better platforms that allow people to curate data easily and extend relevant applications to incorporate such curation" (Abadi et. al, 2013). This data curation exercise repositions the need of database management in a simple, lightweight and just-in-time fashion. These are variables and requirements driven by human factors embedded with (personal) electronic health records (EHR) in support of quality of life, becoming a core asset of the digital economy (McAfee, 2012).

CONCLUSION

There appears to be a significant level of concern about people using wearable devices in relation to their security and privacy and this has been expressed in several online forums and magazines. There are suggestions that organisations, such as health insurance companies, could be using these devices to detect not only activity but also inactivity of their members and this could have adverse outcomes in terms of premiums for some individuals. In this chapter we also highlight the massive movement towards wearable devices. These devices are not considered medical devices and therefore do not need to go through the stringent controls to be registered, and this greatly reduces development costs as well as reducing their time to market. This massive push for cheaper devices to assist people in achieving health and wellness has resulted in companies rushing products to market without much concern for security of the product or the privacy of individual users.

Other issues such as unauthorised video capture also raise concerns about privacy. This problem in particular probably serves as a reminder that not all privacy issues can be solved by technology and that there are certain unpleasant, human nature factors that come into play. These cannot be controlled through the use of technology but are still very much a product of the miniaturisation and amalgamation of devices that are associated with the development of wearables. It appears to be an axiom in these days of wearable devices that no conversation is ever private.

In this chapter we also discuss the ownership of data and pose the question; Is it the owner of the data's responsibility to ensure the privacy of the data, and if so, who is the owner of the raw data? Is it the user or is it the company that provides the hardware to capture the data (wearable tech company) or is it the company that provides the software to manage the data? This ownership question is a major problem because ownership implies a level of control over how and when the data is used and most users of wearable technologies want to have some control over how the data is used. This question is largely unanswered with surveys revealing consumers are confused as to who actually owns the data. Issues such as these need to be solved before we can even begin to look at security and privacy issues.

The privacy issues are also in the fore front of the news in the health and medical records domain. Health records are particularly sensitive to most people and many want assurances about ownership and privacy. This is a problem area with personal medical records and we assume that it will become even more problematic when data from wearable devices comes into the mix. This direct link of personal health data into personal health records is a natural progression in patient care. Medical professionals will want to monitor their patients and this will have to be linked to their health records which will also provide a full history of patient care and medical procedures. The questions we pose in this chapter is how do we provide care for people in terms of devices that can monitor vital signs at all hours of the day and night but still maintain a level of privacy that each individual demands and expects?

Wearable technology offers lots of promise for people in all situations and stages of life. The technology has the potential to reduce the cost of medical devices and provide useful feedback loops for people in areas such as physical activity, blood glucose measures and other conditions such as predicting seizures etc.

The issue of data ownership can go a long way in improving these security and privacy issues because at present no one has provided a legal understanding of data ownership. If data ownership is in question, how can we expect any serious attempts in improving security to be conducted because agencies may well ask who is responsible for data security. In other words, who pays?

With improved consumer education about how they can ensure the privacy of their health data when using wearable technology, it will drive changes in the regulation of these devices, such as legislation and policy. These issues need to be addressed if we are to see significant acceptance of these technologies by vast sections of the community.

DISCUSSION POINTS

- Discuss the implications of private health data being made available to third parties
- How does the statement from the U.S. department of health namely: "Health information privacy is an individual's right to control the acquisition, uses, or disclosures of his or her identifiable health data. Confidentiality, which is closely related, refers to the obligations of those who receive information to respect the privacy interests of those to whom the data relate. Security is altogether different. It refers to physical, technological, or administrative safeguards or tools used to protect identifiable health data from unwarranted access or disclosure." Relate to the present state of wearable devices
- Discuss the reasons for the present situation with regards wearable devices and privacy
- Discuss the ethical implications of the use and distribution of private health data.
- Discuss the commercial imperatives for the quick development and deployment of health and fitness wearable devices
- Discuss the pros and cons of wearable devices with respect to their geo-location functions

QUESTIONS

- Who owns the data from wearable devices?
- Is it acceptable for wearable devices to monitor physiological measures at the cost of our individual privacy?
- What is security and privacy when talking about our health data?
- Are users aware that they can change their privacy settings in their wearable technologies?
- Is there any legislation that requires companies protect an individual's health data?
- Why is the ownership of health data such an important issue?
- Is technology that can locate employees while working important or intrusive?
- If data ownership is so important, how can we expect any serious attempts in improving security to be conducted because agencies may well ask who is responsible for data security. In other words, who pays?

REFERENCES

Abadi, . (2013). *The Beckman Report on Database Research, Communication of the ACM*. Beckman Center of the National Academies of Sciences & Engineering.

Alemdar, H., & Ersoy, C. (2010). Wireless sensor networks for healthcare: A Surevy. *Computer Networks*, *54*(15), 2688–2710. doi:10.1016/j.comnet.2010.05.003

Andrews, L., Sahama, T., & Gajanayake, R. (2014). *Contextualising co-creation of value in electronic personal health records*. Paper presented at the 16th International Conference on E-health, Natal, Brazil. doi:10.1109/HealthCom.2014.7001872

Article 29. (2010). *Data Protection Working Party: Opinion 3/210 on the principle of accountability*. Author.

Black, A. S., Sahama, T., & Gajanayake, R. (2014). eHealth-as-a-Service (eHaaS): A data-driven decision making approach in Australian context. *Studies in Health Technology and Informatics*, *205*, 915–919. PMID:25160321

Bratu, B. (2014, January 30). Brain surgeon walked six miles during snowstorm for emergency operation *NBC News*.

Burns, A. J., & Johnson, E. M. (2015). *Securing Health Information*. Paper presented at the IEEE ITPro. doi:10.1109/MITP.2015.13

Chan, M., Esteve, D., Fourniols, J.-Y., Escriba, C., & Campo, E. (2012). Smart Wearable Systems: Current status and future challenges. *Artificial Intelligence in Medicine*, *56*(3), 1370–156. doi:10.1016/j.artmed.2012.09.003 PMID:23122689

Chretien, K. C., & Kind, T. (2013). Social Media as a Tool in Medicine: Ethical, Professional, and Social Implications. *Circulation*, *127*(13), 1413–1421. doi:10.1161/CIRCULATIONAHA.112.128017 PMID:23547180

CITIT. (2014). *Personal data for the public good*. California Institute for Telecommunications and Information Technology.

Cohn, S. P. (2006). *Privacy and confidentiality in the Nationwide Health Information Network*. Retrieved 28th February 2016, from http://www.ncvhs.hhs.gov/060622lt.htm

Denecke, K., Bamidis, P., Bond, C., Gabarron, E., Househ, M., Lau, A. Y. S., & Hansen, M. (2015). Ethical Issues of Social Media Usage in Healthcare. *Yearbook of Medical Informatics*, *10*(1), 137–147. doi:10.15265/IY-2015-001 PMID:26293861

Doughty, K., & Appleby, A. (2016). Wearable devices to support rehabilitation and social care. *Journal of Assistive Technologies, 10*(1). doi:10.1108/JAT-01-2016-0004

European Parliament. (2015). *The internet of things. Opportunities and challenges.* Retrieved 31st December 2015, from http://www.europarl.europa.eu/RegData/etudes/BRIE/2015/557012/EPRS_BRI(2015)557012_EN.pdf

Gajanayake, R., Iannella, R., & Sahama, T. (2011). Sharing with care: an information accountability perspective. *IEEE Internet Computing, 15*(4), 31-38. doi:10.1109/MIC.2011.51

Gajanayake, R., Iannella, R., & Sahama, T. (2014). *Adoption of accountable-eHealth systems by future healthcare professionals: An empirical research model based on the Australian context.* Paper presented at the 16th International Conference on E-health Networking, Application and Services (Healthcom), Natal, Brazil. doi:10.1109/HealthCom.2014.7001892

Gratton, E. (2015). *Health-tracking bracelets and privacy issues.* Retrieved 11th November 2015, from http://www.eloisegratton.com/blog/2014/12/20/health-tracking-bracelets-and-privacy-issues/

Hern, A. (2014). Sir Tim Berners-Lee speaks out on data ownership. *The Guardian.* Retrieved from http://www.theguardian.com/technology/2014/oct/08/sir-tim-berners-lee-speaks-out-on-data-ownership

Hill, K. (2011). *Fitbit Moves Quickly After Users' Sex Stats Exposed.* Retrieved 11th November 2015, from http://www.forbes.com/sites/kashmirhill/2011/07/05/fitbit-moves-quickly-after-users-sex-stats-exposed/

Lee, L., Lee, J., Egelman, S., & Wagner, D. (2016). *Information Disclosure Concerns in The Age of Wearable Computing.* Working paper University of California, Berkeley. Retrieved from https://blues.cs.berkeley.edu/wp-content/uploads/2016/02/camera-ready.pdf

Maddox, T. (2015). *The dark side of wearables: How they're secretly jeopardizing your security and privacy.* Retrieved 11th November 2015, from http://www.techrepublic.com/article/the-dark-side-of-wearables-how-theyre-secretly-jeopardizing-your-security-and-privacy/

McAfee, A., & Brynjolfsson, E. (2012). Bid data: The management revolution. *Harvard Business Review*, *90*(10), 60–68. PMID:23074865

McLellan, C. (2014). *The History of Wearable Technology: A timeline.* Retrieved 6th May 2015 from http://www.zdnet.com/article/the-history-of-wearable-technology-a-timeline/

Nugawela, S., & Sahama, T. R. (2011) Internet usage trends in medical informatics. In *Statistical Concepts and Methods for the Modern World An international conference organised by the Applied Statistical Association of Sri Lanka.* Applied Statistical Association of Sri Lanka and the School of Mathematics and Statistics, The University of Sydney.

Onserve. (2015). *How geolocation data collection can be useful to businesses.* Retrieved 14th of November 2015, from https://www.onserve.ca/how-geolocation-data-collection-can-be-useful-to-businesses/

Piwek, L., Ellis, D. A., Andrews, S., & Joinson, A. (2016). The rise of consumer health wearables: Promises and barriers. *PLoS Medicine, 13*(2), e1001953. doi:10.1371/journal.pmed.1001953 PMID:26836780

Sahama, T. R., & Liang, J. (2012) Impact of the social networking applications for health information management for patients and physicians. In *Quality of Life through Quality of Information - Proceedings of MIE2012.* IOS Press BV.

Sheldon, R. (2014). *Deleting files in the cloud.* Retrieved 15th of November 2015, from https://www.simple-talk.com/cloud/cloud-data/deleting-files-in-the-cloud/

Xu, H. (2011). Information privacy concerns: Linking individual perceptions with institutional privacy assurances. *Journal of the Association for Information Systems, 12*(12), 798–824.

Zdnet. (2015). *Wearables open new avenues for security and privacy invasions.* Retrieved 14th November 2015, from http://www.zdnet.com/article/wearables-open-new-avenues-for-security-and-privacy-invasions/

Zimmermann, C., & Cabinakova, J. (2015). *A conceptualization of accountability as a privacy principle.* Paper presented at the BIS 2015 Workshops. doi:10.1007/978-3-319-26762-3_23

KEY TERMS AND DEFINITIONS

Geolocation Data: The real time identification of the geographic location of objects.

Healthcare Information Technology (HIT): Information technology applied to health and health care. HIT supports information management for health. It also supports the secure exchange of health information between all stakeholders.

Ownership: The rights associated with possessing something, in this case the ownership of data.

Social Media: Computer and other device based tools that allow people share and exchange information such as messages and videos, etc.

Wearable Technology: Wearable devices such activity bracelets that incorporate practical functions such measuring the number of steps taken by an individual wearer. The technology relates to these devices and their connection to the internet. Wearables are an example of devices used as part of the Internet of Things (IoT).

Chapter 8
Wearable Devices:
Ethical Challenges and Solutions

Marc L. Resnick
Bentley University, USA

Alina M. Chircu
Bentley University, USA

ABSTRACT

Today, innovation in and with Information and Communication Technology (ICT) is accelerating as consumers, companies and governments become users and designers of myriad ICT solutions whose ethical implications are not yet well understood. This chapter contributes to the growing body of research on ethical implications of one popular emerging ICT - wearable devices and associated technologies. Ethical challenges stemming from the extensive prevalence and comprehensiveness of wearable devices are related not only to the device design and use but also to the device-supported data collection and analysis and the creation of derivative products and services. Drawing from theories of ICT ethics, this chapter identifies the major ethical challenges posed by wearable devices and provides several guidelines on how these challenges can be addressed through ethically-informed design interventions.

INTRODUCTION

Today, innovation in and with information and communication technology (ICT) is accelerating as consumers, companies and governments become users and designers of myriad ICT solutions whose ethical implications are not yet well understood.

DOI: 10.4018/978-1-5225-1016-1.ch008

While ICT ethicists posit that technology should be used to protect and advance core human values (life, health, happiness, security, resources, opportunities and knowledge) (Bynum, 2011), new ICTs often fail to do so. This chapter discusses wearable devices and associated technologies as one example of such ICT innovation, analyzes the ethical issues they present for individuals, organizations and societies, and proposes solutions for future designs that can help minimize the negative – intended or unintended – consequences of wearable technologies.

A wearable device is any ICT device which can be worn or carried by a user, and which has embedded sensors (to collect information about the user's activities), software (to enable processing of the information), and network connectivity (to enable remote data storage, synchronization, and exchange, as well as additional processing capabilities). Wearable devices include mobile phones and smartphones, activity trackers, wearable GPS trackers, smart watches, smart glasses, and sensor-enhanced objects such as passports with radio-frequency identification (RFID) chips and RFID luggage tags. Wearable devices are part of the emerging Internet of Things (IoT) – interconnected objects, devices, vehicles, and buildings that can exchange information and be controlled remotely, over the Internet. We are only starting to scratch the surface of possible developments in this area, as IoT is expected to include tens of billions of devices in a few short years.

Many companies are viewing wearables as the next growth opportunity, which will generate over $231 billion in service revenue by 2020 (PRNewswire, 2015). Expected benefits form wearables include improved efficiency, productivity, service and engagement across a range of industries such as retail, healthcare and entertainment (PwC, 2014). According to IDC, the number of wearable units worldwide exceeded 45 million in 2015, and is expected to exceed 126 million by 2019 (Llamas, 2015). If we consider only one subset of wearables – those devoted to health self-monitoring – the number of unique commercial offerings is staggering, with over 200 wearable health sensors and almost 100,000 health applications available for purchase (or free download in many instances) (Patterson, 2013).

As the number of wearable devices and device interconnections increases, so do the associated security vulnerabilities (Goodman, 2015) and privacy threats. To analyze these challenges, this chapter draws from theories focused on the social and ethical impacts of ICT. According to a 2012 bibliometric mapping analysis, ICT ethics, also called computer and information ethics, is a relatively new but rapidly evolving field, mimicking the rapid pace of technological development over the last few decades. Technologies such as the Internet and the many Internet-enabled applications such as email, online gaming, blogs, social networking sites, and others have been extensively examined by ICT ethics researchers, especially as they relate to privacy concerns, regulations and laws, and social impacts (Heersmink et al., 2012). However, the research on ethical implications of wearable devices and associated technologies is in its infancy.

Academic researchers, industry practitioners and users alike do not yet fully understand all the emerging ethical issues posed by these emerging technologies (Chircu, 2013; Resnick, 2013). For example, privacy concerns are raised as real-time tracking and location services technologies are developed. Wearable devices such as Google Glass, a technology that allowed users, among others, to record others using head-mounted glasses, create not just privacy issues, but can lead to knowledge and opportunity disparities between adopters and non-adopters, and provide misleading information that misinterprets the context of action (Michael, 2014, 2015). We posit that these emerging ICTs are fundamentally changing the equilibriums that Western society had reached in the privacy versus safety tradeoff, and the privacy versus service tradeoff. For example, in some Western countries, the privacy versus safety equilibrium was based on the idea that law enforcement should balance individual privacy rights with the need for public safety, and obtain specific approvals for surveillance and searches needed in criminal or national security investigations. Advances in technology now create new surveillance opportunities on an unprecedented scale (Michael, 2014, 2015; Martin, 2016), which disrupt this equilibrium. Inexpensive GPS transmitters can be attached to a wide population of potential suspects' vehicles and tracked through a central database. Public cameras or unmanned aerial vehicles can be programmed with recognition technology to track a face or a license plate around the city. And data from wearable devices used by consumers can be captured in real-time during network transmission from the device to the processing or storage location (a server on a cloud, for example) and analyzed after the fact. Data storage and analytics capabilities make it technically feasible to track, model, and even predict behaviors for anyone who spends time in public areas, and identify them with great precision, in real time (Michael, 2014). Similarly, there was a privacy versus service equilibrium – where consumers were able to purchase goods and services from companies without having to worry that all their activities before, during and after the purchase will be tracked. Today, wearable devices and product sensors are disrupting the equilibrium and generating ethical concerns, as data about consumers is collected, analyzed and used not just to support the function of the technology as originally intended, but also to create derivative products and services.

In this environment, consumers are increasingly concerned about the unauthorized use of their personal data, or use of their data (authorized or not) that is contradictory to core human values. A recent survey by the Pew Research Center indicates the majority of adults in the U.S. are concerned about their privacy, and their inability to maintain the security and confidentiality of their personal information (Madden, 2014). In the absence of design or regulatory safeguards, many users choose to actually opt-out from fully using the features of the technology or disclosing information truthfully in order to minimize the potential for future harm (Patterson, 2013; Keith et al., 2014).

In this chapter, we show not only how wearable technologies disrupt the well-established ethical equilibria, but also how companies and policy-makers can help restore them through ethical interventions. The chapter is organized as follows. In the next section, we discuss several ethical theories and findings from current research on ethical implications of emerging ICTs. We then review the key ethical challenges posed by emerging wearable technologies, and we propose ethical interventions designed to solve each one of these challenges. Next, we suggest future research directions and provide conclusions. Last, but not least, we list several discussion points for practitioners and policy-makers, as well as questions that educators can use in a classroom setting.

THEORETICAL BACKGROUND

Researchers have defined ethics, or moral philosophy, as a branch of philosophy concerned with understanding behavior and what makes it right or wrong. The ethics discipline can be further split in several sub-branches: metaethics (the study of moral principles and their source), normative ethics (the study of norms for moral behavior), applied ethics (the study of how moral norms apply in specific situations), and descriptive (or comparative) ethics (the study of how people describe their behavior and actually behave) (Heersmink et al., 2014). Among these, normative ethics has been of particular interest to ICT researchers, since it can offer guidelines for the design of ethical ICTs. Three main categories of normative ethics theories exist: virtues theories, consequentialist (or utilitarian) theories, and Kantian (or deontology, i.e. duty-based) theories. In short, virtues theories assume virtuous characteristics of the individual (which are universal or community defined) lead to ethical actions; consequentialist theories recommend comparing the utility of various outcomes and acting in a way that generates the best consequences – i.e. choosing the action with the highest utility outcome; and Kantian theories emphasize the duty of the moral agent to follow universal laws that treat humans as ends in themselves rather than means (regardless of consequences) (Heersmink et al., 2014; Stahl, 2011; Mingers and Walsham, 2010).

The discourse on new and emerging science and technology ethics is pluralistic in nature and constantly evolving as new scientific discoveries are made and technologies are developed (Heersmink et al., 2014). In particular, ICTs are complex technologies whose inner-workings are not very clear or easy to understand, and which create new, important ethical dilemmas (Mingers and Walsham, 2010). To deal with these problems, both researchers and practitioners in the ICT domain need to understand ethical concepts in order to design and use ethical technologies – and ethical training should be an integral part of educational programs for these individuals (Stahl, 2011; Narayanan, 2013). New approaches, such as anticipatory ethics (Brey, 2012), may be needed to understand ethical implications of emerging technologies and their features, as well as those of the artifacts, systems and procedures that are created using the technology and their applications in different situations. It is also important to understand the inherent ethical problems of a technology (stemming from its features), as well as the ethical consequences of how technology is implemented in artifacts (stemming from specific design choices) and the risks that its actual applications, or use of the artifacts in practice, will be morally problematic (Brey, 2012).

Privacy is an ethical consideration that has emerged at the forefront of ICT ethics research. Privacy is viewed by many as an essential value, or as basic human right (Boehm, 2015; Michael, 2014, 2015; van den Hoven et al., 2012; Weber, 2015). During human evolution, "etiquettes, customs, artifacts, technologies and laws as well as combinations thereof" were devised to protect personal information in the physical world and, more recently, in the virtual world as well (van den Hoven et al., 2012). These protections, however, are not universally available or accepted – and they can differ widely across countries and cultures. In addition, modern ICTs, such as wearables, now threaten the "essential value" of privacy, and users are exposed to many types of "information based harm" (van den Hoven et al., 2012; Weber, 2015). For example, point of view recording technology (through a wearable camera, as those available in mobile phones or Google Glass), affects basic human rights such as image control and freedom (Martin, 2014). When a user's personal information is collected by an organization and then re-used (through aggregation, data mining, or other activities), it creates the potential for harm due to incorrect inferences, bad decisions due to original data errors, relevant information exclusion, or irrelevant information inclusion. Similarly, when the collected information is accessed without authorization – perhaps due to lax data controls within the organization or due to a security breach, it creates potential harm due to breach of confidentiality or insecurity (such as identity theft) (Culnan and Williams, 2009). Bynum (2008) also notes that as computers and computer-like-devices – either stand-alone or connected to networks such as the Internet –gather, store, search compare, retrieve and share personal information, threats to privacy are created if what a user perceives to be "sensitive" information falls in the wrong hands.

This has given rise to a new conceptualization of the privacy concept – from the notion of control over personal information to the notions of restriction of access to private information and privacy in public spaces (real or virtual). In addition, anonymity is mentioned as a tool of ensuring protection when sensitive information is involved. The emerging argument is that privacy and anonymity "can be helpful in preserving human values such as security, mental health, self-fulfillment and peace of mind" (Bynum, 2008). Thus, the definition of privacy is continuously changing, and now covers several moral considerations related to data protection that prevents harm to those providing the data, ensures fairness in data access and use, prevents economic data-based exploitation and other forms of discrimination, and safeguards moral autonomy, while also allowing for creativity and innovation (van den Hoven et al., 2012).

From a policy-making perspective, the ethical challenges posed by new technologies can be resolved by clarifying existing laws and adopting new, technology-specific legislation and regulatory guidelines. Advances in this area are slowly made in the wearables privacy arena, for example – but requirements differ around the globe, or even within a country (as in the case of different requirements at the state level in the U.S.) (Patterson, 2013; Weise, 2015). While international organizations such as the United Nations (UN) have issued declarations on universal human rights, they usually refer to broader concepts, such as human dignity (Boehm, 2015), which can be subject to local interpretation. In the European Union (EU) for example, there is a long tradition for a comprehensive right to privacy for all persons (Boehm, 2015; Weber, 2015). This informs the EU data protection legislation, which provides several rules and guarantees for personal data privacy that apply independently of context and with few restrictions (Boehm, 2015). The EU privacy laws include the concepts of consumer opt-in for data collection, shared responsibility for both data collection and data processing companies, and "right to be forgotten" (NBC News, 2015; Sayer, 2015). In the United States (US), the Fourth Amendment of the US Constitution declares "the right of the people to be secure in their persons, houses, papers, and effects, against unreasonable searches and seizures" (Wex Legal Dictionary, 2016). This right, however, depends on the "reasonable expectation of privacy" concept, which is defined based on what the society is prepared to recognize as acceptable given all the circumstances of the situation. In addition, the so-called "third party doctrine" excludes information disclosed to a third party from the reasonable expectation of privacy (Wex Legal Dictionary, 2016; Martin, 2016). In the US, consumers do not have a say regarding data collection, but can opt-out from some, but not all, information sharing practices (FTC, 2016). Thus, the expectation of privacy in the US is more case-based, time and context dependent and allows for more exclusion (not covering non-US persons, limiting opt-out options, etc.) (Wex Legal Dictionary, 2016; Boehm, 2015; FTC, 2015; Weber, 2015). In addition, while clarifications are added to cover new technologies such as electronic communication (Wex Legal Dictionary, 2016) and new application domains, such as financial or medical information, these changes cannot keep up with the rapid pace of ICT adoption. Even if states such as California are adopting state-level legislation to protect consumers using these new technologies (such as legislation to limit tracking of online activities), there is a lack of national-level protection for consumers adopting new ICTs, and new consumer rights legislation is sorely needed (Michael, 2014, 2015; Weber, 2015). Legislation should also address the ethical design of new technologies as well as penalties companies have to pay in case of unethical data use or unauthorized breaches (Goodman, 2015).

At the managerial level, companies can address threats to privacy in several ways: create a culture of privacy (with support from the top levels in the organization), create privacy governance processes and accountability, and maintain the element of "personal experience" in privacy decisions (rather than shifting the managers' moral responsibility to an opaque system of complex, anonymous procedures) (Culnan and Williams, 2009). They can also institute training programs to educate their employees - scientists studying new technologies, designers of ICT-based artifacts, and marketers promoting the use of the artifacts in practice – about ethical theories (Stahl, 2011) and privacy-enhancing technologies (Narayanan, 2013). Most importantly, however, individuals and organizations need guidelines for understanding the potential ethical challenges brought by new technologies and a set of design principles they can follow to develop ethical ICT-based artifacts. Such principles exist in other areas of ICT development – such as human-computer interfaces, or usability – and are widely adopted by organizations.

Towards this end, researchers are starting to propose privacy principles for specific applications. For example, leading privacy European scholars have suggested creating a community of scientists, technology users and citizens – dubbed FuturICT – that will focus on understanding the problems brought about by the modern society – including the use of technology in modern society (van den Hoven et al., 2012). Using the concept of value-sensitive design, they arrive at several design principles for the knowledge database and the social networks that will support the community: compliance to data protection and privacy regulations, deliberate participation – i.e. deliberate sharing of data for specific purposes, privacy-preserving data transformation (such as obfuscation, anonymization, surrogacy, and randomization), privacy-preserving data aggregation (such as coarse-graining, hierarchical sampling, and recommender systems), pseudonyms and virtual identities, anonymous lab experiments, two-sided transparency, incentivizing mutual data protection (also called co-privacy), and compliance with codes of conduct that are accepted in the community (or the society at large) (van den Hoven et al., 2012).

This "privacy by design" concept – developing data protection safeguards during (not after) the development of a new technology based on a set of universal guidelines – can be very useful for emerging ICTs, and is the basis of the discussion presented in the next sections regarding ethical challenges of one type of emerging ICT – wearable technologies – and potential solutions for these challenges.

ETHICAL CHALLENGES OF WEARABLE TECHNOLOGIES

Innovation in the ICT domain often uses the launch and learn approach. Companies develop a prototype that seems to achieve a novel and useful function, launch it on the market, and use feedback that they receive directly from users and indirectly through social media to modify it. Feedback from government agencies may uncover unmet legal requirements. Famous examples of this include disputes between Uber (a multinational transportation network company that connects users with drivers through a mobile app) and city governments regarding safety standards and licensing (Begley, 2015) as well as Google's dispute with the European Union regarding privacy and the newly established "right to be forgotten." (NBC News, 2015).

Ethical concerns can slip through this process unnoticed. Government agencies may not get involved because ethical guidelines are not written into specific laws. Developers may not be aware of ethical considerations, or may think they are not as important as usability and functionality considerations. Companies may fear that adopting stricter ethical policies will stifle innovation, reduce value-creation, and ultimately impair their ability to successfully compete in the marketplace. Users may not be aware of a technology's ethical implications or the consequences of their technology use on ethical outcomes. Competing interests between stakeholders such as between employers and employees, parents and children, insurers and policyholders, and marketers and customers can present innovators with contradictory feedback.

Many users carry their mobile devices and other wearables at all times, even in bed. They bring their mobile devices and wearables everywhere they go, including home, work, and play, even the bathroom. They use their devices to communicate with all kinds of people, including family, friends, coworkers, even their pets. Wearables (or mobile ICT more generally) have become truly ubiquitous. They enable not only user communication, but also data collection. Companies collect and aggregate individual data points about users' home and work lives, social and work relationships, health, finances, and entertainment behaviors. This "big data" may become accessible to marketers, government agencies, or hackers with malevolent intent. Unfortunately, the identity paradox of big data suggests that even when personal information is only collected and aggregated anonymously, it can later be associated with an individual because of the incredible specificity and precision of the user models. With minimal effort, an anonymous record of an individual in a particular zip code, age, gender, income, education, and interests can be associated with a specific person by anyone with access to the record.

Ethical challenges emerge from this extensive prevalence and comprehensiveness of wearable ICT in a variety of ways - not just from the way these devices are designed and used, but also from the way data collected by the devices can be analyzed and used to create derivative products (goods or services). The analysis that follows discusses these challenges and some of the reasons why they occur.

Constant Connectivity

An underappreciated challenge that emerges from the constant accessibility of mobile and wearable ICT is that individuals are constantly connected to other people. The pervasiveness of this connectivity is behaviorally salient. Notifications from incoming email, text messages, social media posts, new items on a followed news channel, and other sources can intrude on a user's attention at any time and any place. Even without a notification, there is an ever present temptation to check for updates. This tendency is embedded in the social wiring of a human brain that was not designed for the high volume of information produced by current ICT (Lewis, 2014).

Wearable ICT increases the distraction. The screen is visible without taking a device out of one's pocket or case. Vibration notifications are directly felt on the skin. The Apple Watch instituted its new Taptic Engine that is intentionally designed to feel like a finger tapping on the wrist (Pierce, 2015). This triggers the social instinct with both cognitive and sensory dimensions.

The reverse is also true. There is a constant ability to share one's own activities and status with the social network. Instead of engaging with a physical experience, people take selfies and post it for others to see, share, and comment. Without that external acknowledgment, it is unclear whether an event really occurred. Even important news coverage is evaluated based on how often it is shared on Twitter (Pew Research Center, 2011).

Several specific ethical problems arise from this constant connectivity. The problem most covered in the media is work burnout. Instead of wearables giving employees more flexible work schedules and enabling work-life balance, the technology has simply extended the work day. Even when not engaged in active monitoring and responding to work, the mental distraction is always present. Longitudinal studies conducted so far indicate that this leads to a lower total productivity rather than a higher one. This violates the harm to human capabilities principle of ethics.

A second problem, studied for almost a decade by Muise (Muise et al., 2009), is the relationship jealousy intensification caused by the use of social media such as Facebook. Farrugia (2013) found that there is a positive correlation between

Facebook use and relationship jealousy at all stages of personal relationship development. Utz and Beukeboom (2011) attributes this to the increase in the total volume of information available about a relationship partner and the persistence of that availability. Social media also present a more socially acceptable form of surveillance compared to rifling through a partner's belongings.

Social media-based relationship jealousy is not unique to wearables (or mobile ICT more generally), but mobile access adds two magnifying factors to the problem. Constant connectivity simply adds to the exposure intensity in a simple dose-response risk ratio. In addition, wearables add new types of data, such as video lifelogging and GPS-based location mapping. A jealous individual can now learn what his or her partner (or imagined partner) is doing in more visual and immediate detail. Dr. Muise's research shows that this creates a feedback loop in which more access leads to more jealousy which leads to more monitoring and back again in a self-reinforcing cycle. Relationship jealousy may not only be true for romantic partnerships but can also appear with work teams competing for visibility in their organization, sibling rivalries, and more. Several ethical principles are at stake here, including relational privacy, psychological harm, and consideration for the common good.

User Agreements

Wearable products and associated services usually require consumers to accept user agreements before they can use the product or service. These agreements are notorious for their lack of usability, including small text, extensive length, legal language, challenging user interface design, and hidden risks (Resnick, 2006). On mobile devices, the small screen magnifies these difficulties. This challenges the informed consent principle of ethics.

Users tend to accept user agreements in large majorities despite the shortcomings. To access valuable services provided by wearables, users have no alternatives but to accept the agreements, basically paying for service access with their rights to privacy (Weber, 2015). It is easy for users to engage in optimism bias and assume that their privacy will be adequately protected. They don't understand how extensively user information can be shared among organizations even when companies conform to the language in their agreement. There are information aggregators that create extensive models for each user and sell them to advertisers for targeted marketing campaigns. Users are also unaware that they may be allowing company access to information about their social networks, remote activation of their device cameras and microphones, and access to other sources of very personal information. This challenges the information privacy, informed consent, and autonomy principles of ethics, even when the user actively and voluntarily accepts the user agreement.

User agreements include clauses that allow the host organization to change the policy at their own discretion with minimal dissemination to, or approval from, users. At most, a generic request to "approve changes" is distributed that is equally inscrutable. This challenges the informed consent and user autonomy principles of ethics.

Over time, a learned helplessness could pervade the culture so that the new generation of digital natives accepts a reality in which information privacy no longer exists, without questioning this fact. If the consumer baseline of expectations is set so low, a fundamental shift can be engendered into the entire culture, challenging the consideration for the common good principle of ethics. This is not a far-fetched assumption, but already the current reality. According to a recent survey of over 2,000 consumers in the US and the UK, 80% of consumers between the ages of 20 and 40 think total privacy in the digital world is no longer available, and almost 50% of them would accept behavioral tracking online in order to obtain better offers from companies (Accenture, 2014).

Multi-Tasking

Wearables such as mobile phones and smart watches allow users to multi-task concurrently with other activities they are engaged in. Users instinctively believe that they can be more productive by multi-tasking, despite conclusive evidence that the opposite is true. Ophir, Nass, and Wagner (2009) found that multi-tasking reduces performance and that the presence of the secondary task on the mobile device prevents users from focusing on the primary task. Dean and Webb (2011) found that multi-tasking decreases creativity. There is evidence that long term multi-tasking can lead to a permanent loss of the capacity for focused attention. These issues challenge the harm to human capabilities and psychological harm principles of ethics.

Predictive Modeling

An emerging challenge is that modeling is getting too comprehensive and intrusive. With the available data, even a user that has taken all steps to maintain their anonymity can be identified, as proven in many data de-anonymization papers published over the last decade. In 2006, researchers at a US university popularized this topic by showing that it was possible to de-anonymize, or re-identify anonymous users, using a large, anonymous database of movie ratings from Netflix, a popular movie rentals and streaming provider. As more data becomes publicly available over the Internet, it is easier than ever to find the granularity and volume of data required for successful de-anonymization (TechTarget, 2016). When the model has a user's zip code, age, gender, income, preferences, occupation, etc., it is not hard to figure out who the individual is. The anonymous becomes identifiable – an occurrence also referred to as the Identity Paradox. Even when it doesn't reach this level of prediction, sometimes just the prediction of certain attributes can be problematic. If retailers can predict that a female customer is pregnant based on the modeling of her purchases, they could use this insight to send targeted ads for diapers, possibly informing the customer's family of her pregnancy before she had revealed this herself. Similar problems emerge when a predictive model identifies an individual who is suffering from depression but has not been diagnosed by a physician and may not be aware of the condition himself. These examples violate the informed consent, information privacy, relational privacy, and psychological harm principles of ethics.

In an extensive survey of consumer attitudes, PwC (2014) found that while "consumers across all demographics are leery of the impact wearable technology will have on the privacy and security of their personal information", this effect is most pronounced for sharing personal information with close contacts. According to this survey, people are not comfortable sharing any personal information from wearables with friends and family – but are willing to share data with companies and the government for certain purposes and in exchange for benefits such as monetary rewards, discounts, and more immersive experiences (PwC, 2014). This could be due to the emotional relevance and salience of family interactions compared to the concealed use of personal data by companies. Does this mean that wearable technology developers should prioritize relational privacy over information privacy to companies? This remains an open question.

Geolocation Modeling

The ease with which wearables (or mobile ICT more generally) can incorporate inexpensive and invisible location tracking makes this type of modeling a likely source of ethical challenges. Geolocation modeling involves maintaining a permanent record of a transponder's real-world location to a precision of just a few meters. This is the technology that makes real time maps feasible. The transponder is connected to a mobile device, so the model's accuracy depends on the type of device. Phones are frequently kept on the owner's person and personal fitness trackers are often collocated with the user 24/7/365. Many potential and actual examples of geolocation modeling demonstrate the ethical challenges.

Provider/User

Many wearable devices come preinstalled with a transponder that records of the location of the user. In many cases, users do not know and cannot easily find out whether or not the location record is being used only to provide the immediate service, is maintained long-term for other purposes, or can be deleted. This is in direct violation of the informed consent principle of ethics. When the transponder is on a personal fitness tracker or other wearable device that rarely leaves the user's body, the resulting model can be remarkably accurate. The use of these location models also has ethical challenges. If they are shared with marketers for the purpose of learning a consumer's habits for targeted marketing campaigns, this violates the information privacy principle of ethics. If it is used to profile users who spend time at locations matched with higher financial risk, this could lead to redlining, in violation of the equal treatment principle of ethics.

Law Enforcement/Suspect

The U.S. Supreme Court recently addressed a case where law enforcement placed a transponder on a suspect's motor vehicle. In the past, law enforcement had to expend considerable effort to track a suspect so the general public had a reasonable expectation of privacy. Mobile technology now makes it possible to attach inexpensive and unobtrusive location transponders to a wide population of potential suspects' vehicles and to track them through a central database. Public cameras or unmanned aerial vehicles can be programmed with recognition technology to track a face or a license plate around the city. This results in a significant reduction in privacy for anyone who comes under the scrutiny of law enforcement, even without prior notice. This violates the information privacy principle, freedom of movement principle, and the Fourth Amendment of the Constitution according to the Supreme Court ruling.

Employer/Employee

Another ethical challenge with geolocation emerges from the employer/employee relationship. When an employee uses an employer-owned mobile device, the location model is owned by the employer. Even when the employee is outside the office, on his or her own time, and not engaged in work, his or her location may still be tracked. In one case, an employee was fired for turning off the transponder when outside the office. This violates the autonomy principle of ethics. Even when the pressure to keep the transponder active is informal and indirect, it can violate the information privacy principle of ethics.

Another employer/employee ethical challenge emerges from their competing incentives. For example with health insurance, the employer prioritizes total health care costs higher than the employee would. Both care about the health of the employee, but with different emphases. A fitness tracker or mobile activity logging system could be aligned with either one, or somewhere in between. All three approaches have ethical strengths and weaknesses with respect to the ethical principles of the greater good, information privacy, bodily privacy, and non-discrimination.

Family Members

Another challenge arises between family members, such as between parents and children or between spouses. There are geolocation-based wearables that parents can use to track their children, often without their knowledge. While the legality of this practice depends on specific nuances of how it is done, there are clear ethical information privacy issues. There are also relational privacy challenges because there is evidence that this tracking can interfere with the trust relationships between parents and children.

Equally problematic is when this technology is used between spouses. If an individual is suspicious that his or her spouse may be cheating, a geolocation tracker is a tempting way to test this suspicion. This is in directly violation of the law if it is not done with the spouse's permission. However, the great temptation, the low probability of being caught and the low penalty if one is caught makes it predictable that this use will still occur.

While it can be argued that today's technology merely replaces a job previously done by a human private investigator, some researchers are pointing out that people tend to trust the technology more, and that the technology-based surveillance can be subject to misinterpretation if the context is not properly documented (Michael, 2015, 2016). It would be better if ICT innovators conceive of the potential for this misuse in advance and consider counter-interventions in the design of the wearable system (Brey, 2012).

Marketer/Customer

Marketers rely on geolocation models to target advertising to customers at the ideal time to present a particular offer. At the most basic level, a person walking by a coffee shop can be targeted with an offer for a discounted coffee at that precise moment. When integrated into a longitudinal geolocation model, the system can predict the individual's future path and enhance the precision and timeliness of the offer. If the location is combined with other attributes such as purchase history, demographics, expressed preferences, the offers can be targeted very precisely and persuasively. An individual whose fitness tracker notices high stress levels, a purchasing profile that notices a preference for green tea when under stress, a geolocation model that notices she has stopped at this coffee shop in the past, and a demographic profile that indicates she is a price-conscious shopper, the discounted offer can be exceedingly persuasive. This can violate expectations of information privacy and autonomy principles of ethics.

Disney's Magic Band (Disney, 2016) is a unique application of wearable ICT with geolocation in the context of amusement parks. Currently available at the Walt Disney World Resort in the US, it consists of a bracelet with an embedded radio frequency chip that stores a unique, randomly-selected access code, and sends and receives signals from readers placed throughout the Disney resort. Each visitor's unique code links to a secure, encrypted database that contains detailed information about that specific Disney park visitor, including the visitor's admission ticket, payment information (to facilitate in-park purchases), room access code (if the visitor stays in a Disney property), and access information to a visitor's official park photos, among others. Visitors who wear the band get instant access to park services by simply touching the band to designated short-range readers around the park. However, the band code can also be read by long-range readers without the user's immediate knowledge. This tracking is used not only to provide personalized experiences to the band user, but also to improve report operations. By giving amusement park guests an immersive experience and an immense increase in convenience, the band is hard for them to turn down. But guests are typically unaware of how detailed the tracking is and how the data is used, violating the informed consent principle. Disney can use the bands to generate longitudinal models of the guests that are later used to target advertising or even in real-time inside the park. As with the coffee shop example, the geolocation data can be aggregated with demographics and other sources to craft highly specific and persuasive offers, reducing the guest's autonomy. This is more sensitive because it frequently involves children who need greater protection.

Wearables allow a shopper in a grocery store to access much more information about a food item than could possibly fit on the label. They can look up whether the item is organic, contains GMO ingredients, is grown locally, and its farm to table carbon footprint. More information is not necessarily better, however. Research has shown that consumers often suffer from information overload in which too much information distracts from the important dimensions, causes decision anxiety, and degrades the final choice quality. When considering this additional information, consumers incorrectly think that they are more careful and informed shoppers. This challenges the health principle of ethics. If the device uses the consumer's personal information to target ads for items in the store, it could further violate the principles discussed earlier in this section as well.

SOLUTIONS AND RECOMMENDATIONS

As discussed earlier, managers have several options for ensuring ethical principles are withheld - including promoting an ethical culture, instituting ethical governance systems, and employing ethical design guidelines for ICTs and the corresponding artifacts, systems and procedures. Next, we describe how these tools can be applied to each one of the wearable technology challenges identified in the previous section.

Interventions for Constant Connectivity

Technology and user interaction design can be used to address these challenges. Social networks need to develop more effective policies through which members can protect themselves. The current focus is largely on illegal activities such as stalking and bullying. More emphasis needs to be focused on the less salient but more prevalent problems of everyday relationships and the intensification of destructive tendencies. Another solution is to hard code limits into user access. France has legally banned companies from requiring employees to check email after 6 pm. Social networks can put a maximum on the number of times one user can access the activity stream of another. At the very least, defaults can be set up to provide access only to one's closest connections.

Controls might present new ethical challenges, such as limited user autonomy, so careful design of any new policies needs to consider ethical principles. Turkle (2015), an advocate for changing the way we communicate in the era of ubiquitous device availability, stresses the value of time alone and unplugging from ICT that is valuable in ways that can't be replaced by an app and that individuals do not appreciate well enough instinctively to block into their schedules. ICT can help in reverse, through mechanisms in which it turns itself off.

Interventions for User Agreements

There have been several sets of general guidelines for a more usable and comprehensible design of user agreements (Resnick, 2006). There are also ICT-based solutions such as the Autonomous Privacy Negotiator of Savitskaya (2004). Encryption and anonymity protocols are being developed that allow marketers to target ads to individuals without having access to the individual's identity beyond a coded unique identifier. For example, Affectiva, a provider of emotion recognition software used by over 1,400 brands including Unilever, Mars, and Kellog's (Affectiva, 2016), uses this approach in their emotional modeling service that uses facial recognition through a device's camera to predict the user's emotional state.

Interventions for Multi-Tasking

To prevent multi-tasking, devices can be deactivated by blocking cellular and wi-fi signals or using user-customized or organizational policies. In many workplace meetings, attendees must check their devices at the door when they enter. In social events, attendees put their devices in front of them and the first one to check a notification has to pay the bill. These sound inconsequential but can be effective in part because they don't feel as controlling, thereby minimizing the challenge to the user autonomy principle of ethics.

Interventions for Predictive Modeling

To prevent modeling from causing these overprediction problems, they must be designed with better care towards the consequences of revealing personal information to a customer and/or to her friends and coworkers. Sensitive attributes such as pregnancy or depression could be excluded from any modeling activity, or could be protected by additional safeguards against sharing, for example. User models can also be separated so that no marketer has access to the complete set of user attributes. If these individual model components are kept to a reduced level of specificity, individual identities can remain anonymous. If detailed predictive models are used, marketers should not assume that the targeted individual is the only one who might receive their targeted advertising. To prevent this, they could devise encapsulation mechanisms that keep the targeted message private even after delivery to the wearable device, and authentication mechanisms that require users to confirm their identity or provide consent in order to access the message.

Interventions for Geolocation Modeling

The simplest intervention for solving the ethical challenges of geolocation modeling is for the users to turn off the transponder. But this would prevent users from accessing many of the valuable services provided by mobile and wearable devices. The interaction to turn off the transponder is often hard to accomplish.

Legal rulings can solve some of the law enforcement challenges, particularly those related to the U.S. Fourth Amendment protection from unreasonable search and seizure. They can also prohibit unauthorized tracking from family or employers without consent. But these solutions rely on the compliance of family members and employers with the law. Even one breach can cause a lifetime of harm. More effective interventions remain an open question for wearables (or mobile ICT more generally) developers.

FUTURE RESEARCH DIRECTIONS

Several future research directions exist. In-depth research studies on the perceived value and risks of wearable technologies can be conducted. Existing experiments conducted for information disclosure behavior in mobile applications indicate that even when consumers perceive a benefit from disclosing more personal information, they tend to resist disclosure (or provide inaccurate information) because the perceived risk is also high (Keith et al., 2014). Future studies can investigate whether or not consumers understand the complexity of wearable technologies and the privacy risks they involve, and how their level of understanding affects their information disclosure behavior (as a function of the information type, the use situation, and other factors). In addition, since the consumer perceptions may be dependent on consumer education level (Tan et al., 2014) and perhaps other personal factors, future studies should collect data from diverse user populations. Researchers can also study the determinants of and barriers to adoption of ethical design principles in organizations – both for wearable technologies and for other new ICTs in general. Future research can also investigate the value of designing ethical technologies – from both the consumer and provider perspectives.

CONCLUSION

Emerging ICTs today are developed and used at an accelerating pace by companies, consumers and governments. One unintended consequence of this rapid development is that many emerging ICTs have ethical implications that are not yet well understood. For example, they may fail to protect and advance core human values (life, health, happiness, security, resources, opportunities, and knowledge) (Bynum, 2011). Thus, they expose users to potential harm – during actual use or in the future.

This chapter contributes to the growing body of research on ethical implications of one popular emerging ICT - wearable devices. Drawing from theories of ICT ethics (a relatively new but rapidly evolving field), the chapter identifies the major challenges posed by wearable devices, and provides several guidelines on how these challenges can be addressed through ethically-informed design principles.

As existing ICTs are refined and new ICTs are developed to support the creation of new and improved products and services, technology-related ethical challenges will continue to emerge. We hope that this chapter can serve as an example of how these future ethical challenges can be categorized and analyzed, as a catalyst for discussion among practitioners and policy-makers, and as an educational tool that can help students and practitioners design, manage and use ICTs in an ethical way.

DISCUSSION POINTS

The following discussions points are provided for practitioners and policy makers interested in further exploring these issues:

- What are the ethical challenges facing the wearables industry today? How will these challenges evolve if the industry grows exponentially in the future as the Internet of Things is taking off?
- What are the user needs around wearable technologies and privacy?
- What are the relevant laws and regulations? How can these laws be improved? Are there any gaps that suggest a need for new laws?
- What is the status of our organization's ethical culture, governance system, and specific procedures? How can these be improved?
- What are the ethical challenges inherent in the technologies we develop and use? How can we address them?
- What ethical design principles (if any) are used during new technology development in our organization? How can we encourage adoption and use of such principles?
- What type of ethical training (if any) do we offer our employees? How can we do more in this area?

QUESTIONS

The following questions are suitable for use in an advanced undergraduate or graduate class focused on ethical issues of wearable technologies and other similar emerging ICTs. Using this chapter as a starting point, students are encouraged to gather additional information as needed and apply critical thinking skills in order to answer the questions.

- Wearables like Google Glass (a head-mounted glasses-like device that allowed users to access the Internet and record their environment) have been criticized for infringing on privacy rights though unauthorized recording of events. Do you agree with this assessment? Why or why not?
- Compare and contrast the reasonable expectation of privacy in your own country with those described in this chapter.
- Conduct an inventory of wearable devices you use. What are the main features of the user agreements for each one of them? What are the ethical challenges these agreements pose?
- Does the value of location-based services justify the potential risks from location information disclosure? Explain your reasoning.
- Pick a wearable technology that is popular among your peers. What do you think are its ethical challenges? Do any technology providers address any of these challenges though ethical design features? Why or why not? How can the technology be improved using the interventions outlined in this chapter?

- A provider of wearable technologies wants to aggregate data from its technology users in order to better understand usage patterns, and develop new products and services that can be customized for individual users. Is this ethical? Why or why not? Given your answer, what would be an appropriate course of action for the technology provider?
- A potential employer notices on your resume that you have completed an ICT ethics course, and wants to know more about it. How would you describe the value of the course for your education and future career?

ACKNOWLEDGMENT

Alina M. Chircu would like to acknowledge the premature passing of Prof. Marc L. Resnick during the developing stages of the manuscript.

REFERENCES

Accenture. (2014). *Eighty percent of consumers believe total data privacy no longer exists, Accenture survey finds*. Retrieved March 22, 2016, from https://newsroom.accenture.com/news/eighty-percent-of-consumers-believe-total-data-privacy-no-longer-exists-accenture-survey-finds.htm

Affectiva. (2016). *Technology*. Retrieved March 30, 2016, from http://www.affectiva.com/technology/

Begley, D. (2015, April 11). Uber safety dispute shows balance between personal choice, regulations. *The Houston Chronicle*. Retrieved March 30, 2016 from http://www.houstonchronicle.com/news/transportation/article/Uber-safety-dispute-shows-balance-between-6194128.php

Boehm, F. (2015). *A comparison between US and EU data protection legislation for law enforcement purposes*. European Parliament.

Brey, P. A. E. (2012). Anticipatory ethics for emerging technologies. *NanoEthics*, *6*(1), 1–13. doi:10.1007/s11569-012-0141-7

Bynum, T. (2011). Computer and information ethics. In *The Stanford Encyclopedia of Philosophy*. Retrieved October 1, 2015, from http://plato.stanford.edu/archives/spr2011/entries/ethics-computer/

Chircu, A. M. (2013). *Ethical implications of emerging ICTs*. Presented at the Bentley University's 2013 Fall Research Colloquium on Responsible Innovation: Environmental Sustainability, Financial Accountability, and Information and Communication Technology (ICT) Ethics, Waltham, MA.

Culnan, M. J., & Williams, C. C. (2009). How ethics can enhance organizational privacy: Lessons from the Choicepoint and TJX data breaches. *Management Information Systems Quarterly*, *33*(4), 673–687.

Dean, D., & Webb, C. (2011). Recovering from information overload. *The McKinsey Quarterly*, 1–9.

Disney. (2016). *Unlock the magic with your MagicBand or card*. Retrieved March 30, 2016, from https://disneyworld.disney.go.com/plan/my-disney-experience/bands-cards/

Farrugia, R. C. (2013). *Facebook and relationships: a study of how social media use is affecting long-term relationships*. (Masters Thesis). Rochester Institute of Technology.

FTC. (2016). Privacy choices for your personal financial information. *Federal Trade Commission*. Retrieved March 30, 2016, from https://www.consumer.ftc.gov/articles/0222-privacy-choices-your-personal-financial-information

Goodman, M. (2015). *Future crimes: Everything is connected, everyone is vulnerable, and what we can do about it*. New York, NY: Doubleday.

Heersmink, R., van den Hoven, J., & Timmermans, J. (2014). Normative issues report. *ETICA Project*. Retrieved October 1, 2015, from http://www.etica-project.eu/deliverable-files

Heersmink, R., van den Hoven, J., van Eck, N. J., & van den Berg, J. (2012). Bibliometric mapping of computer and information ethics. *Ethics and Information Technology*, *13*(3), 241–249. doi:10.1007/s10676-011-9273-7

Keith, M. J., Babb, J. S., & Lowry, P. B. (2014). A longitudinal study of information privacy on mobile devices. In *Proceedings of the 47th Hawaii International Conference on System Science*. Los Alamitos, CA: IEEE Computer Society. doi:10.1109/HICSS.2014.391

Lewis, C. (2014). *Irresistible apps: Motivational design patterns for apps, games, and web-based communities*. New York, NY: Apress Publishing. doi:10.1007/978-1-4302-6422-4

Llamas, R. T. (2015). *Worldwide wearables 2015-2019 forecast*. IDC.

Madden, M. (2014). *Public Perceptions of Privacy and Security in the Post-Snowden Era*. Pew Research Center.

Martin, K. (2016). Data aggregators, consumer data, and responsibility online: Who is tracking consumers and should they stop? *The Information Society, 32*(1), 51–63. doi:10.1080/01972243.2015.1107166

Michael, K. (2014). Redefining surveillance: Implications for privacy, security, trust and the law. *Issues Magazine*. Retrieved March 20, 2016, from http://www.issuesmagazine.com.au/article/issue-december-2014/redefining-surveillance-implications-privacy-security-trust-and-law.html

Michael, K. (2015). Sousveillance: Implications for privacy, security, trust, and the law. *IEEE Consumer Electronics Magazine, 4*(2), 92–94. doi:10.1109/MCE.2015.2393006

Mingers, J., & Walsham, G. (2010). Towards ethical information systems: The contributions of discourse ethics. *Management Information Systems Quarterly, 34*(4), 833–854.

Muise, A., Christofides, E., & Desmarais, S. (2009). More information than you ever wanted: Does Facebook bring out the green-eyed monster of jealousy. *Cyberpsychology & Behavior, 12*(4), 441–444. doi:10.1089/cpb.2008.0263 PMID:19366318

Narayanan, A. (2013). Privacy technologies: An annotated syllabus. In *Proceedings of PETS 2013 - The 13th Privacy Enhancing Technologies Symposium*.

NBC News. (2016, February 11). *Google 'Right to be forgotten' to be applied more widely*. Retrieved March 30, 2016, from http://www.nbcnews.com/tech/tech-news/google-right-be-forgotten-will-be-applied-more-widely-n516656

Ophir, E., Nass, C., & Wagner, A. D. (2009). Cognitive control in media multitaskers. *Proceedings of the National Academy of Sciences of the United States of America, 106*(97), 15583–15587. doi:10.1073/pnas.0903620106 PMID:19706386

Patterson, H. (2013). Contextual expectations of privacy in self-generated health information flows. In *Proceedings of TPRC 41: The 41st Research Conference on Communication, Information and Internet Policy*. Retrieved October 1, 2015 from http://ssrn.com/abstract=2242144

Pew Research Center. (2011). *How Mainstream Media Outlets Use Twitter*. Journalism and Media Technical Report. Retrieved August 1, 2015, from http://www.journalism.org/2011/11/14/how-mainstream-media-outlets-use-twitter

Pierce, D. (2015). How Apple designed its Watch to free us from our iPhones. *Wired, 23*(5), 98–105.

PRNewswire (2015). *M2M and wearable devices to help IoT service providers earn $231 billion in revenue according to 'The M2M, IoT & wearable technology ecosystem: 2015 - 2030'*. Author.

PwC. (2014). *The Wearable Future.* Price Waterhouse Coopers. Retrieved August 1, 2015, from http://www.pwc.com/cis

Resnick, M. (2013). *Ethical ICT to restore the privacy equilibrium.* Presented at the Bentley University's 2013 Fall Research Colloquium on Responsible Innovation: Environmental Sustainability, Financial Accountability, and Information and Communication Technology (ICT) Ethics, Waltham, MA.

Resnick, M. L. (2006). Risk Communication for legal, financial, and privacy agreements and mass media. In M. Wogalter (Ed.), *Handbook of Warnings*. Mahwah, NJ: Lawrence Erlbaum Associates, Inc.

Rose, F. (2015). The attention economy 3.0. *Milken Institute Review*, *17*(3), 42–50.

Savitskaya, Y. (2004). *Privacy negotiator for electronic commerce.* (Unpublished Masters Thesis). Florida International University, Miami, FL.

Sayer, P. (2015, December 16). EU privacy law to require opt-in and make data processors share in responsibility. *PCWorld*. Retrieved March 30, 2016, from http://www.pcworld.com/article/3015661/eu-privacy-law-to-require-opt-in-and-make-data-processors-share-in-responsibility.html

Stahl, B. C. (2011). Teaching ethical reflexivity in information systems: How to equip students to deal with moral and ethical issues of emerging information and communication technologies. *Journal of Information Systems Education*, *22*(3), 253–260.

Tan, A. Z. Y., Chua, W. Y., & Chang, K. T. T. Location based services and information privacy concerns among literate and semi-literate users. In *Proceedings of the 47th Hawaii International Conference on System Science*. Los Alamitos, CA: IEEE Computer Society. doi:10.1109/HICSS.2014.394

TechTarget. (2016). *De-anonymization (deanonymization)*. Retrieved March 21, 2016, from http://whatis.techtarget.com/definition/de-anonymization-deanonymization

Turkle, S. (2015). *Reclaiming conversation: The power of talk in the digital age.* New York, NY: Penguin Press.

Utz, S., & Beukeboom, C. J. (2011). The role of social network sites in romantic relationships: Effects on jealousy and relationship happiness. *Journal of Computer-Mediated Communication*, *16*(4), 511–527. doi:10.1111/j.1083-6101.2011.01552.x van den Hoven, J., Helbing, D., Pedrescri, D., Domingo-Ferrer, J., Gianotti, F., & Christen, M. (2012). *FuturICT – the road towards ethical ICT.* arXiv 1210.8181v1

Weber, R. H. (2015). The digital future – A challenge for privacy? *Computer Law & Security Report, 31*(2), 234–242. doi:10.1016/j.clsr.2015.01.003

Weise, E. (2015, December 14). New EU privacy rule could cost U.S. firms billions. *USA Today.* Retrieved March 20, 2016, from http://www.usatoday.com/story/life/web-to-watch/tech-gaming/2015/12/14/eu-european-union-privacy-directive-google-facebook/77314554/

Wex Legal Dictionary. (2016). Retrieved March 20, 2016, from https://www.law.cornell.edu/wex

KEY TERMS AND DEFINITIONS

Activity Tracker: A wearable device that collects data about user's daily activities, such as steps walked, exercise, sleep, and others. Activity trackers are often paired with a smartphone or computer application that allows the user to run reports and analyze the data. Popular brands included Fitbit, Garmin, Polar, Misfit, and Jawbone.

Big Data: A data set characterized by large volume (size of data set), high velocity (speed of collection and transfer), high variety (diversity of structure and formats), and variable veracity (accuracy, or quality of data points).

Ethics: A branch of philosophy concerned with understanding behavior and what makes it right or wrong.

Internet of Things (IoT): The growing set of interconnected, sensor-equipped objects, devices, vehicles, and buildings that can exchange information and be controlled remotely, over the Internet.

Radio-frequency Identification (RFID): A wireless technology used to transmit data over short distances using electromagnetic fields. It can be used to automate data transmission between an object equipped with an RFID tag and an RFID reader.

Smart Watch: A computerized device, worn like a watch, with advanced activity tracking and smartphone interaction features, among others.

Smartphone: A mobile phone with computer-like features and user interface. Smartphones offer users the ability to place and receive calls, text, browse the Internet, and run various applications ("apps"). Smartphones require a supporting mobile (cellular) network with data transmission capabilities.

Wearable Device: A device that can be worn or carried by a user and has embedded sensors (to collect information about the user's activities), software (to enable processing of the information), and network connectivity (to enable remote data storage, synchronization, and exchange, as well as additional processing capabilities).

Chapter 9
What Can People Do with Your Spatial Data?
Socio–Ethical Scenarios

Roba Abbas
University of Wollongong, Australia

Katina Michael
University of Wollongong, Australia

M. G. Michael
University of Wollongong, Australia

ABSTRACT

Location-Based Services (LBS) provide value-added solutions to users based on location or position information and other contextual data. They enable the collection of GPS data logs or location chronicles, and may be deployed on a range of devices, many of which presently come in the form of commercially available product solutions with corresponding applications. This chapter presents the outcomes of an observational study of LBS users, which was designed to gauge user perspectives in relation to LBS socio-ethical dilemmas. The focus is on the outcomes of a spatial analysis exercise, which resulted in the development of a series of scenarios (in map format) that demonstrate varying LBS usability contexts. The scenarios range across various risk levels, and can be used as further input into consultative practices that are centered on the socio-ethical implications of LBS usage. Additionally, the results of the LBS observational study can be utilized to inform the need for LBS regulation. Future research directions are proposed, allowing for the study to be extended to wider contexts.

DOI: 10.4018/978-1-5225-1016-1.ch009

INTRODUCTION

Location-based services (LBS) provide value-added solutions to users based on location or position information, and on other contextual data. They enable the collection of GPS data logs or location chronicles, and may be deployed on a range of devices, many of which presently come in the form of commercially available product solutions. These include, but are not limited to, in-car/vehicle data loggers, dedicated handheld or wearable GPS devices, and GPS- or location-enabled smart phones. In considering the socio-ethical (including privacy and security) issues pertaining to LBS usage, it is important examine user perspectives regarding the technology, and in particular their attitudes regarding location disclosure. This chapter presents a series of socio-ethical scenarios that allow such attitudes to be gauged, thereby spatially reporting on the outcomes of an observational study of LBS users, previously analyzed in Abbas (2010) and Abbas (2011). A summary of this earlier analysis is offered, and a series of spatial maps are put forward as an alternative, visual, representation of the thematic outcomes. Future research directions, such as the regulatory and public policy implications of the study, are discussed.

BACKGROUND: WILLINGNESS TO DISCLOSE LOCATION INFORMATION

This chapter, in essence, focuses on the socio-ethical dilemmas associated with LBS usage, from the perspective of the users themselves. Literature in this domain is primarily focused on location disclosure amongst social relations, such as friends and family, and specifically on the willingness of users to reveal location information to individuals, both within their social circle and extending also to strangers.

Prior ethics and social implications literature address the complexities associated with the themes of control, trust, privacy and security. These complexities arise from the intimate relationships between those themes and their sporadic presentation in relevant scholarship. There are few studies that simultaneously cover all four themes. Specifically, there is a lack of research that covers the *socio-ethical dilemmas* and *usability* related factors of location tracking and monitoring. Whilst previous studies have addressed one or more themes related to control, trust, privacy and security, in many cases they have not done so concurrently and/or explicitly.

Several studies have, however, been conducted that concentrate specifically on the attitudes of users with respect to location information disclosure, monitoring and tracking amongst social relations, which may include *friends*, *parents*, *other family members*, *employers*, and *strangers* (Levin et al. 2008, pp. 81-82), all of whom can be considered "friends" in the social networking environment. A major focus of these studies is on the collection of GPS/location data, and on the readiness of a user to disclose location information to members in a given social context, in addition to the consequent social implications of revealing such sensitive personal location information and of tracking activities in general. These studies have been identified and discussed in Abbas (2011), and are summarized in Table 1. It is noteworthy that this chapter is not intended to provide a complete literature review on location disclosure amongst social relations; rather a number of representative examples are given.

When collectively compared, the studies reveal common methodological characteristics; that is, the majority of the research is focused on some form of observational or field study, in which location information is gathered using a suitable LBS application and usability issues are examined, after which a reflection or interview process follows. Thus in examining control, trust, privacy and security related issues, any study on LBS socio-ethical dilemmas must address issues of usability and location disclosure amongst social relations, thereby enabling the themes and associated socio-ethical challenges to be practically, as opposed to theoretically, explored. For a detailed discussion of literature pre-2011, refer to Abbas (2011).

Further studies in this field, published since Abbas (2011), have persisted in a similar manner, examining location disclosure in relation to a particular theme, and/ or a specific social relation. In terms of theme, studies based on privacy calculus models are prominent. Two common and demonstrative examples are offered. Sun et al. (2015) maintain that individuals' willingness or intention to disclose information in the location-based social networking (LBSN) environment is relative to the link between perceived benefits and the possible privacy threats, whereby gender specific differences play an important role. The authors provide a review of literature on information disclosure and privacy, and their interview-based study employs the privacy calculus model to quantitatively understand information disclosure intentions.

Zhao et al. (2012) similarly utilize a privacy calculus model to assess disclosure behaviors in the LBSN environment, reporting that the disclosure of location-related information is relative to perceived benefits and privacy risks. The results of Zhao et al.'s study show that the existence of privacy controls and privacy policies aid in alleviating users' privacy concerns.

More recent research into location disclosure amongst social relations follows a similar approach to those summarized in Table 1. For example, Bentley et al. (2015) present a system for location-sharing between "strong-tie social relationships" (Bentley et al, 2015:4) i.e. friends and family members, to aid in planning and coordinating location-related events. The study provided the option for the participants (20 in total) to record a voicemail diary at the end of each day, and an interview was conducted at the completion of the 21-day exercise. Bentley et al's study found that certain

Table 1. Summary of studies concerning location disclosure amongst social relations

Author(s)	Research Focus	Methodology
Consolvo et al. (2005)	Users' willingness to disclose location information to individuals in their social circle & the ensuing privacy implications.	Three-phased study utilizing experience sampling method over two-week period, requiring users to respond to hypothetical requests, diary component and reflection task.
Michael et al. (2006)	Implications of GPS monitoring on an individual.	Recording of GPS data log over two-week period, while simultaneously reflecting on the process through daily diary entries.
Anthony et al. (2007)	Users' readiness to disclose location information, upon receiving requests, in specific contexts and with various individuals.	Employed experience sampling methodology over one-week period, in which participants were asked to respond to pager requests by completing the corresponding questionnaire, after which an interview was conducted.
Brown et al. (2007)	Trial of the 'Whereabouts Clock' (WAC), a device that provides family members with location details about each other, to determine attitudes regarding usability, tracking and integration into specific households.	Tracking of family members using mobile phones over six-month period, where location information was displayed on the WAC. Supportive interviews were performed at one-week intervals.
Iqbal & Lim (2007)	The privacy risks of GPS data collection and profiling using telematics systems.	Experiment involving collection of GPS data from volunteers and analysis/ processing of this data to generate profiles and draw inferences.
Barkhuus et al. (2008)	Trial of 'Connecto', a friend-finder application running on a mobile phone that enables automatic location & status updates amongst social groups, to reveal nature of usability amongst individuals and impact on behavior.	Two-week study conducted, in which participants were required to integrate the application into their daily life, while completing a daily diary entry and two interviews at one-week intervals.
Seeburger & Schroeter (2009)	Usability & functionality tests of 'Disposal Maps', a mobile-phone based location sharing software.	Usability tests were performed over three-week period using iPhone running Disposable Maps application.
Toch et al. (2009)	Trial of 'Locaccino', a Facebook-based LBS application facilitating location sharing amongst individuals, to examine their sharing preferences and privacy settings.	Phased field study over four-week period involving a survey prior to the trial, deployment of application, use of application and survey at conclusion of trial.
Tsai et al. (2009)	Trial of 'Locyoution', a Facebook-based location sharing application with an additional software component, to establish the importance of feedback in relation to location sharing & privacy concerns.	Phased field trial over four-week period involving initial survey, installation of system, use of system and survey at completion of trial.
Boesen et al. (2010)	Use of LBS for tracking purposes amongst family members and the resulting implications.	Phased observational study of four families over two-week period, which included initial interview, diary recording tracking activities, interview to gauge attitudes regarding diaries and a practical location tracking exercise.

continued on following page

Table 1. Continued

Author(s)	Research Focus	Methodology
Jedrzejczyk et al. (2010)	Trial of the 'Buddy Tracker' mobile location sharing application to explore the effect of feedback on users' conduct and therefore impact of acceptance.	Field trial conducted over three-week period, focus group and interview.
Mancini et al. (2010)	Implications of accurate location tracking through trial of 'Buddy Tracker' mobile location sharing application.	Mobile phone-based field study over three-week period based on experience sampling method and supplementary interview process.
Tang et al. (2010)	Comparison of the impact of social-driven (one-to-many) versus purpose-driven (one-to-one) forms of location disclosure.	Two-week user investigation entailing multiple components, such as an initial survey, location data logging task and interviews based on logs.
Fusco et al. (2010; 2011)	Impact of location-based social networking (LBSN) on trust for five types of relationships among friends.	Focus group methodology, relying on user responses to a number of scenarios.
Gasson et al. (2011)	Privacy implications of data mining and profiling using GPS data.	Tracking exercise conducted over six-week period, involving the collection of GPS data logs.

features of the application were beneficial and decreased stress levels, and while privacy was raised as a possible concern it was not particularly prevalent given that the social relations of interest were friends and family members.

It is evident in recent studies, however, that there is an increased recognition of the need to concentrate on participants from diverse age groups. For instance, a study by Thomas et al. (2013) recruited 86 participants from the older adult population for a one-week LBS usability study, requiring participants to complete question-naires prior to, and post, LBS use. Detailed interviews were also conducted for 20 selected participants. The study focused on the concerns of this participant group, and whereas participants were initially concerned about the privacy-invasive na-ture of the technology prior to using the technology, they were less so after usage. However, other concerns were also expressed, in particular, a perception that the technology would be considered, not as socially positive, but rather as assistive, implying its user's infirmity.

In all of the aforementioned studies, there is an apparent lack of examination of the spatial component; that is, the power of geographic information system mapping has not been harnessed, particularly as a means of analyzing the location chronicles of users (where collected) in order to emphasize thematic and descriptive findings. Explicitly, the use of spatial scenarios and illustrations in conjunction with the thematic mapping presented in Abbas (2011) is yet to be explored.

This chapter attempts to build on the original thematic mapping exercise by demonstrating the merits of spatial analysis and mapping in understanding the socio-ethical implications of LBS, as articulated by LBS users. Prior to presenting the spatial analysis technique and corresponding maps, a summary of the thematic results, published in Abbas (2011), is provided in the following section.

OBSERVATIONAL STUDY OF LBS USERS: SUMMARY OF THEMATIC FINDINGS

Abbas (2011) offers an observational study methodology that allows for LBS user attitudes to be gauged, the research design of which is based largely on the aforementioned literature (pre-2011) and on relevant socio-technical studies. The research thematically depicts the socio-ethical implications of LBS, demonstrating the benefits and concerns of LBS usage from the perspective of users. The study requested that participants maintain, over a 2-week period, a digital location chronicle, comprising a global positioning system data log, a daily diary entry component and a personal reflection exercise. The primary intention was for participants to observe, reflect and record their experiences during and at the completion of the participant observation, in order to reveal the ensuing collective consequences of LBS usage.

The research was essentially built on the LBS usability study conducted by Abbas (2010), and as a result focuses on the Gen-Y or young adult participant group, widely recognised as eager users of technological solutions, including location-based social networking applications. The crux of the research is the significance of LBS usage in a given social context, whereby participants were prompted to reflect on their willingness to be monitored or tracked by a partner, parent, friend, employer and/or stranger. The 2011 study found that the users' willingness to grant access to location details is reliant on a number of factors; notably, the level of trust within a specific relationship, the perceived privacy threat, the degree of desired control, and the perceived personal security and safety threats.

These outcomes are the result of a qualitative, thematic analysis, focusing on the diary entries and personal reflections gathered from participants, and are therefore reliant on excerpts obtained directly from the diary entries and/or user reflections. The results are grouped by relationship type (e.g. partner) and the dominant theme for that type (e.g. trust), and principally exhibit the benefits and concerns of LBS usage in each of the respective relationship types. The benefits and concerns emerging from the study are summarized in Figure 1.

The thematic analysis results can further be reinforced through the development of socio-ethical dilemmas in the form of a series of spatial scenarios, based on both the thematic narrative and the corresponding participant GPS data logs. The injec-

Figure 1. User perspectives on the benefits and concerns of LBS usage

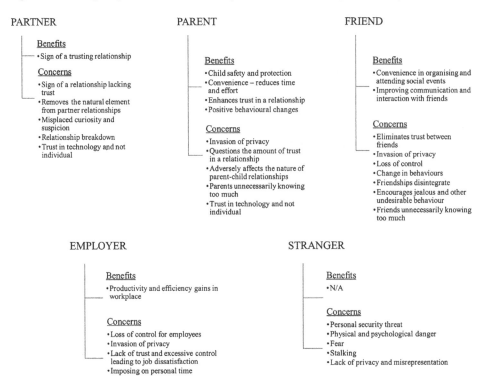

tion of the spatial element provides graphical scenarios with a multitude of advantages. The spatial component and its significance is the focus of the remainder of this chapter.

OBSERVATIONAL STUDY OF LBS USERS: SOCIO-ETHICAL FINDINGS AND SPATIAL SCENARIOS

The Use of Scenarios

In ICT research, scenarios are employed to evaluate potential futures and manage "future uncertainty" (Bria et al. 2001, p. 26). As such, and in the context of technology and telecommunications, Bria et al. (2001, p. 26) define a scenario as "a tool to explore a possible, plausible future by identifying key technical and social developments required for it to be realized." It is not to be used as a means of forecasting the future, but rather for developing an appreciation of a future state of affairs.

While personalized LBS applications offer recommendation and prediction features to users (Bao et al. 2015), Camponovo et al. (2005:3) states that scenario planning, unlike the traditional form of forecasting, is useful for examining "a broad range of potential futures", as opposed to limiting the assessment to a single possibility. In the information systems discipline, specifically in relation to systems development, scenarios are valuable in that they provide a way in which system complexities can be resolved and analyzed (Alexander, 2004). Furthermore, scenarios can be presented in forms ranging from simple stories through to complicated analyses. Fundamental to all forms of scenarios are that they are built on a series of actions and involve storytelling (Alexander 2004).

Story-based scenarios have been used in studies relating to the ethical and social implications of technology for many years, for example, in the fields of computer ethics (Artz, 1998) and artificial intelligence (Epstein, 2000). Significant to this chapter, scenarios have been favored in previous LBS-related studies. For instance, Perusco and Michael (2007) rely on scenarios for the explanation of a possible future state in relation to LBS applications. The authors present their scenarios in short-story format, in order to reveal the ethical challenges associated with LBS, employing the Track, Analyze, Image, Decide, Act (TAIDA) scenario-planning framework, whilst analysis adheres to the deconstruction approach (Perusco and Michael 2007). Dobson and Fischer (2007, p. 320) also present "visions of the future", in which two conflicting scenarios are offered, exploring the "beautiful" and "dark" visions that can possibly be achieved with the use of digital and human tracking technologies.

Other relevant studies also feature scenarios. For example, Sheng et al. (2008, p. 355) adopt a scenario-based approach in order to examine "the emerging u-commerce [ubiquitous-commerce] phenomenon", addressing prospective issues that have not yet materialized. Damiani et al. (2007) outline an LBS usage scenario to examine LBS security requirements. Patel (2004) provides a scenario concerning location tracking of teenagers. Hansen et al. (2005) explore two healthcare-related scenarios relevant to location-aware applications, and Tatli et al. (2005) describe a number of LBS use case examples, in order to assess the associated security challenges.

Ghinita (2013) makes use of scenarios and usability contexts to highlight the potential for LBS applications to be privacy-invasive. Yu et al. (2015) propose two prototype applications, which detail varying LBS usage scenarios in a University campus setting. The corresponding scenarios are put forward in narrative form, and are supported by the graphical (map) application prototypes. The intention of Yu et al.'s work is to identify the power of predictive LBS applications in encouraging 'meet-up' opportunities based on the relative location of individuals. Additionally, Aloudat (2011) made use of vignettes in a survey of user attitudes regarding the deployment of LBS in specific emergency situations, producing scenarios that represent LBS in both a positive and a less desirable light.

In these studies, the scenarios, visions and use cases, were created to provide insights into various aspects of LBS and location-aware applications. As such, the scenarios were forms of input or data that required further analysis. The fundamental contribution of this chapter, however, is that the scenarios are the result of the spatial analysis of participant location chronicles, enabling practical reinforcement of the thematic results summarized above, and in greater detail in Abbas (2011). The spatial analysis process is detailed in the following sections.

Spatial Analysis

In an article examining the varying methodologies and methods of spatial analysis, Baur et al. (2014) provide an in-depth critique on the idea of the 'space' in spatial analysis, describing space as a "multi-level phenomenon" whereby the varying spatial layers are inextricably linked (p.15). The author argues that a wide range of methods exist for spatial analysis, which currently require some form of assimilation. While this is beyond the focus of this chapter, Baur et al.'s research provides an appreciation for the complexities associated with the concepts of space and spatial analysis, and flags the significance of recognizing that many forms and methods of spatial analysis exist.

For the purpose of this chapter, spatial analysis is defined as a technique whereby a geographic information system (GIS) application is utilized in the analysis of spatial data. Taylor and Blewitt (2006:8) define GIS as "the overall name for a continuum of systems ranging from those that display maps for visualization purposes... to those that provide very powerful spatial and statistical analysis of spatial and related data and those providing full immersive virtual environments..." With respect to this investigation, spatial analysis activities were conducted using MapInfo Professional, a "mapping and geographic analysis application" that offers "location intelligence" capabilities (Pitney Bowes, 2012).

Spatial analysis "ranges from a simple query about the spatial phenomenon to complicated combinations of attribute queries, spatial queries, and alterations of original data" (Chou 1997: 15). This investigation involved conducting spatial queries through the manipulation of the raw GPS logs in order to deliver scenarios that were supportive and representative of the socio-ethical narrative resulting from the thematic analysis process detailed in Abbas (2011). A phased spatial analysis process was devised to ensure the consistent and systematic creation of the spatial scenarios.

Figure 2. Spatial analysis process

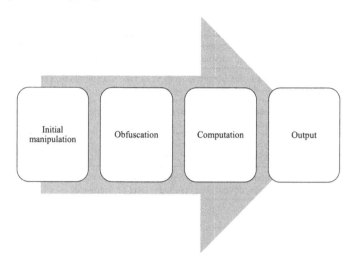

Phases of Spatial Analysis

The stages of spatial analysis (see Figure 2) adopted for this research included initial manipulation, obfuscation, computation and output, devised using relevant literature and the MapInfo software application. *Initial manipulation* was the preliminary stage of the data analysis process and it focused on the preparation of raw participant GPS data logs. This stage involved selecting participant data logs containing sufficient records and exporting those logs into CSV file format to be utilized by MapInfo. The CSV file was then imported into MapInfo by creating the relevant database table.

The subsequent stage involved the *obfuscation* of participant data in order to maintain location privacy and to ensure that the data cannot be linked to a specific participant or individual. Obfuscation is a necessary technique that involves the intentional degradation of location information quality, for the purpose of protecting privacy (Duckham and Kulik 2005). Brush et al. (2010) examine the usefulness of various obfuscation methods, and identify five distinct types of obfuscation. These include, deleting, randomizing, discretizing, subsampling and mixing. Adapted from the work of Brush et al. (2010), Table 2 summarizes these obfuscation methods. With respect to LBS the obfuscation of location details must attempt to balance the location privacy of the individual with functionality/usefulness (Duckham and Kulik 2005).

In the context of this investigation, however, maintaining an acceptable degree of location quality (for functionality purposes) was not a significant issue as the focus was predominantly on the creation of scenarios supporting the thematic results

Table 2. Overview of obfuscation methods

Obfuscation Method	Description
Deleting	Involves the removal of data within a certain level of proximity from an individual's home or other significant locations.
Randomizing	Entails the random movement of GPS data points by a specified amount in order to conceal exact location.
Discretizing	Conceals exact location in favor of providing a square or region in which the actual location exists.
Subsampling	Involves selective removal of data points to create deliberate gaps in location information, providing only partial details of a particular route.
Mixing	Entails combining GPS data of multiple individuals within a specified reason, deliberately creating a level of confusion.

Adapted from Brush et al. (2010).

of the observational study. As a result, a combination of four defined obfuscation techniques was employed, namely deleting, randomizing, subsampling and mixing. Discretizing did not apply due to the fact that it would detract from presentation on the two-dimensional maps presented in this chapter, and potentially affect the ability to comprehend the depicted scenario.

Once the data had been sufficiently obfuscated, the *computation* process followed through the creation of various map layers in the GIS application, each of which contained specific types of information that combine to produce the overall map. An example is provided in Figure 3. Computation activities involved:

1. Importing all relevant country and state boundaries and datasets (in this instance, for Australia and New South Wales respectively),
2. Overlaying this data with a random selection of participant GPS logs on which the necessary obfuscation method(s) had been performed,
3. Creating the simple queries required for depicting the sequence of events in a given scenario, and
4. Inserting all additional labels, titles and aesthetic details to result in a comprehensible layered map.

It should be noted that this exercise was chiefly concerned with displaying each scenario in the most simplistic and understandable form, rather than on justifying the selection of specific computational methods.

The final stage within the spatial analysis process was *output* in which the layered maps were exported into a two-dimension map as illustrated in this chapter, with each map representing a single scenario.

Figure 3. Computation of obfuscated participant location information using Map-Info layers

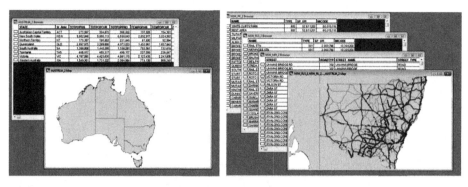

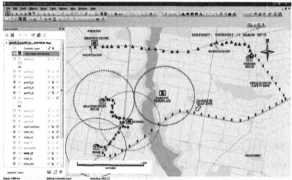

Corresponding spatial scenario
produced using computational
techniques & aesthetic elements

SOCIO-ETHICAL SCENARIOS

The following scenarios are established as representative of the socio-ethical dilemmas pertaining to LBS. They are intended to reinforce the thematic mapping, and to allow for further investigation of LBS socio-ethical implications by exploiting the potential of spatial mapping. The scenarios represent a variety of LBS usability contexts, ranging from those generally perceived by observational study participants as positive and involving less risk, through to less desirable notions entailing increased risk levels. The risk levels themselves are the standard risk categories adapted from Emergency Management Australia (2004), and range from the low/minor risk level to the extreme/catastrophic form. The corresponding scenarios cover consumer (monitoring of family and friends), business (employee monitoring), and government (emergency management) LBS applications or usability contexts, thereby ensuring that a comprehensive set of scenarios is representatively portrayed. Figure 4 illustrates the socio-ethical scenarios and the associated risk levels.

Figure 4. Socio-ethical scenarios and corresponding risk levels

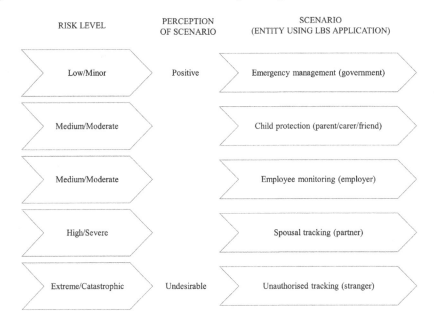

The spatial scenarios are portrayed below in a geographic information systems map format and contain the following components: the sequence of events in each situation (narrative), the equivalent map legend, and the actual spatial scenario modelled using participant GPS data logs.

Scenario One: Emergency Management (Government)

1. On Monday morning, 15th March 2010, a bush fire is blazing near the University of Wollongong, Australia. At 8:33am, the danger zone is identified depending on distance from the fire and its severity.
2. Emergency services personnel receive timely information from location-enabled mobile devices in the vicinity. Individuals within the defined danger zone receive frequent alerts and evacuation procedures based on proximity to an emergency zone, and other factors such as mode of transport, speed and direction.
3. Emergency services personnel initiate their response using the provided information, and the situation is managed in the appropriate manner.

Figure 5. Scenario one legend

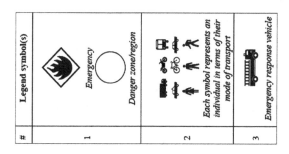

Figure 6. Scenario one depicting an emergency management situation, derived from obfuscated participant GPS data logs

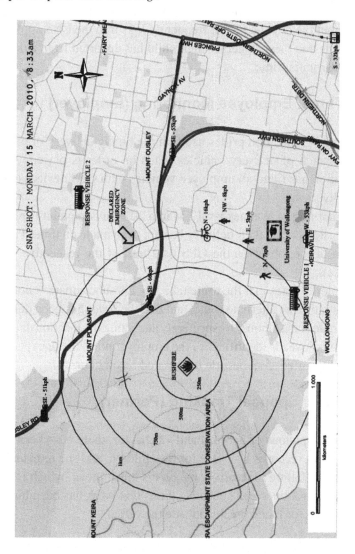

Scenario Two: Child Protection (Parent/Carer/Friend)

1. On Thursday 11 March 2010, a child makes various journeys throughout the day, such as attending school between 9am and 3pm, going from school to grandmother's house for after school care from 3pm to 4pm and travelling to a friend's house from 4pm to 5pm unaccompanied. At 5:30pm, the child departs the friend's house and travels by train to a local shopping center, remaining there until 7pm.
2. The child is equipped with a GPS wristwatch that records their whereabouts and journeys made throughout the day as a set of geographical coordinates. The location data, through a real-time feed, is transmitted to the corresponding subscription-based LBS application and updated on a map that contains defined safety zones within a certain distance from specified points of interest.
3. Throughout the day the parent frequently logs into the LBS application from work/home and views whether their child has departed from a defined safety zone at particular time.

Scenario Three: Employee Monitoring (Employer)

1. A catering organization prides itself on the timely delivery of orders and the quick dispatch of delivery vehicles when an order is placed. As such, the organization has fitted all employee vehicles with GPS devices to coordinate daily deliveries.
2. On the morning of Wednesday 17 March 2010, a complaint is received from a loyal customer that their delivery has not been made on time. The employer, from the office, observes the GPS data trail of the respective vehicle (and employee).
3. The employer notes that the route taken by his subordinate is not the optimal path, but rather an alternate route, and that the order has been delivered some forty minutes late. Upon retrospectively analyzing the location data, the unproductive employee is identified, as the employer notes the unexpected stop-off at a nearby coffee shop outside designated lunch hours.

Scenario Four: Spousal Tracking (Partner)

1. A wife is suspicious of her husband's behavior; there have been many hours spent at work recently, less time for the children, and she remains puzzled by her partner's failure to return home on his lunch break, which is part of their typical daily routine. Her husband claims that work has been busy and there is rarely time for lunch breaks outside the office.

Figure 7. Scenario two legend

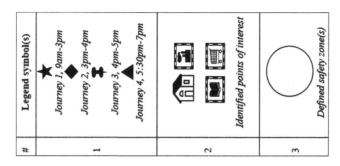

Figure 8. Scenario two depicting a child monitoring situation, derived from obfuscated participant GPS data logs

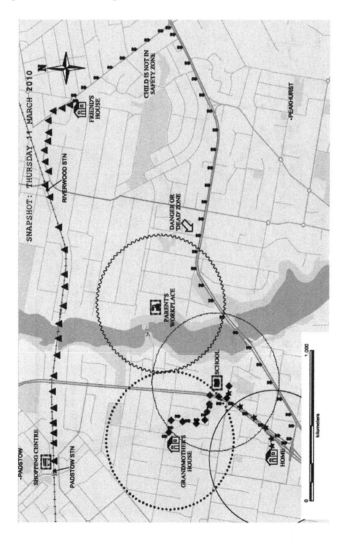

Figure 9. Scenario three legend

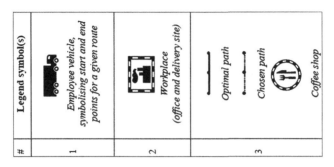

Figure 10. Scenario three depicting an employee monitoring situation, derived from obfuscated participant GPS data logs

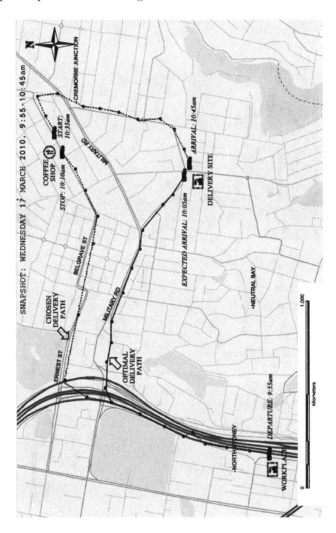

Figure 11. Scenario four legend

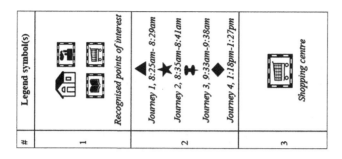

Figure 12. Scenario four depicting a spousal tracking situation, derived from ob-fuscated participant GPS data logs

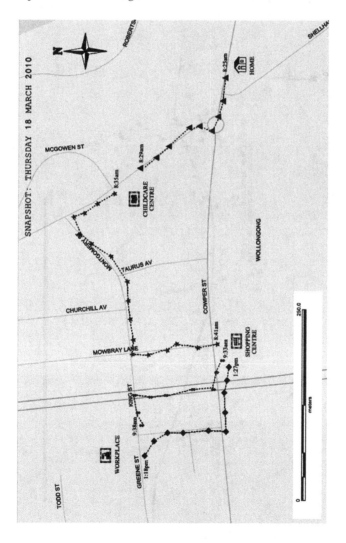

Figure 13. Scenario five legend

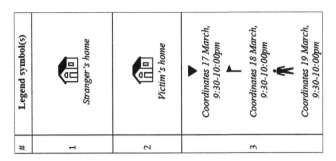

Figure 14. Scenario five depicting an unauthorized tracking situation, derived from obfuscated participant GPS data logs over three days

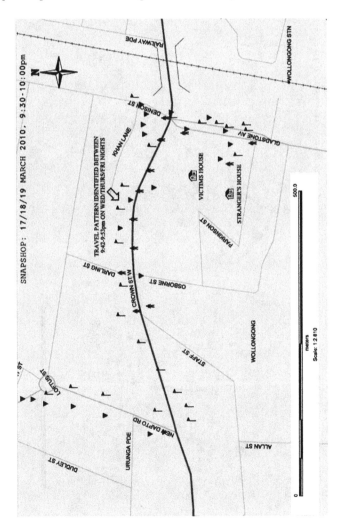

2. The wife, fed up with the deteriorating situation, installs location-tracking software on her husband's mobile phone, and is able to monitor his daily activities and journeys. This includes the journey to the childcare center in the morning to drop off their toddler, followed by his path to work, and back home in the afternoon.

3. Upon monitoring her husband's location chronicle via an online system for a week, the wife notes her partner's late arrival to work and repeated daily trips to the local shopping center. On Thursday 18 March 2010, the wife decides to surprise her husband on his lunch break at the shopping center and confront him with his location data log, demanding an explanation.

Scenario Five: Unauthorized Tracking (Stranger)

1. The stranger identifies the victim, who lives within close walking distance of his home. The stranger has, on many occasions, attempted to capture the attention of the individual, but all previous efforts have failed.

2. A GPS tracking device is covertly installed under the victim's vehicle in the early hours of the morning.

3. The stranger consistently views the location of the victim, noting a pattern on Wednesday, Thursday, and Friday nights, as the victim can be found taking a similar path between 9:42pm and 9:53pm. This information has set the stage for a 'chance' meeting away from the victim's home.

SOLUTIONS AND RECOMMENDATIONS

The LBS observational study involved an examination and presentation of the socio-ethical dilemmas pertaining to LBS usage. Through the creation of a series of scenarios, multiple usability contexts were evaluated and compared. The authors use this public consultation process with prospective consumers/users as a basis for influencing LBS regulatory choices and policy. For instance, Figure 15 depicts the collective user perspective on the need for LBS regulation.

The scenarios, and associated thematic analysis summarized earlier in the chapter, suggested that in regulating LBS, the positive and less desirable usability contexts must be simultaneously recognized and factored into any given LBS regulatory framework. That is, potentially positive uses, such as LBS for emergency situations, must be supported. However, more sinister uses, such as cyber/physical stalking and unauthorized access to location information, should be prohibited by law. Yet, at the same time it is recognized that flexibility and choice for users is paramount and should be maintained in a chosen regulatory framework. That is,

Figure 15. User perspective on the need for LBS regulation

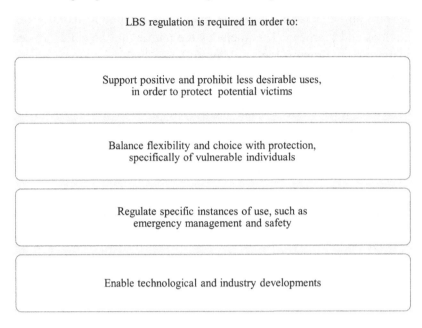

LBS regulation is required in order to:

> Support positive and prohibit less desirable uses, in order to protect potential victims

> Balance flexibility and choice with protection, specifically of vulnerable individuals

> Regulate specific instances of use, such as emergency management and safety

> Enable technological and industry developments

any suggested framework must recognize that restricting potentially dangerous LBS solutions from use might prevent legitimate everyday uses of LBS, which is an objectionable outcome. Rather, attention should be paid to supporting regulation in specific instances and usability contexts. For example, the emergency services context is a situation in which regulation may prove necessary, given that emergency and public safety applications affect all citizens.

In developing a regulatory regime for LBS, a number of supplementary factors should be considered:

1.   In addition to the user perspective presented in this paper and in related work, alternate stakeholder perspectives must be accounted for; namely, the viewpoints of industry and government bodies,

2.   Any proposed regulatory response should incorporate and reflect on multiple approaches to regulation, such as legislation (laws), co-regulation through supporting technological mechanisms (technical guidelines, standards and embedded regulatory instruments), and self-regulation through policies/codes (internal organizational policies/codes of practice and ethical/moral codes of conduct). Only then can a comprehensive regulatory response be proposed that will account for the innumerable usability contexts.

Comprehensive and well-considered regulatory regimes understandably take time to develop and enforce, but in the meantime there are immediate benefits to be garnered from the results presented throughout this chapter. These include, in the first instance, educational materials and public awareness campaigns based both on the thematic and, importantly, on the spatial analyses. It should be noted that while the spatial (map) scenarios presented within this chapter are two-dimensional for illustrative purposes, they are in actual fact layered three-dimension maps that may be also be displayed in an interactive manner. This is particularly valuable for educational purposes in that the full potential of LBS applications becomes apparent.

Secondly, the results of the observational study can be utilized as further input into wider consultative processes to encourage collaboration amongst industry stakeholders. An example established by the authors is a discussion paper (refer to Appendix 1) that transforms the spatial scenarios into an equivalent series of storyboards (see Figure 16) for consultation by industry and government stakeholders.

The discussion paper and associated consultation process was intended to provoke responses from industry and government participants regarding the need for LBS regulation in Australia based on the identified socio-ethical dilemmas. As such, the storyboards range from the positive through to the less desirable uses of LBS, and

Figure 16. Discussion paper storyboards

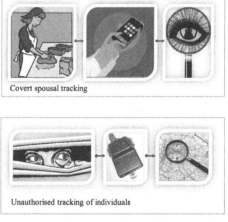

offer a simplified introduction to the various LBS usability contexts. They also provide valuable information for developers of LBS applications (namely, industry) that may be considered in application development processes. The results from the consultation process are beyond the scope of this chapter. This is nonetheless an example demonstrating the manner in which the outcomes of the LBS observational study can be exploited.

FUTURE RESEARCH DIRECTIONS

It is recommended that the both the thematic and spatial outcomes of the LBS observational study of users be utilized as the basis for future research. It is crucial that further research follow a stringent human research ethics clearance process prior to engaging with LBS stakeholders, and it should be noted that this research[1] forms only phase one of a broader study on LBS regulation in Australia. The remaining components of the study include collaboration and consultation with industry stakeholders (phase two) and government agencies (phase three), thereby representing all stakeholders in the LBS value chain. For further reading, refer to Abbas et al. (2013, 2014; 2015a; 2015b), and Abbas (2010; 2011).

The three research phases collectively enable the varying perspectives (user, industry and government) to be used as a means of informing policy-making and regulatory processes. As such, there are numerous suggestions for further research.

In a broad sense, the research covered the technical, social and environmental issues pertaining to LBS, notably privacy and security considerations. This chapter, in particular, spatially illustrated the LBS socio-ethical dilemmas from the perspective of users in the Australian context. It is suggested that future research examines international/alternative contexts to allow comparisons to be made. Additionally, the study concentrated on Gen-Y users; therefore, it may be valuable to focus on an alternative sample to identify any similarities and/or discrepancies.

The theoretical/methodological design of this research was socio-technical in nature, addressing the social, technical and environmental factors in the LBS ecosystem within the Australian context. The process of engagement with participants was largely consultative, based on the unification of socio-technical theory, the social informatics perspective and policy-making approaches. Future research could involve assessing the validity of the process in international contexts and for alternative emerging, particularly wearable, technologies. This can then be supplemented by cross-cultural comparisons.

Another important pragmatic direction would involve developing tools and materials to disseminate research outcomes to diverse audiences, an example of which was given in the preceding section. This may comprise awareness/educational campaigns for users, materials to aid in the policy-making and regulatory processes, and design/development recommendations that feed into the establishment of ethically sound LBS solutions.

CONCLUSION

This chapter offered the results of an LBS observational study, which was designed to articulate the socio-ethical concerns pertaining to LBS from the perspective of users. A series of socio-ethical scenarios were presented in spatial (map) format, and covered a range of LBS usability contexts, ranging from those associated with minor levels of risk such as emergency management through to high risk situations such as unauthorized tracking by a stranger. Importantly, the scenarios demonstrated that LBS could be employed in many situations to generate benefits for users and other members of society. However, the covert and unauthorized applications raised serious concerns among the participants. These outcomes are significant as they inform LBS regulatory choices in that they enable user perspectives to be articulated and gauged. The findings significantly stipulate that any regulatory regime must: support positive and prohibit the less desirable uses of LBS, balance flexibility/ choice with protection, regulate specific instances of use, while concurrently enabling technological and industry progression. Further research is required in this domain to ensure that the outcomes of this study are transformed into pragmatic tools and materials for use by various stakeholders.

DISCUSSION POINTS

- Pros and cons of location disclosure in commercial, business and government settings.
- Security risks associated with "strangers" or "third parties" acquiring GPS data logs or other sensor-based systems.
- Social implications of sharing location-based data with your social network.
- Policy and regulatory implications of LBS usage.
- Role of users in the development of location-based wearable applications.
- Importance of scenarios in examining the socio-ethical dilemmas associated with LBS usage.
- Striking a balance between positive and less desirable uses of LBS.

QUESTIONS

- What is more important when considering LBS usage: flexibility/choice or protection of location data? Discuss.
- Identify one stakeholder in the LBS value chain, and describe their function.
- Develop a socio-ethical scenario focused on LBS usage in a given context. Your answer should focus on the sequence of events and on the socio-ethical implications of LBS usage in the chosen context.
- Select a commercial LBS application, and critique in terms of the benefits and concerns. Consider design improvements to ensure that the application is ethically sound.

REFERENCES

Abbas, R. (2010). Location-based services: an examination of user attitudes and socio-ethical scenarios. In *Proceedings of the IEEE symposium on technology and society: social implications of emerging technologies 2010, 7–9 June 2010* (pp. 1-9). doi:10.1109/ISTAS.2010.5514620

Abbas, R. (2011). The social implications of location-based services: An observational study of users. *Journal of Location Based Services*, 5(3/4), 156–181. doi:10.1080/17489725.2011.637970

Abbas, R., Michael, K., & Michael, M. G. (2014). The regulatory considerations and ethical dilemmas of location-based services (LBS): A literature review. *Information Technology & People*, 27(1), 2–20. doi:10.1108/ITP-12-2012-0156

Abbas, R., Michael, K., & Michael, M. G. (2015a). Using a social-ethical framework to evaluate location-based services in an internet of things world. *International Review of Information Ethics*, 22(12), 42–73.

Abbas, R., Michael, K., Michael, M. G., & Nicholls, R. (2013). Sketching and validating the location-based services (LBS) regulatory framework in Australia. *Computer Law & Security Report*, 29(5), 576–589. doi:10.1016/j.clsr.2013.07.014

Abbas, R., Michael, K., Michael, M. G., & Nicholls, R. (2015b). Key government agency perspectives on location-based services regulation. *Computer Law & Security Report*, 31(6), 736–748. doi:10.1016/j.clsr.2015.08.004

Alexander, I. (2004). Introduction: Scenarios in System Development. In I. Alexander & N. Maiden (Eds.), *Scenarios, Stories, Use Cases through the Systems Development Lifecycle* (pp. 3–24). West Sussex, UK: John Wiley & Sons Ltd.

Aloudat, A. (2011). *Location-Based Mobile Phone Service Utilisation for Emergency Management in Australia*. (PhD Thesis). School of Information Systems and Technology, Informatics, University of Wollongong.

Anthony, D., Kotz, D., & Henderson, T. (2007). Privacy in location-aware computing environments. *Pervasive Computing*, 6(4), 64–72. doi:10.1109/MPRV.2007.83

Artz, J. M. (1998). The role of stories in computer ethics. *Computers & Society*, 28(1), 11–13. doi:10.1145/277351.277354

Barkhuus, L., Brown, B., Bell, M., Hall, M., Sherwood, S., & Chalmers, M. (2008). From Awareness to Repartee: Sharing Location within Social Groups. In *CHI 2008* (pp. 497-506).

Baur, N., Hering, L., Raschke, A. L., & Thierbach, C. (2014). Special issue: Spatial analysis in the social sciences and humanities. towards integrating qualitative, quantitative and cartographic approaches. *Historische Sozialforschung*, 39(2), 7–50.

Bentley, F. R., Chen, Y. Y., & Holz, C. (2015). Reducing the stress of coordination: sharing travel time information between contacts on mobile phones, In *CHI 2015*. doi:10.1145/2702123.2702208

Boesen, J., Rode, J. A., & Mancini, C. (2010). The domestic panopticon: location tracking in families. In *UbiComp'10* (pp. 65-74). doi:10.1145/1864349.1864382

Bria, A., Gessler, F., Queseth, O., Stridh, R., Unbehaun, M., Wu, J., Zander, J. & Flament, M. (2001, December). 4th generation wireless infrastructures: scenarios and research challenges. *IEEE Personal Communications*, 25-31.

Brown, B., Taylor, A. S., Izadi, S., Sellen, A., Kaye, J., & Eardley, R. (2007). Locating family values: a field trial of the whereabouts clock. In *UbiComp '07 Proceedings of the 9th International Conference on Ubiquitous Computing* (pp. 354-371). doi:10.1007/978-3-540-74853-3_21

Camponovo, G., Debetaz, S., & Pigneur, Y. (2005). A comparative analysis of published scenarios for m-business. In *Proceedings of the Third International Conference on Mobile Business, M-Business 2004*.

Chou, Y. H. (1997). *Exploring Spatial Analysis in Georgraphic Information Systems*. Sante Fe, NM: Onword Press.

Consolvo, S., Smith, I. E., Matthews, T., LaMarca, A., Tabert, J., & Powledge, P. (2005). Location disclosure to social relations: why, when, & what people want to share. In *CHI 2005* (pp. 81-90).

Damiani, M. L., Bertino, E., & Perlasca, P. (2007). Data security in location-aware applications: An approach based on RBAC. *International Journal of Information and Computer Security*, *1*(1/2), 5–38. doi:10.1504/IJICS.2007.012243

Dobson, J. E., & Fisher, P. F. (2007). The panopticon's changing geography. *Geographical Review*, *97*(3), 307–323. doi:10.1111/j.1931-0846.2007.tb00508.x

Duckham, M., & Kulik, L. (2005). A formal model of obfuscation and negotiation for location privacy. *Pervasive*, *2005*, 152–170.

Epstein, R. G., & Kumar, D. (2000). Stories and plays about the ethical and social implications of artificial intelligence. *Intelligence*, *11*(Fall), 17–19. doi:10.1145/350752.350758

Fusco, S. J., Michael, K., Aloudat, A., & Abbas, R. (2011). Monitoring people using location-based social networking and its negative impact on trust: an exploratory contextual analysis of five types of "friend" relationships. In *IEEE Symposium on Technology and Society (ISTAS11)*. Chicago: IEEE. doi:10.1109/ISTAS.2011.7160597

Fusco, S. J., Michael, K., Michael, M. G., & Abbas, R. (2010). Exploring the social implications of location based social networking: an inquiry into the perceived positive and negative impacts of using lbsn between friends. In *9th International Conference on Mobile Business (ICMB2010)*(pp. 230-237). Athens, Greece: IEEE. doi:10.1109/ICMB-GMR.2010.35

Gasson, M. N., Kosta, E., Royer, D., Meints, M., & Warwick, K. (2011). Normality mining: Privacy implications of behavioral profiles drawn from GPS enabled mobile phones. *IEEE Transactions on Systems, Man and Cybernetics. Part C, Applications and Reviews*, *41*(2), 251–261. doi:10.1109/TSMCC.2010.2071381

Ghinita, G. (2013). Privacy for location-based services, Volume 4 of synthesis lectures on information security, privacy and trust. Morgan & Claypool Publishers.

Iqbal, M. U., & Lim, S. (2007). Privacy implications of automated GPS tracking and profiling. In K. Michael & M. G. Michael (Eds.), *From Dataveillance to Überveillance and the Realpolitik of the Transparent Society (Workshop on the Social Implications of National Security, 2007), University of Wollongong, IP Location-Based Services Research Program (Faculty of Informatics) and Centre for Transnational Crime Prevention (Faculty of Law)* (pp. 225-240).

Jedrzejczyk, L., Price, B. A., Bandara, A. K., & Nuseibeh, B. (2010). On the Impact of Real-Time Feedback on Users' Behaviour in Mobile Location-Sharing Applications. In *Symposium On Usable Privacy and Security (SOUPS)*. doi:10.1145/1837110.1837129

Levin, A., Foster, M., West, B., Nicholson, M. J., Hernandez, T., & Cukier, W. (2008). *The Next Digital Divide: Online Social Network Privacy.* Ryerson University, Ted Rogers School of Management, Privacy and Cyber Crime Institute. Retrieved from www.ryerson.ca/tedrogersschool/privacy/Ryerson_Privacy_Institute_OSN_Report.pdf

Mancini, C., Jedrzejczyk, L., Thomas, K., Price, B. A., Bandara, A. K., Rogers, Y., & Nuseibeh, B. (2010). Predators and prey: ubiquitous tracking, privacy and the social contract. In *UbiComp 2010.*

Michael, K., McNamee, A., Michael, M. G., & Tootell, H. (2006). Location-based intelligence – modeling behavior in humans using GPS. In *IEEE International Symposium on Technology and Society(pp.*1-8*).* New York: IEEE. doi:10.1109/ISTAS.2006.4375889

Patel, D. P. (2004). Should teenagers get lojacked against their will?: An argument for the ratification of the United Nations convention on the rights of the child. *Howard Law Journal*, *47*(2), 429–470.

Perusco, L., & Michael, K. (2007). Control, Trust, Privacy, and Security: Evaluating Location-Based Services. *IEEE Technology and Society Magazine*, *26*(1), 4–16. doi:10.1109/MTAS.2007.335564

Pitney Bowes. (2012). *Mapinfo Professional.* Retrieved from http://www.pbinsight.com.au/products/location-intelligence/applications/mapping-analytical/mapinfo-professional/

Seeburger, J., & Schroeter, R. (2009). Disposable maps: ad hoc location sharing. In OZCHI'09 (pp. 377-380). doi:10.1145/1738826.1738902

Sheng, H., Fui-Hoon Nah, F., & Siau, K. (2008). An experimental study on ubiquitous commerce adoption: Impact of personalization and privacy concerns. *Journal of the Association for Information Systems*, *9*(6), 344–376.

Sun, Y., Wang, N., Shen, X. L., & Zhang, J. X. (2015). Location information disclosure in location-based social network services: Privacy calculus, benefit structure, and gender differences. *Computers in Human Behavior*, *52*, 278–292.

Tang, K. O., Lin, J., Hong, J., Siewiorek, D. P., & Sadeh, N. (2010). Rethinking location sharing: exploring the implications of social-driven vs. purpose-driven location sharing. In *UbiComp 2010.* doi:10.1145/1864349.1864363

Tatli, E. I., Stegemann, D., & Lucks, S. (2005). Security challenges of Location-Aware Mobile Business. In *The Second IEEE International Workshop on Mobile Commerce and Services, 2005. WMCS '05*. doi:10.1109/WMCS.2005.23

Taylor, G., & Blewitt, G. (2006). *Intelligent Positioning: GIS GPS Unification*. West Sussex, UK: John Wiley & Sons Ltd. doi:10.1002/0470035668

Thomas, L., Little, L., Briggs, P., McInnes, L., Jones, E., & Nicholson, J. (2013). Location tracking: Views from the older adult population. *Age and Ageing*, *42*(6), 758–763. doi:10.1093/ageing/aft069 PMID:23761455

Toch, E., Cranshaw, J., Drielsma, P. H., Tsai, J. Y., Kelley, P. G., Springfield, J., & Sadeh, N. (2009). Empirical models of privacy in location sharing. In *UbiComp '10* (pp. 129-138). doi:10.1145/1864349.1864364

Tsai, J. Y., Kelley, P. G., Drielsma, P. H., Cranor, L. F., Hong, J., & Sadeh, N. (2009). *Who's viewed you? The impact of feedback in a mobile location-sharing application*. Boston, MA: CHI.

Yu, Z., Wang, H., Guo, B., Gu, T., & Mei, T. (2015). Supporting serendipitous social interaction using human mobility prediction. *IEEE Transactions on Human-Machine Systems*, *45*(6), 811–818. doi:10.1109/THMS.2015.2451515

Zhao, L., Lu, Y., & Gupta, S. (2012). Disclosure intention of location-related information in location-based social network services. *International Journal of Electronic Commerce*, *16*(4), 53–90. doi:10.2753/JEC1086-4415160403

KEY TERMS AND DEFINITIONS

Data Log: Record of data over time and in relation to location.

GPS (Global Positioning System): A constellation of 24 satellites that orbit the Earth. With the aid of ground receivers, three or more satellites can pinpoint a person's geographic location between 100 and 10 meters. GPS chipsets can come embedded in various devices, including wearables, mobiles, tablets, etc.

Location Chronicle: A sequential record of an individual's whereabouts.

Policy: An enforceable set of organizational rules and principles used to aid decision-making that have penalties for non-compliance, such as the termination of an employee's contract with an employer.

Regulation: The use of rules and limitations to constrain behavior.

Scenario: A Tool used to examine a possible future in the form of a sequence of events.

Socio-Ethical: Expresses in human judgments our ideas about the ethical nature of the human community.

Spatial: Relates to a specific space.

Thematic: Relates to a specific topic/subject.

User: An individual that employs a particular application.

ENDNOTE

[1]   This research was supported under the Australian Research Council's Discovery Projects funding scheme (project DP0881191). The views expressed herein are those of the authors and are not necessarily those of the Australian Research Council. The University of Wollongong Human Research Ethics Committee (HREC) Approval No is HE09/062.

APPENDIX: DISCUSSION PAPER

UNIVERSITY OF WOLLONGONG LOCATION-BASED SERVICES IN AUSTRALIA: CONSULTATION PAPER

Background Information

Location-based Services (LBS) provide a means of positioning, tracing and tracking individuals and objects, for purposes such as emergency management, employee monitoring, and consumer convenience amongst others. The LBS industry is characterised by a multitude of vendors, all of whom assume a vital role in the value chain. Stakeholders range from technical vendors involved in the development of LBS, external entities such as government and standardisation bodies, to consumers who utilise the solutions.

Our research has thus far recognised the need for extensive collaboration between stakeholders within the LBS value chain in Australia. Essentially, we are attempting to facilitate a consultation process, in which all stakeholders can contribute valuable feedback and comments, in an attempt to address the implications associated with the introduction of location-based services, and help shape the future of the industry. The ultimate objective of this process is to produce a detailed report which examines the factors that will contribute to the success of the LBS industry. This report can be used internally by your organisation to drive the LBS design and development process, allowing you to recognise the conditions and requirements for ethically-sound LBS applications.

The research will specifically focus on the varying uses or applications of location-based services in the Australian market, and consider the implications of each application. As such, *we request that you to consider the scenarios presented below in story-board format*. The interview process will allow you to provide commentary and opinions regarding the implications of each scenario, and discuss your organisation's approach where relevant.

Issues for Consultation: Potential Uses of Location-Based Services in Australia

Respondents were shown the storyboard images reproduced in Figure 16.

How to Respond

- To schedule an interview, please email using the provided details or wait for our follow-up.
- Appended to this paper is a consent form and participant information sheet for your reference.

Chapter 10
Societal Implications of Wearable Technology:
Interpreting "Trialability on the Run"

Katina Michael
University of Wollongong, Australia

Deniz Gokyer
University of Wollongong, Australia

Samer Abbas
University of Wollongong, Australia

ABSTRACT

This chapter presents a set of scenarios involving the GoPro wearable Point of View (PoV) camera. The scenarios are meant to stimulate discussion about acceptable usage contexts with a focus on security and privacy. The chapter provides a wide array of examples of how overt wearable technologies are perceived and how they might/might not be welcomed into society. While the scenario is based at the University of Wollongong campus in Australia, the main implications derived from the fictitious events are useful in drawing out the predicted pros and cons of the technology. The scenarios are interpreted and the main thematic issues are drawn out and discussed. An in depth analysis takes place around the social implications, the moral and ethical problems associated with such technology, and possible future developments with respect to wearable devices.

DOI: 10.4018/978-1-5225-1016-1.ch010

INTRODUCTION

This chapter presents the existing, as well as the potential future, implications of wearable computing. Essentially, the chapter builds on the scenarios presented in an *IEEE Consumer Electronics Magazine* article entitled: "Trialability on the Run" (Gokyer & Michael, 2015). In this chapter the scenarios are interpreted qualitatively using thick description and the implications arising from these are discussed using thematic analysis. The scenario analysis is conducted through deconstruction, in order to extract the main themes and to grant the reader a deeper understanding of the possible future implications of the widespread use of wearable technology. First, each of the scenarios is analyzed to draw out the positive and the negative aspects of wearable cameras. Second, the possible future implications stemming from each scenario context are discussed under the following thematic areas: privacy, security, society, anonymity, vulnerability, trust and liberty. Third, direct evidence is provided using the insights of other research studies to support the conclusions reached and to identify plausible future implications of wearable technologies, in particular use contexts in society at large.

The setting for the scenario is a closed-campus environment, (a large Australian University). Specific contexts such as a lecture theatre, restroom, café, bank, and library, are chosen to provide a breadth of use cases within which to analyze the respective social implications. The legal, regulatory, and policy-specific bounds of the study are taken from current laws, guidelines and normative behavior, and are used as signposts for what should, or should not, be acceptable practice. The outcomes illustrate that the use cases are not so easily interpretable, given the newness of the emerging technology of wearable computing, especially overt head-mounted cameras, that draw a great deal of attention from bystanders. Quite often resistance to the use of a head-mounted camera is opposed without qualified reasoning. "Are you recording me? Stop that please!" is a common response to audio-visual body-worn recording technology in the public space by individuals (Michael & Michael, 2013). Yet companies such as Google have been able to use fleets of cars to gather imagery of homes and streets, with relatively little problem.

There are, indeed, laws that pertain to the misuse of surveillance devices without a warrant, to the unauthorized recording of someone else whether in a public or private space, and to voyeuristic crimes such as upskirting. While there are laws, such as the *Workplace Surveillance Act*, 2005 (NSW), asserting a set of rules for surveillance (watching from above), the law regarding sousveillance (watching from below) is less clear (Clarke, 2012). We found that, while public spaces like libraries and lecture theatres have clear policy guidelines to follow, the actual published policies, and the position taken by security staff, do not in fact negate the potential to indirectly record another. Several times, through informal questioning, we found the strong line "you cannot do that because we have a policy that says you are not allowed to record someone", to be unsubstantiated by real enforceable university-wide policies. Such shortcomings are now discussed in more detail against scenarios showing various sub-contexts of wearable technology in a closed-campus setting.

BACKGROUND

The term *sousveillance* has been defined by Steve Mann (2002) to denote a recording done from a portable device such as a head-mounted display (HMD) unit in which the wearer is a participant in the activity. In contrast to wall-mounted fixed cameras typically used for surveillance, portable devices allow *inverse surveillance*: recordings from the point of view of those being watched. More generally, point of view (POV) has its foundations in film, and usually depicts a scene through the eyes of a character. Body-worn video-recording technologies now mean that a wearer can shoot film from a first-person perspective of another subject or object in his or her immediate field of view (FOV), with or without a particular agenda.

During the initial rollout of Google Glass, explorers realized that recording other people with an optical HMD unit was not perceived as an acceptable practice, despite the fact that the recording was taking place in a public space. Google's apparent blunder was to assume that the device, worn by 8,000 individuals, would go unnoticed, like shopping mall closed-circuit television (CCTV). Instead, what transpired was a mixed reaction by the public—some nonusers were curious and even thrilled at the possibilities claimed by the wearers of Google Glass, while some wearers were refused entry to premises, fined, verbally abused, or even physically assaulted by others in the FOV (see Levy, 2014).

Some citizens and consumers have claimed that law enforcement (if approved through the use of a warrant process) and shop owners have every right to surveil a given locale, dependent on the context of the situation. Surveilling a suspect who may have committed a violent crime or using CCTV as an antitheft mechanism is now commonly perceived as acceptable, but having a camera in your line of sight record you—even incidentally—as you mind your own business can be disturbing for even the most tolerant of people.

Wearers of these prototypes, or even of fully-fledged commercial products like the Autographer (see http://www.autographer.com/), claim that they record everything around them as part of a need to lifelog or quantify themselves for reflection. Technology such as the Narrative Clip may not capture audio or video, but even still shots are enough to reveal someone else's whereabouts, especially if they are innocently posted on Flickr, Instagram, or other social media. Many of these photographs also have embedded location and time-stamp metadata stored by default.

A tourist might not have malicious intent by showing off in front of a landmark, but innocent bystanders captured in the photo could find themselves in a predicament given that the context may be entirely misleading.

Wearable and embedded cameras worn by any citizen carry significant and deep personal and societal implications. A photoborg is one who mounts a camera onto any aspect of the body to record the space around himself or herself (Michael & Michael, 2012). Photoborgs may feel entirely free, masters of their own destiny; even safe that their point of view is being noted for prospective reuse. Indeed, the power that photoborgs have is clear when they wear the camera. It can be even more authoritative than the unrestricted overhead gazing of traditional CCTV, given that sousveillance usually happens at ground level. Although photoborgs may be recording for their own lifelog, they will inevitably capture other people in their field of view, and unless these fellow citizens also become photoborgs themselves, there is a power differential. Sousveillance carries with it huge socioethical, environmental, economic, political, and spiritual overtones. The narrative that informs sousveillance is more relevant than ever before due to the proliferation of new media.

Sousveillance grants citizens the ability to combat the powerful using their own evidentiary mechanism, but it also grants other citizens the ability to put on the guise of the powerful. The evidence emanating from cameras is endowed with obvious limitations, such as the potential for the impairment of the data through loss, manipulation, or misrepresentation (Michael, 2013). The pervasiveness of the camera that sees and hears everything can only be reconciled if we know the lifeworld of the wearer, the context of the event being captured, and how the data will be used by the stakeholder in command.

Sousveillance happens through the gaze of the one wearing the camera, just like a first-person shooter in a video game. In 2003, *WIRED* published an article (Shachtman, 2003) on the potentiality to lifelog everything about everyone. Shachtman wrote:

The Pentagon is about to embark on a stunningly ambitious research project designed to gather every conceivable bit of information about a person's life, index all the information and make it searchable... The embryonic LifeLog program would dump everything an individual does into a giant database: every e-mail sent or received, every picture taken, every Web page surfed, every phone call made, every TV show watched, every magazine read... All of this—and more—would combine with information gleaned from a variety of sources: a GPS transmitter to keep tabs on where that person went, audio-visual sensors to capture what he or she sees or says, and biomedical monitors to keep track of the individual's health... This gigantic amalgamation of personal information could then be used to "trace the 'threads' of an individual's life."

This goes to show how any discovery can be tailored toward any end. Lifelogging is meant to sustain the power of the individual through reflection and learning, to enable growth, maturity and development. Here, instead, it has been hijacked by the very same stakeholder against whom it was created to gain protection.

Sousveillance also drags into the equation innocent bystanders going about their everyday business who just wish to be left alone. When we asked wearable 2.0 pioneer Steve Mann in 2009 what one should do if bystanders in a recording in a public space questioned why they were being recorded without their explicit permission, he pointed us to his "request for deletion" (RFD) web page (Mann, n.d.). This is admittedly only a very small part of the solution and, for the most part, untenable. One just needs to view a few minutes of the Surveillance Camera Man Channel (http://tinyurl.com/lsrl6u9) to understand that people generally do not wish to be filmed in someone else's field of view. Some key questions include:

1. In what context has the footage been taken?
2. How will it be used?
3. To whom will the footage belong?
4. How will the footage taken be validated and stored?

TRIALABILITY ON THE RUN

In this section, plausible scenarios of the use of wearable cameras in a closed campus setting are presented and analyzed in the story "Trialability on the Run". Although the scenarios are not based directly on primary sources of evidence, they do provide conflicting perspectives on the pros and cons of wearables. As companies are engaged in ever-shorter market trialing of their products, the scenarios demonstrate what can go wrong with an approach that effectively says: "Let's unleash the product now and worry about repercussions later; they'll iron themselves out eventually—our job is solely to worry about engineering." The pitfalls of such an approach are the unexpected and asymmetric consequences that ensue. For instance, someone wearing a camera breaches my privacy, and, although the recorded evidence has affected no one else, my life is affected adversely. Laws, and organizational policies especially, need quickly to respond as advances in technologies emerge.

"Trialability on the Run" is a "day in the life" scenario that contains 9 parts, set in a closed-campus in southern New South Wales. The main characters are Anthony, the owner and wearer of the head-mounted GoPro (an overt audio-visual recording device), and his girlfriend Sophie. The narrator follows and observes the pair as they work their way around the campus in various sub-contexts, coming into contact with academic staff, strangers, acquaintances, cashiers, banking personnel, librarians, fellow university students and finally security personnel. Anthony takes the perspective that his head-mounted GoPro is no different from the mounted security surveillance cameras on lampposts and building walls, or from the in-lecture theatre recordings captured by the Echo360 (Echo, 2016), or even from portable smart phone cameras that are handheld. He is bewildered when he draws so much attention to himself as the photoborg camera wearer, since he perceives he is performing exactly the same function as the other cameras on campus and has only the intent of capturing his own lifelog. Although he is not doing anything wrong, Anthony looks different and stands out as a result (Surveillance Camera Man, 2015). His girlfriend, Sophie, is not convinced by Anthony's blasé attitude and tries to press a counter argument that Anthony's practice is unacceptable in society.

Scenario 1: The Lecture

Context

In this scenario, the main character, Anthony, has arrived at the lecture theatre, in which the lesson had already begun, intending to record the lecture instead of taking notes. Being slightly late, he decided to sit in the very front row. All the students and eventually the lecturer saw the head-mounted camera he was wearing. The lecturer continued his lecture without showing any emotion. Some students giggled at the spectacle and others were very surprised with what they observed, as it was quite probable that it was the first time that they were seeing someone wearing a camera to record a lecture. The students were generally not bothered by the head-mounted recording device in full view, as it was focused on the lecture material and the lecturer, so proceedings continued, as they otherwise would have, had the body-worn camera not been present. Students are very used to surveillance cameras on campus; this was just another camera as far as they were concerned, and besides no one objected: they were too busy taking notes and listening to instruction about the structure and form of the final examination in their engineering coursework.

Wearable User Rights and Intellectual Property

In some of the lecture theatres on university campuses, there are motion sensor-based video cameras that make full audio-visual recordings of the lectures (Echo, 2016). Lecturers choose to record their lectures in this manner as available evidence of educational content covered for students, especially for those who were unable to attend the lecture, for those for whom English is a second language or for those who like to listen to lecture content as a form of revision. In this regard, there are no policies in place to keep the students from making audio-visual recordings of the lecture in the lecture theatres.

Lecture theatres are considered public spaces and many universities allow students to attend lectures whether or not they are enrolled in that particular course or subject. Anyone from the public could walk into lectures and listen, as there is no keycard access. Similar to centrally organized Echo 360 audio-visual recordings, Anthony is taping the lecture himself and he does not see any problems with distributing the recording to classmates if someone asks for it to study for the final examination. After all, everyone owns a smartphone and anyone can record the lecture with the camera on their smartphones or tablet device.

This scenario raises a small number of questions that need to be dealt with foremost, such as "What is the difference between making a recording with a smartphone and with a head-mounted camera?" or, "Does it only start being a problem when the recording device is overt and can be seen?" If one juxtaposes the surveillance camera covertly integrated into a light fixture, with an overt head-mounted camera, then why should the two devices elicit such a different response from bystanders?

These questions do not, however, address the fact that an open discussion is required on whether or not we are ready to see a great deal of these sousveillers in our everyday life, and if we are not, what are we prepared to do about it? Mann (2005) predicted the use of sousveillance would grow greatly when the sousveillance devices acquired non-traditional uses such as making phone calls, taking pictures, and having access to the Internet. This emergence produces a grey area, generating the requirement for laws, legislation, regulations and policies having to be amended or created to address specific uses of the sousveillance devices in different environments and contexts. Clarke (2014) identifies a range of relevant (Australian) laws to inform policy discussion and notes the inadequacy of current regulation in the face of rapidly emerging technology.

Scenario 2: The Restroom

Context

In the restroom scenario, Anthony walked into a public restroom after his lecture, forgetting that his head-mounted camera was still on and recording. While unintentionally recording, Anthony received different reactions from the people present in the restroom, all of whom saw the camera and suspected some foul play. The first person, who was leaving as Anthony was entering the restroom, did not seem to care; another tried to ignore Anthony and left as soon as he was finished. The last person became disturbed by the fact that he was being recorded in what he obviously deemed to be a private place. Later that day when Anthony searched for lecture recordings on the tape, he got a sense of wrongdoing after realizing that, in the restroom, he had accidentally left the camera on in record mode. He was surprised, upon hindsight, that he did not get any major reactions, such as an individual openly expressing their discontent or the fact he did not get any specific questions or pronouncements of discomfort. If it were not for the facial expressions to which Anthony was privy, he would not have been able to tell that anybody was upset, as there was no verbal cue or physical retaliation. Of course, the innocent bystanders, going about their business, would not have been able to assume that the camera was indeed rolling.

Citizen Privacy, Voyeurism, and a Process of Desensitization

Restrooms, change rooms, and shower blocks on campus are open to the public, but they are also considered private spaces given that people are engaged in private activities (e.g. showering), and are, at times, not fully clothed. The natural corollary, then, would lead to the expectation that some degree of privacy should be granted. Can anyone overtly walk into a public toilet sporting a camera and record you while you are trying to, for modesty's sake, do what should only be done in the restroom? Is the body-worn technology becoming so ubiquitous that no one even says a word about something that they can clearly see is ethically or morally wrong? Steve Mann has argued that surveillance cameras in the restroom are an invasion of privacy more abhorrent than body-worn cameras owned by everyday people. The direct approachability of the photoborg differs from an impersonal CCTV.

There is a long discussion to be had on personal security. For instance, will we all, one day, be carrying such devices as we seek to lifelog our entire histories, or acquire an alibi for our whereabouts should we be accused of a given crime, as portrayed in film in the drama "The Entire History of You" (Armstrong and Welsh, 2011)? It is very common to find signs prohibiting the use of mobile phones in leisure centers, swimming pools and the like. There remains, however, much to be argued around safety versus privacy trade-offs, if it is acceptable practice to rely on closed circuit television (CCTV) in public spaces.

University campuses are bound by a number of laws, at federal or state level, including (in this case) the *Privacy Act 1998 (Cth)*, the *Surveillance Devices Act 2007(NSW)*, and the *Workplace Surveillance Act 2005 (NSW)*. This scenario points out that even when there cannot possibly be surveillance cameras in restrooms or change rooms, the *Surveillance Devices Act 2007 (NSW)* does not specify provisions about sousveillance in those public/private spaces. In Clarke's (2014) assessment of the *NSW Crimes Act (1900)*, the voyeurism offences provisions exist relating to photographs. They pertain to photographs that are of a sexual and voyeuristic nature, usually showing somebody's private parts. These photographs are also taken without the consent of the individual and/or taken in places where a person would reasonably expect to be afforded privacy (toilets, showers, change rooms etc). When a person claims to have had his or her privacy breached, however, exceptions to this rule apply if s/he is a willing participant in the activity, or if circumstances indicate that the persons involved did not really care if they were seen by onlookers (Clarke, 2014). It is even less likely to be illegal, if the act was conducted in a private place, but with doors open in full view (Clarke, 2014). Thus, the law represents controls over a narrow range of abuses (Clarke, 2014), and, unless they find themselves in a predicament and seek further advice, the general populace is unaware that the law does not protect them entirely, and depends on the context.

Scenario 3: The Corridor

Context

This scenario depicts a conversation occurring with Sophie (Anthony's girlfriend and fellow undergraduate coursework student). In the corridor, Anthony bumps into their mutual friend, Oxford, as they vacate the lecture theatre. Throughout the conversation, Anthony demonstrates confidence in his appearance. He believed wearing a head-mounted camera was not a problem and so consequently, he did not think he was doing anything wrong. On the other hand, Sophie was questioning whether or not body-worn cameras should be used without notifying the people in their vicinity. Oxford, an international student, became concerned about the possible future uses of the recording that featured him. His main concern was that he did not want the footage to be made publicly available given how he looked and the clothing he was wearing. Although Oxford had no objection to Anthony keeping the footage for his personal archives, he did not wish for it to be splattered all over social media.

Trust, Disproportionality, and Requests for Deletion

The two student perspectives of "recording" a lifelog are juxtaposed. Anthony is indifferent as he feels he is taping "his" life as it happens around him through time. Oxford, on the other hand, believes he has a right to his own image, and that includes video (Branscomb, 1994). Here we see a power and control dominance occurring. The power and control is with the photoborg who has the ability to record, store and share the information gathered. On the other hand, the bystander is powerless and at the mercy of the photoborg, unless he/she voices otherwise explicitly. In addition, bystanders may not be so concerned with an actual live recording for personal archives, but certainly are concerned about public viewing. Often lifelogs are streamed in real-time and near real-time, which does not grant the bystander confidence with respect to acceptable use cases.

In the scenario, Sophie poses a question to those who are being incidentally recorded by Anthony's GoPro to see whether there is an expectation among her peers to get individual consent prior to a recording taking place. Oxford, the mutual acquaintance of the protagonists, believes that consent is paramount in this process. This raises a pertinent question: what about the practice of lifelogging? Lifeloggers could not possibly have the consent of every single person they encounter in a daily journey. Is lifelogging acceptable insofar as lifeloggers choose not to share recordings online or anywhere public? Mann (2005) argues that a person wishing to do lifelong sousveillance deserves certain legal protections against others who might attempt to disrupt continuity of evidence, say for example, while going through immigration. On the other hand, Harfield (2014) extends the physical conception of a private space in considering the extent to which an individual can expect to be private in a public space, defining audio-visual recording of a subject without their consent in public spaces as a moral wrong and seeing the act of sousveillance as a moral intrusion against personal privacy.

In the scenario, Sophie pointed out that if someone wanted to record another individual around them, they could easily do so covertly using everyday objects with embedded covert cameras, such as a pen, a key fob, a handbag or even their mobile phone. Sophie was able to put into perspective the various gazes from security cameras when compared to sousveillance. The very thought about the mass surveillance she was under every moment provided a sobering counterbalance, allowing her to experience tolerance for the practice of sousveillance. Yet for Oxford, the security cameras mounted on the walls and ceilings of the Communications Building, provided a level of safety for international students. Oxford clearly justified "security cameras for security reasons", but could not justify additional "in your face" cameras. Oxford did not wish to come across a sousveiller because the recordings could be made publicly available on the Internet without his knowledge. Further, a clear motive for the recordings had not been conveyed by the camera holder (Michael et al., 2014).

Between 1994 and 1996, Steve Mann conducted a *Wearable Wireless Webcam* experiment to visually record and continuously stream live video from his wearable computer to the World Wide Web. Operating 24 hours a day (on and off), this had the effective purpose of capturing and archiving day-to-day living from the person's own perspective (Mann, 2005). Mann has argued that in the future, devices that captured lifelong memories and shared them in real-time would be commonplace and worn continuously (Mann, 2013).

It is true that almost everywhere we go in our daily lives someone, somewhere, is watching. But in the workplace, especially, where there is intent to watch an employee, the law states that individuals must be notified that they are being watched (Australasian Legal Information Institute, 2015). When it comes to sousveillance will this be the case as well? In Australia, the use, recording, communication or publication of recorded information from a surveillance device under a warrant is protected data and cannot be openly shared according to the *Surveillance Device Act 2004 (Cth)*. In the near future when we are making a recording with an overt device, a prospective sousveillance law might posit: "You can see that I am recording you but this is for personal use only and as long as I do not share this video with someone you cannot do or say anything to stop me." Mann (2005) claims that sousveillance, unlike surveillance, will require, and receive, strong legal support through dedicated frameworks for its protection, as well as for its limitation (Mann & Wassell, 2013).

A person can listen to, or visually monitor, a private activity if s/he is a participant in the activity (Australasian Legal Information Institute, 2014). However, this Act forbids a person to install, use or maintain an optical surveillance device or a listening device to record a private activity whether the person is a party to the activity or not. The penalties do not apply to the use of an optical surveillance device or listening device resulting in the unintentional recording or observation of a private activity (*Surveillance Devices Act, 1998* (WA)). Clarke (2014) combines optical surveillance device regulation with the regulation for listening devices and concludes that a person can listen to conversations if they are a participant in the activity but cannot make audio or visual recordings. The applications of the law cover only a limited range of situations and conditions may apply for prosecutions.

Scenario 4: Ordering at the Café

Context

Anthony and Sophie approached the counter of a café to place their orders and Anthony soon found himself engaged in a conversation with the attendants at the serving area about the camera he was wearing. He asked the attendants how they felt about being filmed. The male attendant said he did not like it very much and the female barista said she would not mind being filmed. The manager did not comment about any aspect of the head-mounted GoPro recording taking place but he did make some derogatory comments about Anthony's behavior to Sophie. The male attendant became disturbed about the idea of someone recording him while he was at work and he tried to direct Anthony to the manager, knowing that the manager would not like it either, and it would disturb him even more. Conversely, however, the female barista was far from upset about the impromptu recording, acting as if she was on a reality TV show, and taken by the fact that someone seemed to show some interest to her, overcoming the normal daily routine.

Exhibitionism, Hesitation, and Unease

People tend to care a great deal about being watched over or scrutinized and this is reflected in their social behaviors and choices, which are altered as a result without them even realizing (Nettle et. al., 2012). Thus, some people who generally do not like being recorded (like the male attendant), might be subconsciously rejecting the idea of having to change their behaviors. Others, like the manager, simply ignore the existence of the device and others still, like the female attendant, feel entirely comfortable in front of a camera, even playing up and portraying himself or herself as someone "they want to be seen as".

Anthony did not understand why people found the camera on his head disturbing with the additional concerns about being recorded. In certain cases where people seemed to show particular interest, Anthony decided to engage others about how they felt about being filmed and tried to understand what their reactions were to constant ground-level surveillance. Anthony himself had not been educated with respect to campus policy or the laws pertaining to audio-visual recording in a public space. Anthony was unaware that in Australia, surveillance device legislation differs greatly between states but, broadly, audio and/or visual recording of a private activity is likely to be illegal whatever the context (Clarke, 2014). An activity is, however, only considered to be "private" when it is taking place inside a building, and in the state of New South Wales this includes vehicles. People, however, are generally unaware that prohibitions may not apply if the activity is happening outside a building, regardless of context (Clarke, 2014).

If people were to see someone wearing a head-mounted camera as they were going about their daily routine, it would doubtless gain their attention, as it is presently an unusual occurrence. When we leave our homes, we do not expect pedestrians to be wearing head-mounted cameras, nor, (although increasingly we know we are under surveillance in taxis, buses, trains, and other forms of public transport), do we expect bus drivers, our teachers, fellow students, family or friends to be wearing body-worn recording devices. Having said that, policing has had a substantial impact on raising citizen awareness of body-worn audio-visual recording devices. We now have mobile cameras on cars, on highway patrol police officer helmets, and even on the lapels of particular police officers on foot. While this has helped to decrease the number of unfounded citizen complaints against law enforcement personnel on duty, it is also seen as a retaliatory strategy to everyday citizens who now have a smartphone video recorder at hand 24x7.

Although the average citizen does not always feel empowered to question one's authority to record, everyone has the right to question the intended purpose of the video being taken of him or her, and how or where it will be shared. In this scenario, does Anthony have the right to record others as he pleases without their knowledge, either of him making the recording, or of the places where that recording might end up? Would Anthony get the same reaction if he were making the recordings with his smartphone? Owners of smart phones would be hard-pressed to say that they have never taken visual recordings of an activity where there are bystanders in the background that they do not know and from whom they have not gained consent. Such examples include children's sporting events, wedding receptions, school events, attractions and points of interest and a whole lot more. Most photoborgs use the line of argumentation that says: "How is recording with a GoPro instead of a smartphone any different"? Of course, individuals who object to being subjected to point of view surveillance (PoVS) have potential avenues of protection (including trespass against property, trespass against the person, stalking, harassment etc.), but these protections are limited in their applications (Clarke, 2014). Even so, the person using PoVS technology has access to far more protection than the person they are monitoring even if they are doing so in an unreasonable manner (Clarke, 2014).

Scenario 5: Finding a Table at the Café

Context

In this scenario, patrons at an on-campus café vacated their chairs almost immediately after Anthony and Sophie sat down at the large table. Anthony and Sophie both realized the camera was driving people away from them. Sophie insisted at that point in the scenario, that Anthony at least stopped recording if he was unwilling to take off the device itself. After Cygneta and Klara (Sophie's acquaintances) had joined them at the table, Anthony, interested in individual reactions and trying to prove a point to Sophie, asked Klara how she felt about being filmed. He received the responses that he had expected. Klara did not like being filmed one bit by something worn on someone's head. Moreover, despite being a marketing student, she had not even heard of Google Glass when Anthony tried to share his perspective around the issue by bringing up the technology in conversation. This fell on deaf ears, he thought, despite Cygneta's thought that visual data might well be the future of marketing strategies. Anthony tried to make an argument that if a technology like Google Glass was to become prevalent on campus in a couple of years that they would not have any say about being recorded by a stranger. Sophie supported Anthony from a factual standpoint reinforcing that there were no laws in Australia prohibiting video recordings in public. That is, across the States and Territories of

Australia, visual surveillance in public places are not subject to general prohibitions except when the person(s) would reasonably expect their actions to be private if they were engaging in a private act (NSW); or if the person(s) being recorded had a strong case for expecting he/she would not be recorded (Victoria, WA, NT); and in SA, Tasmania and ACT legislations for recording other people subject to various provisos (Clarke, 2014).

The reactions of Klara and Cygneta got Sophie thinking about gender and if men were more likely than women to get enthralled by technological devices. She could see this happening with drones and wearable technologies like smart watches - and came to the realization that the GoPro was no different. Some male surfers (including Anthony) and skateboard riders had well and truly begun to use their GoPros to film themselves doing stunts, then sharing these on Instagram. She reflected on whether or not people, in general, would begin to live a life of "virtual replays" as opposed to living in the moment. When reality becomes hard to handle, people tend to escape to a virtual world where they create avatars and act "freely", leading to the postponement of the hardships of real life, and some may even become addicted to this as being a more exciting lifestyle. These issues are further explored in the following popular articles: Ghorayshi (2014), Kotler (2014) and Lagorio (2006).

Novelty and Market Potential

The patrons at the first table appeared to find the situation awkward and they rectified this problem by removing themselves from the vicinity of Anthony and his camera. Klara did not possess adequate knowledge about emerging wearable technology, and she claimed she would not use it even if it were readily available. But once wearable computers like Google Glass permeated the consumer market, Cygneta, who seemed like she 'kept up with the Joneses', said she would likely start using it at some point, despite Klara's apparent resistance. While smartphones were a new technology in the 1990s, currently close to one third of the world's population are using them regularly, with 70% projected by 2020 (Ericsson, 2015). One reason this number is not bigger is low-income countries with widespread rural populations and vast terrains: the numbers are expected to rise massively in emerging markets. By comparison wearable computers are basically advanced versions of existing technology and thus uptake of wearable technologies will likely be seamless and even quicker. As with smartphone adoption, as long as they are affordable, wearable computers such as Digital Glass and smartwatches can be expected to be used as much as, or even more than, smartphones, given they are always attached to the body or within arm's reach.

Scenario 6: A Visit to the Bank

Context

When Sophie and Anthony visited the bank, Anthony sat down as Sophie asked for assistance from one of the attendants. Even if Anthony was not the one who needed help, he thought people working at the bank seemed to be more friendly than usual towards him. He was asked, in fact, if he wanted some assistance with anything, and when he confirmed he did not, no further questioning by the bank manager was conducted. He thought it strange that everyone was so casual about his camera, when everyone else that day had made him feel like a criminal. Again, he was acutely aware that he was in full view of the bank's surveillance camera but questioned if anyone was really watching anyway. The couple later queued up at the ATM where Anthony mentioned that had he had some disingenuous intentions: he could be filming people and acquiring their PINs so easily. No one had even attempted to cover up their PIN entry, even though there were now signs near the keypad to "cover up". This entire situation made Sophie feel very uncomfortable and slightly irritated by Anthony. It was after all a criminal act to shoulder surf someone's PIN, but to have it on film as well to replay later was outrageous. It seemed to her that, no matter how much advice people get about protecting their identity or credit from fraud, they just don't seem to pay attention. To Anthony's credit, he too, understood the severity of the situation and admittedly felt uncomfortable by the situation in which, with no malicious intent, he had accidentally found himself.

Security

This scenario illustrates that people in the workplace who are under surveillance are more likely to help clients. Anthony's camera got immediate attention and a forward request: "Can I help you?" When individuals become publicly self-aware that they are being filmed, then their propensity to help others generally increases. The feeling of public self-awareness created by the presence of a camera triggers the change in behavior in accordance with a pattern that signifies concerns with any damage that could be done to reputation (Van Bommel et. al., 2012).

Anthony also could not keep himself from questioning the security measures that the bank should be applying given the increase in incidence of cheap embedded cameras in both stationary and mobile phones. When queuing in front of the ATM for Sophie's cash withdrawal, Anthony noticed that he was recording, unintentionally, something that could easily be used for criminal activities and he started seeing the possible security breaches which would come with emerging wearables. For example, video evidence can be zoomed in to reveal private data. While some believe that personal body worn recording devices protect the security of the individual wearer from mass surveillance, rectifying some of the power imbalances, in this instance the recording devices have diminished security by their very presence. It is a paradox, and while it all comes down to the individual ethics of the photoborg, it will not take long for fraudsters to employ such measures.

Scenario 7: In the Library

Context

After the ATM incident, Anthony began to consider more deeply the implications of filming others in a variety of contexts. It was the very first time he had begun to place himself in other people's shoes and see things from their perspective. In doing this, he became more cautious in the library setting. He avoided glaring at the computer screens of other users around him, as he could then record what activities they were engaged in online, what they were searching for on their Internet browser, and more. He attracted the attention of certain people he came across in the library, because obviously he looked different, even weird. For the first time that day, he felt like he was going to get into serious trouble when he was talking to the librarian who was questioning him about his practice. The librarian claimed that Anthony had absolutely no right to record other people without their permission, as it was against campus policies. Anthony did take this seriously, but he was pretty sure there was no policy against using a GoPro on campus. When Anthony asked the librarian to refer him to the exact policy and university web link, despite clearly stating that his actions were a breach of university rules, the librarian could not provide a link. She did say, however, that she would be calling the library management to convey to them that she suspected that someone was in the library in breach of university policy. While this conversation was happening, things not only began to become less clear for Anthony, but he could sense that things were escalating in seriousness and that he was about to get into some significant trouble.

Campus Policies, Guidelines, and Normative Expectations

The questions raised in this scenario are not only about privacy but also about the issues around the University's willingness to accept certain things as permitted behavior on campus property. Token inappropriate filming of other individuals was presently a hot news item, as many young women were victims of voyeuristic behavior, such as upskirting with mobile phone cameras, and more. Yet, many universities simply rely on their "Student Conduct Rules" for support outside criminal intent. For example, a typical student conduct notice states that the students have a responsibility to conduct themselves in accordance with:

1. Campus Access and Order Rules,
2. IT Acceptable Use Policy, and
3. Library Code of Conduct.

However, none of these policies typically provide clear guidelines on audio-visual recordings by students.

Campus policies here are approved by the University Council, and various policies address only general surveillance considerations about audio-visual recordings. The Campus Access and Order Rules specifies that University grounds are private properties (University of Wollongong, 2014), and under the common law regarding real property, the lawful occupiers of land have the general right to prevent others from being on, or doing acts on, their land, even if an area on the land is freely accessible to the public (Clarke, 2014). It is Clarke's latter emphasis which summarises exactly the context of a typical university setting which can be considered a closed-campus but open to the public.

The pace of technological change poses challenges for the law, and deficiencies in regulatory frameworks for Point of View Surveillance exist in many jurisdictions in Australia (Clarke, 2014). Australian universities as organizations are also bound (in this case) by the *Workplace Surveillance Act 2005 (NSW)* and the *Privacy and Personal Information Protection Act 1998 (NSW)* (Australasian Legal Information Institute, 2016), which again do nothing to specify what is permitted in terms of rules or policies about sousveillance in actions committed by a student on campus grounds.

Scenario 8: Security on Campus

Context

Security arrived at the scene of the incident and escorted Anthony to the security office. By this stage Anthony believed that this might well become a police matter. Security did not wish to ask Anthony questions about his filming on campus but ostensibly wanted to check whether or not Anthony's GoPro had been stolen. There had been a spate of car park thefts, and it was for this that Anthony was being investigated. Anthony then thought it appropriate to ask them several questions about the recordings he had made, to which security mentioned the *Surveillance Devices Act 2007 (NSW)* and how they had to put signage to warn people about the cameras and the fact that activity was being recorded. Additionally, Anthony was told that CCTV footage could be shared only with the police, and that cameras on campus were never facing people but were facing toward the roadways, and footpaths. When Anthony reminded the security about Google Glass and asked if they had a plan for when Glass would be used on the campus, the security manager replied that everything would be thought about when the time arrived. Anthony left to attend a lecture for which he was once again late.

Security Breaches, the Law, and Enforcement

Anthony was not satisfied with the response of the security manager about campus rules pertaining to the filming of others. While Anthony felt very uncomfortable about the footage he had on his camera, he still did not feel that the university's security office provided adequate guidance on acceptable use. The security manager had tended to skirt around providing a direct response to Anthony, probably because he did not have any concrete answers. First, the manager brought up the Video Piracy Policy topic and then the University's IT Acceptable Use Policy. Anthony felt that those policies had nothing to do with him. First, he was sure he was not conducting video piracy in any way, and second, he was not using the university's IT services to share his films with others or exceed his Internet quota, etc. Somehow, the manager connected this by saying that the recording might contain copyrighted material on it, and that it should never be transferred through the university's IT infrastructure (e.g. network). He also shared a newspaper article with Anthony that was somehow supposed to act as a warning message but it just didn't make sense to Anthony how all of that was connected to the issue at hand.

Scenario 9: Sophie's Lecture

Context

Arriving at the lecture theater after the lecture had already begun, Anthony and Sophie opened the door and the lecturer noticed the camera mounted on Anthony's head. The lecturer immediately became infuriated, asking Anthony to remove the camera and to leave his classroom. Even after Anthony left the class, the lecturer still thought he might be being recorded through the lecture theatre's part-glass door and so he asked Anthony to leave the corridor as well. The entire time, the GoPro was not recording any of the incidents. The incident became heated, despite Anthony fully accepting the academic's perspective. It was the very last thing that Anthony had expected by that point in the day. It was absolutely devastating to him.

Ethics, Power, Inequality, and Non-Participation

Every student at an Australian university has academic freedom and is welcome to attend lectures whether or not they are enrolled in the subject. However, it is the academic instructor's right to privacy to keep a student from recording his or her class. A lecturer's classes are considered "teaching material" and the lecturer owns the intellectual property of his/her teaching material (University of Wollongong, 2014). In keeping with the aforementioned statements, any recording of lectures should be carried out after consulting with the instructor. Some lecturers do not even like the idea of Echo 360, as it can be used for much more than simply recording a lecture for reuse by students. Lecture recordings could be used to audit staff or surveil whether staff are doing their job properly, display innovative teaching techniques, possess poor or good knowledge of content, and stick to time or take early marks. Some faculty members also consider the classroom to be a sacred meeting place between them and students and would never wish for a camera to invade this intimate gathering. Cameras and recordings would indeed stifle a faculty member's or a student's right to freedom of speech if the video was ever to go public. It would also mean that some students would simply not contribute anything to the classroom if they knew they were being taped, or that someone might scrutinize their perspectives and opinions on controversial matters.

POSSIBLE FUTURE IMPLICATIONS DRAWN FROM SCENARIOS

In the scenarios, in almost every instance, the overt nature of Anthony's wearable recording device, given it was head-mounted, elicited an instantaneous response. Others displayed a variety of responses and attitudes including that:

1. They liked it,
2. They did not mind it,
3. They were indifferent about it,
4. They did not like it and finally,
5. They were disturbed by it.

Regardless of which category they belonged to, however, they did not explicitly voice their feelings to Anthony, although body language and facial expressions spoke volumes. In this closed campus scenario, the majority of people who came into contact with Anthony fell under the first two categories. It also seems clear that some contexts were especially delicate, for instance, taking the camera (while still recording) into the restroom, an obviously private amenity. It is likely that individuals in the restroom would have had no problem with the GoPro filming outside the restroom setting.

Research into future technologies and their respective social implications is urgent, since many emerging technologies are here right now. Whatever the human mind can conjure is liable to be designed, developed, and implemented. The main concern is how we choose to deal with it. In this final section, issues drawn from the scenarios are speculatively extended to project future implications when wearable computing has become more ubiquitous in society.

Privacy, Security, and Trust

Privacy experts claim that while we might once have been concerned, or felt uncomfortable with, CCTV being as pervasive as it is today, we are shifting from a limited number of big brothers to ubiquitous little brothers (Shilton, 2009). The fallacy of security is that more cameras do not necessarily mean a safer society, and statistics, depending on how they are presented, may be misleading about reductions in crime in given hotspots. Criminals do not just stop committing crime (e.g. selling drugs) because a local council installs a group of multi-directional cameras on a busy public route. On the contrary, crime has been shown to be redistributed or relocated to another proximate geographic location. In a study for the United Kingdom's Home Office (Gill & Spriggs, 2005), only one area of the 14 studied saw a drop in the number of incidents that could be attributed to CCTV.

Questions of trust seem to be the biggest factor militating against wearable devices that film other people who have not granted their consent to be recorded. Many people may not like to be photographed for reasons we don't quite understand, but it remains their right to say, "No, leave me alone." Others have no trouble being recorded by someone they know, so long as they know they are being recorded prior to the record button being pushed. Still others show utter indifference, claiming that there is no longer anything personal out in the open. Often, the argument is posed that anyone can watch anyone else walk down a street. This argument fails however: watching someone cross the road is not the same as recording them cross the road, whether by design or by sheer coincidence. Handing out requests for deletion every time someone asks whether they've been captured on camera is not good enough. Allowing people to opt out "after the fact" is not consent-based and violates fundamental human rights including the control individuals might have over their own image and the freedom to go about their life as they please (Bronitt & Michael, 2012).

Laws, Regulations, and Policies

At the present time, laws and regulations pertaining to surveillance and listening devices, privacy, telecommunications, crimes, and even workplace relations require amendments to keep pace with advancements in wearable and even implantable sensors. The police need to be viewed as enforcing the laws that they are there to upkeep, not to don the very devices they claim to be illegal. Policies in campus settings, such as universities, also need to address the seeming imbalance in what is, and is not, possible. The commoditization of such devices will only lead to even greater public interest issues coming to the fore. The laws are clearly outdated, and there is controversy over how to overcome the legal implications of emerging technologies.

Creating new laws for each new device will lead to an endless drafting of legislation, which is not practicable, and claiming that existing laws can respond to new problems is unrealistic, as users will seek to get around the law via loopholes in a patchwork of statutes. Cameras provide a power imbalance. Initially, only a few people had mobile phones with cameras: now they are everywhere. Then, only some people carried body-worn video recorders for extreme sports: now, increasingly, many are using a GoPro, Looxcie, or Taser Axon glasses. These devices, while still nascent, have been met with some acceptance, in various contexts including some business-centric applications. Photoborgs might feel they are "hitting back" at all the cameras on the walls that are recording 24×7, but this does not cancel out the fact that the photoborgs themselves are doing exactly what they are claiming a fixed, wall-mounted camera is doing to them.

Future Implications

All of the risks mentioned above are interrelated. If we lack privacy, we lose trust; if we lack security, we feel vulnerable; if we lose our anonymity, we lose a considerable portion of our liberty and when people lose their trust and their liberty, then they feel vulnerable. This kind of scenario is deeply problematic, and portends a higher incidence of depression, as people would not feel they had the freedom to act and be themselves, sharing their true feelings. Implications of this interrelatedness are presented in Figure 1.

Since 100% security does not exist in any technological system, privacy will always be a prominent issue. When security is lacking, privacy becomes an issue, individuals become more vulnerable and the anonymity of an individual comes into question. A loss of anonymity limits people's liberty to act and speak as they want and eventually people start losing their trust in each other and in authorities. When the people are not free to express their true selves, they become withdrawn and despite a high-tech community, people may enter a state of despondency. The real

Figure 1. Major implications of wearables: the utopian and dystopian views

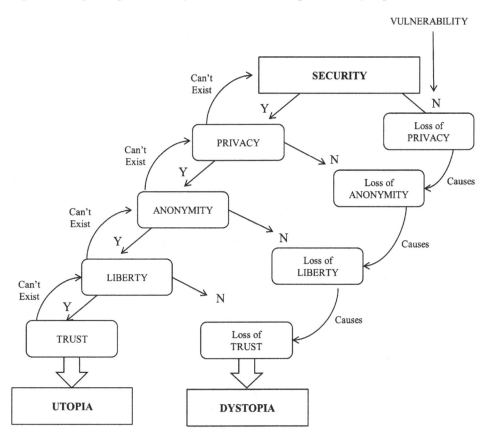

question will be in the future when it is not people who are sporting these body-worn devices, but automated data collection machines like Knightscope's K5 (Knightscope, 2016). These will indeed be mobile camera surveillance units, converging sousveillance and surveillance in one clean sweep (Perakslis et al., 2014).

Future Society

Mann (2013) argues that wearable sousveillance devices that are used in everyday life to store, access, transfer and share information will be commonplace, worn continuously and perhaps even permanently implanted. Michael and Michael (2012, p. 195) in their perception of the age of Überveillence state:

There will be a segment of the consumer and business markets who will adopt the technology for no clear reason and without too much thought, save for the fact that the technology is new and seems to be the way advanced societies are heading. This segment will probably not be overly concerned with any discernible abridgement of their human rights nor the small print 'terms and conditions agreement' they have signed, but will take an implant on the promise that they will have greater connectivity to the Internet, and to online services and bonus loyalty schemes more generally.

Every feature added on a wearable device adds another layer of risk to the pre-existing risks. Currently, we may only have capabilities to store, access, transfer and manipulate the gathered data but as the development of technology continues, context-aware software will be able to interpret vast amounts of data into meaningful information that can be used by unauthorized third parties. It is almost certain that the laws will not be able to keep up with the pace of the technology. Accordingly, individuals will have to be alert and aware, and private and public organizations will need to set rules and guidelines to protect their employees' privacy, as well as their own.

Society's ability to cope with the ethical and societal problems that technology raises has long been falling behind the development of such technology and the same can be said for laws and regulations. With no legal protection and social safe zone, members of society are threatened with losing their privacy through wearable technology. When the technology becomes widespread, privacy at work, in schools, in supermarkets, at the ATM, on the Internet, even when walking, sitting in a public space, and so on, is subject to perishability.

The future is already here and, since the development of technology is seemingly unstoppable, there is more to come, but for any possible futures that may come, there needs to be a healthy human factor. "For every expert there's an equal and opposite expert" (Sowell, 1995, p. 102; also sometimes attributed to Arthur C. Clarke). So even as we are enthusiastic about how data collected through wearable technology will enhance the quality of our daily life, we also have to be cautious to think about our security and privacy issues in an era of ubiquitous wearable technology. In this sense, creating digital footprints of our social and personal lives with the possibility of them being exposed publicly do not seem to coincide with the idea of a "healthy society".

One has to ponder: where next? Might we be arguing that we are nearing the point of total surveillance, as everyone begins to record everything around them for "just in case" reasons such as insurance protection, establishing liability, and complaint handling (much like the in-car black box recorder unit can clear you of wrongdoing in an accident)? How gullible might we become to think that images and video footage do not lie, even though a new breed of hackers might manipulate and tamper with digital reality to their own ends. The überveillance trajectory refers to the ultimate potentiality for embedded surveillance devices like swallowable pills with onboard sensors, tags, and transponder IDs placed in the subdermal layer of the skin (Michael & Michael, 2013). Will the new frontier be surveillance of the heart and mind?

DISCUSSION POINTS

- Does sound recording by wearable devices present any ethical dilemmas?
- Are wearable still cameras more acceptable than wearable video cameras?
- What should one do if bystanders of a recording in a public space question why they are being recorded?
- What themes are evident in the videos and the comments on Surveillance Camera Man Channel at http://www.liveleak.com/c/surveillancecameraman?
- What is the difference between making a recording with a smartphone and with a head mounted camera?
- If one juxtaposes a surveillance camera covertly integrated into a light fixture, with an overt head-mounted camera, then why should the two devices elicit a different response from bystanders?
- In what ways is a CCTV in a restroom any different from a photoborg in a restroom?
- Are there gender differences in enthusiasm for certain wearables? Who are the innovators of these technologies?
- What dangers exist around Internet addiction, escapism, and living in a virtual world?
- Are we nearing the point of total information surveillance? Is this a good thing? Will it decrease criminal activity or are we nearing a *Minority Report* style future?
- Will the new frontier be surveillance of the heart and mind beyond anything Orwell could have envisioned?
- How can the law keep pace with technological change?
- Can federal and state laws be in contradiction over the rights of a photoborg? How?
- Watch the movie *The Final Cut.* Watch the drama *The Entire History of You.* What are the similiarities and differences? What does such a future mean for personal security and national security?
- Consider in small groups other scenarios where wearables would be welcome as opposed to unwelcome.
- In which locations should body-worn video cameras never be worn?

QUESTIONS

- What is meant by *surveillance, sousveillance* and *überveillance*?
- What is a *photoborg*? And what is "point of view" within a filming context?
- Research the related terms *surveillance, dataveillance*, and *überveillence.*

- What does Steve Mann's "Request for Deletion" webpage say? Why is it largely untenable?
- Why did Google decide to focus on industry applications of Glass finally, and not the total market?
- Are we ready to see many (overt or covert) sousveillers in our everyday life?
- Will we all be photoborgs one day, or live in a society where we need to be?
- Do existing provisions concerning voyeurism cover all possible sousveillance situations?
- If lifelogs are streamed in real-time and near real-time what can bystanders shown do about the distribution of their images (if they are ever find out)?
- Is lifelong lifelogging feasible? Desirable? Should it be suspended in confidential business meetings, going through airport security and customs or other areas? Which areas?
- Should citizens film their encounters with police, given police are likely to be filming it too?
- Should the person using PoVS technology have more legal protection than persons they are monitoring?
- Are wearables likely to be rapidly adopted and even outpace smartphone use?

REFERENCES

Armstrong, J., & Welsh, B. (2011). The Entire History of You. In B. Reisz (Ed.), *Black Mirror*. London, UK: Zeppetron.

Australasian Legal Information Institute. (2014). *Workplace Surveillance Act, 2005 (NSW)*. Retrieved June 6, 2016, from http://www.austlii.edu.au/au/legis/nsw/consol_act/wsa2005245/

Australasian Legal Information Institute. (2015). *Surveillance Devices Act, 1998 (WA)*. Retrieved June 6, 2016, from https://www.slp.wa.gov.au/legislation/statutes.nsf/main_mrtitle_946_currencies.html

Australasian Legal Information Institute. (2016). *Privacy and Personal Information Protection Act 1998*. Retrieved June 6, 2016, from http://www.austlii.edu.au/au/legis/nsw/consol_act/papipa1998464/

Branscomb, A. W. (1994). *Who Owns Information? From Privacy to Public Access*. New York, NY: BasicBooks.

Bronitt, S., & Michael, K. (2012). Human rights, regulation, and national security (introduction). *IEEE Technology and Society Magazine, 31*(1), 15–16. doi:10.1109/MTS.2012.2188704

Clarke, R. (2012). *Point-of-View Surveillance*. Retrieved from http://www.roger-clarke.com/DV/PoVS.html

Clarke, R. (2014). Surveillance by the Australian media, and its regulation. *Surveillance & Society, 12*(1), 89–107.

Echo. (2016). *Lecture capture: Video is the new textbook*. Retrieved from http://echo360.com/what-you-can-do/lecture-capture

Ericsson. (2015). *Ericsson Mobility Report*. Retrieved June 6, 2016, from http://www.ericsson.com/mobility-report

Fernandez Arguedas, V., Izquierdo, E., & Chandramouli, K. (2013). Surveillance ontology for legal, ethical and privacy protection based on SKOS. In *IEEE 18th International Conference on Digital Signal Processing (DSP)*.

Ghorayshi, A. (2014). *Google Glass user treated for internet addiction caused by the device*. Retrieved June 6, 2016, from https://www.theguardian.com/science/2014/oct/14/google-glass-user-treated-addiction-withdrawal-symptoms

Gill, M., & Spriggs, A. (2005). *Assessing the impact of CCTV*. London: Home Office Research, Development and Statistics Directorate.

Gokyer, D., & Michael, K. (2015). Digital wearability scenarios: Trialability on the run. *IEEE Consumer Electronics Magazine, 4*(2), 82–91. doi:10.1109/MCE.2015.2393005

Harfield, C. (2014). Body-worn POV technology: Moral harm. *IEEE Technology and Society Magazine, 33*(2), 64–72. doi:10.1109/MTS.2014.2319976

Knightscope. (2016). Advanced physical security technology. *Knightscope: K5*. Retrieved from http://knightscope.com/

Kotler, S. (2014). *Legal heroin: Is virtual reality our next hard drug*. Retrieved June 6, 2016, from http://www.forbes.com/sites/stevenkotler/2014/01/15/legal-heroin-is-virtual-reality-our-next-hard-drug/#225d03c27472

Lagorio, C. (2006). *Is virtual life better than reality?* Retrieved June 6, 2016, from http://www.cbsnews.com/news/is-virtual-life-better-than-reality/

Levy, K. (2014). A surprising number of places have banned Google Glass in San Francisco. *Business Insider, 3*. Retrieved from http://www.businessinsider.com/google-glass-ban-san-francisco-2014-3

Mann, S. (2002). *Sousveillance*. Retrieved from http://wearcam.org/sousveillance.htm

Mann, S. (2005). Sousveillance and cyborglogs: A 30-year empirical voyage through ethical, legal, and policy issues. *Presence (Cambridge, Mass.)*, *14*(6), 625–646. doi:10.1162/105474605775196571

Mann, S. (2013). Veillance and reciprocal transparency: Surveillance versus sousveillance, AR glass, lifeglogging, and wearable computing. In *IEEE International Symposium on Technology and Society (ISTAS)*. Toronto: IEEE.

Mann, S. (n.d.). *The request for deletion (RFD)*. Retrieved from http://wearcam.org/rfd.htm

Mann, S., & Wassell, P. (2013). *Proposed law on sousveillance*. Retrieved from http://wearcam.org/MannWassellLaw.pdf

Michael, K. (2013). Keynote: The final cut—Tampering with direct evidence from wearable computers. In *Proc. 5th Int. Conf. Multimedia Information Networking and Security (MINES)*.

Michael, K., & Michael, M. G. (2012). Commentary on: Mann, S. (2012): Wearable computing. In M. Soegaard & R. Dam (Eds.), *Encyclopedia of human-computer interaction*. The Interaction-Design.org Foundation. Retrieved from https://www.interaction-design.org/encyclopedia/wearable_computing.html

Michael, K., & Michael, M. G. (2013a). Computing ethics: No limits to watching? *Communications of the ACM*, *56*(11), 26–28. doi:10.1145/2527187

Michael, K., Michael, M. G., & Perakslis, C. (2014). Be vigilant: There are limits to veillance. In J. Pitt (Ed.), *The computer after me*. London: Imperial College London Press. doi:10.1142/9781783264186_0013

Michael, M. G., & Michael, K. (Eds.). (2013b). *Überveillance and the social implications of microchip implants: Emerging technologies (Advances in human and social aspects of technology)*. Hershey, PA: IGI Global.

Nettle, D., Nott, K., & Bateson, M. (2012). 'Cycle thieves, we are watching you': Impact of a simple signage intervention against bicycle theft. *PLoS ONE*, *7*(12), e51738. doi:10.1371/journal.pone.0051738 PMID:23251615

Perakslis, C., Pitt, J., & Michael, K. (2014). Drones humanus. *IEEE Technology and Society Magazine*, *33*(2), 38–39.

Ruvio, A., Gavish, Y., & Shoham, A. (2013). Consumer's doppelganger: A role model perspective on intentional consumer mimicry. *Journal of Consumer Behaviour*, *12*(1), 60–69. doi:10.1002/cb.1415

Shactman, N. (2003). A spy machine of DARPA's dreams. *Wired.* Retrieved from http://archive.wired.com/techbiz/media/news/2003/05/58909?currentPage=al

Shilton, K. (2009). Four billion little brothers?: Privacy, mobile phones, and ubiquitous data collection. *Communications of the ACM*, *52*(11), 48–53. doi:10.1145/1592761.1592778

Sowell, T. (1995). *The Vision of the Anointed: Self-congratulation as a Basis for Social Policy*. New York, NY: Basic Books.

Surveillance Camera Man. (2015). *Surveillance Camera Man.* Retrieved from https://www.youtube.com/watch?v=jzysxHGZCAU

Tanner, R. J., Ferraro, R., Chartrand, T. L., Bettman, J., & van Baaren, R. (2008). Of chameleons and consumption: The impact of mimicry on choice and preferences. *The Journal of Consumer Research*, *34*(6), 754–766. doi:10.1086/522322

University of Wollongong. (2014a). *Campus Access and Order Rules*. Retrieved from http://www.uow.edu.au/about/policy/UOW058655.html

University of Wollongong. (2014b). *Ownership of Intellectual Property*. Retrieved from http://www.uow.edu.au/about/policy/UOW058689.html

University of Wollongong. (2014c). *Student Conduct Rules*. Retrieved from http://www.uow.edu.au/about/policy/UOW058723.html

Van Bommel, M., van Prooijen, J., Elffers, H., & Van Lange, P. (2012). Be aware to care: Public self-awareness leads to a reversal of the bystander effect. *Journal of Experimental Social Psychology*, *48*(4), 926–930. doi:10.1016/j.jesp.2012.02.011

KEY TERMS AND DEFINITIONS

Body-Worn Video (BWV): These are cameras that are embedded in devices that can be worn on the body to record video, typically by law enforcement officers.

Closed-Campus: Refers to any organization or institution that contains a dedicated building(s) on a bounded land parcel offering a range of online and offline services, such as banking, retail, sporting. Closed campus examples include schools and universities.

Closed-Circuit Television (CCTV): Also referred to as video surveillance. CCTV is the use of video cameras to transmit a signal to a specific place. CCTV cameras can be overt (obvious) or covert (hidden).

Digital Glass: Otherwise referred to as wearable eyeglasses which house multiple sensors on board. An example of digital glass is Google Glass. The future of digital glass may well be computer-based contact lenses.

Lifelogging: When a user decides to log his/her life using wearable computing or other devices, that have audio-visual capability. It is usually a continuous stream of a recording 24/7.

Personal Security Devices: These are devices that allegedly deter perpetrators from attacking others because they are always on gathering evidence, and ready to record. PSDs may have an on-board alarm alerting central care services for further assistance.

Policy: An enforceable set of organizational rules and principles used to aid decision-making that have penalties for non-compliance, such as the termination of an employee's contract with an employer.

Private Space: Somewhere geographically that one has an expectation of privacy, naturally. Some examples include: the home, the backyard, and the restroom.

Public Space: Somewhere geographically where there is no expectation of privacy save for when someone holds a private conversation in a private context.

Sousveillance: The opposite of surveillance from above, which includes *inverse surveillance*, also sometimes described as person-to-person surveillance. Citizens can use sousveillance as a mechanism to keep law enforcement officers accountable for their actions.

Surveillance: "Watching from above" such as CCTV from business buildings. For behaviors, activities, or other changing information to be under the watchful eye of authority, usually for the purpose of influencing, managing, directing, or protecting the masses.

Chapter 11
Model Course Syllabus:
Management of Security Issues in Wearable Technology

Michelle C. Antero
Zayed University, UAE

ABSTRACT

This chapter briefly introduces some historical and contemporary context before proposing a model course syllabus to implement a course in Management of Security Issues in Wearable Technology. The course syllabus is developed in line with the IS2010 curriculum recommended by the peak bodies (ACM and AIS) for a degree in Information Systems, Computer Information Systems or Management Information Systems. The design further follows the guidelines developed by the Accreditation Board of Engineering and Technology (ABET) that advocates that Course Learning Outcomes (CLOs) be developed for the list of topics covered by the material. In addition, the syllabus provides a basis for enterprise training relevant to managers and security specialists. The chapter also provides some general pedagogical guidelines on how each topic can be discussed and activities appropriate to the learners. It also uses Gluga et al.'s (2013) assessment criteria, based on Bloom's (1956) taxonomy to measure the depth of knowledge.

INTRODUCTION

Technological advances in microchips, mobile technology, wireless networks, sensors, location-based services, and the prevalence of mobile applications have made possible the widespread availability of a whole range of wearable technology.

DOI: 10.4018/978-1-5225-1016-1.ch011

Early applications of wearable technologies were conceived in 1955 and developed in 1961 when Thorpe and Shannon developed a shoe-mounted roulette wheel prediction system (Thorpe, 1998). The mass production of the microchip in the 1980s made it possible to increase computing capabilities and opened up opportunities to develop wearable technology. Pioneering work by Steve Mann in the 1980s and early 1990s (Mann, 1995s) introduced the "wearable wireless webcam" to the world and, in 1996, the USA's Defense Advanced Research Project Agency (DARPA) launched a wearable technology workshop looking towards "Wearables in 2005" (Rhodes & Mase, 2006).

A year later, in 1997, the first head-mounted display (DARPA, 1997) was developed for tactical military purposes. By the late 2000s, we began to see the availability of consumer wearable technology and the ability to sync information between the wearable technology and mobile phones. For example, the collaboration between Nike and Apple in 2006 created Nike+iPod (Apple, 2006). Nike+iPod was the first product to synchronize information collected from sensors in Nike shoes with an iPod application, and it ultimately changed a runner's experience. By 2014, the Consumer Electronic show in Las Vegas was showcasing smart watches, activity trackers, head-mountable cameras and a whole range of other wearable technology for the mass market (Gibbs & Arthur 2014).

The spike in the demand and growth of the availability of wearable technologies in recent years provides motivation to understand the security risks associated with these devices. As these devices become pervasive, individuals and organizations need to be made aware of the security and privacy risks posed by wearable technology. As a new academic discipline focused on this particular research agenda has emerged, there is a corresponding need to develop a model curriculum to guide academics as they discuss these issues in the classroom or in enterprise-wide training courses.

WEARABLE TECHNOLOGY AND ITS SECURITY AND PRIVACY RISKS

Wearable technology builds on the vision that body-worn technology augments a human's physical and analytical capabilities with computing power to engage in superhuman activities (Pedersen, 2014). Wearable technology refers to clothing or accessories that utilize the power of computing and electronics to enable the exchange data between objects without human intervention. The interoperability of these devices with existing technologies has made it possible to have a seamless exchange of data and a push toward connectedness.

Since Thorpe and Shannon's shoe-mounted roulette wheel prediction system (Thorpe,1998) and USA's Defense Advanced Research Project Agency (DARPA)'s first digital glasses, much progress has been made to augmenting reality through wearable technology thanks to the rapid technological developments. Industry professionals attribute the progress of wearable computing to Steve Mann and recognize him to be "father of wearable computing" (Schofield, 2001). His contributions to the development of various elements of wearable technology range from topics in the technical aspects of wearable technology (Mann, 1997; Mann, 2003), to the impact on the social aspects, such as the loss of ability to have control of the information retrieved in surveillance (Mann, 2001).

Developments in human-computer interaction (HCI) interfaces paved the way for wearable technology to provide new ways of communicating and interacting with the environment (Heingartner, 2009; Lumsden & Brewster, 2003; Mann, 2003). The developments of HCI have come in the form of hand gestures, facial recognition, eye tracking and other forms of communicating beyond traditional methods of using the keyboard and mouse. Through the constant interaction and communication between the wearable technology and other computing applications, wearable technology has enabled the collection, interpretation and analysis of different types of data to achieve a particular purpose. Some of the data extracted collect specific information about

1. The wearer and their activities (i.e., inward data), or
2. The wearer's environment (i.e., outward data).

The extent to which data is collected and analyzed for a particular purpose is in varying degrees, and depends on the wearable technology. Digital skin technologies (c.f., Noh et al. 2013) make it possible to collect inward data to monitor a user's health data (e.g., heart rate, blood oxygen, temperature) without human interference. Activity trackers (e.g., Fitbit, pedometers) can collect inward data to monitor activities (Harrison, 2014). The analysis of such activities can range from decision-making concerning online self-quantifications (Sjöklint, 2014); or addressing sedentary and inactive lifestyles using self-regulation (Harrison, 2014). Technological advances in smart watches have the advantage of collecting both inward and outward data from a consistent observation point. The smart watch allows users to collect data as is it is in continuous contact with the skin, on a specific part of the body (i.e., the wrist), and can combine this with contextual information (e.g., geo-location) to sense the user's environment (Reza, Price & Petre, 2015). Smart watches can also combine user's health data with galvanic skin response, which can accurately be used to identify physiological arousal (Reza, Price & Petre, 2015). Some of these smart watches interact directly with mobile applications to communicate and share information, thus combining the inward data and outward data and visualizing this for users to analyze the data. Similarly, wearable headset devices have the ability to collect and interpret inward data to interact with, and control, outward data. For example, Emotiv's EPOC headset uses scalp electroencephalography (EEG) to read facial expressions and emotions and transmit data to computers wirelessly (Heingartner, 2009). Google Glass was envisioned to have the capability of sensing what its users were doing internally and retrieving the information needed to increase productivity (Metz, 2015), thereby utilizing inward and outward data as well.

As these devices provide new forms of transmitting and interpreting data to interact with various computing devices and the Internet of things (IoT), they also pose questions about surveillance & privacy (Pedersen 2014). Data collected from activity trackers has been used in corporate settings to monitor their employees' whereabouts to gain information for a particular purpose. Some companies have seen this as a way encourage employees to have an active lifestyle to reduce health insurance premiums (Everett, 2015); others wanted to determine the strength of working relationships between individuals based on geo-location data and activities (Tsubouchi, Kawajiri and Shimosaka, 2013). While research suggests that this type of monitoring negatively impacts the employees' health and wellbeing (Everett, 2015), the data availability doesn't prevent companies from using it. Moreover, data collected has not only been used internally but has also been shared with third parties, for instance for market research purposes (Mancuso & Stuth, 2015). Unfortunately, the data sharing can be done with or without the explicit knowledge of the individuals because of the ambiguity of the privacy policies of the vendors selling these wearable technologies (Singer & Perry, 2015) or because of the policies of the companies where the employee works.

An even more pressing concern is the security risks associated with the wearable technology, which includes, but goes beyond, the security risks of mobile devices. Geo-location data pinpoints the exact location of an individual at any given time. While the data is useful for tactical military operations to locate targets (DARPA, 1997), this can also be used by individuals with malicious intent to harm another person. Additionally, personal information and health information stored on the devices can be targeted because it provides information about a particular person or used for identity theft.

There is a need to understand the impact of the security and privacy challenges in wearable technology to manage them effectively. From the literature reviewed briefly above, we can see several issues that can variously be addressed by students, researchers and organizations. Students can investigate the answers to the following indicative questions ranging from the technological to the social and ethical:

What are the underlying technologies that power wearables and provide us with superhuman capabilities? How are these technologies connected to provide us a seamless transfer of data? Why is it necessary to collect the data and share it with others? How can we guard these data as wearable technologies communicate with other computing devices? Who are the guardians of the data? Who guards the guardians so that they comply with international and local regulations that protect the privacy of the data? What are the social, professional and ethical issues with sharing data? When will the companies realize that the tradeoffs of data collection and pushing the limits of privacy can be counterproductive?

Such questions, and many more, can be explored within the proposed model course syllabus.

MODELING THE COURSE SYLLABUS

This model course syllabus is developed in line with the recommendations of the IS2010 Curriculum Guidelines in Information Systems (Topi et al., 2010). Endorsed by both the peak bodies in Computer and Management Information Systems, namely, the Association of Computing Machinery (ACM) and the Association for Information Systems (AIS), this remains the latest and most widely accepted reference curriculum for designing IS degrees and individual courses. There are also curriculum guidelines developed for computer science programs (ACM/IEEE, 2013) which have a more technical focus and objective but these too include the new knowledge area of *Information Assurance and Security* in recognition of the critical importance of this in today's world. Issues such as platform security and policy and governance are covered within this knowledge area, and authentication, ethics, trust and vulnerabilities are core topics. These areas are built into the syllabus described in this chapter.

The syllabus design also complies with the Accreditation Board of Engineering and Technology's (ABET) Computing Accreditation Commission's (CAC) accreditation criteria for programs in Computing (ABET 2016a). It follows the accreditation boards' criteria to ensure that the proposed course meets the quality standards set by the board. ABET's general guidelines suggest that courses should align with a particular program-level educational objective and identify specific course learning outcomes (CLOs). Program-level student learning outcomes are defined as statements that "describe what students are expected to know and be able to do by the time of graduation" (ABET 2016b), and each course develops specific knowledge, skills and behaviors towards their overall achievement. In addition to the conceptual content, and in line with the principles of national and international qualifications frameworks (ETF, 2006), both a knowledge and a skills focus are incorporated in the design by specifying a course in measurable outcome terms.

In order to advance learning sooner, it takes into account an analogical pedagogy, which provides students with a quick way to build new knowledge (Paulson, 2014; Mitri, 2012; Gentner & Kurtz, 2006) by mapping a base domain (i.e., IS2010 courses) to a target domain (i.e., Managing Security Issues in Wearable Technology). Accordingly, this model course syllabus references the educational objectives developed as part of the curriculum for a degree in Information Systems, Management Information Systems or Computer Information Systems (Topi et al., 2010).

The model course is expected to build on previous knowledge established particularly from the following IS2010 core courses: *Foundations of Information Systems; Data and Information Management; IT Infrastructure; IS Strategy, Management and Acquisition.* The syllabus addresses "Understanding, managing and controlling IT risks", which is a core high-level outcome of the IS2010 curriculum, and is specifically proposed as an elective course in Topi et al. (2010).

The learning outcomes selected for this model course syllabus is based on the learning outcomes extracted from the core and elective courses identified in Topi et al.'s (2010) guidelines. These outcomes were assessed for applicability to the proposed course of Managing Security in Wearable Technology. Subsequently, these outcomes were then adapted to design the course level educational objectives of Managing Security in Wearable Technology.

The following CLOs were created both to follow the educational program requirements for Information Systems degrees (Topi et al., 2010) and to be relevant to information security management practitioners and managers. Learners would normally be University students, but short course adaptions for professionals are potentially accommodated within the design. The set of course learning outcomes is:

1. Learners should be able to understand the different IT infrastructure components of wearable technology and the implications of its design for security;
2. Learners should be able to evaluate and manage wearable technologies, in relation to the processes, components, or programs to meet desired needs and effectively integrate them into the user environment;
3. Learners should be able to explain the importance of designing a secure organizational information infrastructure, in terms of how data is stored and managed, for wearable technologies;
4. Learners should be able to determine appropriate strategies to assure the confidentiality, integrity and availability of information in wearable technology;

5. Learners should be able to implement and evaluate the best practices and standards for the security of wearable technology;
6. Learners should be able to explain and demonstrate management and technical concepts in securing wearable technologies;
7. Learners should be able to perform a risk assessment to analyze a security problem associated with wearable technology and define the necessary techniques appropriate to mitigate the risk;
8. Learners should be able to examine and explain the impact of wearable technology on individuals and organizations, in relation to the ethical, legal, security and global policy issues; and
9. Learners should be able to aware of emerging technology that enables wearable technology to communicate, collaborate and interact in new ways.

These model CLOs include verbs focusing on both conceptual and applied knowledge, and would be selected and tailored according to the specific focus of individual programs.

COURSE MAPPING

This proposed course features a set of knowledge areas, which are mapped accordingly to CLOs previously identified. The knowledge areas were selected from the seven (7) core courses proposed by the peak bodies (Topi et al., 2010). From this set of core topics, knowledge areas were selected for relevance to the proposed course, spanning IS/IT broadly, since IS programs, as well as corporate training, can have a more management or technical focus. This selection, therefore, included reference to the Computer Science (ACM/IEEE, 2013) and to the IT model curriculum (Lunt et al., 2008). The selection of knowledge areas identified by the peak bodies in both technically and managerially focused disciplines ensures that the student can develop the necessary range of competence relevant to wearable technology as it relates both to an academic program and to professional life.

The syllabus builds on the foundation concepts identified as a core topic with the addition of domain specific knowledge areas. It thus extends the IT Risk Management elective course proposed in IS2010 as applied to this emerging technology. These knowledge areas were subsequently mapped to topics gleaned from a wider literature review and then mapped to learning objectives that are in line with security and privacy issues for wearable technology.

Table 1 lists the knowledge areas, the wearable technology topic domain, a short description of the topic, and the relevant CLOs.

Table 1. Recommended topics as relevant to the wearable technology domain

Knowledge Areas	Wearable Technology Topic	Short Description	CLO Mapping
Networking (NET)	Hardware Architecture	Provides an overview and importance of a reliable network to connect wearable technology across platforms successfully	1, 2, 8, 9
IT Fundamentals (ITF)	Software Standards	Ensures interoperability and seamless transfer of data across multiple technological devices do not compromise the security and privacy of users	2, 3, 4, 8, 9
Human-computer interaction (HCI)	Technology Designs	Designs a safe and user-friendly interface to ensure that users can provide input and receive output from the wearable devices.	1, 2, 3, 4, 9
Information Assurance and Security (IAS)	Protection Mechanisms	Ensures that the proper protection mechanisms are in place to manage and control the access of information used in wearable technology	2, 3, 4, 5, 6
Information Management (IM)	Security Management Practices	Discusses the security management practices and the development of standards and guidelines for compliance	5, 6, 7
Social and Professional Issues (SP)	Social, Professional and Ethical Issues	Explains the social consequences of using wearable technologies from the perspective of individuals and organizations	1,2, 8

Due to the varied needs of each university in terms of number of lectures and time allotted for each class, instead of putting the topics in a weekly format, the list suggests a percentage of time dedicated to discuss the topic. From the wearable technology topics above, Table 2 lists an outline of topics, the percentage of time for the topic, and a proposed reading list. The reading lists were primarily selected from the book chapters in this book, which themselves point to further indicative readings in specific areas. An additional set of readings was also identified to supplement the chapters of the book to provide the instructors with a starting point for their own reading lists, which can easily be replaced to tailor their university's need and as new work emerges.

RECOMMENDED ACTIVITIES

The suggested format for each of these discussion topics is that the instructor provides

1. A lecture to put things in context;
2. An activity that applies the concepts; and
3. A post-exercise discussion to answer additional questions.

Model Course Syllabus

Table 2. Weekly outline and suggested readings

Wearable Technology Topic	% Time	Suggested Readings with Short Description
Overview of Wearable Technology and its Security & Privacy Issues	10	• Chapter 1 The Promise and Perils of Wearable Technologies • Mann, S. (1997) describes the role of technological developments in the computing industry and how he utilized the same to create wearable technology. He has demonstrated in various ways how technological systems can be blamed for the irrationality of actions and be subjected to lack of freedom to make decisions.
Security Management Practices	20	• Chapter 2 The Risk of Wearable Technologies to Individuals and Organizations • Chapter 6 Privacy Dangers of Wearables and the Internet of Things • Zhou, et al., (2015) discusses the network architecture of a cloud-assisted, wireless, wearable technology to determine the how several security techniques can help preserve data privacy.
Protection Mechanisms: Data Security and Privacy	35	• Chapter 3 Watch What You Wear: Smartwatches and Sluggish Security • Chapter 4 Confidential Data Storage Systems for Wearable Platforms • Chapter 5 Authenticity Challenges of Wearable Technologies • Chapter 7 Security, Privacy and Ownership Issues with the use of Wearable Health Technologies • Liang, et. al., (2015) discusses the unique challenges posed by the cloud-computing model with wearable technology and provides some encryption solutions to handle data aggregations in private.
Social, Professional and Ethical Issues	30	• Chapter 8 Wearable Devices: Ethical Challenges and Solutions • Chapter 9 What Can People Do With Your Spatial Data?: Socio-Ethical Scenarios • Chapter 10 Societal Implications of Wearable Technology: Interpreting Trialability on the Run • Mancuso & Stuth (2015) suggest that wearable devices can be used for purposes of market research. Data from device records the geo-position of an individual, the frequency and length of time in a particular position, and biometrics. • Singer, R. & Perry, A (2015) provides a comparative review of privacy policies of popular wearable devices. It presents an account of what data is collected and shared. It then provides guidelines in the language of privacy policies to restrict the information shared, explain the consequences of sharing in a social network and the parameters of aggregated data • Mann, S. (2003) describes the wearable technology he experimented on over 30 years where to highlight the role of technology which undermines the person's ability to be free or to make decisions.
Future Directions of Wearable Technology	5	• Chapter 12 Conclusions – Where Next for Wearables?

The activities below target the CLOs (as identified in Table 1). The instructor can spend 2/3 of the time on lectures and 1/3 of the time on activities and post-exercise discussion.

The following section lists recommended activities for each of the discussion topics. This list is not an exhaustive list of activities but simply ideas on what could be done for a particular topic. Videos, guest speakers, product demonstrations and comparisons, debates or mock trials, discussion boards and wikis and so on allow different forms of engagement with the issues. One of the advantages of wearable technology is that using it in the classroom naturally lends itself to many possibilities to enhance learning (Bower, 2015). It also allows learners to engage with the wearable technology first hand, collaborate in real time and provide a range of pedagogical uses (Bower 2015, Martin, 2014). Instructors should capitalize on the use of wearable technology and build exercises that leverage its strengths.

Engaging students in active and useful learning tasks (e.g., writing papers, problem-based projects or experiential exercises) allow students to learn toward a particular learning objective (Armstrong, 1968). As the instructor sees fit, structured lab exercises can be designed specifically to reinforce and support the lecture material. These exercises have been found to aid in motivating students and to learn effectively (Gluga et al., 2013; Armstrong, 1968; Goel et al., 2006; Sherman et al., 2004). Alternatively, students can also take a case-based approach using practitioner provided content (c.f., Goel 2006, Martin, 2004) instead of lab exercises. A case-based approach has been found to encourage students to have engaging discussions based on a particular objective and find a solution (Boehrer & Linsky 1990; Christensen & Hansen, 1987). The application of theoretical concepts in exercises provides students with the experiential knowledge and are more likely able to apply such concept in other scenarios (Moreno, 2008). Below are some examples of exercises for the themes identified.

Overview of Wearable Technology and Security Issues

The topic focuses on providing the background information on hardware architecture, software standards and designs of wearable technology. Since the technological architecture of each technology may vary, the instructor could bring in background material relevant to the selected wearable technology. This overview should be able to provide students with the context for discussing wearable technology and the security issues. Since the availability of wearable technology varies yearly, the instructor can find the appropriate devices that suit the interest of the student.

- The instructor can showcase various wearable technologies and have a comparative analysis of the hardware architecture and software standard used across these technologies. This activity primarily targets the student's ability to understand the similarity and differences of the wearable technology's systems architecture, which builds on one of the learning objectives identified in IS 2010.4 IT infrastructure core course (Topi et al., 2010).

- The discussion can cover topics that discuss the importance of having a reliable network, interoperability across the devices and the optimization of the user interface to capture the data at the access points. This activity highlights the importance of an infrastructure solution based on standard technological components, and builds on the learning objectives of IS 2010.4 IT infrastructure core course (Topi et al., 2010).

Protection Mechanisms: Data Security and Privacy

The discussion topic focuses on the importance of ensuring data security and privacy.

- Students can compare features of wearable technology (e.g., basic information, storage capacity), where the data is stored (e.g., local or remote storage) and what type of data is stored (e.g., geo-location, activity). This activity specifically builds on the learning objective of understanding how data is stored and accessed as part of IS2010.2 Data and Information Management (Topi et al., 2010). It also provides the context of the type of information that is stored and students can be asked to assess the varying levels of privacy that can be considered when sharing this information with others.
- After identifying where the data is stored, students can determine the weaknesses of these access points, which can then be linked the concept of how different tools can be used to ensure data security and privacy (c.f., Sherman 2004). This activity builds on the learning objective of understanding principles of data security and identifying data security risks as part of IS2010.2 Data and Information Management (Topi et al., 2010).
- Students can analyze the data captured by these wearable devices and evaluate how one's privacy can be compromised as these activities provide geolocation, health data, and other personal information. This activity builds on students' knowledge of how to secure information systems resources, as identified in IS 2010.1 Foundations of Information Systems. It also addresses the objective of identifying risks and appropriate strategies to assure confidentiality, integrity and availability of information and processes as identified in the IT Security and Risk Management Elective course (Topi et al., 2010).

Security Management Practices

This topic focuses on the understanding and implementation of security management practices.

- Learning activities can focus on developing awareness campaigns or compliance programs within the context of information management. This focuses on the understanding best practices and regulatory requirements that govern information assurance procedures and controls as identified in the IT Audit and Controls course (ACM & AIS 2010).

Social, Professional, and Ethical Issues

This topic looks at security and privacy issues from an individual, organizational and societal context. This can be discussed in terms of region-specific data protection laws such as European General Data Protection Regulation (EU 2012), or the California Online Privacy Protection Act 2003 (OAG 2003). The state of California, in the US, has an active legislature in terms of passing laws related to the online data collection and privacy laws. They have made efforts to regulate the data practices in companies that utilize the Internet (e.g., Apple, Google, Hewlett-Packard, Microsoft) (Evans, 2015). Other jurisdictions have analogous initiatives, and students can be asked to discover and report these. One of the difficulties of an ethics class is the lack of students' familiarity in making ethical decisions. One way to overcome this difficulty is to employ an ethical framework that can guide the discussion. For instance, students can go through a series of questions as defined by the doing ethics technique (Simpson et al. 2003) to guide the discussion.

The discussion looks at the various trade-offs from collecting the data from the wearable device and the impact to an individual and/or organization requiring the data. This activity is also linked to the ethical concerns that wearable technologies raise and is in line with the objectives in IS 2010.1 Foundations of Information Systems. The students' discussion can be guided by the following questions, as recommended by Simpson et al. (2003):

(1) What is going on? What are the facts?; (2) What are the issues? ; (3) Who is affected?; (4) What are the ethical issues and implications? (5) What can be done about it? What options are there?; and (6) Which option is best? Why?

Future Directions of Wearable Technology

This topic will also vary based on emerging social and technological developments related to wearable technology. Due to the evolving nature of technology, this topic allows the instructor to have the flexibility to add emerging technology in the discussion through the inclusion of newer readings and commercially available devices.

- This discussion can look into the impact of new technological developments in wearable technology. Students can be asked to research trends and to "show and tell" regarding emerging products or predictions as a final activity. The future of technology is largely dependent on the market trends. Students can also be encouraged to explore other websites on wearable technology (e.g., http://wearcam.org/ (Steve Mann's website), or blogs on developing tech strategies that instructors or students find relevant.

These exercises can be done in public laboratories, which provide access to resources, not necessarily available on student machines, or in specialized labs specifically set-up to support special computing requirements. The use of laboratories is in line with the general guidelines from ABET (ABET, 2016a), which suggest that adequate facilities should be made available to students to support the learning outcomes. Students are therefore recommended to have the opportunity to use the necessary learning materials in either a structured, public or specialized laboratory. These laboratories should set up with the flexibility to adopt new technology as it rapidly changes since there is a pressing need for universities to remain current (Goel et al. 2006). Partnerships with local industry and government entities are helpful in this area, and with specialized lab facilities, designing short courses for practitioners and managers, with research projects or internships based around specialized labs or equipment, become attractive options.

EVALUATION CRITERIA

Using international learning standards provides students with the transparency regarding the learning goals that students are measured against (Gluga et. al. 2013). Having a measurable evaluation mitigates the problem of lack of standardization in comparable outcomes (McGettrick, 2005). Following the guidelines from ABET (2016b), appropriate assessments should also be included to determine the extent to which these outcomes are met. An appropriate assessment should be chosen by the instructor based on the individual university's requirements and should measure the extent to which the individual student meets the outcomes. These assessments can come in various forms, such as a specialized term project (cf. Harrison, 2006; Martin, 2004), written or practical examinations and can be done in on- or off- campus settings. Specific assessments and weight of the assessments are not included in this proposal as these can vary by institution and instructor. Instead, this provides a way to use the CLOs as a way to specifically design assessments to ensure that they address what the learner should be able to do, and have a metric or benchmark to assess achievement.

The effectiveness of the assessments can also be measured to gauge students' performance. Their effectiveness can be evaluated using Gluga et al.'s (2013) criteria which adapted Bloom's (1956) taxonomy to measure the expected learning against student's performance regarding:

1. Knowledge and comprehension; or
2. Synthesis and evaluation.

The first set of criteria is associated with competence at a lower level learning, and the second set is associated with higher-level learning. Depending on whether the course is taught at junior or senior levels, the requirement can be adapted to assess e.g. *comprehension* via correct descriptions of concepts, or synthesis, such as formulating a technically sound ethical or legal security policy. It is also important to note that the reliability of the scores gathered depends on the nature of the examination. For example, a take-home examination will provide lower reliability scores compared to supervised, closed-book final exams since take-home examinations allow students to seek help (Gluga et al., 2013).

Based on the evaluation criteria applied to the assessments, learning activities can also be evaluated regarding the extent to which the objectives are met. Building on the guidelines set by the ACM and the AIS (Topi et al., 2010) which specify five (5) levels of knowledge, these levels can be used to measure the depth of knowledge in learning activities. Bloom's (1956) taxonomy was used to measure the learning activities' impact on students' performance as previously used by Gluga et al. (2013) to measure the effectiveness of assessment. The application of the same criteria for assessments to the learning activities ensures that students have the opportunity to learn in class the areas they will eventually be assessed on.

Table 3 lists the learning activities identified in the prior section mapped to the CLO and evaluated in terms of depth of knowledge using ACM/AIS (Topi et al., 2010) guidelines; impact on student's performance using Bloom's (1956) Taxonomy; and level of learning achieved using Gluga et al.'s (2013) criteria.

As seen from the assessment of the learning activities chosen, the list provides variety in terms of the depth of understanding, the impact on students' performance and the level of learning achieved. It provides instructors with the ability to tailor their exercises depending on the level of standards they would like to push their students towards.

Table 3. Learning activity's objectives and evaluation criteria

Learning Activity with Behavioral Objectives	CLO	Depth of Knowledge	Impact on Students' Performance	Level of Learning
List the characteristics of wearable technology; Compare and Contrast hardware architecture and software standard	1, 2	1 Awareness and 2 Literacy	1 Knowledge recognition; 1 Differentiation in Context	Lower level of learning achieved
Discuss the importance of having a reliable network, interoperability across the devices and the optimization of the user interface to capture the data at the access points.	2, 3	3 Concept/ Use Skill	2 Comprehension Translation/ Extrapolation Use of Knowledge	Lower level of learning achieved
Identify and compare the different features of wearable technology (e.g., basic information, storage capacity) and where the data is stored	3	1 Awareness and 2 Literacy	1 Knowledge recognition; and 1 Differentiation in Context	Lower level of learning achieved
Given the set of weaknesses in these access points, apply the concept of different tools	4, 6, 7	3 Concept/ Use Skill 4 Detailed Understanding and Application Ability	2 Comprehension Translation/ Extrapolation Use of Knowledge 3 Application Knowledge	Lower level of learning achieved
Analyze the data and evaluate how one's privacy can be compromised	7	5 Advanced	4 Analysis 6 Evaluation	Higher level of learning achieved
Design and develop and awareness campaign or compliance program	4, 8	4 Detailed Understanding and Application Ability	3 Application Knowledge	Higher level of learning achieved
The discussion looks at the various trade-offs from collecting the data from the wearable device and the impact to an individual and/or organization requiring the data.	7, 8	5 Advanced	5 Synthesis 6 Evaluation	Higher level of learning achieved
Come up with new knowledge regarding the impact of new technological developments in wearable technology.	7, 8, 9	5 Advanced	5 Synthesis 6 Evaluation	Higher level of learning achieved

CHALLENGES AND FUTURE DIRECTIONS TO MODIFY THE COURSE SYLLABUS

The proposed model curriculum discussed provides the framework for instructors to guide the discussion around the impact of the security and privacy challenges in wearable technology. It provides a list of several topic areas that will continue to be relevant in spite of the changes in the technology. These topics are subsequently mapped to meet specific course learning objectives that can be used to measure the depth of knowledge from the course.

One of the challenges of developing the model course syllabus for managing the security issues of wearable technology is that the rate of change inherent in technology requires the flexibility to include and replace topics as the technology matures. As such, this model course outline was developed in line with the standardized curriculum recommendations from international accreditation boards and built on key core concepts from, and in line with, the program objectives of a model curriculum in Information Systems.

While the additional reading list is indicative only, and can be replaced with updated literature, recommended activities can still provide ideas for the instructors to engage their students in active learning as measured against assessment criteria. While this is a non-exhaustive list of activities, the selection of lab exercises and case-based studies presented a realistic target for achievement in both lower- and higher-level learning, relevant both to students and practitioners. It also utilizes the inherent ability of wearable technology to engage students and incorporate these technologies into exercises that are tied to measurable assessment criteria.

As the field of wearable technology explores the infinite possibilities of augmenting reality, students learn to uncover various components that enable wearable technology to augment our human capabilities with the superhuman processing of the computer. It provides them with opportunities to explore new ways to interact and transfer data seamlessly so that we can share data with others for various purposes. It gives them tools and techniques gained from security best practices so that they can successfully meet their obligation to guard the data so that they comply with international and local regulations. It provides them with the knowhow to protect the confidentiality, integrity and availability of information, while analyzing the tradeoffs between the information gained from sharing the data, and the social, professional and ethical issues that sharing raises. Additionally, the security and privacy risks from wearable technology need to be managed effectively. As emerging technological developments push the limits of wearable technology, students should be able to uncover, explore and understand the hidden dangers inherent in the ability to interact and communicate seamlessly with other technologies.

REFERENCES

ABET. (2016a). *Accreditation Policy and Procedure Manual (APPM), 2016 – 2017. Accreditation Board for Engineering and Technology.* Retrieved from http://www. abet.org/accreditation/accreditation-criteria/accreditation-policy-and-procedure-manual-appm-2016-2017/#criteria

ABET. (2016b). *Criteria for Accrediting Computing Programs, 2016-2017.* Accreditation Board for Engineering and Technology. Retrieved from http://www. abet.org/accreditation/accreditation-criteria/criteria-for-accrediting-computing-programs-2016-2017/

ACM/IEEE. (2013). *Curriculum Guidelines for Undergraduate Degree Programs in Computer Science.* Retrieved from http://www.acm.org/education/CS2013-final-report.pdf

Apple. (2006). *Nike and Apple Team Up to Launch Nike+iPod: Global Collaboration Brings the Worlds of Sports & Music Together Like Never Before.* Retrieved from http://www.apple.com/pr/library/2006/05/23Nike-and-Apple-Team-Up-to-Launch-Nike-iPod.html

Armstrong, R. J., Cornell, R. D., Kraner, R. E., & Roberson, E. W. (Eds.). (1968). *A systematic approach to Developing and Writing Behavioral Objectives: A Handbook Designed to Increase the Communication of Laymen and Educators.* Tucson, AZ: Educational Innovators Press.

Bloom, B. S. (1956). *Taxonomy of educational objectives. The classification of educational objectives. In Handbook 1: Cognitive domain.* New York, NY: Longmans Green.

Boehrer, J., & Linsky, M. (1990). Teaching with cases: Learning to question. In M. D. Svinicki (Ed.), *New Directions for Teaching and Learning: No. 42, The changing face of college teaching.* San Francisco: Jossey-Bass. doi:10.1002/tl.37219904206

Bower, M., & Sturman, D. (2015, October). What are the educational affordances of wearable technologies? *Computers & Education, 88,* 343–353. doi:10.1016/j. compedu.2015.07.013

Christensen, C. R., & Hansen, A. J. (1987). *Teaching and the Case Method.* Boston: Harvard Business School.

DARPA. (1997). *Head-Mounted Displays.* Defense Advanced Research Projects Agency. Retrieved from http://www.darpa.mil/about-us/timeline/headmounted-displays

ETF. (2006). *A Review of International and National Developments in the Use of Qualifications Frameworks.* European Training Foundation. Retrieved from http://www.etf.europa.eu/pubmgmt.nsf/(getAttachment)/4B4A9080175821D1C125715 40054B4AF/$File/SCAO6NYL38.pdf

EU. (2012). *Proposal for a Regulation of the European Parliament and of the Council on the protection of individuals with regard to the processing of personal data and on the free movement of such data (General Data Protection Regulation).* European Commission. Retrieved from http://ec.europa.eu/justice/data protection/document/review2012/com_2012_11_en.pdf

Evans, G. J. (2015). Regulating Data Practices: How State Laws can Shore Up the FTC's Authority to Regulate Data Breaches, Privacy, and More. *Administrative Law Review, 67*(1), 187–219.

Everett, C. (2015). Can wearable technology boost corporate wellbeing? *Occupational Health, 67*(8), 12–13.

Gentner, D., & Kurtz, K. J. (2006). Relations, Objects, and the Composition of Analogies. *Cognitive Science, 30*(4), 609–642. doi:10.1207/s15516709cog0000_60 PMID:21702828

Gibbs, S., & Arthur, C. (2014). CES 2014: Why wearable technology is the new dress code. *The Guardian.* Retrieved from https://www.theguardian.com/technology/2014/jan/08/wearable-technology-consumer-electronics-show

Gluga, R., Kay, J., Lister, R., Charleston, M., Harland, J., & Teague, D.M. (2013). A conceptual model for reflecting on expected learning vs. demonstrated student performance. In *Proceedings of the 15th Australasian Computing Education Conference (ACE2013).* Australian Computer Society, Inc.

Goel, S., Gangolly, J., Baykal, A., Hobbs, J., Pon, D., Bloniarz, P., & Schuman, S. P. et al. (2006). Innovative Model for Information Assurance Curriculum: A Teaching Hospital. *Journal of Educational Resources in Computing, 6*(3). doi:10.1145/1243481.1243483

Harrison, D. (2014). Tracking physical activity: problems related to running longitudinal studies with commercial devices. In *Proceedings of the 2014 ACM International Joint Conference on Pervasive and Ubiquitous Computing: Adjunct Publication* (UbiComp '14 Adjunct). ACM. http://dx.doi.org.esc-web.lib.cbs.dk/10.1145/2638728.2641320

Harrison, W. (September, 2006). A term project for a course on computer forensics. *ACM Journal of Educational Resources in Computing, 6*(3), Article 6.

Heingartner, D. (2009). Mental Block. *IEEE Spectrum, 46*(1), 42–43. doi:10.1109/MSPEC.2009.4734313

Liang, X., Zhang, K., Shen, X., & Lin, X. (2015). Security and privacy in mobile social networks: challenges and solutions. *IEEE Wireless Communications, 22*(2), 136 – 144.

Lumsden, J., & Brewster, S. (2003). A paradigm shift: alternative interaction techniques for use with mobile & wearable devices. In *Proceedings of the 2003 conference of the Centre for Advanced Studies on Collaborative research* (CASCON '03). IBM Press.

Lunt, B. M., Ekstrom, J. J., Gorka, S., Hislop, G., Kamali, R., Lawson, E., & Reichgelt, H. et al. (2008). *Curriculum guidelines for undergraduate degree programs in information technology. Technical report*. New York, NY: ACM.

Mancuso, J., & Stuth, K. (2015). The Internet of All Things. *Marketing Insights, 27*(2), 16–17.

Mann, S. (1997, February). Wearable Computing: A First Step Toward Personal Imaging. *Cybersquare Computer, 30*(2), 25–32. doi:10.1109/2.566147

Mann, S. (2001, May–June). Wearable computing: Toward humanistic intelligence. *IEEE Intelligent Systems, 16*(3), 10–15. doi:10.1109/5254.940020

Mann, S. (2003). Existential Technology: Wearable Computing Is Not the Real Issue! *Leonardo, 36*(1), 19–25. doi:10.1162/0024094033321152239

Mann, S. (2015). *Wearable Wireless Webcam*. [blog]. Retrieved from http://wearcam.org

Mann, S. (1995). *An experiment in connectivity*. Retrieved from http://wearcam.org/myview.html

Martin, T. (2004). Experiences Teaching a Course on Wearable and Ubiquitous Computing. In *Proceedings of the Second IEEE Annual Conference on Pervasive Computing and Communications Workshops (PERCOMW'04)*. doi:10.1109/PERCOMW.2004.1276941

McGettrick, A. (2005). Grand challenges in computing: Education–a summary. *The Computer Journal, 48*(1), 42–48. doi:10.1093/comjnl/bxh064

Metz, R. (2015). Google Glass Is Dead; Long Live Smart Glasses. *MIT's Technology Review, 118*(1), 79–82.

Mitri, M. (2012). Applying analogical reasoning techniques for teaching XML document querying skills in database classes. *Journal of Information Systems Education*, *23*(4), 385–394. Retrieved from http://search.proquest.com/docview/1432294615?accountid=15192

Moreno, R., & Ortegano-Layne, L. (2008). Do Classroom Exemplars Promote the Application of Principles in Teacher Education? A Comparison of Videos, Animations, and Narratives. *Educational Technology Research and Development*, *56*(4), 449–465. doi:10.1007/s11423-006-9027-0

Noh, S. (2014). Ferroelectret film-based patch-type sensor for continuous blood pressure monitoring. *Electronics Letters*, *50*(3), 1–2. doi:10.1049/el.2013.3715

OAG. (2003). *Online Privacy Act of 2003*. Office of Attorney General. Retrieved April 27, 2016 https://oag.ca.gov/privacy/privacy-laws

Paulson, E. (2013). Analogical Processes and College Developmental Reading. *Journal of Developmental Education*, *37*(3).

Pedersen, I. (2014). Are Wearables Really Ready to Wear?. *IEEE Technology and Society Magazine*, *33*(2), 16–18. doi:10.1109/MTS.2014.2319911

Reza, R., Price, B., & Petre, M. (2015). Wearables: Has the Age of Smartwatches Finally Arrived?. *Communications of the ACM, 58*(1), 45-47. Business Source Complete, EBSCOhost (accessed May 1, 2016).

Rhodes, B., & Kenji, M. (2006). Wearables in 2005. *IEEE Pervasive Computing / IEEE Computer Society [and] IEEE Communications Society*, *5*(1), 92–95. doi:10.1109/MPRV.2006.21

Schofield, J. (2001). From man to borg -- is this the future. *The Guardian*. Retrieved from https://www.theguardian.com/technology/2001/aug/02/onlinesupplement.gadgets

Sherman. (2004). Developing and Delivering Hands-On Information Assurance Exercises: Experiences with the Cyber Defense Lab at UMBC. Presented at the 2004 IEEE Workshop on Information Assurance and Security. West Point, NY: United States Military Academy. Retrieved from http://www.cisa.umbc.edu/papers/ShermanWestpoint2004.pdf

Singer, R. W., & Perry, A. J. (2015). Wearables: The Well-Dressed Privacy Policy. *Intellectual Property & Technology Law Journal*, *27*(7), 24–27.

Sjöklint, M. (2014). The measurable me: The influence of self-quantification on the online user's decision-making process. In *Proceedings of the 2014 ACM International Symposium on Wearable Computers: Adjunct Program* (ISWC '14 Adjunct). ACM. http://dx.doi.org.esc-web.lib.cbs.dk/10.1145/2641248.2642737

Thorpe, E. O. (1998). The Invention of the First Wearable Computer. In 2nd IEEE International Symposium on Wearable Computers (p. 4). Washington, DC: IEEE Computer Society. Retrieved from http://dl.acm.org/citation.cfm?id=858031

Topi, H., Valacich, J. S., Wright, R. T., Kaiser, K., Nunamaker, J. F. Jr, Sipior, J. C., & de Vreede, G. J. (2010). IS 2010: Curriculum guidelines for undergraduate degree programs in information systems. *Communications of the Association for Information Systems*, *26*, 18.

Tsubouchi, K. (2015). Fine-grained social relationship extraction from real activity data under coarse supervision. In *Proceedings of the 2015 ACM International Symposium on Wearable Computers* (ISWC '15). ACM. doi:10.1145/2802083.2808402

Zhou, J., Cao, Z., Dong, X., & Lin, X. (2015). *Security and Privacy in Cloud-Assisted Wireless Wearable Communications: Challenges, Solutions and Future Directions*. IEEE Wireless Communications.

KEY TERMS AND DEFINITIONS

Accreditation: A process that recognizes someone or something is qualified to perform or achieve a particular activity.

Case-Based Teaching: The use of case studies to explain a particular concept or scenario for teaching in the classroom.

Course Learning Outcomes (CLOs): Statements that "describe what students are expected to know and be able to do by the time of graduation."

Course: A series of lectures or lessons in a particular subject

Curriculum: A group of courses that comprise a discipline of study in a school or university.

Privacy: The non-disclosure of information about/belonging to a person except as permitted by that person to parties and for purposes agreed to by that person.

Taxonomy: Technique of classification.

APPENDIX: ACRONYMS

ABET: Accreditation Board of Engineering and Technology
ACM: Association of Computing Machinery
AIS: Association for Information Systems
CAC: Computing Accreditation Commission
CLOs: Course Learning Outcomes
DARPA: Defense Advanced Research Project Agency
EU: European Union
HCI: Human Computer Interface
IoT: Internet of Things

Chapter 12
Conclusions:
Where Next for Wearables?

Don Kerr
University of the Sunshine Coast, Australia

John Gammack
Zayed University, UAE

ABSTRACT

This chapter provides a contemporary example of how data from wearable devices can be used for "big data" type research. It then asked the question of data policies for the use of data generated by wearable devices. This is followed by an overview of the chapters in the book and how they fit within the general theme of the book. In addition, each chapter is categorised into whether it is social research or more technical type research. The chapter also includes concluding suggestions on the possible future research agenda for privacy and security within the subject domain of the use of wearables. In addition, insights into the future of wearables in relation to ethical considerations, privacy, security and data ownership is also given.

INTRODUCTION

Scientists announce that there is a global sleep crisis and describe how age, gender and the amount of natural light people are exposed to affects sleep patterns in 100 countries around the world (ABC News, 2016). A curious reader may well ask, "How did they get all that data?". The answer is from smartphone apps linked to wearable activity devices. While some readers may consider this to be very useful research, others may consider the information obtained to be a violation of people's

DOI: 10.4018/978-1-5225-1016-1.ch012

privacy. In this particular study, 6,000 people were asked to send anonymous data about their age, gender, country of residence and time zone to the researchers (ABC News, 2016). As the authors of chapters in this book have brought to light, however, new possibilities enabled by gathering data from wearables may have undesirable social and personal impacts.

Here, the asking of permission to undertake the study was merely a courtesy by the research team, since the data obtained in a study such as this can easily be obtained without any written consent. This is because it is just "out there in the cloud" and controlled by organizations who have accountability neither to its sources nor to its end users, and who can, in fact, on-sell the data to the highest bidder.

Welcome to the world of wearable devices, a world where security and privacy can be traded off against getting the latest device out to market in the quickest possible time in order to increase market share and maximize profits. As the chapters in this book have demonstrated, the use of wearable devices potentially compromises their users' security and privacy. The collected data, whether medical, geographical, or personal, and in video, audible, or other precisely specified forms, can end up being a uncontrolled resource whereby anyone can access the data for any reason. In addition to privacy concerns, there is also a range of security issues associated with smart wearable devices. These concerns are very real and have implications for end users, for enterprises, and for society as a whole.

As is understood by security experts, the machine-to-machine communication in the wearable area is not as secure as it is in other parts of the Internet. Any Bluetooth communication between devices (such as a fitness bracelet and a smartphone) can be easily accessible to third parties. At present, much of the communications between devices is not encrypted and can easily be intercepted. Moreover, as described in various chapters of this book, the privacy and security issues associated with wearables have been demonstrated to be problematic, both from a technical point of view and from a social or policy view. The dangers noted raises management problems, not just for enterprises and custodians of data but for government and lawmakers regulating society as well.

This final chapter is divided into the following sections. The next section provides an overview of each chapter and how the content of the chapter fits into the research themes of the book. The issues involved in wearables cover technical aspects, particularly around security issues, along with managerial and wider social issues, issues relevant to the privacy and freedoms of individuals, enterprises and society at large. The various chapters were selected to represent this range of research. The second section, titled, "What have we learned?", attempts to abstract lessons from all the chapters to provide a general view of what has been learned from research across these various areas. The final section discusses the issue of "What is next?" and attempts to provide an overview of possible research directions in the future.

SUMMARY OF THE CHAPTERS AND THEIR CONTRIBUTION

Specific evidence of the issues outlined in the first section of this chapter is given in the following summaries of chapters in the book. This section provides a summary of each chapter and how the chapter fits into the overall theme of the book.

The Promise and Perils of Wearable Technologies

The first chapter, by John Gammack and Andrew Marrington, is titled "The Promise and Perils of Wearable Technologies". This chapter introduces the field of wearables and foreshadows some of the themes explored in depth in later chapters. In this first chapter, the authors describe emerging technologies and devices in the wearable arena. These devices include smart gadgets, garments, jewelery, and other devices worn on the user's body. The authors also discuss high profile wearable devices such as the Apple Watch, Google Glass, and FitBit and describe how they have captured both the headlines and the public imagination. Describing briefly some other emerging categories, some of the basic technologies are sketched to indicate areas of hidden danger.

The authors suggest that wearable technology has the potential to change the world even more profoundly than other mobile technologies, noting, however, that the appearance of such high profile wearable devices in the end-consumer market also requires the serious consideration of the implications of such technologies. The chapter concludes that the implications for security and privacy of individuals and organizations, and the potential dangers to both society and the economy, must be considered and addressed in order for wearable technology to successfully deliver upon its many promises. The chapter ends on a positive note, suggesting that addressing such concerns can still lead towards a positive "wearable future", and that mindful users can adopt wearable technology with confidence.

The Risks of Wearable Technologies to Individuals and Organizations

The second chapter, written by Sarra Berrahal and Nourredine Boudriga, is titled "The Risks of Wearable Technologies to Individuals and Organizations". In this chapter the authors discuss the advancements in wearable and integrated sensing devices and how they have provided new capabilities. In particular, they describe the opportunities in enabling advanced remote applications including sensing, monitoring, and tracking systems and states. The authors suggest that wearable systems can be used to provide social and economic well-being for individuals by assisting them in the performance of their daily duties and for organizations by keeping their employees connected to each other anytime and anywhere. The authors indicate that this will enhance employee productivity.

The authors, however, also suggest that because wearable devices are mainly wireless in nature, it renders them exposed to security attacks that may even threaten the life of individuals and the security of an organization. They provide a comprehensive study, examining the benefits of wearable technologies and their related security and privacy issues. The authors further discuss the major policies that can be used to mitigate the risk posed by wearable technologies and the proposed techniques to assist users' safety in hazardous workplaces. The chapter is relevant to the management and enterprise aspects of the field and provides discussions on digital investigations of security incidents with respect to wearable technologies.

Watch What You Wear

The third chapter, written by Joseph Ricci, Ibrahim Baggili and Frank Breitinger is titled, "Watch What You Wear: Smartwatches and Sluggish Security". In this chapter the authors observe that the form factor of devices continues to shrink, and discuss some of the security issues arising from this continuing miniaturization. This is evidenced by smartphones and, more recently, smartwatches. The authors observe that the adoption rate of small computing devices is "staggering" and that security issues need to be addressed. In particular, they argue that stronger attention to these devices is needed from the cybersecurity and forensics communities.

In their chapter these authors comprehensively dissect smartwatches by providing a historical roadmap of smartwatches followed by an exploration of the smartwatch marketplace. They also outline existing smartwatch hardware, operating systems and software and, reviewing the relevant literature, further elaborate on the uses of smartwatches and the security and forensic implications of smartwatches. Their chapter concludes with a discussion on the future research directions in smartwatch security and forensics. This chapter advocates a technical approach to addressing the problems as well as providing an insight into the demand of such devices by consumers.

Confidential Data Storage Systems for Wearable Platforms

The fourth chapter, by Mingzhong Wang and Donald Kerr, is titled "Confidential Data Storage Systems for Wearable Platforms". This chapter examines confidentiality in data storage systems. In this chapter, the sensitivity of the data collected is specifically acknowledged. The authors argue that this sensitivity of collected data should make security and privacy protection one of the first priorities in the advancement of wearable technologies.

The chapter also details a study on encryption-based confidentiality protection for data storage systems in wearable platforms. The authors first conducted a review of existing storage solutions in consumer wearable products and explored a two-tier, (local flash memory and remote cloud storage), storage system in wearable platforms. Then encryption-based confidentiality protection and implementation methods for both flash memory and remote cloud storage are examined. This chapter recognizes both the social dimension of wearable security issues as well as investigating the technical constraints and reasons for those security and privacy issues. Possible solutions are also explored.

Authenticity Challenges of Wearable Technologies

The fifth chapter is titled "Authenticity Challenges of Wearable Technologies" by Filipe da Costa and Filipe de Sá-Soares. In this chapter the security challenges raised by wearable technologies with respect to the authenticity of information and subjects is discussed. This chapter firstly looks at the capabilities of wearable technology and then provides an authenticity analysis framework for wearable devices. This original framework includes graphic classification classes of authenticity risks in wearable devices that are expected to improve the awareness of users with regard the risks of using those devices. The object of this is to allow individuals to moderate their behaviors and take into account the inclusion of controls aimed to protect authenticity.

Building on the results of the application of the framework to a list of wearable devices, a solution is presented to mitigate the risk for authenticity based on digital signatures. This research concentrates on the social and policy aspects of wearables and provides a possible solution to the data ownership problem, or at least to enable end-users to be aware of where the data is going.

Privacy Dangers of Wearables and the Internet of Things

In chapter six, titled "Privacy Dangers of Wearables and the Internet of Things", Scott Amyx looks at the privacy dangers of wearables in relation to the Internet of Things (IoT). In this chapter concerns are identified regarding data privacy issues related to wearables and the IoT. Again, this is related to both enterprise management and to social themes.

In his chapter, the author discusses the managerial implications of data security and offers some enterprise solutions to the complex concerns arising from the aggregation of the massive amounts of data derived from wearables and IoT devices. Consumer and employee privacy concerns are elucidated, as are the problems facing managers, as data management and security become an increasingly important part of business operations. The chapter also examines trending issues in the areas of data protection and the IoT, and contains thought-provoking discussion questions pertaining to business, wearables/IoT data, and to privacy issues.

Security, Privacy, and Ownership Issues with the Use of Wearable Health Technologies

In the seventh chapter titled "Security, Privacy and Ownership Issues with the use of Wearable Health Technologies" by Donald Kerr, Kerryn Butler-Henderson and Tony Sahama, the discussion focuses on the use of mobile or wearable health technologies to collect health data. The fact that users are often connected 24/7 through devices such as activity-measuring wearables means that there is a higher risk of data theft or the misappropriation and use of health data. In the chapter it is shown that a majority of users' state that security and privacy of their data is a primary concern.

The authors suggest that data ownership is often a misunderstood topic in wearable technology and that many users are simply unaware of who owns the data collected by a device, what that data can be used for, and who can receive that data. The authors note that many countries are reviewing privacy governance in an attempt to clarify data privacy and ownership, but also pose the question, 'is it too late?' The chapter explores the concepts of security and privacy of data from mobile and wearable technology, giving specific examples. It also suggests a series of implications for the future of health related wearable technologies. This research is primarily social in that it discusses policy issues relevant to society.

What Can People Do with Your Spatial Data?

The eighth chapter is titled "What Can People Do With Your Spatial Data?: Socio-Ethical Scenarios". In this chapter, authored by Roba Abbas, Katina Michael and M.G. Michael, Location-Based Services (LBS) are discussed. These services can provide value-added solutions to users based on location or positional information, and on other contextual data available from wearable or other mobile devices. The authors indicate that these services enable the collection of GPS data logs or location chronicles, and may be deployed on a range of devices, many of which presently come in the form of commercially available product solutions with corresponding applications.

The chapter presents the outcomes of an observational study of LBS users, which was designed to gauge user perspectives in relation to LBS socio-ethical dilemmas. The focus is on the outcomes of a spatial analysis exercise, which resulted in the development of a series of scenarios (in map format). These scenarios demonstrate varying LBS use contexts and are centered on the socio-ethical implications of

LBS usage. The scenarios display a range in terms of risk levels, and the potential is shown for these scensrios to be used as further input into consultative practices. The authors show how the results of the LBS observational study can be utilized to inform the need for LBS regulation, and that the findings have relevant implications for designing appropriate legislation and policies. Future research directions are proposed, allowing for the study to be extended to wider contexts with the focus being towards the social.

Wearable Devices: Ethical Challenges and Solutions

The ninth chapter is titled "Wearable Devices: Ethical Challenges and Solutions" written by Alina Chircu with the late Marc Resnick. In this chapter the authors discuss the acceleration of innovation in and through information and communication technology (ICT) with consumers, companies and governments. As these stakeholders increasingly become users and designers of a myriad of ICT solutions, it is critical that their ethical implications also become well understood. The chapter looks at the growing body of research on ethical implications of wearable devices and associated technologies.

The authors suggest that many ethical challenges stem from the extensive prevalence of wearable devices. These challenges are related not only to the device design and use, but also to the device-supported data collection and analysis, and, further, to the creation of derivative products and services. The authors take a social view of the problem using theories associated with ICT ethics and identify the major ethical challenges posed by wearable devices. From this they provide several guidelines on how these challenges can be addressed through ethically-informed design interventions. This chapter highlights a much needed research area, namely ethical considerations in the use of wearable devices. If users of wearable devices are to become comfortable with, and confident in, the use of wearables, such ethical challenges need to be addressed, and solutions identified.

Societal Implications of Wearable Technology

The tenth chapter is titled "Societal Implications of Wearable Technology" and is authored by Daniz Goyker, Katina Michael and Sam Abbas. This chapter presents a set of scenarios involving the GoPro wearable point of view (PoV) camera. The authors used these scenarios to stimulate discussion about acceptable usage contexts with a focus on security and privacy. The chapter provides a wide array of examples of how overt wearable technologies are perceived and how they might, or might not, be welcomed into society.

The scenarios are acted out in an Australian University, which represents many typical social situations found elsewhere. Key implications derived from the fictitious events are useful in drawing out the predicted pros and cons of the technology. The authors discuss and interpret the main thematic issues, followed by an in-depth analysis of their social implications. In particular, they explore the moral and ethical problems associated with use of such technology, and consider possible future developments with respect to these wearable devices becoming common in society. Again, this is a socially focused research area, and it will be interesting to see how people's responses to being videoed or unintentionally recorded in some way changes over time, both in terms of societal norms and legislative developments.

Model Course Syllabus: Management of Security Issues in Wearable Technology

The eleventh chapter is titled "Model Course Syllabus: Management of Security Issues in Wearable Technology" and is authored by Michelle Antero. This chapter looks at some historical and contemporary context before proposing a model course syllabus to implement a course in Wearable Technology. The course syllabus is developed in line with the IS2010 curriculum recommended by the peak bodies (ACM and AIS) for a degree in Information Systems, Computer Information Systems or Management Information Systems. The author states that the design further follows the guidelines developed by the Accreditation Board of Engineering and Technology (ABET) and that this accreditation board advocates that course learning outcomes be developed for the list of topics covered by the material.

The syllabus can be focused in various ways, depending on scheduled time and content scope, and is also related to the chapter themes in this book along with other indicative readings. In addition, the syllabus provides a basis for enterprise training relevant to managers and to security specialists. The chapter also provides some general pedagogical guidelines on how each topic can be discussed and suggests activities appropriate to the learners. This chapter provides a practical outcome for the book as it shows a way forward with respect to educating people in the relevant concerns about security and privacy in the wearables space.

Conclusions: Where Next for Wearables?

The final chapter is the present one and is titled "Conclusions: Where's Next?", summarizing the individual chapters before abstracting key lessons and extending to suggest future broad research directions.

WHAT HAVE WE LEARNED?

As can be seen from the chapter summaries above, research into privacy and security with wearable technologies can be looked at in terms both of social factors and technical issues, each variously relevant to enterprise and government policies and management. The social factors include ethical issues such as overt video recording of people undertaking their daily activities; authenticity issues with the data provided and policies associated with data ownership, and various ethical implications of data usage derived from wearables using location based services. Wearables research can also be directed more towards technical aspects such data storage systems and keeping data secure from attack. Both approaches are vital in ensuring that wearable devices can be used with confidence. However, it should also be noted that even if technical solutions are found and data is protected from interception, it does not alter the concerns authors in this book have expressed about the data usage policy issues and the ethical concerns about incidental recording of an individual's daily activity.

It will be interesting to see where these concerns may lead and how they are nuanced. For example, the concern may not be as ethically problematic in countries that have adopted wide-ranging CCTV surveillance of their population, and to which their citizens have become accustomed. However, it would seem that this area is heavily dependent on the context, as the hypothetical instance of a GoPro unintentionally recording while the user was in the men's bathroom would attest. Police or surgeons wearing Google Glass-like devices may be socially acceptable; so-called "Glassholes" would not be. A doctor using identifiable medical data is appropriate; perhaps a researcher should not have such access.

It appears that until policy decisions are made about who actually owns the data and ethical considerations about the use of data are resolved, that concerns about privacy and security will persist. Research into authenticity could help, and the chapter by Filipe da Costa and Filipe de Sá-Soares is very relevant in this regard. If users have the option to authenticate data usage from third parties and allow or disallow the use of their data, a major portion of the problem could be solved. On the other hand users may decide to opt out of authentication procedures, thus making the informed use of data problematic from a legal perspective.

There is no doubt that the accumulation of vast amounts of data from wearables could help with very large scale global research projects in a variety of areas, as the study outlined at the start of this chapter illustrated. These "Big Data" type research projects could have useful results for the entire human race. Under this scenario, any hindrance to the large-scale use of such big data sets could be thought of as reducing the possibility of medical and/or social breakthroughs in whole-of-population research projects. The ethical dilemmas raised in various chapters juxtapose some individual rights against a wider potential social good, but the discussions, and the supporting research, remains to be done.

Judging by the large number of sales of wearable devices over the past few years, the benefits of the technology are apparent to a large section of the population. No doubt the most common applications of the technology, namely high functioning smartwatches and activity bracelets, can have massive implications for public health, both positively and negatively. The positive implications may be in terms of large population trials, greater awareness of their own activity by individuals, better safety in the workplace and better management of disease to name just a few. On the other hand, the negative implications could relate to a lack of privacy and security with possible consequences for individuals including higher health insurance premiums for recorded inactivity or even death through hacking of vital medical devices. Whilst many individuals may prioritize fashion (or payment convenience), and either don't know or don't care about the risks and dangers, as was illustrated in different chapters, to continue such behavior is not without risk. Vulnerabilities remain and are liable to be exploited.

WHERE NEXT FOR WEARABLES?

This book has identified various issues and concerns with the design and use of wearable technologies. Building on the variety of empirical research studies and conceptual perspectives of the individual authors, there is still a lot more valuable research to be done, both in social and in technical areas. A social or soft research focus might emphasize, for instance, data usage policies, as well as new ethical issues arising in contexts that were not even possible before the advent of wearables. It is, for example, apparent that an individual's right to privacy could be compromised if there are no mechanisms or laws in place to determine the authenticity of data, who actually owns that data and the rights to its use. Policies will need to be developed to address the lack of a clear direction as to the ownership of the data collected and how the data should be used, as well as other amendments to privacy legislation required by scenarios indicated in earlier chapters. Data from devices such as activity monitors can, in principle, be on-sold to anyone. The implications for this could be quite profound for certain individuals with respect to GPS tracking and its risks, or publicizing indications of an individual's physical condition. Again, numerous issues raised in the discussion points of individual chapters suggest relevant research questions in such areas.

The other broad area of research adopts from a more technical focus. A cursory glance shows how much can be done with respect to improving security safeguards, in particular the implementation of standard security measures that are already in use in other parts of the digital ecosystem -with encryption being one pertinent example. The case for end-to-end security, and for end-to-end authentication, has been described in different chapters in this book, and the technical issues involved suggest another part of the wearables research agenda implied by issues raised.

This book has provided an overview of some key technical, privacy, security and ethical problems relevant to wearable technology and has also provided suggestions and approaches for further discussion and research. The specific directions that future research might pursue naturally depends the researchers' interest areas. However, this research needs to be long-ranging both in social and technical terms, and a pressing need for effective legislation provides another imperative to direct priorities. Research also needs to be done quickly to ensure confidence by end users of wearable devices and to allow for more user insight and accountability by companies researching, developing, manufacturing and marketing these devices.

The book's initial premise was that wearables have promise but also hold perils. Individual chapters detailed many specific areas in which these are being, or might be, realized. The title of the book, however, suggests that the security issues, at least, can be managed, and education, awareness raising, and effective design of devices and of systems can be achieved to mitigate some of the hidden dangers that the various authors have identified.

Although there are systemic links between security, privacy and social freedoms, we hope that readers do not think that only a dystopia is inevitable. The use of wearable technologies and the resultant increase in the amount of analyzable data from a whole-of-population perspective can provide major benefits for all. The sleep research vignette at the start of this chapter is one example of the possibilities in obtaining better insights into general population trends by analyzing big data from wearable devices. Such possibilities can lead to major public health and social breakthroughs that can have a lasting effect on the well-being of the human race.

REFERENCES

ABC News. (2016). *Scientists using smartphone app to study slumber patterns warn of 'global sleep crisis'*. Retrieved from http://www.abc.net.au/news/2016-05-07/scientists-using-smartphone-app-warn-of-global-sleep-crisis/7393490

Compilation of References

Abadi, . (2013). *The Beckman Report on Database Research, Communication of the ACM*. Beckman Center of the National Academies of Sciences & Engineering.

Abbas, R. (2010). Location-based services: an examination of user attitudes and socio-ethical scenarios. In *Proceedings of the IEEE symposium on technology and society: social implications of emerging technologies 2010, 7–9 June 2010* (pp. 1-9). doi:10.1109/ISTAS.2010.5514620

Abbas, R. (2011). The social implications of location-based services: An observational study of users. *Journal of Location Based Services*, *5*(3/4), 156–181. doi:10.1080/17489725.2011.637970

Abbas, R., Michael, K., & Michael, M. G. (2014). The regulatory considerations and ethical dilemmas of location-based services (LBS): A literature review. *Information Technology & People*, *27*(1), 2–20. doi:10.1108/ITP-12-2012-0156

Abbas, R., Michael, K., & Michael, M. G. (2015a). Using a social-ethical framework to evaluate location-based services in an internet of things world. *International Review of Information Ethics*, *22*(12), 42–73.

Abbas, R., Michael, K., Michael, M. G., & Nicholls, R. (2013). Sketching and validating the location-based services (LBS) regulatory framework in Australia. *Computer Law & Security Report*, *29*(5), 576–589. doi:10.1016/j.clsr.2013.07.014

Abbas, R., Michael, K., Michael, M. G., & Nicholls, R. (2015b). Key government agency perspectives on location-based services regulation. *Computer Law & Security Report*, *31*(6), 736–748. doi:10.1016/j.clsr.2015.08.004

ABC News. (2016). *Scientists using smartphone app to study slumber patterns warn of 'global sleep crisis'*. Retrieved from http://www.abc.net.au/news/2016-05-07/scientists-using-smartphone-app-warn-of-global-sleep-crisis/7393490

ABET. (2016a). *Accreditation Policy and Procedure Manual (APPM), 2016 – 2017. Accreditation Board for Engineering and Technology*. Retrieved from http://www.abet.org/accreditation/accreditation-criteria/accreditation-policy-and-procedure-manual-appm-2016-2017/#criteria

Compilation of References

ABET. (2016b). *Criteria for Accrediting Computing Programs, 2016-2017.* Accreditation Board for Engineering and Technology. Retrieved from http://www.abet.org/accreditation/accreditation-criteria/criteria-for-accrediting-computing-programs-2016-2017/

Accenture. (2014). *Eighty percent of consumers believe total data privacy no longer exists, Accenture survey finds.* Retrieved March 22, 2016, from https://newsroom.accenture.com/news/eighty-percent-of-consumers-believe-total-data-privacy-no-longer-exists-accenture-survey-finds.htm

ACM/IEEE. (2013). *Curriculum Guidelines for Undergraduate Degree Programs in Computer Science.* Retrieved from http://www.acm.org/education/CS2013-final-report.pdf

Affectiva. (2016). *Technology.* Retrieved March 30, 2016, from http://www.affectiva.com/technology/

Akram, S., Javaid, N., Ahmad, A., Khan, Z. A., Imran, M., Guizani, M., & Ilahi, M. et al. (2015). A Fatigue Measuring Protocol for Wireless Body Area Sensor Networks. *Journal of Medical Systems, 39*(12), 1–15. doi:10.1007/s10916-015-0338-8 PMID:26490151

Al Ameen, M., & Kwak, K. (2011). Social Issues in Wireless Sensor Networks with Healthcare Perspective. *The International Arab Journal of Information Technology, 8*(1), 52–58.

Al Ameen, M., Liu, J., & Kwak, K. (2012). Security and Privacy Issues in Wireless Sensor Networks for Healthcare Applications. *Journal of Medical Systems, 36*(1), 93–101. doi:10.1007/s10916-010-9449-4 PMID:20703745

Alemdar, H., & Ersoy, C. (2010). Wireless sensor networks for healthcare: A Surevy. *Computer Networks, 54*(15), 2688–2710. doi:10.1016/j.comnet.2010.05.003

Alexander, I. (2004). Introduction: Scenarios in System Development. In I. Alexander & N. Maiden (Eds.), *Scenarios, Stories, Use Cases through the Systems Development Lifecycle* (pp. 3–24). West Sussex, UK: John Wiley & Sons Ltd.

Aloudat, A. (2011). *Location-Based Mobile Phone Service Utilisation for Emergency Management in Australia.* (PhD Thesis). School of Information Systems and Technology, Informatics, University of Wollongong.

Alshurafa, N., Eastwood, J. A., Pourhomayoun, M., Nyamathi, S., Bao, L., Mortazavi, B., & Sarrafzadeh, M. (2014, June). *Anti-cheating: Detecting self-inflicted and impersonator cheaters for remote health monitoring systems with wearable sensors.* Paper presented at 11th International Conference on Wearable and Implantable Body Sensor Networks (BSN), Zurich, Switzerland. doi:10.1109/BSN.2014.38

Anderson, R. (2001). Why information security is hard - an economic perspective. *Seventeenth Annual Computer Security Applications Conference.* Doi:10.1109/ACSAC.2001.991552

Andrews, L., Sahama, T., & Gajanayake, R. (2014). *Contextualising co-creation of value in electronic personal health records.* Paper presented at the 16th International Conference on E-health, Natal, Brazil. doi:10.1109/HealthCom.2014.7001872

Anthony, D., Kotz, D., & Henderson, T. (2007). Privacy in location-aware computing environments. *Pervasive Computing, 6*(4), 64–72. doi:10.1109/MPRV.2007.83

Antonopoulos, C. P., Voros, N. S., Hey, S., Anastasolpoulou, P., & Bideaux, A. (2015). Secure and Efficient WSN Communication Infrastructure. In Cyberphysical Systems for Epilepsy and Related Brain Disorders (pp. 163-188). Berlin: Springer International. doi:10.1007/978-3-319-20049-1_9

Apple Inc. (2015). *Apple Watch User Guide. Version 1.0*. Retrieved from https://manuals.info. apple.com/MANUALS/1000/MA1708/en_US/apple_watch_user_guide.pdf

Apple Inc. (n.d.). *Privacy*. Retrieved from http://www.apple.com/au/privacy/approach-to-privacy/

Apple. (2006). *Nike and Apple Team Up to Launch Nike+iPod: Global Collaboration Brings the Worlds of Sports & Music Together Like Never Before*. Retrieved from http://www.apple.com/pr/library/2006/05/23Nike-and-Apple-Team-Up-to-Launch-Nike-iPod.html

Armstrong, J., & Welsh, B. (2011). The Entire History of You. In B. Reisz (Ed.), *Black Mirror*. London, UK: Zeppetron.

Armstrong, R. J., Cornell, R. D., Kraner, R. E., & Roberson, E. W. (Eds.). (1968). *A systematic approach to Developing and Writing Behavioral Objectives: A Handbook Designed to Increase the Communication of Laymen and Educators*. Tucson, AZ: Educational Innovators Press.

Article 29. (2010). *Data Protection Working Party: Opinion 3/210 on the principle of accountability*. Author.

Artz, J. M. (1998). The role of stories in computer ethics. *Computers & Society, 28*(1), 11–13. doi:10.1145/277351.277354

Auchard, E. (2015, September 16). Cisco router break-ins bypass cyber defenses. *Reuters*. Retrieved from http://www.bbc.com/news/technology-28602997

Australasian Legal Information Institute. (2014). *Workplace Surveillance Act, 2005 (NSW)*. Retrieved June 6, 2016, from http://www.austlii.edu.au/au/legis/nsw/consol_act/wsa2005245/

Australasian Legal Information Institute. (2015). *Surveillance Devices Act, 1998 (WA)*. Retrieved June 6, 2016, from https://www.slp.wa.gov.au/legislation/statutes.nsf/main_mrtitle_946_currencies.html

Australasian Legal Information Institute. (2016). *Privacy and Personal Information Protection Act 1998*. Retrieved June 6, 2016, from http://www.austlii.edu.au/au/legis/nsw/consol_act/papipa1998464/

Aviv, A. J., Sapp, B., Blaze, M., & Smith, J. M. (2012) Practicality of Accelerometer Side-Channel on Smartphones.*Proceedings of the 28th Annual Computer Security Applications Conference (ACSAC'12)*. Orlando, FL: ACM.

Compilation of References

Bagci, I., Pourmirza, M., Raza, S., Roedig, U., & Voigt, T. (2012). *Codo: confidential data storage for wireless sensor networks*. Paper presented at the IEEE 9th International Conference on Mobile Adhoc and Sensor Systems (MASS), Las Vegas, NV.

Baggili, I., Oduro, J., Anthony, K., Breitinger, F., & McGee, G. (2015, August). Watch What You Wear: Preliminary Forensic Analysis of Smart Watches. *Availability, Reliability and Security (ARES), 2015 10th International Conference*, (pp. 303-311).

Ballve, M. (2013). Wearable Gadgets Are Still Not Getting The Attention They Deserve: Here's Why They Will Create A Massive New Market. *Business Insider*. Retrieved from http://www.businessinsider.com/wearable-devices-create-a-new-market-2013-8

Barkhuus, L., Brown, B., Bell, M., Hall, M., Sherwood, S., & Chalmers, M. (2008). From Awareness to Repartee: Sharing Location within Social Groups. In *CHI 2008* (pp. 497-506).

Baur, N., Hering, L., Raschke, A. L., & Thierbach, C. (2014). Special issue: Spatial analysis in the social sciences and humanities. towards integrating qualitative, quantitative and cartographic approaches. *Historische Sozialforschung, 39*(2), 7–50.

Begley, D. (2015, April 11). Uber safety dispute shows balance between personal choice, regulations. *The Houston Chronicle*. Retrieved March 30, 2016 from http://www.houstonchronicle.com/news/transportation/article/Uber-safety-dispute-shows-balance-between-6194128.php

Ben Aissa, A., Abercrombie, R. K., Sheldon, F. T., & Mili, A. (2009, April). Quantifying security threats and their impact. In *Proceedings of the 5th Annual Workshop on Cyber Security and Information Intelligence Research: Cyber Security and Information Intelligence Challenges and Strategies* (p. 26). ACM.

Bentley, F. R., Chen, Y. Y., & Holz, C. (2015). Reducing the stress of coordination: sharing travel time information between contacts on mobile phones, In *CHI 2015*. doi:10.1145/2702123.2702208

Berrahal, S., Boudriga, N., & Chammem, M. (2015). WBAN-Assisted Navigation for Firefighters in Indoor Environments. *Ad Hoc & Sensor Wireless Networks Journal, 28*(5).

Berrahal, S., & Boudriga, N. (2014). A Smart QoS- based Traffic Management for WBANs. In *Proceedings of the 14th International Symposium on Communications and Information Technologies (ISCIT 2014)*. doi:10.1109/ISCIT.2014.7011892

Bigelow, P. (2015, May 20). General Motors says it owns your car's software. *Autoblog*. Retrieved from https://www.gov.uk/government/news/cyber-security-myths-putting-a-third-of-sme-revenue-at-risk

Billinghurst, M., & Starner, T. (1999). Wearable devices: New ways to manage information. *Computer, 32*(1), 57–64. doi:10.1109/2.738305

Black, A. S., Sahama, T., & Gajanayake, R. (2014). eHealth-as-a-Service (eHaaS): A data-driven decision making approach in Australian context. *Studies in Health Technology and Informatics, 205*, 915–919. PMID:25160321

Bloom, B. S. (1956). *Taxonomy of educational objectives. The classification of educational objectives. In Handbook 1: Cognitive domain.* New York, NY: Longmans Green.

Boehm, F. (2015). *A comparison between US and EU data protection legislation for law enforcement purposes.* European Parliament.

Boehrer, J., & Linsky, M. (1990). Teaching with cases: Learning to question. In M. D. Svinicki (Ed.), *New Directions for Teaching and Learning: No. 42, The changing face of college teaching.* San Francisco: Jossey-Bass. doi:10.1002/tl.37219904206

Boesen, J., Rode, J. A., & Mancini, C. (2010). The domestic panopticon: location tracking in families. In *UbiComp'10* (pp. 65-74). doi:10.1145/1864349.1864382

Bower, M., & Sturman, D. (2015, October). What are the educational affordances of wearable technologies? *Computers & Education, 88,* 343–353. doi:10.1016/j.compedu.2015.07.013

Brady, S. (2016). *IBM Watson x Marchesa Twitter Dress Lights Up the Met Gala Red Carpet.* Retrieved from http://www.brandchannel.com/2016/05/02/ibm-watson-met-gala-050216/

Brannon, S. K., & Song, T. (2008). Computer Forensics: Digital Forensic Analysis Methodology. *Computer Forensics Journal, 56*(1), 1–8.

Branscomb, A. W. (1994). *Who Owns Information? From Privacy to Public Access.* New York, NY: BasicBooks.

Bratu, B. (2014, January 30). Brain surgeon walked six miles during snowstorm for emergency operation *NBC News.*

Brey, P. A. E. (2012). Anticipatory ethics for emerging technologies. *NanoEthics, 6*(1), 1–13. doi:10.1007/s11569-012-0141-7

Bria, A., Gessler, F., Queseth, O., Stridh, R., Unbehaun, M., Wu, J., Zander, J. & Flament, M. (2001, December). 4th generation wireless infrastructures: scenarios and research challenges. *IEEE Personal Communications,* 25-31.

Brodkin, J. (2008). *Gartner: Seven cloud-computing security risks.* Retrieved from http://www.infoworld.com/article/2652198/security/gartner--seven-cloud-computing-security-risks.html

Bronitt, S., & Michael, K. (2012). Human rights, regulation, and national security (introduction). *IEEE Technology and Society Magazine, 31*(1), 15–16. doi:10.1109/MTS.2012.2188704

Brown, B., Taylor, A. S., Izadi, S., Sellen, A., Kaye, J., & Eardley, R. (2007). Locating family values: a field trial of the whereabouts clock. In *UbiComp '07 Proceedings of the 9th International Conference on Ubiquitous Computing* (pp. 354-371). doi:10.1007/978-3-540-74853-3_21

Buergy, C., & Kenn, H. (2013). Wearable systems for industrial augmented reality applications. In *Proceedings of the 2013 ACM conference on Pervasive and ubiquitous computing adjunct publication.* doi:10.1145/2494091.2499568

Compilation of References

Bureau of Justice Statistics. (2011, November 30). *Identity Theft Reported by Households Rose 33 Percent from 2005 to 2010.* Retrieved from http://www.bjs.gov/content/pub/press/itrh0510pr.cfm

Burns, A. J., & Johnson, E. M. (2015). *Securing Health Information.* Paper presented at the IEEE ITPro. doi:10.1109/MITP.2015.13

Bynum, T. (2011). Computer and information ethics. In *The Stanford Encyclopedia of Philosophy.* Retrieved October 1, 2015, from http://plato.stanford.edu/archives/spr2011/entries/ethics-computer/

Camponovo, G., Debetaz, S., & Pigneur, Y. (2005). A comparative analysis of published scenarios for m-business. In *Proceedings of the Third International Conference on Mobile Business, M-Business 2004.*

Casey, E. (2004). *Digital Evidence and Computer Crime* (2nd ed.). Academic Press.

Casio. (n.d.). *Operation Guide 1138 1173 Casio* [PDF document]. Retrieved from Casio Support Online Web site: http://support.casio.com/storage/en/manual/pdf/EN/009/qw1173.pdf

Chalykoff, J., & Kochan, T. (2006). Computer-Aided Monitoring: Its Influence On Employee Job Satisfaction And Turnover. *Personnel Psychology, 42*(4), 807-834. 10.1111/j.1744-6570.1989.tb00676.x

Chang, A. (2013, June 19). *Smart Locks: Wired.* Retrieved from Wired: http://www.wired.com/2013/06/smart-locks/

Chan, M., Estève, D., Fourniols, J. Y., Escriba, C., & Campo, E. (2012). Smart wearable systems: Current status and future challenges. *Artificial Intelligence in Medicine, 56*(3), 137–156. doi:10.1016/j.artmed.2012.09.003 PMID:23122689

Charara, S. (2015). *Ringly CEO: Keep smart jewellery simple with no screens or steps.* Retrieved from http://www.wareable.com/meet-the-boss/ringly-ceo-christina-mercando-smart-jewellery-2016

Chessa, S., & Maestrini, P. (2003). *Dependable and secure data storage and retrieval in mobile, wireless networks.* Paper presented at the International Conference on Dependable Systems and Networks.

Chinaculture.org. (2010). *The Story of the Chinese Abacus: The Abacus with Chinkang Beads.* Retrieved from http://www.chinaculture.org/classics/2010-04/20/content_383263_4.htm

Chircu, A. M. (2013). *Ethical implications of emerging ICTs.* Presented at the Bentley University's 2013 Fall Research Colloquium on Responsible Innovation: Environmental Sustainability, Financial Accountability, and Information and Communication Technology (ICT) Ethics, Waltham, MA.

Choi, J. J. U., Ae Chun, S., & Cho, J. W. (2014, June). Smart SecureGov: mobile government security framework. In *Proceedings of the 15th Annual International Conference on Digital Government Research* (pp. 91-99). ACM.

Chou, Y. H. (1997). *Exploring Spatial Analysis in Georgraphic Information Systems.* Sante Fe, NM: Onword Press.

Chretien, K. C., & Kind, T. (2013). Social Media as a Tool in Medicine: Ethical, Professional, and Social Implications. *Circulation, 127*(13), 1413–1421. doi:10.1161/CIRCULATIONAHA.112.128017 PMID:23547180

Christensen, C. R., & Hansen, A. J. (1987). *Teaching and the Case Method.* Boston: Harvard Business School.

Cirilo, C. (2008). *Computação Ubíqua: definição, princípios etecnologias.* Retrieved from: http://www.academia.edu/1733697/Computacao_Ubiqua_definicao_principios_e_tecnologias

CITIT. (2014). *Personal data for the public good.* California Institute for Telecommunications and Information Technology.

Clarke, R. (2012). *Point-of-View Surveillance.* Retrieved from http://www.rogerclarke.com/DV/PoVS.html

Clarke, R. (2014). Surveillance by the Australian media, and its regulation. *Surveillance & Society, 12*(1), 89–107.

Cohn, S. P. (2006). *Privacy and confidentiality in the Nationwide Health Information Network.* Retrieved 28th February 2016, from http://www.ncvhs.hhs.gov/060622lt.htm

Collins. (2015). *Collins English Dictionary – Complete and Unabridged.* Retrieved October 8 2015 from http://www.thefreedictionary.com/artifact

Consolvo, S., Smith, I. E., Matthews, T., LaMarca, A., Tabert, J., & Powledge, P. (2005). Location disclosure to social relations: why, when, & what people want to share. In *CHI 2005* (pp. 81-90).

Cook, J. (2014, October 6). FBI Director: China Has Hacked Every Big US Company. *Business Insider.* Retrieved from http://www.businessinsider.com/fbi-director-china-has-hacked-every-big-us-company-2014-10

Covill, M. (2015, May 22). *Watches2U Will Smartwatches Become Future.* Retrieved from TechnologyTell: http://www.technologytell.com/apple/150314/watches2u-will-smartwatches-become-future/

Coyle, S., Benito-Lopez, F., Byrne, R., & Diamond, D. (2010). On-Body Chemical Sensors for Monitoring Sweat. In A. Lay-Ekuakille (Ed.), *Wearable and Autonomous Biomedical Devices and Systems for Smart Environments.* Berlin: Springer-Verlag. doi:10.1007/978-3-642-15687-8_9

Culnan, M. J., & Williams, C. C. (2009). How ethics can enhance organizational privacy: Lessons from the Choicepoint and TJX data breaches. *Management Information Systems Quarterly, 33*(4), 673–687.

Compilation of References

Cyr, B., Horn, W., Miao, D., & Specter, M. (2014). *Security Analysis of Wearable Fitness Devices (Fitbit)*. Massachusetts Institute of Technology. Retrieved from https://courses.csail.mit.edu/6.857/2014/files/17-cyrbritt-webbhorn-specter-dmiao-hacking-fitbit.pdf

Damiani, M. L., Bertino, E., & Perlasca, P. (2007). Data security in location-aware applications: An approach based on RBAC. *International Journal of Information and Computer Security*, *1*(1/2), 5–38. doi:10.1504/IJICS.2007.012243

Danova, T. (2014, April 29). *global-smartwatch-sales-set-to-explode-2014-3*. Retrieved from Business Insider: http://www.businessinsider.com/global-smartwatch-sales-set-to-explode-2014-3

DARPA. (1997). *Head-Mounted Displays*. Defense Advanced Research Projects Agency. Retrieved from http://www.darpa.mil/about-us/timeline/headmounted-displays

Darwish, A., & Hassanien, A. E. (2011). Wearable and implantable wireless sensor network solutions for healthcare monitoring. *Sensors (Basel, Switzerland)*, *11*(6), 5561–5595. doi:10.3390/s110605561 PMID:22163914

Davenport, T. H. & Kirby, J. (2015, June). Beyond Automation – Strategies for remaining gainfully employed in as era of very smart machines, *Harvard Business Review*.

Dean, D., & Webb, C. (2011). Recovering from information overload. *The McKinsey Quarterly*, 1–9.

Dehghantanha, A., Udzir, N. I., & Mahmod, R. (2010). Towards a Pervasive Formal Privacy Language. In *Advanced Information Networking and Applications Workshops (WAINA), 2010 IEEE 24th International Conference* (pp. 1085-1091). Doi:10.1109/WAINA.2010.26

Deitrick, C. (2015, June 11). *Consumer Reports*. Retrieved 10 4, 2015, from Consumer Reports: http://www.consumerreports.org/cro/news/2015/06/smartphone-thefts-on-the-decline/index.htm

Denecke, K., Bamidis, P., Bond, C., Gabarron, E., Househ, M., Lau, A. Y. S., & Hansen, M. (2015). Ethical Issues of Social Media Usage in Healthcare. *Yearbook of Medical Informatics*, *10*(1), 137–147. doi:10.15265/IY-2015-001 PMID:26293861

Dhillon, G., & Backhouse, J. (2000). Technical opinion: Information system security management in the new millennium. *Communications of the ACM*, *43*(7), 125–128. doi:10.1145/341852.341877

di Pietro, R., & Mancini, L. V. (2003). Security and Privacy Issues of Handheld and Wearable Wireless Devices. *Communications of the ACM*, *46*(9), 75–79. doi:10.1145/903893.903897

Diesburg, S. M., Meyers, C. R., Lary, D. M., & Wang, A.-I. A. (2008). *When cryptography meets storage*. Paper presented at the 4th ACM international workshop on Storage security and survivability, Alexandria, VA. Retrieved from http://dl.acm.org/citation.cfm?doid=1456469.1456472

Diesburg, S. M., & Wang, A.-I. A. (2010). A survey of confidential data storage and deletion methods. *ACM Computing Surveys*, *43*(1), 1–37. doi:10.1145/1824795.1824797

Disney. (2016). *Unlock the magic with your MagicBand or card*. Retrieved March 30, 2016, from https://disneyworld.disney.go.com/plan/my-disney-experience/bands-cards/

Disterer, G., & Kleiner, C. (2013). BYOD Bring Your Own Device. *Procedia Technology, 9*, 43–53. doi:10.1016/j.protcy.2013.12.005

Dobson, J. E., & Fisher, P. F. (2007). The panopticon's changing geography. *Geographical Review, 97*(3), 307–323. doi:10.1111/j.1931-0846.2007.tb00508.x

Dohrn-van Rossum, G. (1996). *History of the Hour: Clocks and Modern Temporal Orders* (T. Dunlap, Trans.). Chicago, IL: The University of Chicago Press.

DoNothingBox LLC. (2013). *Open Source Watch*. Retrieved from http://oswatch.org

Doughty, K., & Appleby, A. (2016). Wearable devices to support rehabilitation and social care. *Journal of Assistive Technologies, 10*(1). doi:10.1108/JAT-01-2016-0004

Duckham, M., & Kulik, L. (2005). A formal model of obfuscation and negotiation for location privacy. *Pervasive, 2005*, 152–170.

Duval, S., Hoareau, C., & Hashizume, H. (2009). Humanistic Needs as Seeds in Smart Clothing in Cho, G. (Ed) Smart Clothing Technology and Applications (pp. 153–188). Boca Raton, FL: CRC Press. doi:10.1201/9781420088533-c7

Echo. (2016). *Lecture capture: Video is the new textbook*. Retrieved from http://echo360.com/what-you-can-do/lecture-capture

Ecosystem. (n.d.). *American Heritage® Dictionary of the English Language, Fifth Edition*. Retrieved October 11 2015 from http://www.thefreedictionary.com/ecosystem

Edwards, B. (2012, April 15). *Story: Slideshow: PC Mag Digital Group*. Retrieved from PC Mag Digital Group: http://www.pcmag.com/slideshow/story/296609/the-digital-watch-a-brief-history/2

Ellouze, N., Allouche, M., Ben Ahmed, H., Rekhis, S., & Boudriga, N. (2013). Securing Implantable Cardiac Medical Devices: Use of Radio Frequency Energy Harvesting. In *Proceedings of the International Workshop on Trustworthy Embedded Devices (TrustED 2013) in conjunction with CCS 2013*. Berlin, Germany: ACM. Doi:10.1145/2517300.2517307

Ellouze, N., Allouche, M., Ben Ahmed, H., Rekhis, S., & Boudriga, N. (2014). Security of implantable medical devices: Limits, requirements, and proposals. *Security and Communication Networks, 7*(12), 2475–2491. doi:10.1002/sec.939

eMarketer. (2015, June 11). *Putting Smart Watch Adoption in Perspective: eMarketer*. Retrieved from eMarketer: http://www.emarketer.com/Article/Putting-Smart-Watch-Adoption-Perspective/1012595#sthash.RzZiBqXh.dpuf

Epstein, R. G., & Kumar, D. (2000). Stories and plays about the ethical and social implications of artificial intelligence. *Intelligence, 11*(Fall), 17–19. doi:10.1145/350752.350758

Ericsson. (2015). *Ericsson Mobility Report*. Retrieved June 6, 2016, from http://www.ericsson.com/mobility-report

Compilation of References

ETF. (2006). *A Review of International and National Developments in the Use of Qualifications Frameworks.* European Training Foundation. Retrieved from http://www.etf.europa.eu/pubmgmt. nsf/(getAttachment)/4B4A9080175821D1C12571540054B4AF/$File/SCAO6NYL38.pdf

EU. (2012). *Proposal for a Regulation of the European Parliament and of the Council on the protection of individuals with regard to the processing of personal data and on the free movement of such data (General Data Protection Regulation).* European Commission. Retrieved from http://ec.europa.eu/justice/data protection/document/review2012/com_2012_11_en.pdf

European Commission. (1995). *Directive 95/46/EC of the European Parliament and of the Council.* Retrieved from http://eur-lex.europa.eu/legal-content/en/TXT/?uri=CELEX:31995L0046

European Parliament. (2015). *The internet of things. Opportunities and challenges.* Retrieved 31st December 2015, from http://www.europarl.europa.eu/RegData/etudes/BRIE/2015/557012/EPRS_BRI(2015)557012_EN.pdf

Evans, G. J. (2015). Regulating Data Practices: How State Laws can Shore Up the FTC's Authority to Regulate Data Breaches, Privacy, and More. *Administrative Law Review, 67*(1), 187–219.

Everett, C. (2015). Can wearable technology boost corporate wellbeing? *Occupational Health, 67*(8), 12–13.

Fanthorpe, L., & Fanthorpe, P. (2007). *Mysteries and Secrets of Time* (Vol. 11). Dundurn Press Toronto.

Fantz, A. (2015, March 23). As ISIS threats online persist, military families rethink online lives. *CNN.* Retrieved from http://www.cnn.com/2015/03/23/us/online-threat-isis-us-troops

Farrugia, R. C. (2013). *Facebook and relationships: a study of how social media use is affecting long-term relationships.* (Masters Thesis). Rochester Institute of Technology.

Federal Trade Commission. (2013, July 2). *Enforcement Case Proceedings in the Matter of HTC America Inc.* Retrieved from https://www.ftc.gov/enforcement/cases-proceedings/122-3049/htc-america-inc-matter

Fernandez Arguedas, V., Izquierdo, E., & Chandramouli, K. (2013). Surveillance ontology for legal, ethical and privacy protection based on SKOS. In *IEEE 18th International Conference on Digital Signal Processing (DSP).*

Fernando, N., Loke, S. W., & Rahayu, W. (2013). Mobile cloud computing: A survey. *Future Generation Computer Systems, 29*(1), 84–106. doi:10.1016/j.future.2012.05.023

Finklea, K. (2014, January 16). Identity Theft: Trends and Issues. *Congressional Research Service.* Retrieved from https://www.fas.org/sgp/crs/misc/R40599.pdf

Fitbit Inc. (2015). *Fitbit Charge Product Manual. Version 1.1.* Retrieved from https://staticcs.fitbit.com/content/assets/help/manuals/manual_charge_en_US.pdf

Ford Motor Company. (2015, September 17). *Media Center: Ford.* Retrieved from Ford: https://media.ford.com/content/fordmedia/fna/us/en/news/2015/09/17/new-ford-smart-watch-apps.html

FTC. (2016). Privacy choices for your personal financial information. *Federal Trade Commission.* Retrieved March 30, 2016, from https://www.consumer.ftc.gov/articles/0222-privacy-choices-your-personal-financial-information

Fujitsu Limited. (2012, January 19). *Fujitsu Uses Private Cloud for Communications Platform to Integrate Global Communications.* Retrieved from http://www.fujitsu.com/global/about/resources/news/press-releases/2012/0119-02.html

Fusco, S. J., Michael, K., Aloudat, A., & Abbas, R. (2011). Monitoring people using location-based social networking and its negative impact on trust: an exploratory contextual analysis of five types of "friend" relationships. In *IEEE Symposium on Technology and Society (ISTAS11).* Chicago: IEEE. doi:10.1109/ISTAS.2011.7160597

Fusco, S. J., Michael, K., Michael, M. G., & Abbas, R. (2010). Exploring the social implications of location based social networking: an inquiry into the perceived positive and negative impacts of using lbsn between friends. In *9th International Conference on Mobile Business (ICMB2010)* (pp. 230-237). Athens, Greece: IEEE. doi:10.1109/ICMB-GMR.2010.35

Fuster, G. G. (2014). *The Emergence of Personal Data Protection as a Fundamental Right of the EU.* Cham, Switzerland: Springer International. doi:10.1007/978-3-319-05023-2

Gajanayake, R., Iannella, R., & Sahama, T. (2011). Sharing with care: an information accountability perspective. *IEEE Internet Computing, 15*(4), 31-38. doi:10.1109/MIC.2011.51

Gajanayake, R., Iannella, R., & Sahama, T. (2014). *Adoption of accountable-eHealth systems by future healthcare professionals: An empirical research model based on the Australian context.* Paper presented at the 16th International Conference on E-health Networking, Application and Services (Healthcom), Natal, Brazil. doi:10.1109/HealthCom.2014.7001892

Gao, Y., Li, H., & Luo, Y. (2015). An empirical study of wearable technology acceptance in healthcare. *Industrial Management & Data Systems, 115*(9), 1704–1723.

Gartner. (2014). *Gartner Says Worldwide Information Security Spending Will Grow Almost 8 Percent in 2014 as Organizations Become More Threat-Aware.* Retrieved from http://www.gartner.com/newsroom/id/2828722

Gasson, M. N., Kosta, E., Royer, D., Meints, M., & Warwick, K. (2011). Normality mining: Privacy implications of behavioral profiles drawn from GPS enabled mobile phones. *IEEE Transactions on Systems, Man and Cybernetics. Part C, Applications and Reviews, 41*(2), 251–261. doi:10.1109/TSMCC.2010.2071381

Geier, B. (2005, August 12). NASA wants you to make a smartwatch app for astronauts. *Fortune.* Retrieved from http://fortune.com

Gentner, D., & Kurtz, K. J. (2006). Relations, Objects, and the Composition of Analogies. *Cognitive Science, 30*(4), 609–642. doi:10.1207/s15516709cog0000_60 PMID:21702828

Compilation of References

Ghinita, G. (2013). Privacy for location-based services, Volume 4 of synthesis lectures on information security, privacy and trust. Morgan & Claypool Publishers.

Ghorayshi, A. (2014). *Google Glass user treated for internet addiction caused by the device.* Retrieved June 6, 2016, from https://www.theguardian.com/science/2014/oct/14/google-glass-user-treated-addiction-withdrawal-symptoms

Gibbs, S. (2015, August 28). *Technology: The Guardian.* Retrieved from The Guardian: http://www.theguardian.com/technology/2015/aug/28/apple-watch-smartwatch-sales-analysis

Gibbs, S., & Arthur, C. (2014). CES 2014: Why wearable technology is the new dress code. *The Guardian.* Retrieved from https://www.theguardian.com/technology/2014/jan/08/wearable-technology-consumer-electronics-show

Gill, M., & Spriggs, A. (2005). *Assessing the impact of CCTV.* London: Home Office Research, Development and Statistics Directorate.

Glasseshistory. (n.d.). *History of Eyeglasses and Sunglasses.* Retrieved from http://www.glasseshistory.com/

Glisson, W. B., Andel, T., McDonald, T., Jacobs, M., Campbell, M., & Mayr, J. (2015). *Compromising a Medical Mannequin.* Retrieved from http://arxiv.org/pdf/1509.00065

Gluga, R., Kay, J., Lister, R., Charleston, M., Harland, J., & Teague, D.M. (2013). A conceptual model for reflecting on expected learning vs. demonstrated student performance. In *Proceedings of the 15th Australasian Computing Education Conference (ACE2013).* Australian Computer Society, Inc.

Goel, V. (2014, June 29). Facebook Tinkers with Users' Emotions in News Feed Experiment, Stirring Outcry. *New York Times.* Retrieved from http://www.nytimes.com/2014/06/30/technology/facebook-tinkers-with-users-emotions-in-news-feed-experiment-stirring-outcry.html?_r=0

Goel, S., Gangolly, J., Baykal, A., Hobbs, J., Pon, D., Bloniarz, P., & Schuman, S. P. et al. (2006). Innovative Model for Information Assurance Curriculum: A Teaching Hospital. *Journal of Educational Resources in Computing, 6*(3). doi:10.1145/1243481.1243483

Gokyer, D., & Michael, K. (2015). Digital wearability scenarios: Trialability on the run. *IEEE Consumer Electronics Magazine, 4*(2), 82–91. doi:10.1109/MCE.2015.2393005

Goldfarb, Z., & Tumulty, K. (2013, May 10). IRS admits targeting conservatives for tax scrutiny in 2012 election. *The Washington Post.* Retrieved from http://www.washingtonpost.com/business/economy/irs-admits-targeting-conservatives-for-tax-scrutiny-in-2012-election/2013/05/10/3b6a0ada-b987-11e2-92f3-f291801936b8_story.html

Goldstein, M., & Perlroth, N. (2015, March 15). Authorities Closing In on Hackers Who Stole Data From JPMorgan Chase. *The New York Times.* Retrieved from http://www.nytimes.com/2015/03/16/business/dealbook/authorities-closing-in-on-hackers-who-stole-data-from-jpmorgan-chase.html

Goodman, M. (2015). *Future crimes: Everything is connected, everyone is vulnerable, and what we can do about it*. New York, NY: Doubleday.

Google Inc. (n.d.). *GLASS FAQ*. Retrieved from https://sites.google.com/site/glasscomms/faqs

Google. (n.d.). *Glass Explorers*. Retrieved from https://sites.google.com/site/glasscomms/glass-explorers

Gordon, L. A., Loeb, M. P., & Lucyshin, W. (2003). Information Security Expenditures and Real Options: A Wait-and-See Approach. *Computer Security Journal, 19*, 2. Retrieved from http://papers.ssrn.com/sol3/papers.cfm?abstract_id=1375460

Gratton, E. (2015). *Health-tracking bracelets and privacy issues*. Retrieved 11th November 2015, from http://www.eloisegratton.com/blog/2014/12/20/health-tracking-bracelets-and-privacy-issues/

Greenwald, G. (2013, June 6). NSA collecting phone records of millions of Verizon customers daily. *The Guardian*. Retrieved from http://www.theguardian.com/world/2013/jun/06/nsa-phone-records-verizon-court-order

Grupp, L. M., Caulfield, A. M., Coburn, J., Swanson, S., Yaakobi, E., Siegel, P. H., & Wolf, J. K. (2009). *Characterizing flash memory: Anomalies, observations, and applications.* Paper presented at the 42nd Annual IEEE/ACM International Symposium on Microarchitecture.

Gürses, S., & del Alamo, J. M. (2016, March/April). Privacy Engineering: Shaping an Emerging Field of Research and Practice. *IEEE Security and Privacy, 14*(2), 40–46. doi:10.1109/MSP.2016.37

Hager, E. B. (2011, July 22). Explosions in Norway. *The New York Times*. Retrieved from http://www.nytimes.com

Hammond, T. (2015, October 8). *The dark side of wearables: How they're secretly jeopardizing your security and privacy*. Retrieved from http://www.techrepublic.com/article/the-dark-side-of-wearables-how-theyre-secretly-jeopardizing-your-security-and-privacy/

Hardekopf, B. (2015, January 13). The Big Data Breaches of 2014. *Forbes*. Retrieved from http://www.forbes.com/sites/moneybuilder/2015/01/13/the-big-data-breaches-of-2014/

Harfield, C. (2014). Body-worn POV technology: Moral harm. *IEEE Technology and Society Magazine, 33*(2), 64–72. doi:10.1109/MTS.2014.2319976

Harrison, D. (2014). Tracking physical activity: problems related to running longitudinal studies with commercial devices. In *Proceedings of the 2014 ACM International Joint Conference on Pervasive and Ubiquitous Computing: Adjunct Publication* (UbiComp '14 Adjunct). ACM. http://dx.doi.org.esc-web.lib.cbs.dk/10.1145/2638728.2641320

Harrison, W. (September, 2006). A term project for a course on computer forensics. *ACM Journal of Educational Resources in Computing, 6*(3), Article 6.

Compilation of References

Hartman, L. P. & Bucci, G. (1999). The Economic and Ethical Implications of New Technology on Privacy in the Workplace. *Business and Society Review.* DOI: 10.1111/0045-3609.00021

Hasanain, A. (2014). *Eyewear and challenges to existing privacy paradigms and laws.* (Unpublished Masters Thesis). Zayed University, Abu Dhabi, UAE.

Hawkins, S. (2015, March 20). *How Smart Watches Can Help Improve Your Health: Intermountain Health Care.* Retrieved from Intermountain Health Care: https://intermountainhealthcare.org/blogs/2015/03/how-smart-watches-can-help-improve-your-health/

Heersmink, R., van den Hoven, J., & Timmermans, J. (2014). Normative issues report. *ETICA Project.* Retrieved October 1, 2015, from http://www.etica-project.eu/deliverable-files

Heersmink, R., van den Hoven, J., van Eck, N. J., & van den Berg, J. (2012). Bibliometric mapping of computer and information ethics. *Ethics and Information Technology, 13*(3), 241–249. doi:10.1007/s10676-011-9273-7

Hein, B. (2015, June 9). *Apple Watch Now Has Over 6000 Apps: Cult of Mac.* Retrieved from Cult of Mac: http://www.cultofmac.com/325765/apple-watch-now-has-over-6000-apps/

Heingartner, D. (2009). Mental Block. *IEEE Spectrum, 46*(1), 42–43. doi:10.1109/MSPEC.2009.4734313

Hern, A. (2014). Sir Tim Berners-Lee speaks out on data ownership. *The Guardian.* Retrieved from http://www.theguardian.com/technology/2014/oct/08/sir-tim-berners-lee-speaks-out-on-data-ownership

Hill, K. (2011). *Fitbit Moves Quickly After Users' Sex Stats Exposed.* Retrieved 11th November 2015, from http://www.forbes.com/sites/kashmirhill/2011/07/05/fitbit-moves-quickly-after-users-sex-stats-exposed/

Holman, D., Chisick, C., & Totterdell, P. (2002). The Effects of Performance Monitoring on Emotional Labor and Well-Being in Call Centers. *Motivation and Emotion, 26*(1), 57-81. Retrieved from http://link.springer.com/article/10.1023/A:1015194108376

Huang, J., Badam, A., Chandra, R., & Nightingale, E. B. (2015). *WearDrive: Fast and Energy-Efficient Storage for Wearables.* Paper presented at the 2015 USENIX Annual Technical Conference (USENIX ATC 15), Santa Clara, CA. Retrieved from https://www.usenix.org/conference/atc15/technical-session/presentation/huang-jian

Hurford, R. D. (2009). Types of smart clothes and wearable technology. In J. McCann & D. Bryson (Eds.), *Smart clothes and wearable technology* (pp. 25–44). Cambridge: Woodhead Publishing. doi:10.1533/9781845695668.1.25

Hurley, C. (2004). *WarDriving: Drive, Detect, Defend: A Guide to Wireless Security.* Rockland, MD: Syngress Publishing.

Iqbal, M. U., & Lim, S. (2007). Privacy implications of automated GPS tracking and profiling. In K. Michael & M. G. Michael (Eds.), *From Dataveillance to Überveillance and the Realpolitik of the Transparent Society (Workshop on the Social Implications of National Security, 2007), University of Wollongong, IP Location-Based Services Research Program (Faculty of Informatics) and Centre for Transnational Crime Prevention (Faculty of Law)* (pp. 225-240).

Irum, S., Ali, A., Khan, F. A., & Abbas, H. (2013). A hybrid security mechanism for intra-WBAN and inter-WBAN communications. *International Journal of Distributed Sensor Networks*.

ISO/IEC. (2014). *ISO/IEC 27000 – Information technology – Security techniques – Information security management systems – Overview and vocabulary*. International Organization for Standardization/International Electrotechnical Commission.

Jackson Higgins, K. (2014, October 21). White Hat Hackers Fight For Legal Reform. *Dark Reading (Information Week)*. Retrieved from http://www.darkreading.com/white-hat-hackers-fight-for-legal-reform/d/d-id/1316838

Jawbone. (n.d.). *Jawbone UP24 Support*. Retrieved from https://help.jawbone.com/up24

Jayanathi, A. (2015, September 1). 19 latest healthcare data breaches. *Becker's Health IT & CIO Review*. Retrieved from http://www.beckershospitalreview.com/healthcare-information-technology/19-latest-healthcare-data-breaches.html

Jedrzejczyk, L., Price, B. A., Bandara, A. K., & Nuseibeh, B. (2010). On the Impact of Real-Time Feedback on Users' Behaviour in Mobile Location-Sharing Applications. In *Symposium On Usable Privacy and Security (SOUPS)*. doi:10.1145/1837110.1837129

Jobst, B. C. (2010). Electrical stimulation in epilepsy: Vagus nerve and brain stimulation. *Current Treatment Options in Neurology*, *12*(5), 443–453. doi:10.1007/s11940-010-0087-4 PMID:20842599

Johnson, M. E. (2009). Data Hemorrhages in the Health-Care Sector. In R. Dingledine & P. Golle (Eds.), Lecture Notes in Computer Science: Vol. 5628. *Financial Cryptography and Data Security* (pp. 71–89). doi:10.1007/978-3-642-03549-4_5

Judicial Watch. (2015, July 22). *New Documents Show IRS Used Donor Lists to Target Audits*. Retrieved from http://www.judicialwatch.org/press-room/press-releases/judicial-watch-new-irs-documents-used-donor-lists-to-target-audits

Kakria, P., Tripathi, N. K., & Kitipawang, P. (2015, December). A Real-Time Health Monitoring System for Remote Cardiac Patients Using Smartphone and Wearable Sensors. *International Journal of Telemedicine and Applications*. PMID:26788055

Kamara, S., & Lauter, K. (2010). Cryptographic Cloud Storage. In R. Sion, R. Curtmola, S. Dietrich, A. Kiayias, J. Miret, K. Sako, & F. Sebé (Eds.), Financial Cryptography and Data Security (Vol. 6054, pp. 136-149). Springer Berlin Heidelberg. doi:10.1007/978-3-642-14992-4_13

Compilation of References

Karlovsky, B. (2014, May 07). *Smartphones represent the greatest IT security risk to business: Good Mobility Index*. Retrieved from PC Advisor: http://www.pcadvisor.co.uk/news/enterprise/smartphones-represent-the-greatest-it-security-risk-to-business-good-mobility-index-3515300/

Karlsson, S., & Lugn, A. (n.d.). *The history of Bluetooth*. Retrieved from: http://www.ericsson-history.com/changing-the-world/Anecdotes/The-history-of-Bluetooth-/

Keith, M. J., Babb, J. S., & Lowry, P. B. (2014). A longitudinal study of information privacy on mobile devices. In *Proceedings of the 47th Hawaii International Conference on System Science*. Los Alamitos, CA: IEEE Computer Society. doi:10.1109/HICSS.2014.391

Kent, K., Chevalier, S., Grance, T., & Dang, H. (2006). *Guide to integrating forensic techniques into incident response*. NIST Special Publication, 800-886.

Kesh, S., & Ratnasingam, P. (2007). A knowledge architecture for IT security. *Communications of the ACM, 50*(7), 103–108. doi:10.1145/1272516.1272521

Kirkham, R., & Greenhalgh, C. (2015). Social Access vs. Privacy in Wearable Computing: A Case Study of Autism. *Pervasive Computing, IEEE, 14*(1), 26–33. doi:10.1109/MPRV.2015.14

Klann, M. (2009). Tactical Navigation Support for Firefighters: The LifeNet Ad-Hoc Sensor-Network and Wearable System. In *Proceedings of Mobile Response: 2nd International Workshop on Mobile Information Technology for Emergency Response*. Berlin: Springer.

Klann, M., Riedel, T., Gellersen, H., Fischer, C., Oppenheim, M., Lukowicz, P., . . . Visser, O. (2007). Lifenet: an ad-hoc sensor network and wearable system to provide firefighters with navigation support. In Proceedings Of UbiComp: Demos Extended Abstracts.

Knightscope. (2016). Advanced physical security technology. *Knightscope: K5*. Retrieved from http://knightscope.com/

Knowles, R. (2014). *The wearables revolution is coming – security professionals must be ready*. Retrieved from http://www.techradar.com/news/world-of-tech/future-tech/the-wearables-revolution-is-coming-security-professionals-must-be-ready-1227542

Kotler, S. (2014). *Legal heroin: Is virtual reality our next hard drug*. Retrieved June 6, 2016, from http://www.forbes.com/sites/stevenkotler/2014/01/15/legal-heroin-is-virtual-reality-our-next-hard-drug/#225d03c27472

Kress, B. (2015). Optics for Smart Glasses, Smart Eyewear, Augmented Reality, and Virtual Reality Headsets. In W. Barfield (Ed.), *Fundamentals of Wearable Computers and Augmented Reality* (2nd ed.). Boca Raton, FL: CRC Press. doi:10.1201/b18703-8

Lagorio, C. (2006). *Is virtual life better than reality?* Retrieved June 6, 2016, from http://www.cbsnews.com/news/is-virtual-life-better-than-reality/

LaMarche, J., Cheney, K., Roth, K., & Sachs, O. (2012). *Home Energy Management: Products & Trends*. Fraunhofer Center for Sustainable Energy Systems Marco Pritoni, Western Cooling Efficiency Center. Retrieved from http://cdn2.hubspot.net/hub/55819/docs/lamarcheetal_2012_aceee.pdf

Lamkin, P. (2015, May 11). *Tech: Forbes*. Retrieved from Forbes: http://www.forbes.com/sites/paullamkin/2015/05/11/101-million-smartwatch-shipments-by-2020-with-apple-and-google-leading-the-way/

Larson, E. (2015, October 7). T-Mobile, Experian Sued Over Data Hack Affecting 15 Million. *Bloomberg*. Retrieved from http://www.bloomberg.com/news/articles/2015-10-07/t-mobile-experian-sued-over-hack-on-15-million-customers

LaValle, S., Lesser, E., Shockley, R., Hopkins, M. S., & Krushwitz, N. (2010). Big Data, Analytics and the Path From Insights to Value. *Sloan Review, Winter Research Feature*. Retrieved from http://sloanreview.mit.edu/article/big-data-analytics-and-the-path-from-insights-to-value

Lee, L., Lee, J., Egelman, S., & Wagner, D. (2016). *Information Disclosure Concerns in The Age of Wearable Computing*. Working paper University of California, Berkeley. Retrieved from https://blues.cs.berkeley.edu/wp-content/uploads/2016/02/camera-ready.pdf

Leventhal, A. (2008). Flash storage memory. *Communications of the ACM, 51*(7), 47–51. doi:10.1145/1364782.1364796

Levin, A., Foster, M., West, B., Nicholson, M. J., Hernandez, T., & Cukier, W. (2008). *The Next Digital Divide: Online Social Network Privacy*. Ryerson University, Ted Rogers School of Management, Privacy and Cyber Crime Institute. Retrieved from www.ryerson.ca/tedrogersschool/privacy/Ryerson_Privacy_Institute_OSN_Report.pdf

Levy, K. (2014). A surprising number of places have banned Google Glass in San Francisco. *Business Insider, 3*. Retrieved from http://www.businessinsider.com/google-glass-ban-san-francisco-2014-3

Lewis, C. (2014). *Irresistible apps: Motivational design patterns for apps, games, and web-based communities*. New York, NY: Apress Publishing. doi:10.1007/978-1-4302-6422-4

Liang, X., Zhang, K., Shen, X., & Lin, X. (2015). Security and privacy in mobile social networks: challenges and solutions. *IEEE Wireless Communications, 22*(2), 136 – 144.

Li, M., Wenjing, L., & Kui, R. (2010). Data security and privacy in wireless body area networks. *Wireless Communications, IEEE, 17*(1), 51–58. doi:10.1109/MWC.2010.5416350

Liu, H., Saroiu, S., Wolman, A., & Raj, H. (2012, June). Software abstractions for trusted sensors. In *Proceedings of the 10th International Conference on Mobile Systems, Applications, and Services* (pp. 365-378). Ambleside, UK: ACM.

Llamas, R. T. (2015). *Worldwide wearables 2015-2019 forecast*. IDC.

Compilation of References

Lumsden, J., & Brewster, S. (2003). A paradigm shift: alternative interaction techniques for use with mobile & wearable devices. In *Proceedings of the 2003 conference of the Centre for Advanced Studies on Collaborative research* (CASCON '03). IBM Press.

Lunt, B. M., Ekstrom, J. J., Gorka, S., Hislop, G., Kamali, R., Lawson, E., & Reichgelt, H. et al. (2008). *Curriculum guidelines for undergraduate degree programs in information technology. Technical report.* New York, NY: ACM.

Lymberis, A. (2004). *Wearable ehealth systems for personalised health management: state of the art and future challenges* (Vol. 108). IOS press.

Madden, M. (2014). *Public Perceptions of Privacy and Security in the Post-Snowden Era.* Pew Research Center.

Maddox, T. (2015). *The dark side of wearables: How they're secretly jeopardizing your security and privacy.* Retrieved 11th November 2015, from http://www.techrepublic.com/article/the-dark-side-of-wearables-how-theyre-secretly-jeopardizing-your-security-and-privacy/

Mahadev, S., Bahl, P., Caceres, R., & Davies, N. (2009). The Case for VM-Based Cloudlets in Mobile Computing. *Pervasive Computing, IEEE, 8*(4), 14–23. doi:10.1109/MPRV.2009.82

Malik, M. Y. (2012). An Outline of Security in Wireless Sensor Networks: Threats, Countermeasures and Implementations. In N. Zaman, K. Ragab, & A. Abdullah (Eds.), Wireless Sensor Networks and Energy Efficiency: Protocols, Routing and Management (pp. 507-527). Hershey, PA: Information Science Reference. doi:10.4018/978-1-4666-0101-7.ch024

Mancini, C., Jedrzejczyk, L., Thomas, K., Price, B. A., Bandara, A. K., Rogers, Y., & Nuseibeh, B. (2010). Predators and prey: ubiquitous tracking, privacy and the social contract. In *UbiComp 2010.*

Mancuso, J., & Stuth, K. (2015). The Internet of All Things. *Marketing Insights, 27*(2), 16–17.

Mann, S. (1995). *An experiment in connectivity.* Retrieved from http://wearcam.org/myview.html

Mann, S. (2001, July 1). A GNU/Linux Wristwatch Videophone. *Linux Journal.*

Mann, S. (2002). *Sousveillance.* Retrieved from http://wearcam.org/sousveillance.htm

Mann, S. (2015). *Wearable Wireless Webcam.* [blog]. Retrieved from http://wearcam.org

Mann, S. (n.d.). *The request for deletion (RFD).* Retrieved from http://wearcam.org/rfd.htm

Mann, S., & Wassell, P. (2013). *Proposed law on sousveillance.* Retrieved from http://wearcam.org/MannWassellLaw.pdf

Mann, S. (1997). Wearable computing: A first step toward personal imaging. *Computer, 30*(2), 25–32. doi:10.1109/2.566147

Mann, S. (2001, May–June). Wearable computing: Toward humanistic intelligence. *IEEE Intelligent Systems, 16*(3), 10–15. doi:10.1109/5254.940020

Mann, S. (2003). Existential Technology: Wearable Computing Is Not the Real Issue! *Leonardo*, *36*(1), 19–25. doi:10.1162/002409403321152239

Mann, S. (2005). Sousveillance and cyborglogs: A 30-year empirical voyage through ethical, legal, and policy issues. *Presence (Cambridge, Mass.)*, *14*(6), 625–646. doi:10.1162/105474605775196571

Mann, S. (2013). Veillance and reciprocal transparency: Surveillance versus sousveillance, AR glass, lifeglogging, and wearable computing. In *IEEE International Symposium on Technology and Society (ISTAS)*. Toronto: IEEE.

Marquardt, P., Verma, A., Carter, H., & Traynor, P. (2011) (sp)iPhone: Decoding Vibrations From Nearby Keyboards Using Mobile Phone Accelerometers. In *Proceedings of ACM Conference on Computer and Communications Security, CCS, 2011*. Chicago, IL: ACM. doi:10.1145/2046707.2046771

Marrington, A. D., Mohay, G. M., Clark, A. J., & Morarji, H. L. (2007) Event-based computer profiling for the forensic reconstruction of computer activity. In AusCERT Asia Pacific Information Technology Security Conference (AusCERT2007): Refereed R&D Stream.

Marrington, A., Baggili, I., Mohay, G., & Clark, A. (2011). CAT Detect (Computer Activity Timeline Detection): A tool for detecting inconsistency in computer activity timelines. *Digital Investigation*, *8*, S52–S61. doi:10.1016/j.diin.2011.05.007

Martin, K. & Freeman, R. E. (2003). Some Problems with Employee Monitoring. *Journal of Business Ethics*, *43*(4), 353-361.

Martin, K. (2016). Data aggregators, consumer data, and responsibility online: Who is tracking consumers and should they stop? *The Information Society*, *32*(1), 51–63. doi:10.1080/019722 43.2015.1107166

Martin, T. (2004). Experiences Teaching a Course on Wearable and Ubiquitous Computing. In *Proceedings of the Second IEEE Annual Conference on Pervasive Computing and Communications Workshops (PERCOMW'04)*. doi:10.1109/PERCOMW.2004.1276941

Mayer, A., Niemietz, M., Mladenov, V., & Schwenk, J. (2014, November). Guardians of the Clouds: When Identity Providers Fail. In *Proceedings of the 6th edition of the ACM Workshop on Cloud Computing Security* (pp. 105-116). Scottsdale, AZ: ACM.

McAfee, A., & Brynolfsson, E. (2012, October). Big Data: The Management Revolution. *Harvard Business Review*. Retrieved from https://hbr.org/2012/10/big-data-the-management-revolution/ar

McAfee, A., & Brynjolfsson, E. (2012). Bid data: The management revolution. *Harvard Business Review*, *90*(10), 60–68. PMID:23074865

McCann, J. (2009). End-user based design of innovative smart clothing. In J. McCann & D. Bryson (Eds.), *Smart clothes and wearable technology*. Boca Raton, FL: CRC Press/Woodhead Publishing Limited. doi:10.1533/9781845695668.1.45

Compilation of References

McEnore, P. (2014, August 12). *Feds bust wordwide smartphone theft ring based in Twin Cities*. Retrieved from Star Tribune: http://www.startribune.com/feds-bust-worldwide-smartphone-theft-ring-based-in-twin-cities/270960821/

McGettrick, A. (2005). Grand challenges in computing: Education–a summary. *The Computer Journal, 48*(1), 42–48. doi:10.1093/comjnl/bxh064

McGrath, M. (2014, February 26). Target Profit Falls 46% On Credit Card Breach And The Hits Could Keep On Coming. *Forbes*. Retrieved from http://www.forbes.com/sites/maggiemcgrath/2014/02/26/target-profit-falls-46-on-credit-card-breach-and-says-the-hits-could-keep-on-coming/

McHugh, M. (2016). *How L'Oreal Built a UV-Measuring Temporary Tattoo*. Retrieved from http://www.wired.com/2016/01/how-loreal-built-a-uv-measuring-temporary-tattoo/

McLellan, C. (2014). *The History of Wearable Technology: A timeline*. Retrieved 6th May 2015 from http://www.zdnet.com/article/the-history-of-wearable-technology-a-timeline/

Mell, P. M., & Grance, T. (2011). *SP 800-145. The NIST Definition of Cloud Computing*. Retrieved from http://nvlpubs.nist.gov/nistpubs/Legacy/SP/nistspecialpublication800-145.pdf

Menezes, A. J., Van Oorschot, P. C., & Vanstone, S. A. (1996). *Handbook of applied cryptography*. CRC Press. doi:10.1201/9781439821916

Metz, R. (2015). Google Glass Is Dead; Long Live Smart Glasses. *MIT's Technology Review, 118*(1), 79–82.

Miaoui, Y., Boudriga, N., & Abaoub, E. (2015). Economics of Privacy: A Model for Protecting Against Cyber Data Disclosure Attacks. In *Proceedings of the 3rd Information Systems International Conference*. doi:10.1016/j.procs.2015.12.165

Michael, K. (2014). Redefining surveillance: Implications for privacy, security, trust and the law. *Issues Magazine*. Retrieved March 20, 2016, from http://www.issuesmagazine.com.au/article/issue-december-2014/redefining-surveillance-implications-privacy-security-trust-and-law.html

Michael, K., & Michael, M. G. (2012). Commentary on: Mann, S. (2012): Wearable computing. In M. Soegaard & R. Dam (Eds.), *Encyclopedia of human-computer interaction*. The Interaction-Design.org Foundation. Retrieved from https://www.interaction-design.org/encyclopedia/wearable_computing.html

Michael, K. (2013). Keynote: The final cut—Tampering with direct evidence from wearable computers. In *Proc. 5th Int. Conf. Multimedia Information Networking and Security (MINES)*.

Michael, K. (2015). Sousveillance: Implications for privacy, security, trust, and the law. *IEEE Consumer Electronics Magazine, 4*(2), 92–94. doi:10.1109/MCE.2015.2393006

Michael, K., McNamee, A., Michael, M. G., & Tootell, H. (2006). Location-based intelligence – modeling behavior in humans using GPS. In *IEEE International Symposium on Technology and Society(pp.1-8)*. New York: IEEE. doi:10.1109/ISTAS.2006.4375889

Michael, K., & Michael, M. G. (2013a). Computing ethics: No limits to watching? *Communications of the ACM*, *56*(11), 26–28. doi:10.1145/2527187

Michael, K., Michael, M. G., & Perakslis, C. (2014). Be vigilant: There are limits to veillance. In J. Pitt (Ed.), *The computer after me*. London: Imperial College London Press. doi:10.1142/9781783264186_0013

Michael, M. G., & Michael, K. (Eds.). (2013b). *Überveillance and the social implications of microchip implants: Emerging technologies (Advances in human and social aspects of technology)*. Hershey, PA: IGI Global.

Milosevic, B., & Farella, E. (2015, May). Wearable Inertial Sensor for Jump Performance Analysis. In *Proceedings of the 2015 workshop on Wearable Systems and Applications* (pp. 15-20). ACM. doi:10.1145/2753509.2753512

Mingers, J., & Walsham, G. (2010). Towards ethical information systems: The contributions of discourse ethics. *Management Information Systems Quarterly*, *34*(4), 833–854.

Mitri, M. (2012). Applying analogical reasoning techniques for teaching XML document querying skills in database classes. *Journal of Information Systems Education*, *23*(4), 385–394. Retrieved from http://search.proquest.com/docview/1432294615?accountid=15192

Mittal, S., & Vetter, J. S. (2015). A Survey of Software Techniques for Using Non-Volatile Memories for Storage and Main Memory Systems. *Parallel and Distributed Systems, IEEE Transactions on,* (99). doi:10.1109/TPDS.2015.2442980

Monrose, F., & Rubin, A. D. (2000). Keystroke dynamics as a biometric for authentication. *Future Generation Computer Systems*, *16*(4), 351–359. doi:10.1016/S0167-739X(99)00059-X

Moore, G. (1965). Moore's law. *Electronics Magazine*. Retrieved from http://www.extremetech.com/extreme/210872-extremetech-explains-what-is-moores-law

Moreno, R., & Ortegano-Layne, L. (2008). Do Classroom Exemplars Promote the Application of Principles in Teacher Education? A Comparison of Videos, Animations, and Narratives. *Educational Technology Research and Development*, *56*(4), 449–465. doi:10.1007/s11423-006-9027-0

Motti, V. G., & Caine, K. (2014). Users' Privacy Concerns About Wearables: impact of form factor, sensors and type of data collected [PDF]. *Financial Cryptography and Data Security Proceedings*. Retrieved from http://fc15.ifca.ai/preproceedings/wearable/paper_2.pdf

Muise, A., Christofides, E., & Desmarais, S. (2009). More information than you ever wanted: Does Facebook bring out the green-eyed monster of jealousy. *Cyberpsychology & Behavior*, *12*(4), 441–444. doi:10.1089/cpb.2008.0263 PMID:19366318

Narayanan, A. (2013). Privacy technologies: An annotated syllabus. In *Proceedings of PETS 2013 - The 13th Privacy Enhancing Technologies Symposium*.

Compilation of References

NBC News. (2016, February 11). *Google 'Right to be forgotten' to be applied more widely*. Retrieved March 30, 2016, from http://www.nbcnews.com/tech/tech-news/google-right-be-forgotten-will-be-applied-more-widely-n516656

Neild, D. (2015, September 16). *Apple Watch Vs. Samsung Gear S2 Comparison*. Retrieved from Gizmag: http://www.gizmag.com/apple-watch-vs-samsung-gear-s2-comparison/39399/

Nettle, D., Nott, K., & Bateson, M. (2012). 'Cycle thieves, we are watching you': Impact of a simple signage intervention against bicycle theft. *PLoS ONE*, *7*(12), e51738. doi:10.1371/journal.pone.0051738 PMID:23251615

Neumann, P. G. (2014). Risks and myths of cloud computing and cloud storage. *Communications of the ACM*, *57*(10), 25–27. doi:10.1145/2661049

Neurowear. (n.d.). *Projects / shippo*. Retrieved from http://www.neurowear.com/projects_detail/shippo.html

Nike Inc. (2013). *Nike+ FuelBand SE User's Guide*. Retrieved from https://support-en-us.nike-plus.com/ci/fattach/get/853467/1406073309/

Noh, S. (2014). Ferroelectret film-based patch-type sensor for continuous blood pressure monitoring. *Electronics Letters*, *50*(3), 1–2. doi:10.1049/el.2013.3715

Nugawela, S., & Sahama, T. R. (2011) Internet usage trends in medical informatics. In *Statistical Concepts and Methods for the Modern World An international conference organised by the Applied Statistical Association of Sri Lanka*. Applied Statistical Association of Sri Lanka and the School of Mathematics and Statistics, The University of Sydney.

Nyambura-Mwaura, H. (2014, November 6). Africa fast off blocks in adopting Internet of Things - industry group. *Reuters*. Retrieved from http://www.reuters.com/article/2014/11/06/africa-tech-idUSL6N0SW5O920141106

OAG. (2003). *Online Privacy Act of 2003*. Office of Attorney General. Retrieved April 27, 2016 https://oag.ca.gov/privacy/privacy-laws

Onserve. (2015). *How geolocation data collection can be useful to businesses*. Retrieved 14th of November 2015, from https://www.onserve.ca/how-geolocation-data-collection-can-be-useful-to-businesses/

Open Effect. (2016). *Every Step You Fake: A Comparative Analysis of Fitness Tracker Privacy and Security Ver.0.3*. Retrieved from https://openeffect.ca/reports/Every_Step_You_Fake.pdf

Ophir, E., Nass, C., & Wagner, A. D. (2009). Cognitive control in media multitaskers. *Proceedings of the National Academy of Sciences of the United States of America*, *106*(97), 15583–15587. doi:10.1073/pnas.0903620106 PMID:19706386

Oracle. (2015, April). *Oracle Technology Network: Topics: Security*. Retrieved from Oracle.com: http://www.oracle.com/technetwork/topics/security/poodlecve-2014-3566-2339408.html

Otto, C. A., Jovanov, E., & Milenkovic, A. (2006). A WBAN-based System for Health Monitoring at Home. In *Proceedings of the 3rd IEEE-EMBS International Summer School and Symposium on Medical Devices and Biosensors*. MIT. doi:10.1109/ISSMDBS.2006.360087

Owusu, E. (n.d.). ACCessory: password inference using accelerometers on smartphones. *Proceedings of the Twelfth Workshop on Mobile Computing Systems & Applications*. New York, NY: ACM. doi:10.1145/2162081.2162095

Page, C. (2015). *Samsung and LG smartwatches leave sensitive data open to hackers*. Retrieved from http://www.v3.co.uk/v3-uk/news/2413018/samsung-and-lg-smartwatches-leave-sensitive-data-open-to-hackers

País, E. (2011, July 23). Horror en la isla de Utoya: "Debéis morir, debéis morir todos". *El País*. Retrieved from http://internacional.elpais.com

Palmeri, C. (2016, January 10). Why Disney Won't Be Taking Magic Wristbands to Its Chinese Park. *Bloomberg*. Retrieved from http://www.bloomberg.com/news/articles/2016-01-10/why-disney-won-t-be-taking-magic-wristbands-to-its-chinese-park

Parker, D. B. (1998). *Fighting computer crime: A new framework for protecting information*. John Wiley & Sons, Inc.

Patel, D. P. (2004). Should teenagers get lojacked against their will?: An argument for the ratification of the United Nations convention on the rights of the child. *Howard Law Journal*, *47*(2), 429–470.

Patel, S., Chen, B. R., Buckley, T., Rednic, R., McClure, D., Tarsy, D., & Bonato, P. et al. (2010, August). Home monitoring of patients with Parkinson's disease via wearable technology and a web-based application. In *Proceedings of the 32nd Annual International Conference of the IEEE EMBS*.

Patterson, H. (2013). Contextual expectations of privacy in self-generated health information flows. In *Proceedings of TPRC 41: The 41st Research Conference on Communication, Information and Internet Policy*. Retrieved October 1, 2015 from http://ssrn.com/abstract=2242144

Paulson, E. (2013). Analogical Processes and College Developmental Reading. *Journal of Developmental Education*, *37*(3).

Pearce, M., Zeadally, S., & Hunt, R. (2013). Virtualization: Issues, security threats, and solutions. *ACM Computing Surveys*, *45*(2), 17. doi:10.1145/2431211.2431216

Pearse, D. (2015, August 25). *Wearable Sensors Help Diagnose Depression: Article: Horizon Magazine*. Retrieved from Horizon Magazine: http://horizon-magazine.eu/article/wearable-sensors-help-diagnose-depression_en.html

Pebble Technology. (n.d.). *Pebble Help Center*. Retrieved from http://help.getpebble.com/?b_id=8309

Compilation of References

Pedersen, I. (2014). Are Wearables Really Ready to Wear?. *IEEE Technology and Society Magazine, 33*(2), 16–18. doi:10.1109/MTS.2014.2319911

Perakslis, C., Pitt, J., & Michael, K. (2014). Drones humanus. *IEEE Technology and Society Magazine, 33*(2), 38–39.

Perusco, L., & Michael, K. (2007). Control, Trust, Privacy, and Security: Evaluating Location-Based Services. *IEEE Technology and Society Magazine, 26*(1), 4–16. doi:10.1109/MTAS.2007.335564

Pew Research Center. (2011). *How Mainstream Media Outlets Use Twitter*. Journalism and Media Technical Report. Retrieved August 1, 2015, from http://www.journalism.org/2011/11/14/how-mainstream-media-outlets-use-twitter

Philips. (2015). *What Hue Does: About Hue: Meet Hue*. Retrieved from Meet Hue: http://www2.meethue.com/en-us/about-hue/what-hue-does/

Pierce, D. (2015, September 30). *LG Watch Urbane Cellular Connected: Wired*. Retrieved from Wired: http://www.wired.com/2015/09/lg-watch-urbane-cellular-connected/

Pierce, D. (2015). How Apple designed its Watch to free us from our iPhones. *Wired, 23*(5), 98–105.

Pitney Bowes. (2012). *Mapinfo Professional*. Retrieved from http://www.pbinsight.com.au/products/location-intelligence/applications/mapping-analytical/mapinfo-professional/

Piwek, L., Ellis, D. A., Andrews, S., & Joinson, A. (2016). The rise of consumer health wearables: Promises and barriers. *PLoS Medicine, 13*(2), e1001953. doi:10.1371/journal.pmed.1001953 PMID:26836780

Polsonetti, C. (2015). Know the Difference Between IoT and M2M. *Automation World*. Retrieved from http://www.automationworld.com/cloud-computing/know-difference-between-iot-and-m2m

Ponemon Institute. (2011, November). *Reputation Impact of a Data Breach U.S. Study of Executives & Managers*. Retrieved from https://www.experian.com/assets/data-breach/white-papers/reputation-study.pdf

Ponemon, L. (2009, February 9). *The Cost of a Lost Laptop*. Ponemon Institute LLC. Retrieved from Intel.com: https://www-ssl.intel.com/content/dam/doc/white-paper/enterprise-security-the-cost-of-a-lost-laptop-paper.pdf

Ponemon, L. (2010). *Missing a Laptop? Join the Billion-Dollar Club*. Ponemon Institute.

Privacy Gift Shop. (n.d.). *Stealth Wear*. Retrieved from https://privacygiftshop.com/collections/stealth-wear

PRNewswire (2015). *M2M and wearable devices to help IoT service providers earn $231 billion in revenue according to 'The M2M, IoT & wearable technology ecosystem: 2015 - 2030'*. Author.

PwC. (2014). *The Wearable Future*. Price Waterhouse Coopers. Retrieved August 1, 2015, from http://www.pwc.com/cis

Rainie, L., & Madden, M. (2015, March). Americans' Privacy Strategies Post-Snowden [PDF]. *Pew Research*. Retrieved from http://www.pewinternet.org/files/2015/03/PI_AmericansPrivacyStrategies_0316151.pdf

Ramli, S. N., Ahmad, R., Abdollah, M. F., & Dutkiewicz, E. (2013). A biometric-based security for data authentication in Wireless Body Area Network (WBAN). *Advanced Communication Technology (ICACT), 2013 15th International Conference on.*

Rekhis, S. (2007). *Theoretical Aspects of Digital Investigation of Security Incidents.* (Doctoral Dissertation). Available from CN&S research lab. (CNAS-2008-103)

Rekhis, S., & Boudriga, N. (2011). Logic-based approach for digital forensic investigation in communication Networks. *Computers & Security*, *30*(6), 376–396. doi:10.1016/j.cose.2011.02.002

Resnick, M. (2013). *Ethical ICT to restore the privacy equilibrium.* Presented at the Bentley University's 2013 Fall Research Colloquium on Responsible Innovation: Environmental Sustainability, Financial Accountability, and Information and Communication Technology (ICT) Ethics, Waltham, MA.

Resnick, M. L. (2006). Risk Communication for legal, financial, and privacy agreements and mass media. In M. Wogalter (Ed.), *Handbook of Warnings*. Mahwah, NJ: Lawrence Erlbaum Associates, Inc.

Reza, R., Price, B., & Petre, M. (2015). Wearables: Has the Age of Smartwatches Finally Arrived?. *Communications of the ACM, 58*(1), 45-47. Business Source Complete, EBSCOhost (accessed May 1, 2016).

Rhodes, B. (n.d.). *A brief history of wearable computing.* Retrieved from http://www.media.mit.edu/wearables/lizzy/timeline.html

Rhodes, B., & Kenji, M. (2006). Wearables in 2005. *IEEE Pervasive Computing / IEEE Computer Society [and] IEEE Communications Society, 5*(1), 92–95. doi:10.1109/MPRV.2006.21

Rodrigo, M. A. (1988). Ser Y Conocer: Peculiaridades Informáticas de la Especie Humana. *Cuadernos Salamantinos de Filosofia, 15*, 5–20.

Roggen, D., Magnenat, S., Waibel, M., & Troster, G. (2011). Wearable Computing. *Robotics & Automation Magazine, IEEE, 18*(2), 83–95. doi:10.1109/MRA.2011.940992

Rose, F. (2015). The attention economy 3.0. *Milken Institute Review, 17*(3), 42–50.

Rushby, J. (1981). The Design and Verification of Secure Systems. *ACM Operating Systems Review, 15*(5), 12–21. doi:10.1145/1067627.806586

Ruvio, A., Gavish, Y., & Shoham, A. (2013). Consumer's doppelganger: A role model perspective on intentional consumer mimicry. *Journal of Consumer Behaviour, 12*(1), 60–69. doi:10.1002/cb.1415

Compilation of References

Sacco, A. (2015, August). Nymi Band uses your heartbeat to secure mobile payments. *CIO Digital Magazine*. Retrieved from http://www.cio.com/article/2969293/wearable-technology/nymi-band-uses-your-heartbeat-to-secure-mobile-payments.html

Saha, A. (2015, March 12). *10 Reasons to Buy a Smartwatch: techgyd*. Retrieved from techGYD: http://www.techgyd.com/10-reasons-to-buy-a-smartwatch/15144/

Sahama, T. R., & Liang, J. (2012) Impact of the social networking applications for health information management for patients and physicians. In *Quality of Life through Quality of Information - Proceedings of MIE2012*. IOS Press BV.

Saleem, S., Ullah, S., & Kwak, K. S. (2011). A study of IEEE 802.15. 4 security framework for wireless body area networks. *Sensors (Basel, Switzerland)*, *11*(2), 1383–1395. doi:10.3390/s110201383 PMID:22319358

Samsung Electronics. (2015). *Gear S User Manual. Rev.1.4*. Retrieved from http://downloadcenter.samsung.com/content/UM/201501/20150109141014529/SM-R750_UM_EU_Tizen_Eng_Rev.1.4_150106.pdf

Savitskaya, Y. (2004). *Privacy negotiator for electronic commerce*. (Unpublished Masters Thesis). Florida International University, Miami, FL.

Saxena, N., & Chaudhari, N. S. (2012, October). Secure encryption with digital signature approach for Short Message Service. In *2012 World Congress on Information and Communication Technologies (WICT)*, (pp. 803-806). IEEE. doi:10.1109/WICT.2012.6409184

Sayer, P. (2015, December 16). EU privacy law to require opt-in and make data processors share in responsibility. *PCWorld*. Retrieved March 30, 2016, from http://www.pcworld.com/article/3015661/eu-privacy-law-to-require-opt-in-and-make-data-processors-share-in-responsibility.html

Schell, D. (n.d.). *RFID Keyless Entry And Ignition System Speeds FedEx Couriers*. Retrieved from http://www.bsminfo.com/doc/rfid-keyless-entry-and-ignition-system-speeds-0001

Schofield, J. (2001). From man to borg -- is this the future. *The Guardian*. Retrieved from https://www.theguardian.com/technology/2001/aug/02/onlinesupplement.gadgets

Scholz, M., & Decker, T. R. (2010). A flexible architecture for a robust indoor navigation support device for firefighters. In *Proceedings of the 7th International Conference On Networked Sensing Systems (INSS2010)*. doi:10.1109/INSS.2010.5573554

SDL Customer Journey Analytics. (2015). *Are wearables here to stay?* Retrieved from http://www.sdl.com/Images/SDL_wp_Wearables_SI_A4_hires_tcm94-84978.pdf

Seeburger, J., & Schroeter, R. (2009). Disposable maps: ad hoc location sharing. In OZCHI'09 (pp. 377-380). doi:10.1145/1738826.1738902

Seijts, G., & Crim, D. (2006). What Engages Employees the Most, or the Ten Cs of Employee Engagement. *Ivey Business Journal*. Retrieved from http://iveybusinessjournal.com/publication/what-engages-employees-the-most-or-the-ten-cs-of-employee-engagement/

Shactman, N. (2003). A spy machine of DARPA's dreams. *Wired*. Retrieved from http://archive.wired.com/techbiz/media/news/2003/05/58909?currentPage=al

Shahnazarian, D., Hagemann, J., Aburto, M., & Rose, S. (2013). *Informed Consent in Human Subjects Research*. Office for the Protection of Research Subjects (OPRS), University of Southern California. Retrieved from oprs.usc.edu/files/2013/04/Informed-Consent-Booklet-4.4.13.pdf

Sheldon, R. (2014). *Deleting files in the cloud*. Retrieved 15th of November 2015, from https://www.simple-talk.com/cloud/cloud-data/deleting-files-in-the-cloud/

Sheng, H., Fui-Hoon Nah, F., & Siau, K. (2008). An experimental study on ubiquitous commerce adoption: Impact of personalization and privacy concerns. *Journal of the Association for Information Systems*, *9*(6), 344–376.

Sherbit. (2015a). *The Future of Wearables: Ingestible Sensors*. Retrieved from https://www.sherbit.io/the-future-of-wearables-ingestible-sensors/

Sherbit. (2015b). *iDNA: Why Apple (and Google) Want Your Genetic Information*. Retrieved from https://www.sherbit.io/apple-wants-your-dna/

Sherman. (2004). Developing and Delivering Hands-On Information Assurance Exercises: Experiences with the Cyber Defense Lab at UMBC. Presented at the 2004 IEEE Workshop on Information Assurance and Security. West Point, NY: United States Military Academy. Retrieved from http://www.cisa.umbc.edu/papers/ShermanWestpoint2004.pdf

Shilton, K. (2009). Four billion little brothers?: Privacy, mobile phones, and ubiquitous data collection. *Communications of the ACM*, *52*(11), 48–53. doi:10.1145/1592761.1592778

Singer, S. (2012, December 8). Company envisions vaults for personal data. *New York Times*. Retrieved from http://www.nytimes.com/2012/12/09/business/company-envisions-vaults-for-personal-data.html

Singer, R. W., & Perry, A. J. (2015). Wearables: The Well-Dressed Privacy Policy. *Intellectual Property & Technology Law Journal*, *27*(7), 24–27.

Sjöklint, M. (2014). The measurable me: The influence of self-quantification on the online user's decision-making process. In *Proceedings of the 2014 ACM International Symposium on Wearable Computers: Adjunct Program* (ISWC '14 Adjunct). ACM. http://dx.doi.org.esc-web.lib.cbs.dk/10.1145/2641248.2642737

Smith, C., & Miessler, D. (2015, August). *Website*. Retrieved from http://go.saas.hp.com/fod/internet-of-things

Compilation of References

Solon, O. (2013, August 14). VW Has Spent Two Years Trying to Hide a Big Security Flaw. *Bloomberg Business Review*. Retrieved from http://www.statista.com/statistics/259372/wearable-device-market-value/

Sowell, T. (1995). *The Vision of the Anointed: Self-congratulation as a Basis for Social Policy*. New York, NY: Basic Books.

Srinivasan, V. Stankovic, J. & Whitehouse. K. (2008b). A fingerprint and timing-based snooping attack on residential sensor systems. *ACM SIGBED*, 5(1).

Srinivasan, V., Stankovic, J., & Whitehouse, K. (2008a). Protecting your Daily In-Home Activity Information from a Wireless Snooping Attack. In *Proceedings of the 10th International Conference on Ubiquitous Computing UbiComp'08*. doi:10.1145/1409635.1409663

Stahl, B. C. (2011). Teaching ethical reflexivity in information systems: How to equip students to deal with moral and ethical issues of emerging information and communication technologies. *Journal of Information Systems Education*, 22(3), 253–260.

Starner, T. (2001). The Challenges of Wearable Computing: Part 2. *IEEE Micro*, 21(4), 54–67. doi:10.1109/40.946683

Statista. (2016). *Facts and statistics on Wearable Technology*. Retrieved from http://www.statista.com/topics/1556/wearable-technology/

Stinson, B. (2015, March 14). Nokia's 3310: the greatest phone of all time. *Techradar*. Retrieved from http://www.techradar.com

Strategy Analytics. (2016). *Global Smartwatch Shipments Overtake Swiss Watch Shipments in Q4 2015*. Retrieved from http://tinyurl.com/zma78ek

Subramanian, N., Yang, C., & Zhang, W. (2007). Securing distributed data storage and retrieval in sensor networks. *Pervasive and Mobile Computing*, 3(6), 659–676. doi:10.1016/j.pmcj.2007.06.002

Sultan, N. (2015). Reflective thoughts on the potential and challenges of wearable technology for healthcare provision and medical education. *International Journal of Information Management*, 35(5), 521–526. doi:10.1016/j.ijinfomgt.2015.04.010

Sun, Y., Wang, N., Shen, X. L., & Zhang, J. X. (2015). Location information disclosure in location-based social network services: Privacy calculus, benefit structure, and gender differences. *Computers in Human Behavior*, 52, 278–292.

Surveillance Camera Man. (2015). *Surveillance Camera Man*. Retrieved from https://www.youtube.com/watch?v=jzysxHGZCAU

Sweeney, L. (2000). *Simple Demographics Often Identify People Uniquely*. Retrieved from http://dataprivacylab.org/projects/identifiability/paper1.pdf

Symantec Security Response. (2014, July 30). How safe is your quantified self? Tracking, monitoring, and wearable tech. *Symantec*. Retrieved from http://www.symantec.com/connect/blogs/how-safe-your-quantified-self-tracking-monitoring-and-wearable-tech

Talbot, D. (2015, June 10). Cyber-Espionage Nightmare. *MIT Review*. Retrieved from http://www.technologyreview.com/featuredstory/538201/cyber-espionage-nightmare/

Tan, A. Z. Y., Chua, W. Y., & Chang, K. T. T. Location based services and information privacy concerns among literate and semi-literate users. In *Proceedings of the 47th Hawaii International Conference on System Science*. Los Alamitos, CA: IEEE Computer Society. doi:10.1109/HICSS.2014.394

Tang, K. O., Lin, J., Hong, J., Siewiorek, D. P., & Sadeh, N. (2010). Rethinking location sharing: exploring the implications of social-driven vs. purpose-driven location sharing. In *UbiComp 2010*. doi:10.1145/1864349.1864363

Tanner, R. J., Ferraro, R., Chartrand, T. L., Bettman, J., & van Baaren, R. (2008). Of chameleons and consumption: The impact of mimicry on choice and preferences. *The Journal of Consumer Research*, *34*(6), 754–766. doi:10.1086/522322

Tatli, E. I., Stegemann, D., & Lucks, S. (2005). Security challenges of Location-Aware Mobile Business. In *The Second IEEE International Workshop on Mobile Commerce and Services, 2005. WMCS '05*. doi:10.1109/WMCS.2005.23

Taylor, G., & Blewitt, G. (2006). *Intelligent Positioning: GIS GPS Unification*. West Sussex, UK: John Wiley & Sons Ltd. doi:10.1002/0470035668

TechTarget. (2016). *De-anonymization (deanonymization)*. Retrieved March 21, 2016, from http://whatis.techtarget.com/definition/de-anonymization-deanonymization

Teixeira, A., & de Sá-Soares, F. (2013). A Revised Framework of Information Security Principles. In S. M. Furnell, N. L. Clarke, & V. Katos (Eds.), *Proceedings of the European Information Security Multi-Conference EISMC 2013 —IFIP Information Security Management Workshop*.

Temple, R., & Naziri, J. (2015, July 28). *Best Android Smartwatch apps 2015: Wearables: News: techradar*. Retrieved from techradar: http://www.techradar.com/us/news/wearables/best-android-wear-smartwatch-apps-2015-1281065

Thomas, L., Little, L., Briggs, P., McInnes, L., Jones, E., & Nicholson, J. (2013). Location tracking: Views from the older adult population. *Age and Ageing*, *42*(6), 758–763. doi:10.1093/ageing/aft069 PMID:23761455

Thomaz, E., Parnami, A., Bidwell, J., Essa, I., & Abowd, G. D. (2013, September). Technological approaches for addressing privacy concerns when recognizing eating behaviors with wearable cameras. In *Proceedings of the 2013 ACM international joint conference on Pervasive and ubiquitous computing* (pp. 739-748). New York, NY: ACM. doi:10.1145/2493432.2493509

Thorpe, E. O. (1998). The Invention of the First Wearable Computer. In 2nd IEEE International Symposium on Wearable Computers (p. 4). Washington, DC: IEEE Computer Society. Retrieved from http://dl.acm.org/citation.cfm?id=858031

Compilation of References

Thorsteinsson, G., & Page, T. (2015, January 21). How attached to our smart phones are we? *International Journal of Mobile Learning and Organisation, 8*, 201 - 215. Retrieved from Science Daily: www.sciencedaily.com/releases/2015/01/150121083646.htm

Timberg, C. (2013, November 6). Google encrypts data amid backlash against NSA. *Washington Post*. Retrieved from http://www.washingtonpost.com/business/technology/google-encrypts-data-amid-backlash-against-nsa-spying/2013/09/06/9acc3c20-1722-11e3-a2ec-b47e45e6f8ef_story.html

Toch, E., Cranshaw, J., Drielsma, P. H., Tsai, J. Y., Kelley, P. G., Springfield, J., & Sadeh, N. (2009). Empirical models of privacy in location sharing. In *UbiComp '10* (pp. 129-138). doi:10.1145/1864349.1864364

Topi, H., Valacich, J. S., Wright, R. T., Kaiser, K., Nunamaker, J. F. Jr, Sipior, J. C., & de Vreede, G. J. (2010). IS 2010: Curriculum guidelines for undergraduate degree programs in information systems. *Communications of the Association for Information Systems, 26*, 18.

Torres, J. (2015, June 8). *Samsungs Next Smartwatch Will Have NFC For Samsung Pay: Slash Gear*. Retrieved from Slash Gear: http://www.slashgear.com/samsungs-next-smartwatch-will-have-nfc-for-samsung-pay-08387154/

TRUSTe. (2014, November). *Beta Program for TRUSTe Data Privacy Management Platform Commences at Full Capacity*. Retrieved from https://www.truste.com/about-truste/press-room/beta-program-truste-data-privacy-management-platform-commences-full-capacity/

Tsai, J. Y., Kelley, P. G., Drielsma, P. H., Cranor, L. F., Hong, J., & Sadeh, N. (2009). *Who's viewed you? The impact of feedback in a mobile location-sharing application*. Boston, MA: CHI.

Tsubouchi, K. (2015). Fine-grained social relationship extraction from real activity data under coarse supervision. In *Proceedings of the 2015 ACM International Symposium on Wearable Computers* (ISWC '15). ACM. doi:10.1145/2802083.2808402

Turing, A. M. (1950). Computing Machinery and Intelligence. *Mind. New Series, 59*(236), 433–460. doi:10.1093/mind/LIX.236.433

Turkle, S. (2015). *Reclaiming conversation: The power of talk in the digital age*. New York, NY: Penguin Press.

Uddin, M., Salem, A., Nam, I., & Nadeem, T. (2015, May). Wearable Sensing Framework for Human Activity Monitoring. In *Proceedings of the 2015 workshop on Wearable Systems and Applications* (pp. 21-26). ACM. doi:10.1145/2753509.2753513

Ullah, S., Higgins, H., Braem, B., Latre, B., Blondia, C., Moerman, I., & Kwak, K. et al. (2012). A Comprehensive Survey of Wireless Body Area Networks. *Journal of Medical Systems, 36*(3), 1065–1094. doi:10.1007/s10916-010-9571-3 PMID:20721685

United States Computer Emergency Response Team. (2013, July 22). *DNS Amplification Attacks: Alert (TA13-088A): US-CERT*. Retrieved from US-CERT: https://www.us-cert.gov/ncas/alerts/TA13-088A

University of Wollongong. (2014a). *Campus Access and Order Rules*. Retrieved from http://www.uow.edu.au/about/policy/UOW058655.html

University of Wollongong. (2014b). *Ownership of Intellectual Property*. Retrieved from http://www.uow.edu.au/about/policy/UOW058689.html

University of Wollongong. (2014c). *Student Conduct Rules*. Retrieved from http://www.uow.edu.au/about/policy/UOW058723.html

US Department of Justice. (2014). U.*S. Charges Five Chinese Military Hackers for Cyber Espionage Against U.S. Corporations and a Labor Organization for Commercial Advantage*. Retrieved from http://www.justice.gov/opa/pr/us-charges-five-chinese-military-hackers-cyber-espionage-against-us-corporations-and-labor

US Senate. (2014). *Online Advertising and Hidden Hazards to Consumer Security and Data Privacy*. Retrieved from https://otalliance.org/system/files/files/resource/documents/report_-_online_advertising_hidden_hazards_to_consumer_security_date_privacy_may_15_20141.pdf

USPTO. (2015). *United States Patent Application Publication US 2015/0061837 A1 Reader Communication with Contact Lens Sensors and Display Device*. Retrieved from http://pdfaiw.uspto.gov/.aiw?PageNum=0&docid=20150061837

Utter, C. J., & Rea, A. (2015). The "Bring Your Own Device" Conundrum for Organizations and Investigators: An Examination of the Policy and Legal Concerns in the Policy and Legal Concerns in Light of Investigatory Challenges. *The Journal of Digital Forensics, Security and Law*, 57 - 72.

Utz, S., & Beukeboom, C. J. (2011). The role of social network sites in romantic relationships: Effects on jealousy and relationship happiness. *Journal of Computer-Mediated Communication*, *16*(4), 511–527. doi:10.1111/j.1083-6101.2011.01552.x

Valdes, R., & Chandler, N. (2005, April 13). *Clocks Watches: Gadgets: How Stuff Works*. Retrieved from How Stuff Works: http://electronics.howstuffworks.com/gadgets/clocks-watches/smart-watch.htm

Van Bommel, M., van Prooijen, J., Elffers, H., & Van Lange, P. (2012). Be aware to care: Public self-awareness leads to a reversal of the bystander effect. *Journal of Experimental Social Psychology*, *48*(4), 926–930. doi:10.1016/j.jesp.2012.02.011

van den Hoven, J., Helbing, D., Pedrescri, D., Domingo-Ferrer, J., Gianotti, F., & Christen, M. (2012). *FuturICT – the road towards ethical ICT*. arXiv 1210.8181v1

Venkatraman, K., Vijay Daniel, J., & Murugaboopathi, G. (2013). Various Attacks in Wireless Sensor Network: Survey.[IJSCE]. *International Journal of Soft Computing and Engineering*, *3*(1), 208–211.

Vila, P., & Rodriguez, R. J. (2015). Relay Attacks in EMV Contactless Cards with Android OTS Devices.Hack in the Box 2015, Amsterdam.

Compilation of References

VTT. (2016). *Smart clothing of the future will automatically adjust itself according to the wearer's actual needs.* Retrieved from http://www.vttresearch.com/media/news/smart-clothing-of-the-future

Walton, Z. (2015, November 06). *Wearables: WTVOX.* Retrieved from WTVox: https://wtvox.com/wearables/researchers-able-to-hack-smartwatches/

Wang, H., Tsung-Te, L. T., & Choudhury, R. R. (2015, September). MoLe: Motion Leaks through Smartwatch Sensors. *Annual International Conference on Mobile Computing and Networking.* Paris: Association for Computing Machinery's Special Interest Group on Mobility of Systems, Users, Data, and Computing. doi:10.1145/2789168.2790121

Wang, Q., Ren, K., Yu, S., & Lou, W. (2011). Dependable and Secure Sensor Data Storage with Dynamic Integrity Assurance. *ACM Transactions on Sensor Networks*, *8*(1), 1–24. doi:10.1145/1993042.1993051

Wang, W., Wang, H., Hempel, M., Peng, D., Sharif, H., & Chen, H. H. (2011). Secure stochastic ECG signals based on Gaussian mixture model for e-healthcare systems. *IEEE Systems Journal*, *5*(4), 564–573. doi:10.1109/JSYST.2011.2165597

Weber, R. H. (2015). The digital future – A challenge for privacy? *Computer Law & Security Report*, *31*(2), 234–242. doi:10.1016/j.clsr.2015.01.003

Wei, L., Zhu, H., Cao, Z., Dong, X., Jia, W., Chen, Y., & Vasilakos, A. V. (2014). Security and privacy for storage and computation in cloud computing. *Information Sciences*, *258*, 371–386. doi:10.1016/j.ins.2013.04.028

Weise, E. (2015, December 14). New EU privacy rule could cost U.S. firms billions. *USA Today*. Retrieved March 20, 2016, from http://www.usatoday.com/story/life/web-to-watch/tech-gaming/2015/12/14/eu-european-union-privacy-directive-google-facebook/77314554/

Wex Legal Dictionary. (2016). Retrieved March 20, 2016, from https://www.law.cornell.edu/wex

Williamson, J., Liu, Q., Lu, F., Mohrman, W., Li, K., Dick, R., & Shang, L. (2015, January). Data sensing and analysis: Challenges for wearables. In *Design Automation Conference (ASP-DAC), 2015 20th Asia and South Pacific* (pp. 136-141). IEEE. doi:10.1109/ASPDAC.2015.7058994

Wood, A. (2012, June 22). *News: TechTarget*. Retrieved from TechTarget: http://searchmobile-computing.techtarget.com/news/2240158544/Web-apps-easier-for-IT-to-secure-but-BYOD-users-go-native

Woolaston, V. (2013). Facebook users are committing 'virtual identity suicide' in droves and quitting the site over privacy and addiction fears. *UK Daily Mail*. Retrieved from http://www.dailymail.co.uk/sciencetech/article-2423713/Facebook-users-committing-virtual-identity-suicide-quitting-site-droves-privacy-addiction-fears.html

WTc. (n.d.). *Innovation Worldcup Categories*. Retrieved from: http://www.wearable-technologies.com/innovation-worldcup/categories/

Xu, H. (2011). Information privacy concerns: Linking individual perceptions with institutional privacy assurances. *Journal of the Association for Information Systems*, *12*(12), 798–824.

Xu, Y., Li, W. J., & Lee, K. K. (2008). *Intelligent wearable interfaces*. Hoboken, NJ: John Wiley & Sons. doi:10.1002/9780470222867

Yang, H., Yu, Zo, & Choi. (2016). User acceptance of wearable devices. *Telemat. Inf.*, *33*(2), 256-269.

Yu, Z., Wang, H., Guo, B., Gu, T., & Mei, T. (2015). Supporting serendipitous social interaction using human mobility prediction. *IEEE Transactions on Human-Machine Systems*, *45*(6), 811–818. doi:10.1109/THMS.2015.2451515

Zdnet. (2015). *Wearables open new avenues for security and privacy invasions*. Retrieved 14th November 2015, from http://www.zdnet.com/article/wearables-open-new-avenues-for-security-and-privacy-invasions/

Zhao, L., Lu, Y., & Gupta, S. (2012). Disclosure intention of location-related information in location-based social network services. *International Journal of Electronic Commerce*, *16*(4), 53–90. doi:10.2753/JEC1086-4415160403

Zhao, M., Walker, J., & Wang, C. C. (2012, August). Security challenges for the intelligent transportation system. In *Proceedings of the First International Conference on Security of Internet of Things* (pp. 107-115). ACM. doi:10.1145/2490428.2490444

Zheng, Y.-L., Ding, X. R., Poon, C. C. Y., Lo, B. P. L., Zhang, H., Zhou, X.-L., & Zhang, Y.-T. et al. (2014). Unobtrusive Sensing and Wearable Devices for Health Informatics. *IEEE Transactions on Bio-Medical Engineering*, *61*(5), 1538–1554. doi:10.1109/TBME.2014.2309951 PMID:24759283

Zhou, Z., & Huang, D. (2013). *Efficient and secure data storage operations for mobile cloud computing*. Paper presented at the 8th International Conference on Network and Service Management, Las Vegas, NV.

Zhou, J., Cao, Z., Dong, X., & Lin, X. (2015). *Security and Privacy in Cloud-Assisted Wireless Wearable Communications: Challenges, Solutions and Future Directions*. IEEE Wireless Communications.

Zimmermann, C., & Cabinakova, J. (2015). *A conceptualization of accountability as a privacy principle*. Paper presented at the BIS 2015 Workshops. doi:10.1007/978-3-319-26762-3_23

Zingerle, A., & Kronman, L. (2013). Humiliating Entertainment or Social Activism? Analyzing Scambaiting Strategies Against Online Advance Fee Fraud. *Cyberworlds (CW), 2013 International Conference on, Yokohama* (pp. 352-355).

Zolfagharifard, E. (2014, March 19). Is this the first wearable computer? 300-year-old Chinese abacus ring was used during the Qing Dynasty to help traders. *Daily Mail*. Retrieved from: http://www.dailymail.co.uk

About the Contributors

Andrew Marrington is an Associate Professor and the Acting Associate Dean at the College of Technological Innovation at Zayed University, in the United Arab Emirates. At Zayed University, Dr. Marrington teaches information security management and digital forensics, at the undergraduate and graduate level. Dr. Marrington received his PhD in digital forensics from Queensland University of Technology (QUT), where he studied at the Information Security Institute. Dr. Marrington's primary field of research is digital forensics, although he is also interested in other aspects of information security. He serves on the program committees of various conferences and workshops in digital forensics and information security, and on the editorial boards of several journals in the same field.

Don Kerr, PhD, is an Associate Professor of Information Systems at the University of the Sunshine Coast in Australia. Don worked for 25 years as a principal research scientist for the Queensland Department of Primary Industries before coming to academic in the year 2000. He has conducted both qualitative and quantitative research in both industry and academia over the past 35 years. Most recently he has undertaken research into Information and communications Technology (ICT) workarounds in organizations and ICT security issues. Don has been an editor on two IGI books previous to this one. These two books where titled "Digital Business Security Development: Management Technologies" and "Feral Information Systems Development: Managerial Implications". Don has also published over 130 peer reviewed papers in Information systems and management journals and conferences over the past 20 years, including in journals such as *Decision Support Systems*, the *Australasian Journal of Information systems*, *Knowledge Based Systems and the International Journal of Learning and Change*. He has supervised nine PhD research students to completion.

John Gammack is a Professor in the College of Technological Innovation at Zayed University in Abu Dhabi, UAE. Dr. Gammack received his PhD on the topic of expert knowledge acquisition and modeling from Cambridge University, where he studied at the MRC Applied Psychology Unit. Prior to working at Zayed University, he worked as an academic in China, the UK and Australia, where he was Head of the School of IT at Murdoch University, Perth, and later Head of Management at Griffith University Business School, Queensland. At Griffith he led the User and Societal Needs group of the Institute for Integrated and Intelligent Systems. Professor Gammack's primary field of research is knowledge management and decision support, particularly in the social, cultural and human aspects of their application areas. He is also interested in other aspects of informatics, particularly intelligent information systems interfaces. He has published around 200 books and articles in this general area, including a foundation text, "The Book of Informatics".

* * *

Roba Abbas is an Honorary Fellow with the Faculty of Engineering and Information Sciences at the University of Wollongong, Australia. She completed her Australian Research Council (ARC)-funded Doctor of Philosophy on the topic of Location-Based Services Regulation in 2012, earning special commendations for her thesis titled Location-Based Services Regulation in Australia: A Socio-Technical Approach. Abbas also graduated with first class Honours and Distinction in Information and Communication Technology (majoring in Business Information Systems) from the University of Wollongong Australia in 2006, earning a place on the Faculty of Informatics Dean's Merit List. She has a strong interest in socio-technical theory, social media, and location-enabled technologies. Abbas has co-edited the Privacy and Security Issues in Social Networks section in the Encyclopedia of Social Network Analysis and Mining, and has previously co-edited a special issue in Cases on Information Technology on the Social Implications of Emerging Technologies. Abbas has written numerous papers most recently for Computer Law and Security Review and IT and People. She has also lectured and tutored in ICT, and has over five years industry experience in product management and enterprise information architecture.

Samer Abbas enlisted into the Australian Defence Force in 2010, working specifically in a broad range of electronics, and the repair and maintenance of them. For six years Samer worked as an electronics technician and left the Defence Force at the beginning of 2016. He is a qualified electronics technician and has a Certificate III and a Certificate IV in Electronics and Communications. Samer has recently accepted an offer to commence study at the University of Wollongong and will be studying Writing and English Literature.

Scott Amyx was voted one of the Top 25 Global Speakers by Speaking.com. Scott is a thought-leader, speaker, and author on wearables and the Internet of Things and the CEO of Amyx+McKinsey. He was nominated by the Republic of Korea to represent cutting-edge research and case studies on wearables and the Internet of Things at the ITU Telecom World 2015 in Budapest. He debuted the concept of "The Digital Currency of Happiness" at TechCrunch Beijing 2015. Intel & TBS's America's Greatest Makers look to Scott to recommend the most promising startups. As a thought leader in wearables & IoT, Scott explores the intersection of enterprise implications and consumer decisions of adopting wearables & IoT technologies. He writes for Wired, InformationWeek, IEEE, Wearable Technologies (WT), ReadWrite, TechBeacon, and other leading publications and speaks at global conferences. Scott is the co-author of The Internet of Things and Cyber-Physical Systems Handbook, an academic publication by John Wiley and Sons, scheduled for late 2015 and The Advances in Information Security, Privacy, & Ethics (AISPE) Book Series, a series of academic publications by IGI Global (formerly Idea Group Inc.), scheduled for 2016. Scott has over 18 years of large-scale strategy and implementation experience, managing double digit million dollar projects across multiple verticals. In his last corporate position as VP of Product Management, Scott helped the company be acquired by a Fortune 500 publicly traded company. Scott has also started numerous startups and successfully sold a company. Scott has a master's degree in applied microeconomics/public policy from the University of Chicago. Scott was a national Sloan Fellow at Carnegie Mellon University.

Michelle Antero is an Assistant Professor at Zayed University, College of Technological Innovation, where she is engaged in several research projects on ERP, mobile computing, and sustainable logistics. She received her PhD in Information Systems degree from Copenhagen Business School, Copenhagen, Denmark and her MSc. in Analysis and Management of Information Systems degree from London School of Economics and Political Science (LSE), London, UK. Prior to joining academia, Michelle was as an IT manager in Silicon Valley in California with over 12 years extensive experience in providing management consulting services. She is a Subject Matter Expert (SME) in telecommunications. She has successfully developed and implemented custom billing solutions for Incumbent Local Exchange Carriers (ILECS). She has also managed the systems development of Customer Relationship Management (CRM) systems, web applications and mobile solutions for Communications and High Technology clients. Her research looks at the impact of mobile technologies on a vendor's ability to compete and on a student's ability to learn. She has published in the Information Research Management Journal, the International Journal of Enterprise Information Systems and at international conferences such as AMCIS, ECIS and CENTERIS.

Ibrahim Baggili is the founder and co-director of the University of New Haven's Cyber Forensics Research and Education Group (UNHcFREG) – http://www.unhcfreg.com. He is the Elder Family Endowed Chair of Computer Science and the Assistant Dean of the Tagliatela College of Engineering at the University of New Haven, CT. He was the former editor in chief to the Journal of Digital Forensics, Security and Law. He has published numerous articles in the domain of cybersecurity and forensics and has been nominated and won a number of awards. To learn more about him, you can visit his website http://www.baggili.com.

Sarra Berrahal is a PhD Student at the Engineering School of Communications (SUP'Com, Tunisia), University of Carthage, and member of the Communication Networks and Security (CNAS) research Laboratory at the same University. She is conducting her research activities in the area of wireless body area network, networking, and quality of service.

Noureddine Boudriga received his Ph.D. in Algebraic Topology from University Paris XI (France) and his Ph.D. in Computer Science from University of Tunis (Tunisia). He is currently a full Professor of Telecommunications at the University of Carthage, Tunisia and the Director of the Communication Networks and Security Research Laboratory (CNAS, University of Carthage). He is the recipient of the Tunisian Presidential award in Science and Research (2004). He has served as the General Director and founder of the Tunisian National Digital Certification Agency (2000-2004). He was involved in very active research in communication networks and system security. He authored and co-authored many chapters and books on information security, security of mobiles networks, and communication networks. He published over 300 refereed journal and conference papers. Prof. Boudriga's research interests include networking and internetworking security, security management of electronic services, and security-related theories and formal methods.

Frank Breitinger is an Assistant Professor of Computer Science at the Tagliatela College of Engineering at the University of New Haven, CT (ECECS Department). His research is carried out in the University of New Haven Cyber Forensics Research and Education Group (UNHcFREG, http://www.unhcfreg.com) where he also acts as a Co-Director. Additional information about his work and him is on his website http://www.fbreitinger.de.

Kerryn Butler-Henderson is the Coordinator of the Master of Health Information Management at the University of Tasmania, and National Director of the Health Information Management Association of Australia. She holds positions on a number of national and international committees related to health information management and health informatics. Kerryn is widely published across health information management related research, including in the areas of health data, e-health and workforce issues.

Alina M. Chircu is a Professor and department chair in the Information and Process Management department at Bentley University, USA. She holds a Ph.D. degree in Management Information Systems and bachelor's and master's degrees in Computer Science. She has published articles in journals such as the Journal of Information Systems Education, Business Process Management Journal, Communications of the AIS, Journal of Product Innovation Management, Decision Support Systems, Journal of Management Information Systems, Communications of the ACM, and others, as well as numerous book chapters and conference papers. Her research interests include business process management and the business value and adoption of transformational technologies such as e-business, e-government, mobile, RFID, and emerging Internet of Things technologies.

Filipe da Costa is researcher in the Department of Information Systems at the University of Minho, Portugal. He holds a Licenciatura in Systems Engineering and Computer Science from the University of Minho. He has 8 years of experience as IT consultant in the telecom and enterprise business assurance areas, at a multinational company. His research focuses on information systems security.

Deniz Gokyer completed his Master's of Information Communication Technology degree and his Master's of Information Technology Management degree in the School of Information Systems and Technology at the University of Wollongong. In his final year research project in 2014, he investigated the domain of wearable computing. He examined the social implications of emerging form factors of new wearables with a view to characterizing and predicting the industry's trajectory. He was formerly a research assistant in the Faculty of Engineering and Information Sciences and has previously been an intern for several government agencies in Turkey.

Katina Michael is the editor in chief of IEEE Technology and Society Magazine and the senior editor of IEEE Consumer Electronics Magazine. She is the associate dean international of the Faculty of Engineering and Information Sciences at the University of Wollongong, NSW, Australia, where she specialises in the socio-ethical implications of emerging technologies. She has been responsible for the annual workshop since 2006 on the Social Implications of National Security and has program chaired the International Symposium on Technology and Society in 2010 and 2013 on the respective topics of implantable technologies and wearable technologies. Her most recent book, coedited with MG Michael, is Uberveillance and the Social Implications of Microchip Implants: Emerging Technologies. She holds a PhD degree in automatic identification and location-based services, a master's degree in transnational crime prevention from the University of Wollongong, and a bachelor of information technology from the University of Technology, Sydney.

M. G. Michael, Ph.D. (ACU), M.A (Hons) (MacqUni), M.Theol (SydUni), B.Theol (SCD), B.A.(SydUni), DipProfCouns (AIPC), is an Honorary Associate Professor in the School of Computing and Information Technology at the University of Wollongong, NSW, Australia. Michael is a theologian and historian with cross-disciplinary qualifications in the humanities and who introduced the concept of überveillance into the privacy and bioethics literature. Michael brings with him a unique perspective to Emerging Technologies. His formal studies include Ancient History, Theology, General Philosophy, Political Sociology, Ethics, Linguistics, and Government. He was previously the coordinator of Information & Communication Security Issues at the University of Wollongong and since 2005 has guest-lectured and tutored in Location-Based Services, IT & Citizen Rights, Principles of eBusiness, and IT & Innovation. The focus of his current research extends to modern hermeneutics and the Apocalypse of John; the historical antecedents of modern cryptography; the auto-ID trajectory; data protection, privacy and ethics related issues; biometrics, RFID and chip implants; national security and government policy; dataveillance and überveillance; and more broadly the system dynamics between technology and society. Michael is a member of the American Academy of Religion (AAR) and a life member of the Australian Privacy Foundation (APF). He has guest edited the December 2006 volume of Prometheus, several IEEE Technology and Society Magazine issues in 2010-11, an issue for Information Technology Cases (2011) and more recently the Journal of Location-Based Services. He is also the proceedings editor of four national security workshops sponsored by the Australian Research Council's Research Network for a Secure Australia (RNSA).

Marc Resnick had 25 years of experience in human factors and user experience strategy. His research covered a wide variety of conceptual frameworks and application domains, including enterprise systems, health care information systems, consumer products and social networks. He conducted basic research for the National Science Foundation, and applied research for NASA, large corporations, small businesses, and technology startup companies. Prior to joining Bentley, Dr. Resnick taught at Florida International University, with a focus on human factors, usability, ergonomics, performance management, business strategy, innovation and entrepreneurship. His professional résumé included independent consulting in business planning and entrepreneurship, and he was an active expert witness in human factors, ergonomics, and performance management. Dr. Resnick held a M.S. and PhD from the University of Michigan, Ann Arbor and a B.S. from Tufts University.

Joseph Ricci is an undergraduate in Cyber Systems at University of New Haven, class of 2017. Joseph is also a researcher for University of New Haven's Cyber Forensics Research and Education Group (UNHcFREG). He has presented at Manhattan College about smartwatch security and forensics.

Filipe de Sá-Soares is assistant professor in the Department of Information Systems at the University of Minho, Portugal. He holds a Licenciatura in Systems Engineering and Computer Science, Master of Science in Management Information Systems and Ph.D. in Engineering and Management of Information Systems. He has 20 years of experience teaching introductory and advanced courses in computer science and information systems. His research focuses on information systems security, information systems audit, information systems management and IS/IT education. He is the Managing Editor of the Journal of Information System Security (JISSec).

Tony Sahama is a senior lecturer in the Information Security Discipline, Science and Engineering Faculty, Queensland University of Technology (QUT), Brisbane, Australia. An academic and researcher for more than 25 years, Tony's research interest is in Medical and Health Informatics in particular, Healthcare Information Technology (HIT), Information Accountability (IA) and Clinical Decision Support Systems (CDSS) design and development. Tony possesses PhD in Computer Science (Computer Simulation and Modelling, DACE), and has experience working with researchers in developing customised technology applications for Clinical Decision Support Systems, Data warehousing, Data Integration and IT applications for healthcare decision making processes. Tony's recent work is in developing a black box to solve information security and privacy issues in electronic health records

(EHRs). In addition, Tony also involved in IT educational applications for consumers in the PACT arena (People Accepting Controversial Technologies). Currently, Tony is supervising six PhD level research projects in the Medical Informatics, Health Informatics, eHealth and Health Information Technology research areas. Tony holds professional membership with ACM, IEEE, IBS, ACS, SSAI and HISA.

Mingzhong Wang is a Lecturer in ICT at the University of the Sunshine Coast. He received his PhD in Computer Science from the University of Melbourne. His research interests include large-scale distributed systems, data management, multiagent systems, and information security issues in these fields.

Index

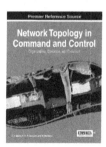

Printed in the United States
By Bookmasters